The Best 300 Professors

By The Princeton Review and RateMyProfessors.com

The Best 300 Professors

By The Princeton Review and RateMyProfessors.com

By Robert Franek, Laura Braswell,
and the Staff of The Princeton Review

PrincetonReview.com

Random House, Inc. New York

The Princeton Review, Inc.
111 Speen Street, Suite 550
Framingham, MA 01701
E-mail: editorialsupport@review.com
1-800-2-Review

ISBN: 978-0-375-42758-9

Editors: Laura Braswell
Production Designer: Kimberly Howie
Production Editor: Meave Shelton

Printed in the United States of America on partially
recycled paper.

10   9   8   7   6   5   4   3   2   1

Editorial
Rob Franek, VP Test Prep Books, Publisher
Laura Braswell, Senior Editor
Selena Coppock, Editor
Meave Shelton, Editor
Calvin Cato, Editor

Random House Publishing Team
Tom Russell, Publisher
Nicole Benhabib, Publishing Manager
Ellen L. Reed, Production Manager
Alison Stoltzfus, Managing Editor

Acknowledgments

My sincere thanks go to the many who contributed to this tremendous project. I would first like to thank all of the professors who participated in this project. I learned something from each one of them. The students who completed our surveys and submitted reviews of professors on RateMyProfessors.com made this project possible. I am also very grateful to the schools that value great professors as much as we do. A special thank you goes to our authors, Jen Adams (who, by the way, is a goddess), Eric Owens, Andrea Kornstein, Calvin Cato, Ann Weil, Jennifer Zbrizher, Brandi Tape, Eric San Juan, Jen Clark, and Eric Ginsberg. Suzette Korchmaros and Evan Schreier deserve many thanks for their incredible dedication to working with thousands of student quotes and professor surveys to produce the professor profiles and the school profiles. Very special thanks go to Robert Franek and Seamus Mullarkey for their editorial commitment to and vision for our editorial endeavors. My continued thanks go to our data collection pro, David Soto, for his successful efforts in collecting and accurately representing the statistical data that appear with each college profile. The enormousness of this project and its deadline constraints could not have been realized without the calm presence of our production marvel Kim Howie and her dedication and focus. Meave Shelton and her careful eyes continue to amaze me. Special thanks also go to Jeanne Krier, our Random House publicist, for the dedicated work she continues to do for all of our books. I would also like to make special mention of Tom Russell, Nicole Benhabib, Alison Stoltzfus, and Ellen Reed, our Random House publishing team, for their continuous investment and faith in our ideas. We are so lucky to have the RateMyProfessors.com team as partners, and their massive amounts of data kept boredom at bay for many weeks on end. Last, I thank my TPR Partner Team, Scott Kirkpatrick, Michael Bleyhl, Paul Kanarek, Brian Healy, and Lev Kaye for their confidence in me and my content team and for their commitment to providing students the resources they need to find the right fit school for them. Again, to all who contributed so much to this publication, thank you for your efforts; they do not go unnoticed.

Laura Braswell
Senior Editor
The Princeton Review

Table of Contents

Introduction

ADVICE FROM THE BEST PROFESSORS

We hope we're not the first to tell you this, but if we are, brace yourself: College classes will be a lot different from your high school classes.

Walking into your first college class will be a little scary. At some larger schools, freshman classes can have as many as 500 students in them, so you might feel lost in a crowd of strangers, and your professor might not even bother to learn your name or care whether you even show up.

And as you work your way through the semester, it might get even scarier if you have managed to make it through most of high school without nailing down a study method and without coming across any truly challenging material. Professors expect you to do a lot of reading and studying on your own time so that you're prepared for the next lesson. In high school you learned new material in class and received homework assignments to help you understand that day's discussion. In college, you'll be responsible for understanding a lot of the material BEFORE the class discusses it; class time will be spent digging deeper into what you should have already read. You will have to prepare.

At some point you might fall behind in your preparation and then feel like it's okay to skip a class or two because no one will notice. And you'll plan to double up on the studying before the next class…only to find that you have to cram for that other exam that you almost forgot about. You may decide to skip the reading altogether and just survive on the notes. You might even think you're getting away with something only to discover, on test day, that the questions on the exam look nothing like what was on the board during lecture.

Let's look at a different scenario. Maybe you'll be lucky enough to walk into a small freshman class where the professor will know your name by the end of the first class; maybe class time will mostly consist of discussion about an interesting topic with no boring lecture to put you to sleep. Don't get too comfortable just yet, because that's no cake walk either. Because your professor will know your name and will have a lot more time to spend critiquing your papers and directing questions at you in class, then you and only you will be responsible for knowing the material and for being able to convey logically your ideas to the class. If you don't know an answer or if you think you can hover under the radar, there will be nowhere to hide, and any absences will be noticeable.

Even a mid-size class with a mix of both of these scenarios will put you in the seat of responsibility. There will be no daily reminders to read those chapters before class next Tuesday. The friend who has helped you with random homework assignments since third grade probably won't be your lab partner. Your chemistry professor is going to assume you don't need a refresher about how to calculate electron charges, so he'll skip over that part of the first chapter even though your last chemistry class was maybe two years ago.

All of those handy crutches that you've leaned on for years will not be there. So how do you survive? Here are a few pieces of advice from our Best Professors.

WHAT ADVICE WOULD YOU GIVE TO STUDENTS?

Paul Anderson, Professor of Mathematics, Albion College
Get help when you need it, do your homework every night, come to class, take detailed notes, and ask questions when you need to.

Sue Barry, Professor, Biological Sciences, Mount Holyoke College
The potential for change is great in all of us if we can learn how to tap in to that potential. I tell my students not to let anyone tell them what it is they cannot do. They should not shortchange themselves.

Randy Beard, Professor, Economics, Auburn University
I tell my students not to panic.

Dara N. Byrme, PhD, Associate Professor, Rhetoric and Intercultural Communication Specialist, John Jay College of Criminal Justice
Support and encouragement from a professor matter just as much as doing the homework. The most powerful thing any young person can learn to do, especially in this century, is to continually learn how to harness the power of language and communication.

Fredrick P. Frieden, PhD, ABPP, Adjunct Associate Professor of Psychology, The College of William & Mary
Take risks. Sometimes it works and sometimes it doesn't.

Joel Richeimer, Professor, Philosophy, Kenyon College
Be totally awake or you will miss what is happening.

Dasan M. Thamattoor, Associate Professor of Chemistry, Colby College
Come regularly to classes, listen carefully to lectures, take good notes, and persevere with a good attitude.

Ronald S. Thomas, PhD, Senior Lecturer in Global Management, College of Business Administration, Northeastern University
Probably the most important thing is an openness to examine new ideas and a curiosity about the world and other people. Active and consistent class participation is a key part of learning. My classes and assignments are demanding of students' time and attention, so good time management is important. Finally, it's essential to make one's best effort in contributing to the work of the team.

Eleanor Townsley, Professor of Sociology, Mount Holyoke College
Curiosity and humor are essential, but so are more practical qualities like diligence, tenacity, and good time management.

10 THINGS YOU NEED TO DO TO SUCCEED IN COLLEGE (AND IN LIFE)

We talked to hundreds of professors, and we specifically asked them about the habits they see in the most successful students. Professors do, after all, see hundreds of students come and go every year, and they also see the transformation that students make over the course of a semester.

We went through all of their answers and pulled out ten actions you can take to make sure you are one of those successful students who doesn't look so lost on the first day of class or who slouches down in the back of the class in the middle of the semester trying to avoid a question the professor has thrown out for discussion. We also don't want you to be the student who just gives up a little after halfway through the class and completely stops going.

The good news is that professors don't want you to be any of those students either, so they gave us some great tips! We've picked out the ones we heard over and over, and we've also given you the information in the professors' own words. We hope it helps get you through some of those tough classes!

1. **Read**—Those college textbooks aren't just for show. In order to understand and appreciate a subject, you'll need to read, and you'll need to read critically. Reading ahead will help you understand the class discussions, and reading for pleasure will help you have a wider appreciation for many different subjects that you can relate to your classes. Increasing your vocabulary never hurts either. There are studies that show a strong vocabulary will make you more successful in your career.

2. **Listen**—One of the easiest ways to learn anything is to simply be quiet and listen. You'll learn more than just the information that is coming out of a person's mouth. You'll start recognizing the importance of body language and nuance in someone's voice tone. You can learn from the questions that other students ask, and you can learn about other people's backgrounds and relationships, which will help you understand people better in general.

3. **Ask**—What is that fear of asking questions? Do we think it's a weakness to show that we don't know everything? Though it might seem like that in a high school classroom, the college classroom is a completely different environment. Questions that you ask will be a key part of your learning experience. Class discussions will give you a deeper understanding of material, and the questions that you ask will help spur on those class discussions. Also going to office hours and asking your professors questions will help build connections with your professor that will help you throughout college and perhaps throughout your life. Professors are there to help you, and they are eager to answer questions.

4. **Prepare**—Unless you have strong study habits, the workload from a full schedule of classes might seem daunting. You will need to know how to outline chapters and how to build and research a thesis. You'll need to learn how to keep up with the readings and not try to cram a semester's worth of learning in the night before an exam. But even making the effort to prepare for each class will help break all of those looming projects, papers, and exams into easier tasks. Do yourself a favor by reading through material before going to class to discuss it. You wouldn't show up to the big game without having practiced any, would you?

5. **Plan**—Having a goal to work toward is always more productive than swimming around in the sea of college. Whether you're working on an essay, a project, a double major, or a job offer, the best way to make sure you do your best is to take some time at the beginning and do some planning. Break the larger task down into smaller tasks and build a schedule and a task list. You will feel more productive working through the smaller pieces and less overwhelmed than if you were to wait to do the work at the last minute. You don't want to be starting a fifteen-page paper two days before it's due.

6. **Organize**—In high school, your classes were all in one place, and most of your friends had the same projects, exams, and deadlines that you did. College is not high school. Classes meet on different days. Exams for different classes will all come at the same time. You may have work to do on a weekend when all of your friends want to do a road trip. The best way to keep track of it all is to stay organized. Also, keeping an organized dorm room helps you keep your roommates happy.

7. **Participate**—With it being so easy these days to zone out and hide inside of our phones and the Internet, make sure you don't forget to participate in the classes and activities that are going on around you. College is about meeting tons of people, networking with people you might work with in the future, and living experiences that you'll remember for the rest of your life. You'll absolutely miss something if you're staring into your phone during class—or even during the break or at the beginning of class. Chat with your classmates—the real people sitting next to you—instead of texting people who you feel safe talking to. Besides, one of those strangers might just be the person who becomes your best friend for the next twenty or thirty years.

8. **Work**—It's not the most fun thing to do, but it's necessary if you want to succeed. Nothing in life worth having is free. The great thing about college work is that you'll reap great rewards. You'll expand your horizons, and you'll work on projects that you'll love, which may lead you toward a successful and interesting career in the future. Some projects will not be fun, but they still have to get done, and working through those will teach you discipline, which you'll need out in the real world beyond campus.

9. **Persevere**—Things will get hard. Yes, college is supposed to be fun, but it's not going to be easy. Some days you'll feel scared and alone, and other days you'll feel overwhelmed and defeated. The best thing you can possibly do on those days is to find a quiet spot on campus (probably in the library) and just hunker down and power through whatever project is giving you trouble. Simply closing the book and

avoiding the project will never make it go away. Perhaps you can find a friend who is having trouble with his or her project and sit down and brainstorm solutions to both problems. Collaboration is one of the many wonderful parts of being in college; never again will you be in such a collaborative learning environment. Even if your project or paper ends up done but not perfect, your professor will appreciate the effort and can help you make it better.

10. **Show up**—You can't learn anything if you never go to class. Some professors might require you to attend class, but some may not care if you show up or not. You're responsible for yourself once you get to college. If you don't show up for class and then fail the exam, it's no one's fault but your own. You can't expect to keep a job where you can just decide not to show up for work on random days. Just know that professors will notice if you show up every day, and put in the effort to participate. They will know your name and face if you show up to their offices with questions and further discussion about the topics. And once they know your name, your ability, and your work ethic, they just might cut you some slack when you really do need it (just don't take advantage of the kindness).

WHAT HABITS DO YOU CONSISTENTLY SEE IN STUDENTS WHO HAVE THE MOST SUCCESS IN YOUR CLASSES?

Soha Abdeljaber, Mathematics Instructor, New Jersey Institute of Technology

Students who have the most success are the ones who come prepared to class. They have their homework and are ready to learn. They come to class with the goal to learn and not just earn credits to graduate.

Dr. David Baker, Associate Professor and Chair, Physics, Austin College

Curiosity, hard work, ownership of their learning, and a sense of adventure.

Elizabeth Barnes, Professor of English and American Studies, The College of William & Mary

Honestly, the most successful students are the ones who pay attention. I could say the ones who ask questions and take notes and volunteer ideas, and that would be true. But that's all part of paying attention.

Dr. Curtis Bennett, Professor of Mathematics, Loyola Marymount University

Students who succeed in my classes are willing to put in a lot of time and come to my office hours. They are willing to take chances and to embrace the idea that even unsuccessful serious attempts at solving problems will help them learn (and are even sometimes a necessary part of learning).

Victoria Brown, Professor, History, Grinnell College

Stick-to-itiveness. Just sheer grit, persistence, and perseverance—hunger to improve their intellectual game and a willingness to shoot intellectual hoop after intellectual hoop to gain that improvement.

Dale F. Burnside, Professor of Biology, Lenoir-Rhyne University

Curiosity, enthusiasm, and self discipline.

Victor L. Cahn, Professor of English, Skidmore College

Most of my best students seem to be very organized. I also respect creativity in almost any form, and I hope that my writing assignments allow students to exercise their talents in this area.

Matthew Carnes, SJ, Assistant Professor, Department of Government, Georgetown University

They're active learners. They question what they read and hear, and they test it against what they know of the world. They look up facts that they doubt or wonder about, and they regularly verbalize their thoughts—whether in class or discussion section, or in office hours, or in informal study groups or conversations with friends. This forces them to form and re-form their opinions and, ultimately, to integrate them into their larger sense of themselves and the world.

Ralph G. Carter, Professor of Political Science, Texas Christian University

They don't miss classes, are well-organized, follow instructions, ask questions, get their work done on time, and learn from their mistakes.

Phillip Cornwell, Professor of Mechanical Engineering, Rose-Hulman Institute of Technology

They have an excellent work ethic. They do not procrastinate and are willing to ask questions after they have engaged the material in a meaningful way. They do all the homework and always come to class prepared.

Susan Croll, Associate Professor of Psychology, Neuropsychology, and Neuroscience, City University of New York—Queens College

The habits that all of my most successful students possess are good attendance, open-minded thinking, and tolerance for the ideas of others.

Yolanda P. Cruz, Robert S. Danforth Professor of Biology, Oberlin College

Curiosity, attentiveness, and persistence.

David B. Daniel, Professor, Psychology, James Madison University

Hard work and flexibility. One can always develop, improve, or even backslide, and it is seldom due to chance. Even if it were, we are each responsible for how we handle things. Conscientiousness. Openness to new ideas. Asking questions without being too self-conscious. Curiosity and willingness to think about things, not just to memorize.

Susan Daniels, Visiting Instructor in Theatre Arts, Mount Holyoke College

Students who have the most success in my class tend to be disciplined, curious, and courageous.

Richard Fleming, Professor of Philosophy, Bucknell University

A desire to do more than is done in the classroom, an appetite for reading, and a passion for asking questions.

Fredrick P. Frieden, PhD, ABPP, Adjunct Associate Professor of Psychology, The College of William & Mary

The best students seem to be very attentive, diligent, and detail-oriented, and they are good writers. They make me know who they are by contributing to the class often.

Steven W. Guerrier, Professor of History, James Madison University

A seriousness of purpose. They enjoy learning, they read and write without coercion, and they understand that they are in college to gain an education.

Joe Irvine, Instructor, Business Law, The Ohio State University

They are diligent, well prepared, and interested in doing well.

Douglas Johnson, Associate Professor, Psychology, Colgate University

They are open to new ideas and come to class prepared to learn, and they ASK when they don't understand something.

Stephen Long, Assistant Professor, Political Science and International Studies, University of Richmond

Students' attitudes have a great effect on their success in my classes. Students who bring themselves fully to class, without distractions like Facebook or text messaging, always perform better than others.

John Warne Monroe, Associate Professor of History, Iowa State University

Students who do well in my class tend to be good readers and have been good readers for a long time.

Nina Moore, Associate Professor, Political Science, Colgate University

The most successful students begin the semester with one or more questions and ideas of their own.

Ronald Pitcock, J. Vaughn & Evelyne H. Wilson Honors Fellow, John V. Roach Honors College, Texas Christian University

Successful students in my classes are risk-takers; they throw themselves fully into everything they do. They are unafraid of making mistakes; in fact, my best students can laugh at the mistakes they make, instead of becoming paralyzed. Successful students do not shy away from working with me. They seek professional relationships with their professors, are open books when it comes to sharing their work and preparation, and most importantly are able to take criticism and advice. They listen well and can apply, very quickly, those lessons to their learning, writing, and research.

John J. Pitney Jr., Professor of Government, Claremont McKenna College

One set of habits is common to just about any job: punctuality, thoroughness, and attention to detail. Another set is more specific to academia: a willingness to search the scholarly literature and an ability to devise topics that either challenge conventional wisdom or fill gaps in the existing research.

🗨 **Aric Rindfleisch,** McManus-Bascom Professor in Marketing, University of Wisconsin—Madison

They attend class regularly, come prepared, and participate actively.

🗨 **Todd Schoepflin,** Associate Professor, Sociology, Niagara University

They come to class with a positive attitude and an open mind. They are willing to participate in discussions and motivated to do the required work throughout the semester.

🗨 **Roberto Serrano,** Harrison S. Kravis University Professor of Economics, Brown University; and Research Professor, Madrid Institute of Advanced Studies (IMDEA)

Hard work and sacrifice. Economic theory is not something one learns without truly applying oneself.

🗨 **Timothy Baker Shutt,** Professor of Humanites, Director of the Integrated Program in Humane Studies, Kenyon College

Eagerness, interest, and commitment.

🗨 **Mark Sibley-Jones,** PhD, University of South Carolina

Effort, effort, effort, and constant eagerness to be intellectually engaged.

🗨 **Bryan W. Van Norden,** Professor, Philosophy, Vassar College

Successful students are highly motivated, but not by grades. Successful students are interested in the topic, and they want to understand it deeply.

🗨 **David Walker,** Professor of English and Creative Writing, Oberlin College

Creativity, persistence, not being satisfied with the easy answers, and a willingness to take risks in the pursuit of truth.

🗨 **Nicole Y. Weekes,** Professor, Neuroscience, Pomona College

Drive, a love of knowledge, dedication, persistence, and resilience.

🗨 **David Wetzel,** Lecturer, University of California—Berkeley
They challenge what I say or ask me to explain further points they don't understand.

🗨 **Jim Whittenburg,** Pullen Professor of History, Lyon G. Tyler Department of History, The College of William & Mary
Above all, reflection. My best students are introspective. Of course, they must be willing to say, orally and in written form, what they think. Fearlessness and competitiveness have their place, but I find that the students who get their hands in the air first are not necessarily the students with the insight. I prefer that students surround a topic, look at it from many angles, then tell me what they think. Of course, sometimes I get all these things—fearlessness, competitiveness, AND reflection in one package.

🗨 **Craig Woodard,** Professor of Biological Sciences, Mount Holyoke College
There is no secret here. Successful students work hard. They come to every class, they study consistently, and they hand in their papers and lab reports on time. Successful students get to know their professors. They ask questions, and they participate in class discussions.

🗨 **Steve J. Wurtzler,** Associate Professor, Cinema Studies, Colby College
A willingness, sometimes a passion, to embrace new experiences and new ideas.

🗨 **Samuel Yamashita,** Henry E. Sheffield Professor of History, Pomona College
The students who do the best in my classes are those willing to devote the time necessary to read, think, and write carefully. They also are fearless and speak up in class discussions, offering their opinions, often on subjects quite new to them.

RateMyProfessors.com Top University Professors List

Each year RateMyProfessors.com publishes its list of Best Professors based on ratings posted by students who use the site. The list is published to shine some love and attention on those professors who bring their A game to class every day and those who have won not only the minds but also the hearts of their students. We love those professors and RMP wants you to know who they are. We have included profiles of some of these professors in with the rest of the Best Professors. (Professors who appear on this list but not in the book chose not to participate in our survey.)

1. David Mease, Business, San Jose State University
2. Dr. Kimora, Criminal Justice, John Jay College of Criminal Justice
3. Kateryna Schray, English, Marshall University
4. Melinda Shoemaker, Psychology, Broward College
5. Stephen Pennell, Mathematics, University of Massachusetts—Lowell
6. Susan Croll-Kali, Psychology, City University of New York—Queens College
7. James O'Keefe, Criminal Justice, St. John's University
8. Melissa Bush, Chemistry, University of North Florida
9. Tony Smith, Communication, St. Petersburg College
10. Todd Schoepflin, Sociology, Niagara University
11. Susan Young, Mathematics, The University of Akron
12. Jimmy Anderson, Health Science, Macon State College
13. Evelyn McClave, English, California State University—Northridge
14. Howard Peter Steeves, Philosophy, DePaul University
15. James White, Music, Pennsylvania State University—Altoona
16. Monica Zima, Computer Science, Miami Dade College
17. Mike Morrison, History, Purdue University
18. Dara Byrne, Speech, John Jay College of Criminal Justice
19. Gerard Callanan, Management, West Chester University of Pennsylvania
20. Dale Burnside, Biology, Lenoir-Rhyne University
21. Soha Abdeljaber, Mathematics, New Jersey Institute of Technology
22. Lea Ramsdell, Languages, Towson University
23. Michallene McDaniel, Social Science, Gainesville State College

24. Joseph Biel, Art, California State University—Fullerton
25. Tom Gufrey, Chemistry, California State University—Long Beach

How to Use RateMyProfessors.com as a Student

What if there were a website where professors could post your grades and comments about your performance as a student in their classroom? What if your parents could read it? Potential employers? Your friends? Public evaluations—like the ones that students post about professors—are sometimes a hard pill to swallow. It's important to know that reading through the reviews of professors on RateMyProfessors.com can really help you decide which professor might best help you understand the material, but you have to remember to use the website as a guide. In the long run, YOU are the most knowledgeable about the way you learn. You should walk into class with an open mind and make sure that you always give your best to the professor—he or she has dedicated his or her life to teaching students just like you.

THE METHODOLOGY FOR THIS BOOK

How do we pick the Best Professors? To determine which professors will be in this book, we use some analysis and a wide range of input from students and college administrators, both quantitative and qualitative. We work to ensure that the professors in the book represent a wide range of subjects and teaching methods as well as institutions by region, character, and type. We created this first Best Professors guide as a resource to give students insight into the college experience and how exceptional professors can enhance it. We culled an initial list of one thousand professors from over forty-two thousand professors, based on our own knowledge and input from thousands of students via The Princeton Review's survey and RateMyProfessors.com. We gathered institutional data from schools, and we surveyed the professors themselves. The survey contains ten open-ended questions relating to teaching methods and student interaction.

Professor profiles are based on survey results, student comments, and interviews. For school profiles, we incorporated school data and quotes from surveyed students.

Our surveying is a continuous process. The survey has more than eighty questions divided into four sections: About Yourself, Your School's Academics/Administration, Students, and Life at Your School. We ask about all sorts of things, such as "How accessible are your professors?" and "How interesting are your professors?" Most questions offer students a five-point grid on which to indicate their answer choices (headers may range from "Excellent" to "Awful"). Eight questions offer students the opportunity to expand on their answers with narrative comment. These essay-type responses are the sources of the student quotations that appear in the school profiles. Once the surveys have been completed and responses stored in our database, every college is given a score (similar to a grade point average) for its students' answers to each question. This score enables us to compare students' responses to a particular question from one college to the next. We use these scores as an underlying data point in our calculation of the ratings that we cross-reference with RateMyProfessors.com data. Certain RateMyProfessors.com data points weigh more heavily, such as the number of student reviews and the overall quality rating. Once we have the professor survey information in hand, we write the professor profiles. Student quotations in each profile are pulled from RateMyProfessors.com because they represent the sentiments expressed by the majority of survey respondents regarding the quality of that professor. To guard against producing a write-up that's off the mark for any particular professor or college, we send professors and contacts at each school a copy of the profiles we intend to publish prior to publication date, with ample opportunity to respond with corrections, comments, and/or outright objections. When we receive requests for changes, we take careful measures to review the suggestions and make appropriate changes when warranted. All quotations in the school profiles are from students' responses to open-ended questions on our survey. We select quotations based on the accuracy with which they reflect overall student opinion about the school's professors.

HOW THIS BOOK IS ORGANIZED

The professors are organized by department and subject to give students a look into classrooms at many different schools and to allow for insight into that major. Following the professor profiles is a section of school profiles; any school that has a professor in the book is included. These profiles are organized alphabetically.

DATA DESCRIPTIONS

Type of school

Whether the school is public or private.

Affiliation

Any religious order with which the school is affiliated.

Environment

Whether the campus is located in an urban, suburban, or rural setting.

Total undergrad enrollment

The total number of degree-seeking undergraduates who attend the school.

Type of school

Whether the school is public or private.

Most common regular class size

The most commonly occurring class size for regular courses.

Tuition

How much in-state and out-of-state tuition costs minus fees and room and board.

Average Indebtedness

The average per-borrower cumulative undergraduate indebtedness of those who borrowed at any time through any loan programs (institutional, state, Federal Perkins, Federal Stafford Subsidized and Unsubsidized, private loans that were certified by your institution, etc.; exclude parent loans).

Nota Bene: The statistical data reported in this book, unless otherwise noted, was collected from the profiled colleges from the fall of 2011. In some cases, we were unable to publish the most recent data because schools did not report the necessary statistics to us in time, despite our repeated outreach efforts. Because the enrollment and financial statistics, as well as application and financial aid deadlines, fluctuate from one year to another, we recommend that you check with the schools to make sure you have the most current information before applying.

About RateMyProfessors.com

RateMyProfessors.com is built for college students, by college students. Choosing the best courses and professors is a rite of passage for every student, and connecting with peers on the site has become a key way for millions of students to navigate this process. The site does what students have been doing forever: checking in with each other—their friends, their brothers, their sisters, their classmates—to figure out who's a great professor.

RateMyProfessors.com is the largest online destination for professor ratings. With 7,500+ schools and more than 13,000,000 entirely student-generated comments and ratings, RateMyProfessors.com is the highest trafficked free site for quickly researching and rating 1,500,000+ professors from colleges and universities across the United States, Canada, and the United Kingdom. More than 4 million college students each month are using RateMyProfessors!

RATEMYPROFESSORS.COM METHODOLOGY

Ratings

All categories are based on a 5 point rating system, with 5 being the best. The Overall Quality rating is the average of a Professor's Helpfulness and Clarity ratings, and is what determines the type of "smiley face" that the professor receives. An overall rating of 3.5 to 5 is considered good (yellow smiley face). An overall rating of 2.5 to 3.4 is considered average (green smiley face). An overall rating of 1 to 2.4 is considered poor (blue sad face). Easiness and Hotness ratings are NOT included when calculating the Overall Quality rating.

Ranking Lists

Professors are ranked according to the following methodology: Each individual professor's rating is first standardized, and subsequently the standardized scores for the years 2008, 2009, and 2010 are weighted, putting more weight on recent years and fewer weight on ratings from the past (15 percent for 2008, 25 percent for 2009, and 60 percent for 2010). Using the weighted score, professors are ranked from high to low. Only professors with thirty ratings or more are included to provide statistical significance. In an attempt to break ties, professors with a greater number of ratings were ranked higher; the rationale is that a larger amount of information typically results in an estimate closer to the true parameter. Nevertheless, ties (i.e., professors with the same score and the same number of ratings) still occur. In that case, if two professors are tied for the same place—say fifth—then the next available rank is seventh.

It should also be noted that school size does not affect the outcome of the lists nor does it give professors from larger schools an advantage over their corollaries from smaller schools. We performed a regression analysis on school size versus number of ratings and found no noteworthy correlation. Here now is a look at how each of the lists were compiled:

Highest Rated Professors

Students on RateMyProfessors rate professors on several dimensions: clarity, helpfulness, easiness, and rater interest (interest level prior to attending the class). However, overall professor quality (which informs the highest rated professor list) is determined by an equal weighting of only two criteria: clarity and helpfulness. A 5 is the highest rating and 1 is the lowest rating for each of the above-mentioned dimensions.

Highest Rated Schools

School rankings are based partially on the above professor ratings. In order to assemble a school's rating, we include both its average professor rating as well as its average campus ratings. We weigh professor ratings and campus ratings equally (50 percent each), which implies that a top school scores high both in terms of academics as well as campus life. Similar to the professor ratings, in order to provide statistical significance, we only admit schools with at least thirty rated professors and thirty campus ratings. Using the resulting scores, schools are ranked from high to low.

1. Data analysis was conducted with the help of Professor Wolfgang Jank, Associate Professor in the Department of Decisions, Operations & Information Technologies at the University of Maryland's Robert H. Smith School of Business.

2. Campus Ratings is a new element on RateMyProfessors that allows students to rate schools based on reputation, location, career opportunities, school library, campus grounds and common areas, Internet speed on campus, campus food, clubs and events, social activities, and whether or not the student is happy with their decision to attend the school.

WE WANT TO HEAR FROM YOU

To all of our readers, we welcome your feedback on how we can improve this book. We hope you will share with us your comments, questions, and suggestions. Or maybe you have a professor you would like to nominate for the next edition. Please contact us at editorialsupport@review.com.

Professor Profiles

Professor Profiles
Table of Contents

Accounting

Anne Clem PhD, Senior Lecturer, Accounting, Iowa State University

Anne Clem, who teaches accounting at Iowa State University, treats her students with respect, and demands the same of them in return. Students claim she "knows your question before you ask it" and "knows her stuff and will help you figure it out if you don't get it."

She brings a relentlessly positive attitude to her classroom, keeping her verbiage simple so that students can understand and "don't tune out, thinking 'this is over my head.'" As one student puts it, she is "incredibly organized and could teach the class blindfolded." Though her lectures are typically on the larger side, she "always makes an effort to teach as if I am in a room of thirty." "If students aren't comfortable asking questions or for clarification, their learning will be seriously limited." Basically, she emphasizes that the only "stupid" question is "the one that you don't ask," and that if all of the students had the answers and understood the material after reading the chapter, "we wouldn't need to be sitting in the classroom."

She is a big proponent of using aids to further studies, and believes that "technology provides so many outside of the classroom resources that are helpful to students with varying learning styles." Her classes include Advanced Accounting Problems and Financial Accounting, which is a large intro class; while many professors dislike teaching such courses, Professor Clem "loves to see the students start to understand a topic that is completely new to them and to begin to see its relevance in the world." She works very hard to help students break down the material in a systematic way that assists in their comprehension. "Accounting is a field which is constantly changing, so we spend a lot of time understanding the conceptual reasoning for the current rules rather than memorizing," she explains.

Dan Hubbard, PhD, CPA, Accounting and Management Information Systems, University of Mary Washington

Dan Hubbard, who teaches accounting and management information systems at the University of Mary Washington, wants students to see how the subject material is relevant to their lives outside of the classroom, and "that they will learn more through their own curiosity and questions than through my lectures."

Every student is a "class of one" for Professor Hubbard, who provides students with "a mirror of their own capacity." He teaches Advanced Accounting, Intermediate Accounting, and Principles of Accounting and Auditing, the latter of which is "fun" because "the students come convinced that 'this is going to be boring,' and I can play intellectual judo and flip them around." Auditing is his "real love" because students learn to really experience the world around them; it is the most "sensual" of business courses. His approach is Socratic and student-centered; he rarely uses a textbook but asks lots of open-ended questions. "There are many 'right' answers in my classes, because I'm infamous for saying, 'It depends,'" he says.

"He is the most unconventional professor you'll ever meet, and that's why it's the best class I've ever taken," says one student. "He allows you to work with others on everything because he wants you to get it right and learn the material," says another. "He is a great man, hilarious, and you actually learn valuable things from him. Take any class you can with him; it will be well worth it."

John M. Janiga, BBA, MBA, JD, LLM in Taxation, CPA, Professor, Accounting, Loyola University Chicago

Professor John M. Janiga, who teaches accounting and tax law at Loyola University Chicago, views teaching as the highest calling of a university or college professor. "It is the one aspect of a professor's work that most directly touches a student's life," he says.

In the classroom, his main goal is to get students to see the importance of taxation in decision-making, and "to develop a conceptual framework for understanding taxation that will serve them well for the rest of their careers." Throughout his twenty-six-year career at Loyola, he has "expended enormous amounts of time and energy into developing, refining, and teaching" his courses, which students view "as ultra-comprehensive and demanding" but "incredibly interesting." "He is extremely friendly, very dedicated to his work, and busts his tail to make all of the information as comprehensible as possible," says one.

It can be difficult to stimulate interest in and understanding of the complexities of accounting, especially in the area of taxation, but one student claims that "every single lecture is fun and interesting." "His lectures are illuminating, the homework is pertinent and helpful, exams are challenging, and the two projects help round out the learning process." Students walk away with a thorough understanding of tax concepts.

Professor Janiga has an extensive background in accounting, economics, finance, and law; for twenty-three years he operated his own tax consulting and preparation business and currently serves "of counsel" to the law firm of Spagnolo & Hoeksema, LLC. As a CPA and an attorney, he tries to incorporate "the best of the teaching methodologies and techniques that I had been exposed to in both the accounting and legal realms, and synthesize them in such a fashion so as to make my courses 'come alive' for my students." For example, he has developed a set of catchy or colorful words or phrases to illustrate certain crucial tax concepts, and many of his former students tell him that "they will never forget a concept we covered simply because of the terminology that I used."

It's a heavy-duty agenda, but Professor Janiga "puts more effort into his class than any other professor I've had at Loyola," one student says. "My hope is that by attacking my work—in my research, in my service activities, in my consulting work, and especially in the classroom—with such a high level of energy, passion, preparedness, values, and professionalism, students will be motivated to pursue growth, excellence, and ethical behavior in all of their pursuits. My belief is that if I model the characteristics of a joyful life to my students, they will recognize and appreciate those characteristics and will be driven to implement them no matter what career path they take," he says.

Mariah Lynch, MBA, MACC, School of Accounting, Moore School of Business, University of South Carolina

Mariah Lynch, a professor of accounting at the University of South Carolina Moore School of Business, wants what she says to stick, whether consciously or not. "They don't know it, but accounting creeps into all of the classes and is an absolutely necessary skill in the business world."

Even though some of the principles are admittedly occasionally "boring," she tries to convince them that they NEED to understand the fundamentals through real-life examples and stories. She has learned that "stories help, being funny doesn't equal unprofessional, and talking down to the students, particularly in the early classes, only disengages them." Students are treated the same as her children: "with respect when deserved, and I really want for them to do well." This "very laid-back and down-to-earth" woman also treats them as adults and doesn't take attendance, telling them to come only if they want but makes it known on the first day that "this is difficult material to learn yourself, and if they'll do their part, I'll do mine, and that will get them through."

In classes such as Managerial Accounting and Communication Skills (or any of her classes, for that matter), she doesn't use PowerPoint, because "if you aren't engaged, you won't do well." Her classes are example-based and very discussion oriented and she will, as time allows, "answer any question I can and apply it to a specific scenario I've experienced or heard." "I still remember what it is like to be a student and try to cater to different learning styles as much as possible given class size and make myself as available as possible given my family situation," she says. "She is extremely approachable and helpful," agree students. "If I could make her teach every accounting class I take from here on out, I would."

Agriculture

George W. Hudler, Professor, Agriculture and Life Sciences, Cornell University

"I want my students to leave each class period and/or complete each assignment having learned just one new piece of information that is so special that they can't wait to teach it to someone else," says George Hudler, professor of agriculture and life sciences at Cornell University.

He certainly has made good on this promise, teaching with passion and humor, "as if what you have to offer is the most important thing your students will learn that day, week, month, or semester." Students find him to be "entertaining and informative," and note that "he puts a lot of time into [his courses]."

Professor Hudler's quirky course offerings include Magical Mushrooms, Mischievous Molds, which is "a light introduction to the world of the fungi" that places a special emphasis on the roles of fungi as decayers of organic matter, as pathogens of plants and animals, and as sources of mind-altering chemicals; it also happens to be the most popular elective course in the college. "Our department chair challenged me to come up with a course that would attract students from other colleges and departments; students who would not normally take a course in our department," he says of its origin. He has since written a book on the subject, and helps to host a "fungus feast" at the end of every course. No wonder students describe him as having "such an infectious love of fungi."

In addition to classroom teaching, he conducts educational programs on tree diseases for plant health care professionals, Christmas tree growers, and golf course superintendents both in New York State and nationally, and brings the personal experiences he encounters to his classroom. He also actively seeks out stories in newspapers or popular magazines that are relevant to the topics he's covered, in order to show students "that the knowledge base I'm asking them to expand has some value in how they live and/or how their environment sustains them."

American Culture

Dr. Bruce Michael Conforth, Program in American Culture, University of Michigan

"Whatever the circumstance of my interaction with students, my primary goal is to use the material under discussion to show students that they have the ability to empower and define themselves." So says Bruce Michael Conforth, a professor of American culture at the University of Michigan. "To me, teaching is about engaging students: sharing my knowledge and experience as a way of helping them understand the American culture(s) they are entering."

Professor Conforth sees the material he presents in this "highly interdisciplinary field" as a vehicle to show students how they are connected to history, culture, other people, and the world. "A piece of historical or cultural information doesn't mean much to students unless they can relate it to their own lives in some way," he says. "Too many times students get used to professors who talk at them rather than engage them. Teaching, indeed all education, is about interaction with your subject matter, those around you, and the world." One student agrees: "Dr. Conforth is the most enlightened, empathic, intelligent, creative, and fun professor I've ever had."

In classes such as Post WWII American Subcultural Movements, The History of American Popular Music, and Survey of American Folklore, he tries to create a safe environment in which all students can express themselves, or disagree with him, and be treated with respect. "My classrooms are learning environments in which we are all on a mutual journey of exploration, and the topics we discuss are as much about life as they are the content of the subject matter." To this end, even in large lectures, he walks around the room, gets in students' faces, and "acts as a provocateur to get them to think outside the box and fully engage the subject, themselves, and their individual learning styles," while making it known that students are in a safe environment.

"Expanding topics is usually not a problem," and he uses his personal and professional experience with the content as a way for "topics to become individual and human, rather than distant and abstract." "I learned so much about people and culture in this class because Bruce was able to make the topic really come alive with personal examples that had relevance for everyone in the class," says a student.

American Politics

Sam Potolicchio, Visiting Assistant Professor, Semester in Washington Program, Georgetown University
Every day that Sam Potolicchio teaches, he strives to let his students feel that the classroom is the place he most wants to be. He follows the "teacher as animator"

school of pedagogy, and believes that in order "to excite the intellectual souls of students, a teacher must know how to match her own passions to the specific needs and wishes of students."

Professor Potolicchio, who teaches American politics and public affairs at Georgetown University, wants to inspire students to think about the world in ways they didn't think were possible, and for them to be able to connect seemingly disparate bodies of information. He is constantly seeking to understand how each student learns things differently so that he can present the material in accessible and entertaining ways. Having taught at every level of the educational system and in many different cultures, he has a "unique panoramic educational vision": "Teaching in a range of situations has added a depth and capaciousness to my pedagogical approach that allows me to understand how to animate a wide range of students."

His course load includes Religion and Politics, United States Political System, and Presidential Rhetoric, and guest lectures by prominent politicians are a regular feature in some of his classes. "I love attempting to understand people, and studying the art of persuasion not only provides a lens into the motivations and methods of our political leaders but it also provides a unique perspective on the American voter and citizenry," he says.

The man that students call "a cross between Matt Damon in *Good Will Hunting* and Robin Williams in *Dead Poets Society*" is "charismatic, brilliant, and presidential." "This is the first time in my life I am sad a class is going to end. Now I am just looking forward to when he becomes president so I get to see him every day again," laments one student.

Ancient Studies

Kerry Muhlestein, Associate Professor of ancient scripture and ancient Near Eastern studies, Brigham Young University

Kerry Muhlestein, who is a professor of Ancient Scripture and Ancient Near Eastern Studies at Brigham Young University, is interested in his students as learners. "My goal is to help students feel excited about learning, help them see their potential as a learner, and help them feel valued as a learner."

Several decades ago, he learned from his teachers that students learn far better from a teacher who cares more about them and their learning than about what others think of him. His areas of expertise are Egypt and Old Testament, and he just finished a year of teaching Old and New Testament courses in a study abroad program in Jerusalem, where he supplements facts and concepts with visits to appropriate sites or activities to illustrate them. "The cultural insights he provides help cement concepts," says a student. "He really knows the scriptures well, especially the Bible, so it was cool that he could tie in the Bible with his lectures," says another. "I love to teach the Old Testament the most because few students understand much of it before the course, and I love seeing the light bulbs come on in their heads as they get something for the first time," he says.

Professor Muhlestein tries to teach mainly by getting the students to ask questions, and starts out every class period by asking what questions students have from the texts they are studying. "At first the questions come slowly, but as we model how to ask and answer questions, the question session often takes up half of the class. In this way we cover much of the material I would cover in the lecture, but in a much more interesting and natural way than if I just spout it out and go through PowerPoints," he says. Students say that he makes you work for your grade, but "is clear on what you need to know and do, so if you will work, you can do well."

Animal Science

Thomas Famula, Professor, Department of Animal Science, University of California—Davis

Thomas Famula, a professor of animal science at the University of California—Davis, stresses the development of writing skills. "Clear thinking is not possible in the absence of clear writing," he says.

It's an admirable devotion for someone who teaches one of the school's most hands-dirtying classes. For twenty years, he has been teaching Animal

Science 1—Domestic Animals and People, which is a course pertaining to the basic biology and husbandry of domestic animals; students learn to milk a cow, set sheep, and clean a horse's hoof. In the classroom, he is admittedly old-fashioned—"I use chalk"—and he loves working with freshmen, who are "so enthusiastic." For larger classes, he is well aware of what is needed to keep everyone's attention: an "element of being able to control them and keep them on task and keep their minds engaged." "Where else do you milk a cow for a final??" says a student of his lab final.

To help the students get into the modern age, he podcasts his lecture, but he "plays games" to punish the students who don't show for class. "I may turn it off and give students information they won't get anywhere else." But why would you want to skip class? Students say this "hilarious" professor conducts a class that is "very entertaining and at the same time educational" and which "keeps his audience riveted." Or, as one student more simply puts it, "Just BIG FAN OF FAMULA!!!!!!"

Anthropology

Kathleen M. Adams, Professor of Anthropology, Loyola University Chicago
Kathleen Adams, professor of anthropology at Loyola University Chicago, learned the value of mentorship early on in her undergraduate career. "Adams is great—especially if you are one of those people that likes to cultivate a relationship with the professor," says a student.

She is passionate about her work and her students, and she mainly seeks to "encourage critical thinking and to teach students to teach themselves." She is "very clear and energetic," insists on involvement and perseverance from her students, and assigns a great deal of reading, but "it's interesting and easy to stay focused…[she] makes anthropology a lot of fun," students say.

Her classes include Globalization and Local Cultures, Anthropology of Tourism, and Anthropology of Museums, all areas that are relevant to her own research, or classes that "will enable students to see the world in new ways." On any given day, she tends to mix up her teaching strategies, offering students a mixture of lecture, discussion, video clips, etc. "She made me want to become an anthropology major. This class is so broad, but she picks the most interesting points to discuss," says a student. Another plus: She is "very understanding on poor grades if you come and talk to her."

Robert Anderson, MD, Professor of Anthropology, Mills College

Students in the classes of Robert Anderson, who teaches anthropology at Mills College in California, explore what it means to live in communities throughout the world in our time as well as in the far distant past. "In learning about other cultures, they come to realize that they can choose how to live their lives," he says.

He has been teaching at Mills for more than fifty-one years; and has been known to be called "Dr. Bob." "A VERY kind professor—great sense of humor and very flexible. He tries to be accommodating if you're in a pinch, but he's never gullible!" says a student. One of his most popular anthropology courses is School Culture and Policy, which shines a light on the importance, challenges, and rewards of educating children. "After twenty-five years of teaching courses in medical anthropology I changed my research, writing, and teaching program to education because I see the future of the United States in jeopardy due to schools failing our children and youth."

He finds the joy of being an anthropologist lies in the fact that that "we study people by living in a community"; this immersion is woven into the classroom, where he is moving away from straight lectures to interactive teaching formats, engaging his students in a richer learning experience. "Dr. Bob's class held my attention and was clearly taught. His exams and grading are fair and if you take decent notes, you should have zero problems," says a student.

John W. Burton, Professor of Anthropology, Connecticut College

"In some ways teaching is impossible; the best you can do is try to inspire someone to learn. Once a student trusts you, the rest follows."

Sage advice from Connecticut College anthropology professor John W. Burton, who sees a large part of his job as simply listening carefully to his students. "Teaching is a discussion, not a lecture. One of the most important goals is to make students feel confident to engage in discussion." In doing this, he "treats students as young anthropologists and never talks down," says a student.

Classes are always open conversations; to see Professor Burton standing at a podium and reading a lecture would be jarring. He wants his students to learn about a new way to see the world and themselves—"that's what anthropology is all about"—and he actively tries to engage student interest, "instead of trying to force info down their throats." He doesn't waste students' time with busywork and doesn't assign research papers until the upper-level classes, when students have a sophisticated understanding about what the discipline is all about. "So much of class time can be wasted with busy projects, and that is a waste of discussion and thinking," he says.

Now in the thirty-fifth year of his career, he teaches Introduction to Social and Cultural Anthropology; Topics in Human Evolution; Language and Symbolism; and Culture and the Human Experience. He admits that most freshmen come to him with very little knowledge of the field; it is his job to get them to step outside the box of their own lives and realize a very basic, and yet extremely challenging idea: that humans are somewhat cultural oddities. "The trick with anthropology is to have third eye and step outside ourselves as we're being ourselves."

It's this perspective (not to mention his mastery of the material) that students appreciate. "How did an intro class change my life?" asks one.

David N. Suggs, Professor, Anthropology, Kenyon College

Kenyon College anthropology professor David Suggs wants to help students to think critically about the world around them and to be able to communicate directly and effectively whether they are speaking or writing.

His entire teaching approach is based on the idea that education should be fun as well as challenging. Professor Suggs has no interest in producing clones of himself; he says that "the first step in becoming a liberally educated person is developing a shameless ability to say 'I don't know' or 'I don't understand.'" Rather, he wants students to know that "it is 'safe' to disagree with me so long as the argumentation which they present is data-based and well-reasoned." A student notices: "[He] likes you not to agree with him as long as you can back up your difference of opinion."

His courses include Anthropology of Alcohol Use and Human Sexuality and Culture, which is an examination of how we construct the "natural" in cultures of sexuality and of how we attribute meaning to sexual belief and behavior. His classroom style is best described as "laid-back lecture and discussion," and he tries to find anecdotes from his own research that he can present in an enjoyable and often humorous fashion as a means to begin exploring concepts. "While anecdotal teaching as an end in itself is merely self-gratifying, using anecdotes to lead students into seeing how you have initially negotiated realities and then subsequently come to understand them in greater depth can be remarkably empowering to them," he says.

Students love his thoughtful, "straightforward and clear" classes; says one, "You'd miss out not taking something with him before graduating."

Art (History)
Bradford R. Collins, Associate Professor, Art History, University of South Carolina

"Only humans make art because only humans do not instinctively know how to be." These are the words of Bradford Collins, an "endlessly intelligent" art history professor at the University of South Carolina, who has been teaching for more than thirty years. Even in reading his words, it is clear that he is passionate about clearly communicating why art history is not a marginal subject in the humanities. "I want to make my students understand that art history is relevant to their lives because it deals in the subject of human values," he says.

His lectures in classes including the History of Modernist Art, the History of American Art, 1900–1990, and the History of European Art After WWII are "captivating and interesting." "Collins is not only the most knowledgeable art history teacher I've ever had, but he is the only one who has fully captured my interest," says a student. His approach is "semi-Socratic"; for example, when the class discusses the idea of progress, which is a central tenet of modernist art, he asks them if they believe in progress. "And I require them to be specific," he adds.

"I never realized WHY art was so valuable," says a student. "The material is so interesting, or maybe he just makes it so. He inspires. He makes a large class feel intimate because he doesn't just lecture, he entertains."

Diana DePardo-Minsky, Assistant Professor, Art and Architectural History, Bard College

Diana DePardo-Minsky, a professor of art and architectural history at Bard College, loves Rome with its infinitely interesting and eternally complex mix of art and history, and aims to inspire a similar passion in her students.

This "dynamic and intelligent" lover of the Eternal City (one student calls her "practically frightening in her excitement") encourages students to trust their instincts when they analyze either visual or verbal information and to take pride in their work through clear articulation of their ideas whether written or spoken. She is committed to primary sources, both textual and material: "Firsthand experience—if possible involving actual handling—connects the past to the present, emphasizing relevance." She makes the material come alive to the students through enthusiasm and immersion; when they cannot visit the works they are studying, she shows them images that she took so she "can choreograph the experience of a piece as it unfolds over time in space." She also enhances secondary texts on the political, theological, or intellectual context of a commission with primary sources so that students understand the art within its culture and how that culture connects to their own. "She has a great way of sequencing the information she gives you in just the right way so you really absorb it," says a student.

Whenever possible, she immerses her students in the culture they are studying, which is a treat for students in classes such as Ancient Roman Art and Architecture, Italian Renaissance Architecture, and Villas of the Hudson Valley. She incorporates anecdotes about favorite professors and other colleagues into her teaching, "so that, when my students read texts, these authors appear as individuals, and they too can feel part of a continuum of comprehension." Most significantly, "I impress upon my students the importance of refining their work into something that they can be proud of, into a work of art worthy of the subject at hand." She often crafts research projects in conjunction with students to allow their personal interests to inform their topics, and she supplements lectures with relevant field trips, films, or food "to keep learning fun—since it is fun." "She truly is a pearl...kind and passionate, she will do all it takes to make you love and learn what she is teaching," says a student.

Leonard Folgarait, Professor, History of Art, Vanderbilt University

At most colleges and universities, there isn't much of a buzz about art history courses beyond the cliques of a few diehard art lovers. That's not the case at Vanderbilt University, though, where Professor Leonard Folgarait teaches a number of courses in the subject. Students call Folgarait the "best professor at Vanderbilt, hands down," which is a pretty impressive claim.

Folgarait is exceedingly humble about all this praise. He's not some larger-than-life personality bouncing around the lecture hall. He is by all accounts "soft spoken," with a dry sense of humor that includes "the occasional semi-funny art history joke." "What makes me interesting is that I don't try to be interesting," Folgarait says. "I try to disappear as a personality. I don't want students to remember if I was funny or mean or whatever. I want them to remember the subject matter." He adds that one of his goals is to convince each batch of students "that to challenge assumed and received knowledge is quite liberating."

Folgarait suspects that his popularity as a professor stems from his ability to convey his own passion about art to his students. "You can remember any material for awhile," he notes, "but if you are passionate it stays with you forever." Students straightforwardly call Folgarait "a dynamic lecturer with a contagious passion for the subject." His emphasis is less on mere facts and "more on learning how to look at art," and he is "very good at leading discussion and encouraging each participant." "Trust me," guarantees one student, "you'll want to go to class." "He makes art history extremely interesting and truly worth studying. There is no attendance but you go anyway because the lecture is so interesting." The word at Vanderbilt is that Folgarait's courses are worth taking "even if art history isn't your cup of tea." "Sometimes, I go sit in on his lectures, even though I'm not in any of his classes anymore," admits one student. "If I still lived in Nashville, I would sit in on his classes just for fun," adds a wistful Vanderbilt alum. "They were that good."

Barrett Tilney, Lecturer, Art History, Georgetown University

Barrett Tilney, who teaches art history at Georgetown University, endeavors to provide a foundation of her subject that instills an interest that goes far beyond the classroom. "My goal is to have students realize that the subject is fun, valuable, and worth learning," she says.

She is passionate about the discipline of art history and enjoys engaging in conversation on any level (lecture and individual discussion) about the subject. The students realize that that the material is relevant, powerful, and interesting, and that Professor Tilney is "laid-back, yet knowledgeable" and "just awesome." "TAKE HER CLASS. You will never regret it. She made me want to major in art history, a subject I'd never even considered before," says a student.

Her classes include Renaissance to Modern Art and Art in the Age of Rembrandt, and she even assigns some projects at the National Gallery, to illustrate the broad appeal of what some consider a niche subject. "Art history is a subject that has the potential to appeal to everyone," she says. She makes lectures "really fun with clever anecdotes and clips that feature famous paintings," and endeavors to create a relaxed environment in which students can feel comfortable to be actively engaged. "I also introduce ways that the works from the past are relevant to contemporary life and interests."

Art (Studio)

Joe Biel, Associate Professor of Studio Art, California State University—Fullerton

It was the piano-teacher mom of Joe Biel, studio art professor at California State University—Fullerton, who gave him the most valuable insight into teaching: "One might have to explain the simplest most basic concept fifty different ways to fifty different students."

It's a daunting lesson to learn at such a young age, but he embraced it fully, and even after twenty one years of teaching, he is always willing to give time to students who want to learn. "I develop a person-to-person dialogue with each student. I don't have blanket formulas but act in accordance with each individual student's particular nature," Professor Biel says. "He is extremely helpful, outgoing. Projects are really straightforward and practical and really help you improve your work," says a student.

He teaches classes such as Foundation Level Design, Advanced Level Figure Painting Class, and Artist Statement, which is a grad level class which helps students talk/write about their work, and he has staged numerous gallery and museum exhibitions in Los Angeles, New York, and Berlin. In assigning his students to a curriculum, he creates projects which have "specific parameters, but an endless number of specific solutions." Projects always have an idea generation component (which takes longer than most students expect), allowing them to develop their own personal ideas in solving the project, and a student can redo any project if they wish. "I also have technical exercises which accompany each project—this allows students to develop a sense of craft while working out their creative ideas."

One student says that "he's fair, intelligent, helpful, knowledgeable, friendly, professional, etc...He's the all-around BEST professor I've ever had the pleasure of encountering."

Daniel Stupar, Professor of Visual Arts, Brown University

Daniel Stupar, who teaches visual arts at Brown University, takes a personal interest in each student, teaching them "how to" skills, and "helping them realize their personal goals without prejudice."

His best students are those who are comfortable challenging status quo presumptions by defining artistic expression on their own terms, and he looks to support this perspective in classes such as Studio Art Foundations. This professional artist, furniture maker, and carpenter sees teaching his students in this way as "a natural extension of my lifestyle," and students agree that he is "incredibly knowledgeable of materials and knows just how to push his students." "Daniel's class was the defining feature of my first semester at Brown. I had always been interested in art, but had not felt as inspired or passionate as I did taking his classes," says one student.

His incredible knowledge of technical art-making skills aside, he stands out because of his clearly laid-out expectations of students, which always run high.

"Regardless of a student's level of ability, Professor Stupar pushes and challenges them, while giving them lots of artistic freedom to explore their passions." He gives students "a lot of freedom," but is also always available to talk in and out of class. This "downright cool" professor's assignments are open-ended and play best to the curious and ambitious, and he is "the perfect professor, friend, and mentor."

Atmospheric and Oceanic Sciences

Jonathan E. Martin, Professor and Chair, Atmospheric and Oceanic Sciences, University of Wisconsin—Madison

Jonathan Martin, who teaches atmospheric and oceanic sciences at the University of Wisconsin—Madison, wants to convey to his students that creating new insight into nature through the scientific method is as creative as any activity in the fine arts. "My goal in the classroom is to dispel the misconception that science is a litany of facts and that scientists are simply custodians of those facts," he says.

During office hours he offers a welcoming environment in which to question ideas and theories, seek deeper understanding of concepts or their origins, and to engage in thoughtful conversations about the material the class is covering. His courses include Introduction to Weather and Climate and The Frontal Cyclone, a synthesis course in which "the audience is captive and will go to any lengths to gain understanding." "I very much enjoy being the person who 'brings it all together' for our students," he says. A student says that he is "one of the most incredible professors out there, [and] this class puts together everything you learned in calculus, physics, and dynamics."

In his classes, he offers clear descriptions of challenging material that "are motivated by an empathy I try to retain for those who do not understand." Before a discussion, he will define all the relevant terms that will be included, to ensure that all are familiar with the necessary vocabulary for the given topic; he also gives a "conceptual explanation of the phenomena at hand before distilling the insights gained from that discussion into elegant mathematics." He engages the class in the Socratic method and is "not afraid to wait an uncomfortably long time for the response I am soliciting. In fact, if it takes a long time, I remind my students that remaining silent and running with the pack ensures mediocrity so I use the delay as a teaching instrument."

Professor Martin tries to approach explanation of challenging ideas from a variety of perspectives and almost always through the use of analogies that can be related to everyday experiences, and brings a sense of humor and humanity to scholarly activity and that is appreciated by students. "He talks about current weather for fifteen minutes every class," say students, and tells "engaging and funny" stories, all using his "great Boston accent." An unbridled enthusiasm barely conceals the fact that he "has a great set of secrets that I intend to share with students."

Biochemistry

Gerald Feigenson, Professor, Biochemistry, Cornell University

Gerald Feigenson is a professor at Cornell University who teaches junior and senior level biochemistry. His courses are typically pretty big—usually around three hundred students. Feigenson is also a serious, cutting-edge researcher and a really interesting guy. For example, he compares teaching classes at an Ivy League school to—of all things—*Enter the Dragon*, a classic 1973 movie starring kung fu icon Bruce Lee. "There's a scene where one of Bruce Lee's high-level students does a bunch of moves," he explains. "Then, Bruce slaps him and says something like, 'you have no emotional content.'" That's the key to lecturing effectively, he says. "You have to capture their attention."

Students call Feigenson "inspiring" and "one of the best teachers at Cornell." He is a "very good lecturer" and an "amazing professor who genuinely cares about teaching." He simplifies what is often complex material so that it's "very understandable and interesting." "You can tell he puts a ton into this class," relates one student, "from the separate word files he creates for the lecture notes to the silly little overheads he prepares and manipulates with forceps." Also great is Feigenson's exam system. "I pick about forty randomly chosen students from the class on the first day," he says. "I say, 'show up at 3:00 P.M. and we'll decide the grading policy. As they walk in the door, I greet them by name (because I've studied their photos) and they're dumbfounded because it's a huge class. We talk for about an hour about the exam policy and they vote." In the next class, Feigenson tells the whole class about the grading system that he and the subcommittee crafted. "Also," he adds, "the word gets out that the professor seems to know everybody's name."

Feigenson's generosity outside the classroom is still another perk. "He goes out of his way for his students." "You can just tell he cares a lot." He's "very helpful in office hours, not condescending," and he "tries hard to get to know his students." Students say that "his extra 'seminars on life' are very worthwhile." Every Friday afternoon, Feigenson holds optional discussions about things that are only tangentially related to biochemistry. Topics include how to find a good undergraduate lab and the finer points of the medical school application process.

Biology

Susan R. Barry, PhD, Professor, Biological Sciences, Mount Holyoke College
Dr. Sue Barry is a professor of biological sciences at Mount Holyoke College and the author of *Fixing My Gaze: A Scientist's Journey into Seeing in Three Dimensions.* She teaches Introductory Biology and Neurobiology, both of which focus on the important theme that organisms, including humans, are in a constant dialogue with their environment and can adapt. From this central tenet, she is able to demonstrate that far fewer behaviors in humans are hard-wired than most people think. "The potential for change is great in all of us if we can learn how to tap into that potential. I tell my students not to let anyone tell them what it is they cannot do. They should not shortchange themselves," she says.

One of the things that Dr. Barry stresses is the need for expansive learning; she has taught courses with her colleagues in a number of departments at MHC and has audited courses in the biology, music, math, and geology departments. "These experiences have all enhanced my teaching...there's no better way to learn than to try to teach the material to someone else."

She believes that personality is necessary in the pedagogical field, and tries to give the students an idea of what she is like as a person by incorporating stories about herself, as well as about how new information was obtained and how new ideas were developed. Students say that "her excitement for the subject is so contagious, that you're bound to become interested in it." To build upon this enthusiasm, she quotes as often as possible from firsthand accounts. "Thus, in my introductory biology class, I will read passages from Darwin's books."

There is another technique that she uses in the classroom: She will pause during lecture to give the students a problem to ponder, then ask them to pass in a written response. "I look over the answers and call on one of the students to describe what she's written. I'll often ask someone to speak who seems insecure or very quiet. I have told the students beforehand that I will only call on someone who has answered correctly so when the student speaks, she can speak with confidence." Perhaps this is why students say the she is "a lot of fun to listen to and time just seems to fly during class."

Jennifer Basil, PhD, Associate Professor, Biology, City University of New York Graduate Center and Brooklyn College

Everyone learns differently; that's why Jennifer Basil, who teaches biology at the City University of New York—Brooklyn College, tries to determine each student's learning style and to approach the subject matter in as many ways as possible for the whole class. "I present ideas in at least three different ways to reach everyone. I aim for long-term learning of concepts, rather than rote memorization. I want them to learn how to learn," she says.

Humor is critical in any classroom, and she believes that humans learn best from stories. "After all, for much of our history we did not have the written word." She tries to make every lecture like a story, so that it keeps the students' interest high, and they are excited to learn. "She has a story for every animal (somebody ate it, or died from it) that helps you remember," says a student. Her classes, which include Zoology and Animal Behavior, may be large, but she gets to know every student all by name, and they appreciate it. "She is so much fun and her love for animals adds to her sweet personality."

She is an avid researcher and has been studying the evolution of brain complexity and behavioral complexity for twenty-five years, using a diversity of animal models. "I've worked with birds, lobsters, octopuses, chambered nautilus, crayfishes, hamsters, you name it!" She sees research as keeping her teaching up to date, and teaching as keeping her research objective ("students have ideas that I do not, and they can be eye opening").

P. Robert Beatty, Lecturer, Department of Molecular and Cell Biology, University of California—Berkeley

P. Robert Beatty, who teaches in the Molecular and Cell Biology Department at the University of California—Berkeley, hopes to make students excited about the joys of science discovery through research. "My primary goal is to elicit enthusiasm in the students by finding the relevance of immunology in their everyday lives," he says.

He loves to teach (having done so for thirteen years at Berkeley) and is even "occasionally funny," in his own modest words ("He makes really boring material interesting," a student puts it). "I try to provide stories from my life or research work that provides relevance for class material." He thinks learning immunology is like "learning a new language," in which "you need to know the new vocabulary so you can "speak" immunology." In classes such as Immunity and Disease and Molecular Immunology Lecture, he will expedite this process by taking examples from current research or disease such as the 2009 influenza pandemic and discussing how the virus caused increased disease. "He's very funny, well-organized, helpful, and just a cool guy. He's got a gift for making complicated material comprehensible." "Don't be afraid! You don't need to know any science beforehand (I didn't), and he's very willing to answer questions," says a student.

John D. Bell, Professor and Dean, Undergraduate Education, Brigham Young University

John D. Bell, who teaches physiology and developmental biology at Brigham Young University, looks to create self-reliant problem solvers.

He cares deeply about his students' learning and makes himself accessible to them, designing courses that are "well-aligned between objective, activities, and assessments; and focused on lots of practice, feedback, and opportunity to demonstrate improvement." His classes include The Science of Biology and Mathematical Modeling; the former because he loves "to help students develop good learning habits early in their college career"; the latter because he enjoys "helping non-math and non-science majors learn to appreciate the wonders of math and its application to creativity and to understanding the world."

Professor Bell's teaching style is to have students prepare by reading before class and then to engage them in class by solving problems related to the reading topic. He provides feedback on their solutions, followed by answers to their questions, clarifications, and then repeated practice. "The classroom is often a very noisy place as two hundred students are working in pairs and trios with me and teaching assistants circulating among them." He also provides brief presentations to add context and clarity to the different topics. "These may involve slides, but not in the conventional sense. The slides often contain tasks for the students to do in class to build their understanding."

Dale F. Burnside, Professor of Biology, Lenoir-Rhyne University

"Stories and examples help students to understand concepts," says Dale Burnside, a professor of biology at Lenoir-Rhyne University, who enthusiastically claims that "biology is fascinating. My mind gets wrapped up with it."

He transmits this devotion to his students, letting them know that he is "actively involved in their learning" and giving them both the foundation and the tools for thinking and solving problems. His courses include Cell Biology ("the complexity of the simplest living units is amazing"), Human Anatomy and Physiology ("Wow! What a wonder of nature and of God"), and Bacteriology ("What amazing creatures! They adapt to every situation"). A former student refers to her experience as "one of the most fun classes ever. He speaks on your level and makes class enjoyable. You won't be skipping his class."

Even after teaching for forty-four years, Professor Burnside still prepares every class to make it "fresh and new." "I am blessed to be in this career. The students are very good to me," he says. His classes are arranged into an organized presentation of basic facts followed by thought provoking questions ideas and student response, which students say "makes learning fun and exciting." "He is serious about his teaching and loves his career choice," says another.

Yolanda P. Cruz, Robert S. Danforth Professor of Biology, Oberlin College

Oberlin College biology professor Yolanda Cruz is "a taskmaster, but apparently in a good way." While each class has a strict agenda ("classroom interactions are formal, organized, practiced (rehearsed) for the most part"), those that take the time to come to her office hours find a professor that is much more personal and relaxed. Her concern for students seeps through at the most surprising of times; those who do poorly in their first exam in one of her classes receive a personal e-mail offering assistance with study habits and note taking. "I'm a hardass. I think students actually respect that. If you demand a lot from them, they rise to the occasion," she says, it seems students do: "She's a very engaged lecturer and she's wonderful one-on-one. You HAVE to take a class with her before you graduate," says one.

Now teaching classes including an introductory course in Organismal Biology, advanced courses in Developmental Biology and in Epigenetics, and a freshman seminar called The Ethics of Biotech, she is an active researcher in the area of embryonic development in mammals. Professor Cruz has "never given the same lecture or exam twice," and she composes each lecture to the material as if it were a "seamless story," "leading discussions and seminars with appropriate historical or political perspective. I rely heavily on handouts so as to concentrate on the thread running through the lecture instead of digressing because of factlets."

One thing that Professor Cruz stresses is laying the foundations of critical thinking and study skills early in each student's college career. Her freshman seminar is writing-intensive, and some courses have drop-in study sessions and peer learning workshops where experienced students help the current ones figure out the best study techniques. In her lower level and intro courses, "students in general have never really had an experience with lectures, and the various reactions go from impressed to overwhelmed, and students need to be able to adjust." Advanced courses are "radically different," utilizing research projects, independent work, and discussion sessions. "I focus more on the student, not in just coming off as clever or smart. I want my students to come to lecture excited about what I will be talking about, not nervous about how overwhelmed they are."

Rachel Fink, Professor, Biological Sciences, Mount Holyoke College

"From my mother I learned that a good teacher cares passionately about her students," says Rachel Fink, a professor in the biological sciences at Mount Holyoke College.

She treasures the time she spends with her students—"they teach me about the world, what it is like to be young, they ask questions that can take a conversation from public policy to the behavior of molecules"—and finds that "being a teacher is NEVER dull." Students know that she cares about their lives, and that she sees the act of teaching as a tool unto itself: "To this day I try to get my shyest students to agree to teach something."

Her courses include The Cellular and Molecular Basis of Development and How Organisms Develop; what is most splendid about the latter course is the way the laboratory experiences are tied to the lecture material. "Since our lab schedule is based on the spawning season of the Pacific purple sea urchin, I always begin the course with a study of fertilization. FedEx delivers the ripe urchins the Tuesday of the second week of the semester, and that afternoon dozens of first-year students add drops of sperm to small beakers of eggs. As one cell cleaves to two, then four, students see that, amazingly, a context for learning mitosis is born." "She always made an effort to visualize processes that were difficult to visualize and explain things in different ways to make sure that we got it," says a student.

In Stem Cells and Regenerative Medicine: Past, Present and Future, which focuses on the science and bioethics of current topics in developmental biology, students take on the persona of a figure in the national/international debate about a topic such as embryonic stem cells, and then play that person in a debate presented to her large intro class. This is one of her favorite ways to get students teaching each other, and show that science is a very human endeavor. In all of her courses one goal is to have students see how ALIVE cells are, and how magnificent are the processes of development. "If even a few undergraduates tingle when thinking of the cells wandering, dividing, and rearranging within their own bodies, I have indeed done my job well."

Amy Frary, Associate Professor, Department of Biological Sciences, Mount Holyoke College

"Plants are a defining part of the landscape and yet they are so often overlooked," says Amy Frary, who teaches in the Department of Biological Sciences at Mount Holyoke College. "Moreover, there is a widely held belief that plants are not worth learning about."

Professor Frary considers it her duty to work hard in the classroom to dispel that misconception. "My goal is for students to leave my class not only knowing structure-function relationships and the particularities of plant sex lives but also with a newfound appreciation for the beauty of plants and the vital role they play in the environment and in our lives," she says. In the process of sharing her love of plants with her students, she hopes to impact their perception of and interaction with the natural world. "Oh what a difference a passionate teacher makes," exclaims a student. "When I signed up for this class I thought plant biology would be boring. On the FIRST DAY, Amy proved me wrong."

In classes such as Introductory Biology: A Green World, Introductory Biology II: How Organisms Develop, and Local Flora, she tries to present the material in a lively and stimulating way that emphasizes her respect for and fascination with the plant world. "Students often feel overwhelmed by terminology and the details of processes so I try to show them that a little logic and common sense will help them understand the material without having to resort to rote memorization." A student says: "She loves her field, that's for sure. It shows in her lectures."

Whenever possible, she will make reference to what one may observe in nature or to practical applications so that students can see how scientific knowledge impacts their lives; during labs, her classes use the local landscape as their laboratory, walking around campus to observe the colors of autumn and how plants prepare for winter. During individual meetings, her aim is to encourage students as much as possible: "[I want] to assuage their fears that the material is too difficult for them or that their ideas/lab reports/grades aren't good enough. My hope is that they leave my office feeling better than they did when they came in."

Dr. David Jaynes, Associate Professor, Biology, James Madison University

David Jaynes, who teaches biology at James Madison University makes the material in his courses accessible to students of any ability. In courses such as Human Anatomy (one of the hardest classes at JMU), Advanced Human Anatomy, and Human Embryology, he conveys the material as clearly as possible, building (very linearly) upon previously covered concepts. "I was surprised the first day because he's such a regular guy and doesn't put on airs. He's very approachable and helpful and so interested in what he teaches," says a student.

His organized approach to the complex topics he covers is what students appreciate the most; for heart anatomy, he starts very generally (e.g., superficial appearance), then adds detail, then gradually moves to internal structure, then function. "I use as many widely understood examples as possible," he says. "Anatomy is really, really time consuming! No professor is going to make this course an easy A. As far as professors go though, Dr. Jaynes is great!" says a student. "He was the best teacher I ever had. The material was tough, but he was always there to help. He is the reason I became a teacher myself." says an alum.

Robert Kosinski, Professor of Biological Sciences, Clemson University

"Students at Clemson are experts at blind memorization, and that's what they tend to do," says Robert J. Kosinski, who is a professor of the biological sciences at Clemson University. "By questioning them, I want to get them past memorization to a true understanding of the material. I try to get them to expect that the material will make sense to them."

This approach comes naturally to someone who truly finds learning enjoyable, and delights in understanding the world. "The pleasure of understanding motivates me, and by my example, I hope to motivate my students to seek understanding in all their studies." He mainly teaches premeds, and tries to be "very organized and not boring." Years of teaching the subject has given him plenty of interesting examples, and he tries to use the ones that are the clearest and most entertaining, and to give the students authentically hard questions to consider. "He keeps your attention through the lecture," says a student.

He prides himself on giving his students a solid preparation for upper-level courses, and loves introducing so many beginning students to the mysteries of biology. A self-proclaimed "old-fashioned lecturer," he tries to keep students engaged through somewhat outrageous and therefore memorable analogies in class. "Dr. Kosinski is a GREAT teacher, and he makes learning about biology entertaining with his silly metaphors in class," says a student.

Though his tests have a reputation for being "VERY hard," he is up-front about what he needs from students, and while students are not always happy with their grades, they usually admit that they got the grade they deserved.

John M. Lammert, Professor, Biology, Gustavus Adolphus College

John M. Lammert, a professor of biology at Gustavus Adolphus College, tries to be a quiet facilitator of his students' learning. "I hope that I am on their side, but that I have high expectation for their work."

An undergraduate professor of his gave the advice to "be a bit of a ham," implying "the creation of a feeling of excitement in the class and teaching lab." Professor Lammert took him up on his advice, and, in courses such as Principles of Biology, Microbes and Human Health, and Immunology, tries to incite these emotions using a Socratic approach, without putting students in the hot seat. "I guide students to help them move up the levels of learning so they become effective critical thinkers. A student who chooses rote memory for learning will not have much success in my classes," he says. "The man knows EVERYTHING. It's unbelievable," adds a student.

Professor Lammert knows that the real test of effectiveness of a professor is the feedback one receives after students graduate and go on to professional and graduate programs or to teaching or to research positions. Students say he is "one of the few profs who will follow a student throughout their college career and is interested in them as a person, not just a student." "He definitely LOVES when you engage in class and show a strong interest in the subject," says another.

Karl J. Niklas, The Liberty Hyde Bailey Professor of Plant Biology, Cornell University

Karl Niklas, who teaches plant biology at Cornell University, wants his students to achieve a full understanding of the material being taught and to think critically.

He respects his students, and has a sense of humor "that moves with the times." He is clear, careful, concise, and heeds his own advice to "always watch your audience to see if they are following what you are saying." Professor Niklas was an adjunct professor at the New York Botanical Garden and has been teaching for thirty-four years at Cornell. He has published four books and over 300 peer-reviewed papers in scientific journals. "Pedagogically speaking, he is a master and a perfect model of effectiveness," says a student.

His courses include Plant Biology 2410: Plant Biodiversity and Evolution and Plant Evolution and the Fossil Record 4480, which is a presentation of general evolutionary principles and a review of the plant fossil record, emphasizing form-function relationships. It's a niche field, for sure, but easily explained. "I think plants are cool (and extremely important to understand evolution and life on Earth)," he says. He uses a casual lecture style "that is designed to keep students entertained but, first and foremost, informed." For example, to illustrate the energy stored in seeds, he burns a peanut in the darkened lecture room. Students say "he works really hard to keep you awake and entertain you. He knows and interacts with all of the students during every lab." "He breaks information down to digestible pieces," and "is so excited about the subject [that he] gets tongue-tied talking about parts in the lecture."

Stan Rachootin, Professor, Biological Sciences, Mount Holyoke College
"There are many ways to make some sense of truly complicated and unexpected things. The goal is to get some of the world more coherent, by finding tools that fit both the problem and one's own way of thinking," says Stan Rachootin, who teaches in the Department of Biological Sciences at Mount Holyoke College.

A true lover of his job, he says he has "the amazing good fortune to teach only what I find fascinating—it can be a structure, a fossil, a person, or an idea." His courses include Evolution, Invertebrate Zoology, Darwin, and Nature Harmoniously Confus'd, which is an introduction to biology that poses questions where there are currently only suggestions of answers. "I illustrate the problems in lab with the plants, microbes, and animals one can find in the campus streams or in a teaspoon of soil." On one of the last days of class, "he lay down on the floor and demonstrated how we evolved out of fish."

He has been teaching for thirty-five years ("there really isn't anything else I could do"), a profession which he basically sees as telling and retelling stories. "Some were first told seventy-five or one-hundred years ago, but then more or less forgotten; many are new." Behind the stories, there are some recurrent themes— for instance, if you think that DNA explains life, you are missing at least half of what ought to be explained." "Stan's classes are story times themselves," says a student. "[His class] takes cell bio, genetics, and developmental bio and puts them together to tell an awesome story."

Beverly Sher, PhD, Visiting Assistant Professor/ Health Professions Advisor, Biology, The College of William & Mary

Beverly Sher, who teaches biology at The College of William & Mary, wants to help students become independent learners. This means encouraging them to ask questions and helping them to evaluate sources of information and devise strategies to find answers. "I want to be a coach as they learn how to learn, not just a source of information." "I'd be happy if I remembered even a third of what Dr. Sher said in class. She knows so much about her field and wants to pass that knowledge to her students," says a student.

Students appreciate her detailed comments on their work, as well as her accessibility. "One of my students called me 'the Instant Netflix of premedical advisors' because I answer e-mail so quickly," she says. She loves working with her students, and it comes through in her teaching and advising. "Professor Sher is simply unparalleled in her ability to engage. As a student in her freshman seminar on emerging diseases I could not wait to come to class," says one.

Professor Sher teaches two sections of Biology 150W: Emerging Diseases, a writing-intensive freshman seminar, every semester; one student calls it the "most rewarding class I have ever taken." Because this area of science changes so quickly, the course stays perpetually fresh, and she loves to point out its relevance to the real world: "We discuss everything from the latest Ebola outbreaks to the U.S. health care reform debate." The course is a discussion-intensive seminar, so she tries to be an informal facilitator of class discussion of the assigned readings. When students bring up topics in class that require expansion or background information, she gets up from the seminar table and draws pictures on the board while she talks. "For example, students often ask about the assay described in Richard Preston's book *The Hot Zone* that involves making virus-producing cells turn green; my informal diagrams on the board help the students understand what the author was trying to convey, as well as introducing an important serological technique." She detests PowerPoint and does not use it in class, as "I find that it kills discussion. In contrast, informal blackboard explanations keep the discussion going."

Trisha Spears, PhD, Department of Biological Science, Florida State University

Trisha Spears, who teaches biological science at Florida State University, has learned that if she is not enthusiastic about the material she's teaching, then she has no right to expect her students to be. "I think my students respond to my teaching because I am enthusiastic and because they know that I truly care whether they learn or not," she says. "She is so passionate about biology and she really taught me how to love it," says a student.

Her main courses are General Biology and Animal Diversity, and she enjoys teaching General Biology to majors who are early in their college career, so "that I can help them maintain the initial high level of interest they have for the subject, and also to expose them to, and have them appreciate, the breadth of interesting biological disciplines." She has taught on and off for more than twenty-eight years, and works to create a small-classroom atmosphere by learning students' names and actively engaging them in their learning. "Dr. Spears was the BEST professor I've ever had. She was helpful, clear, and very passionate about her work," says a student.

She is also a proponent of peer-learning, whereby students form groups of four the second week of class and they work together throughout the semester both in and out of class. "For example, students work as a group to create 'concept maps' of a topic covered in class, or by discussing a journal article that illustrates recent primary research being done that is related to a topic covered in class."

William Weiner, Associate Professor, Applied Biology and Biomedical Engineering, Rose-Hulman Institute of Technology

First impressions matter to William Weiner, who teaches in the Department of Applied Biology and Biomedical Engineering at Rose-Hulman Institute of Technology. It is essential to him that students feel comfortable around him and are willing to see him for extra help, and so he does everything in his power not to come off as intimidating. "I LOVE teaching college students, and I want them to know this. I also hope my students know I will do everything within reason to help them learn," he says.

Having experienced situations as a student where complex topics were explained simply and elegantly, as well as situations where very simple concepts were botched beyond recognition, this "personable" professor places a great importance on how he presents material. He encourages questions and classroom discussion, and "I always try to connect different concepts and help students to appreciate WHY they are learning certain topics and how this material relates to their particular majors." Practical examples are especially helpful in classes such as Electrical Systems, Comparative Anatomy and Physiology, and Essential Biology; in biology courses, he tries to explain key concepts first and then fill in the details, continuously using relevant examples of why a particular concept matters and how it fits in with practical experiences. "He is clear in his explanation and very straightforward and flexible in his schedule," says a student.

At a technical school like Rose-Hulman, students "must be willing to work hard," and his end goal is for students of EVERY technical major "to understand some basic biology and how it interfaces with a student's particular discipline. I love having students leaving this course and commenting on how they never appreciated how exciting biology can be!"

Craig Woodard, Professor of Biological Sciences, Mount Holyoke College

"Students are much more likely to learn difficult concepts if they find the concepts fascinating," says Craig Woodard, a professor of biological sciences at Mount Holyoke College.

In getting students excited about the topics being discussed, he brings his own enthusiasm to the classroom. He works hard keep up with the research literature in the field, and brings to the table the experiences he has as the principal investigator of a genetics/molecular biology research lab. A "very approachable, and straightforward" lecturer, he also puts all his lecture notes online, makes it clear what the quizzes and tests will focus on, "tries to keep the class's stress levels to a minimum." "He treats all his students with respect," and is "always willing to meet with people."

His courses include Genetics & Molecular Biology, Eukaryotic Molecular Genetics, and Biology in the Age of the Human Genome Project, which focuses on the science behind the Human Genome Project and the ways in which it will change our lives. Most of his teaching is done in the traditional lecture style (some case studies are used), which he supplements with animations. He encourages questions and comments from students ("even when it is a large class in a lecture hall"), and students say that "he is incredibly approachable and thoughtful and is passionate about genetics."

Business
David Mease, Associate Professor, San Jose State University
David Mease, who teaches at the College of Business at San Jose State University, simply wants to help his students truly understand the topic.

The man who one student calls "the epitome of what every college professor should be like" primarily teaches statistics and data mining, which are "extremely useful in the current economy due to new technology which makes large amounts of data extremely accessible." "He is very clear on what he wants… uses plenty of examples, and he doesn't try to trick you," says a student.

This organized professor always makes materials available online, including videos of all of his "crystal clear lectures," and he believes that students can generalize well from examples. Whereas many professors prefer to introduce examples only after they have introduced the general concepts and formulas (which often are difficult for students to grasp without context), his teaching style is very example-driven from the start, and he calls upon his experience as a statistician at Google to help make the blackboard come to life for students.

"For instance, when I teach probability, I first work through a number of probability problems with students before introducing any notation or formulas at all," he says.

Ronald S. Thomas, PhD, Senior Lecturer in Global Management, College of Business Administration, Northeastern University

Ronald S. Thomas, a senior lecturer in international business and strategy at Northeastern University's College of Business Administration, helps students develop a global mindset for "a world of extraordinarily rapid change, so they can engage with personal and business issues in a way that transcends the assumptions and values of their own country or culture."

A central focus of his teaching is "a moral commitment to help business students learn to value diversity, thrive in ambiguity, and engage complexity with enthusiasm and compassion." His doctoral degree is in psychological anthropology, so he brings a cross-cultural, historical, and humanistic perspective to all his teaching, and he sees his task not just as transmitting the basic concepts of international management, but as awakening his students' interest and enthusiasm for understanding the deep interplay of social, political, cultural, and economic forces forming the global economy in which they will work. "I help them expand their thinking and develop confidence in expressing their own point of view while remaining open to, and engaging respectfully with, other perspectives," he says.

He teaches classes such as International Business and Global Social Responsibility, Greening the Global Economy with Sustainable Business, Cultural Aspects of International Business, and National Strategies in the Global Economy. Students say he is "insightful, up to date with the world." He uses a mix of class discussion, mini-lectures, case discussions, debates, presentations, projects, and online activities, all of which "help move students to more complex ways of thinking by challenging their preconceptions and taken-for-granted ideas."

He also uses the debate format to enhance elements of the global mindset; however, unlike traditional debating, his student teams must develop a visual presentation to accompany their verbal debates, and must continue responding to questions from the class in online discussions. He works closely with the student teams to help them create effective and persuasive positions, and gives each team substantial written feedback on draft versions. "Students often tell me that being compelled to defend a position which they might not have personally agreed with, while working intensively with teammates from other cultures, is a powerful learning experience they deeply value."

Business Law

Joyce Boland-DeVito, Esq., Professor of Business Law, College of Professional Studies, St. John's University

Joyce Boland-DeVito, a Fulbright Grant recipient and a professor of business law at St. John's University in Queens, New York, has one main goal in her classroom: to have her students set goals for themselves. "I try to prepare my students to be aware of global, national, and local issues and be able to think critically so that they can succeed in their business lives and personal lives."

Though entering her twenty-fifth year of full-time teaching, it's still hard for Professor Boland-DeVito to think of it as work. "It's not just a job for me. It's a mission. I think about my students after I am in the classroom; in particular, how I can help them to be successful," she says. It shows, too. One student says, "She goes above and beyond the call of what a professor's duties are. She helps students with anything and everything that they may need."

She teaches undergraduate students, introducing them to the various types of law and the court system. A former in-house counsel and volunteer arbitrator for Nassau County Court, Professor Boland-DeVito knows that the law will undoubtedly impact students' lives, whether in their professional or personal lives, and she wants them to be prepared. She loves that "the law is ever-changing," and she imbues this excitement into her students through a high energy, positive teaching method that students "simply love." "I had her at 7:30 in the morning and still loved the class!" says one. Students are meant to assess their strengths and interests, and hopefully will learn how they can bring them to the world as a job; fortunately, her corporate background lends her a keen understanding of "the pressures on students outside of her classroom."

Best of all, there are no widgets or train A's and B's in these classes. Professor Boland-DeVito makes the material come alive through relatable, fun examples that often pertain to current events. "For instance, when I tell the class about contracts, I ask them about their favorite singers or band. Then I ask them about what type of contracts would be needed in order for that artist to put on a concert tour."

Arthur Gross-Schaefer, JD, CPA, MAHL, DD, Professor/Rabbi, Marketing and Business Law, Loyola Marymount University

Arthur Gross-Schaefer has been at Loyola Marymount University's College of Business Administrations for more than thirty-three years, held the position of the chair of the Department of Marketing and Business Law, and received numerous awards including being named the university's professor of the year. A primary goal of his teaching has always been to help students open up to the importance of their own acquired wisdom. "I encourage my students to share their knowledge. I want each of them to understand that they are a unique creation with their own set of experiences and views," he says.

This diverse collection of experiences all come together in his classroom, where Gross-Schaefer ("one of the nicest, most humble professors I have ever met at LMU") is an exciting professor who makes room for student expression. Rather than filling students with pre-selected knowledge, he prefers an environment of mutual respect and trust in which students learn from themselves, classmates, and the professor. "I have learned to listen to a student's question not only for its content but for its context. If a student's question is off base or reveals a lack of understanding, I never embarrass or shame a student. I look at it as an opportunity to explore multiple interpretations."

Gross-Schaefer's courses include Legal Environment of Business (in the MBA Program) and the "truly innovative and exciting" Business Ethics and Spirituality, which looks at various applied ethics models and philosophies as well as spiritual practices that can be used to enhance the workplace. He views law as providing students with an understanding of our history, a critical way of thinking about issues and the importance of the power of words. He teaches ethics and spirituality "as critical tools to help students remember who they are, who they wish to be, and how to remain true to their individual values when faced with complex choices and decisions."

According to one of his students, "his background is more than thorough, his love for business law is undeniable, and he truly wants each student to learn the material." His courses are very interactive, and he peppers them with creative ways to learn, such as mock trials, movies, journals, wellness kits, visits to court houses and guest speakers who have been faced with difficult legal/ethical situations. In the end, says Gross-Schaefer, "my goal is to excite the students and always treat them as partners in our learning process."

Tom Hughes, Professor, Business Law, University of South Carolina

"A college professor has very little guidance. I have learned how to teach from remembering what worked well with me when I was a student. I still take courses to constantly update my opinion of what works in the classroom."

And so on the shoulders of giants stands Tom Hughes, who teaches in the Moore School of Business at the University of South Carolina. Now teaching for twenty-four years, he looks to teach each student to care about thought processes, to be careful with language, and to take pride in their approach to learning. He finds the study of law fascinating—the practice "not so much so"—and enjoys discussing where the law may be headed. "The way he teaches his information is superb," says a student. "Take this class and you'll never regret it. The subject material is difficult; however, life lessons learned are more valuable than grade earned."

His courses include Honors Business Law, Honors Fundamentals of Business Inquiry, and Honors Law as a Tool of Social Evolution, and he takes a full Socratic approach to all of them, incorporating classroom discussion whenever possible. "There is no such thing as a bad answer from a student…well almost no such thing," he says. "Law is a seamless web so that expanding a topic involves inclusion of other topics." His classes are notoriously tough ("because there's always the 'what if' scenario for his tests"), but "he really helps you out and knows what he's teaching."

Joe Irvine, Instructor, Business Law, The Ohio State University

Joe Irvine is a seasoned attorney and certified public accountant. As development and tax counsel, he's a fairly big kahuna at The Ohio State University. More or less on the side, he also teaches an upper-level course in business law at Ohio State and, according to students, really excels in the classroom. "My business law class is an overview of the areas of law with which business students should be familiar. It is designed to help students become familiar with general legal concepts and spot legal issues," Irvine relates. "I start class allowing students to tell the joke of the day, within reasonable guidelines, of course. I know the punch lines to every lawyer joke there is." After this introductory diversion, the fun really begins. "Irvine's class is challenging simply because you're expected to know the entire chapter upon arriving to class." "He will cold call students all the time and give you a hard time if you are not prepared," explains one student. "I never simply lecture. That's crazy," Irvine says. "I try to call on everybody at least once every other class," which, by the way, is no small feat with some eighty students in his course. "If too many people don't know the answers," Irvine tells us, "it's time for a surprise quiz."

"I enjoy the material," Irvine declares. "I don't fake it. I want to be excited. I try to go into class excited every day. It's almost like a performance, really." He also demonstrates that he cares about the students in his class. "I learn everyone's name. I don't just teach information. I also try to help students with their careers and with their lives."

"The class is hard but he is very fair," says one student. "I try to reward effort," Irvine adds in this regard. "I allow extra credit." Students report that they really appreciate the way he keeps them on their toes. Irvine is "very enthusiastic and entertaining." "He is pretty funny," too. Certainly, there is "never a dull moment" and, frankly, students wish Irvine would teach more courses. He is "possibly the best teacher I have had in my entire collegiate career," reflects one student. "Professor Irvine is a great teacher, knows his material, and makes the class enjoyable," says a student who admittedly bombed the final. "Trust me, you will learn."

Christopher B. Wolfe, Instructor, Business Law, University of Delaware

Christopher B. Wolfe, who teaches Law and Social Issues in Business and Business Law at the University of Delaware, steeps his students in the foundations of our nation's judicial system. "My goal is to help them understand the larger world…to understand and appreciate their individual rights, freedom and liberty; to understand the individual's relationship to others and to the state; and to understand the basics of the U.S. legal system and various fundamental areas of Law."

He tries to instill in students the calm desire to think logically and accurately and recognize faulty arguments, and to arrive at conclusions based on fact, history, and logic, without being swayed by purely emotional arguments. "Your conclusion can only be as accurate as the presuppositions you bring to the problem," he says. He takes what many students wrongly expect to be a "dry and boring required course," and make it a relevant, practical, thought-provoking and sometimes entertaining subject. "Wolfe makes each class fun and interesting, [so] you won't have any trouble paying attention. Each class is like a performance," says a student.

He is a licensed attorney in Delaware and has maintained a law practice since 1984, and rather than simply presenting a dry lecture on the topic, he tries to use real-life examples which are easily understood by students. Often, he will include props which further demonstrate and illuminate the topic. "For example, when discussing the limitations of eye-witness testimony, I have been known to surprise students by opening and drinking from a beer bottle in class, which the students only later learn was actually 'non-alcoholic'." "He lectures with heart and puts the info into the words of a college kid to make it really easy to understand," says a student. "Add his class! WHAT ARE YOU WAITING FOR??" yells another.

Chemistry

Charlie Bass, McCalla Professor of Chemistry, Wofford College

Charlie Bass, who teaches organic chemistry at Wofford College, prefers to go straight to having his students attempt to solve problems. "That way, I can help them correct misconceptions. I think this is much more effective than watching me solve problems for them."

A believer that positive reinforcement helps students gain confidence and to become willing to work harder, he cares deeply "that my students 'get it.' I will work as hard as I can to help them understand the course material." He uses humor in the classroom to help put students at ease, and although lecture is "necessary," he thinks students really get an understanding of the subject during help sessions, of which he provides many. During these optional sessions, he has students work in small groups on problems distributed through the room on multiple white boards. Once the groups finish their work, they discuss all of the problems as a class. By working in this way my students feel a little less timid as they have the support of their group."

All in all, he looks to disarm the common perceptions of the difficulty of orgo, and to make it "interesting and fun." "Dr. Bass is awesome and makes the incredible pain of learning organic chemistry slightly bearable. Definitely recommend," says one student. "Many students are apprehensive about organic. I chose to teach organic so others would give the subject a chance," he says. "Organic chemistry is an impossible subject, but his funny personality and perseverance in teaching make you comfortable in trying to learn it," says a student.

Stephanie Gould, Assistant Professor, Chemistry, Austin College

The main goal of Stephanie Gould, who teaches chemistry at Austin College, is to instill critical thinking and problem solving abilities in students; the content she uses to teach those important skills is chemistry. "I want students to leave my courses being able to evaluate problems, understand the tools they have to solve those problems, and decide what is the best tool to use," she says.

She believes that patience is a pedagogical virtue; that deep learning happens when a student is being stretched to think critically about a problem. Students may think that this is struggling, but always knowing the answer right away doesn't push students beyond what they've already learned. "I think the key for me as the instructor is to foster the healthy-learning kind of struggling and preempt the type of struggling that causes a student to quit trying." She wants each student to succeed but doesn't change her expectations in order to make this happen. "Having high expectations pushes the students; most of them probably don't appreciate those expectations during the class, but a few years later they do (and I love it when they come tell me so!)" she says.

Each year begins with her telling the students that she is their guide to organic chemistry, but cannot learn for them. "They may choose to do the hard work that is required to learn or not, but I can't make that choice for them. I am here to help and guide." Her classes are admittedly difficult—as organic chemistry often is—and she tries to get the students to understand that some people learn some material faster than others, but they can learn the material. "They have to put in the time it takes them to learn, not how long it takes their friend to learn," she says. She tries not to lecture for more than twenty minutes at a time, interspersing her lecturing with problems for students to work in groups or on their own, which allows her time to go around to everyone and see how they are doing with the material. "I seek to treat each student as an adult."

Thomas Gufrey, Chemistry Instructor, California State University— Long Beach

"Chemophobia" is the term Thomas Gufrey, who teaches chemistry at California State University—Long Beach, uses to describe students' innate fear of the science. He does this by imbuing them with "chemistry literacy" and turning them into "informed voters on chem issues."

In his legendary demonstrations, he uses humor, songs, and poems, and treats students with respect. And, he says, "frankly, I make it very easy to do well if students show up and really try." "It's half chemistry, logic, and critical thinking but half of it is appreciating how important chemistry is." He has taught for more than forty years, and he is constantly soliciting student input and bringing in stories from everyday breakthroughs in chemistry. "I'm lucky to have a job I would do for free," he says.

His only class is General-Ed Chemistry, and he looks for students whose love of chemistry "is buried so deep inside them, they don't know they have it! My job is to 'un-bury' that love of chem!" He is the first to admit that he is "obsessed" with chemistry, and it comes through in his demonstrations. "They learn better when they're having fun," he says. Even though 99 percent of his time is devoted to teaching chemistry, he stresses the need to "be nice to the person next to you. That is what matters most in life. Getting a PhD in chemistry is a most admirable goal. However, helping those in need, being kind and compassionate, and doing as many good deeds as possible for others on a daily basis is far more important than wealth, power, or academic achievement. As Americans we should cherish and defend our rare and precious freedom."

This "real goofball" is "big on explosions" and awards bonus points to students for all sorts of contributions; students say he is "extremely caring and fun and just loves life." "All you have to do is show up and make an effort," says another.

Michael Haaf, Associate Professor, Chemistry, Ithaca College

Ithaca College chemistry professor Michael Haaf's principal objective extends beyond his field. "As a teacher, my goal should not only include helping the students learn and practice chemistry, but should also include helping them learn how to learn anything," he says.

The key lies in supplying students with not just information but also the tools to get the information. In short, he wants to help them to become practiced and excited about learning on their own. "I like to let the students know that they should set high expectations for themselves, and that I will do everything I can to help them realize those expectations."

Preparation is key, no matter how many times one has taught a course ("He explains orgo so well, he makes it seem easy," says a student). "I remember what it felt like to struggle with new material in chemistry courses when I was a student. As a teacher, this helps me to anticipate issues students may have in understanding trickier concepts," he says. "Sometimes, I think it's more difficult for someone to explain material that he or she finds deeply intuitive." A positive attitude and a good sense of humor go a long way in the classroom, and Professor

Haaf offers both in his lectures, breaking up the class using short activities, demonstrations, or guided inquiry-based problems to keep students actively engaged. "His nerdy superhero jokes actually connected with the material he was teaching," says an appreciative student. "He is a wonderful professor and one of the greatest personalities I have ever met," says another.

Charles Kutal, Professor of Chemistry, The University of Georgia

For more than thirty-eight years, Charles Kutal, a chemistry professor at The University of Georgia, has been helping students to master the fundamental concepts, experimental techniques, and critical-thinking skills needed to understand chemistry. Students say that "he knows what he's talking about, and wants that for his students. He is helpful and fair."

Professor Kutal's courses include General Chemistry at both the undergraduate and honors level, and he is always well-prepared for lectures. He does not follow a rigid script, as "the best teaching moments often are spontaneous and the result of a student question." He illustrates key chemical concepts with practical examples that interest students, and continually encourages questions; he also presents material in an interactive lecture (non-PowerPoint) style that engages students. "I am not satisfied until the point that I am trying to make is clear to the class," he says.

As much as possible, he links concepts in the textbook to something tangible, usually an experiment or demonstration in which students are active participants. In "learning by doing," they tear apart a disposable diaper to test the properties of the super-absorbent polymer filler, or explore the rheology of a non-Newtonian fluid by sticking a finger into a slush of corn starch and water. "It may seem impossible at first, but it's not. You will learn a lot from Dr. Kutal, and he makes class pretty interesting," says a student.

Scott B. Lewis, Associate Professor, Chemistry, James Madison University

Scott Lewis, a chemistry professor at James Madison University, wants his students to have some time alone with the material he gives them. Then, after a little mulling it over, they can use their understanding to apply their newfound knowledge to questions or situations. "This pushes them into the realm of critical thinking, which is vital for anyone going into science or medicine," he says.

He lectures in organic chemistry, a topic he considers to be "part art": "Most chemistry can be done with brute force, or with grace and style," he says. Difficult though his subject may be, he loves spending time with students, and will try to stay on something until they have it down. He is not afraid to attempt to explain complex topics in other ways (one student says that he just "gets students"), and never takes it personally if students don't "see" things the same way he does; this just means he must try to "see" it from their angle. "The subject is amazing in how broad it is (everything from plastic to biochem to synthesis to understanding mechanisms). Yet, one small change in the shape of a molecule, or just the direction an atom points in space can completely change the chemistry. A topic this broad yet precise must be explained to others." Students say that he loves when people come to his office hours, and "will take as much time explaining something as you need to understand."

His teaching style is classic; he still hand-draws all structures on the board, and spends a great deal of time trying to get students to speak the "language" of structures, reactions, and mechanisms. "His tests are tougher than the other o-chem professors' as he likes to integrate information, which can be a pain, but it ensures you understand what you're doing," says a student.

Larry Louters, PhD, Professor of Chemistry and Biochemistry, Calvin College

"What is the key concept the student seems to be missing? Where does the confusion and difficulty lie?"

Those are the questions that Calvin College chemistry professor Larry Louters asks himself every day. He loves teaching, and "the students know it"; this trust means that, as complicated as it may seem, they know that he will present the material in a logical fashion, and that he is on their side when it comes to learning the material. "I give students permission to struggle and not like all of the stuff they learn. I tell students if they learn one new thing each day, it is a good day," he says.

His course load includes Fundamentals of Biochemistry and Chemistry for the Health Sciences, which he enjoys because it is filled with students who are apprehensive about chemistry, giving him the challenge of turning it into a positive experience. "I wish he taught other classes besides chemistry so that I could continue taking him," says a student. He also enjoys the contrasting challenge of teaching biochemistry and mentoring undergraduates in research as they prepare for medical or graduate school. He writes an organized set of notes on a white board in order to control the pace of each class, uses PowerPoint and short videos to present biochemical structures and processes, and walks through the classroom and asks a lot of questions. "This is designed to keep the students engaged and to do some formative assessment to see what the students are learning. I often use human physiology or nutrition ideas to solidify biochemical principles." "Take Louters!" says a student.

Steven Pedersen, PhD, University of California—Berkeley

The primary goal of Steven Pedersen, who teaches organic chemistry at the University of California—Berkeley, is to present the material from a conceptual standpoint rather than encouraging rote memorization, whether in a lecture hall environment or in an office-hour setting.

His mantra for teaching the year-long course in organic chemistry is "Learn It To Use It"; in order to facilitate this, he tries to incorporate examples of the practical applications associated with the material being learned. "Organic chemistry is not a subject that comes naturally to anyone. Those students who practice problems and always try to approach them from a conceptual standpoint rather than relying on rote memorization always do well in my classes," he says. "When I expand on a topic I almost always start talking about how the subject is related to an everyday occurrence."

He has been teaching at Berkeley for twenty-seven years, and most recently, has been working with undergraduates to develop innovative laboratory experiments for his laboratory courses. His classes have a delightfully classic feel, as he still presents all his lectures on the chalkboard (which keeps the pace of his lectures fairly even), and his passion for the subject is clear and appreciated:

"Organic chemistry is fundamental to all aspects of life and I enjoy sharing the science behind this subject with undergraduates."

This "excellent" professor "makes you learn conceptually and is very student-oriented." He "expects you to work hard, but he is really helpful and clearly and concisely tells you what you need to know." Students call him out as being "like a 'funny uncle' who doesn't know he's being funny": "mostly no-nonsense, but he'll show his quirky sense of humor every so often."

Karen Pressprich, PhD, Lecturer, Clemson University

"Hopefully my enthusiastic treatment of this fascinating subject will excite a lifelong interest in chemistry," says Clemson University chemistry lecturer Karen Pressprich. "I hope I can help them learn how to learn on their own."

Her pedagogical style relies on the belief that learning is a lot easier if it is conveyed as a story, and if she emphasizes the concepts the details will follow. She views her job in the teaching/learning process as being not only that of a communicator but also that of a facilitator and motivator, empowering and encouraging students to learn. "My role as an instructor is to excite the students' interest in chemistry and to demystify the learning process. While a teacher can distribute a syllabus, deliver lectures, grade exams, and assign grades, all learning is actually done by the student."

Dr. Pressprich is currently teaching three sections of general chemistry and particularly enjoys working with freshman because "they are enthusiastic and open to new study habits." Because many students have never had to use their problem-solving skills until coming into the university setting, she often tries to think out loud as the class works through example problems, modeling how she approaches problems. "It is my hope that this approach provides an example for construction of students' own problem-solving skills," she says. "She's extremely sweet and really cares about her students. She is also funny at times and she keeps the lectures entertaining," says a student.

Students say that she "is so incredibly willing to help," and she often extends office hours and arranges extra conferences, and engages in long and detailed e-mail exchanges with students, making it clear that students "are more than just a number."

Stephen Schvaneveldt, Chemistry, Clemson University

"The trick to teaching is to know when to get out of the way," says Clemson University chemistry professor Stephen Schvaneveldt. "Teaching is basically finding that tricky balance between providing help and resources to the student, but yet not trying to do the work of learning for them."

In teaching General Chemistry and Physical Chemistry, he takes a roll-up-your-sleeves approach; he doesn't think students can learn much just by watching him solve the problems, so he forces them to get their hands dirty. "He is incredibly clear, goes at a very steady pace, and keeps interest through his surprisingly good humor," says a student.

The best advice he ever received was "don't try to be your favorite teacher"; in following that wisdom, he simply takes the material and communicates his interest, fascination, and excitement to his students. "Students know the difference between 'being authentic' and 'play acting'," he says. The end goal is to make sure they have the resources they need, and then convince them that they can master the difficult material if they really set their mind to it. "He puts notes on blackboard for every chapter, complete with pictures and fill-in-the-blanks, which are very helpful to print and fill in during class. He also makes study guides for EACH chapter," says a student of some of these resources. "You can tell he really loves to teach. He does an excellent job of making things clear in his lectures, even something as complicated as chemistry."

Dasan M. Thamattoor, Associate Professor of Chemistry, Colby College

Colby College chemistry professor Dasan M. Thamattoor is aware of the general terror-inspiring nature of his chosen discipline; in accepting the effect that the mention of the word "chemistry" has, he can embrace its mysteries. "I look to teach students a subject that they might otherwise fear in a way that gets them to not only understand it but also enjoy learning about it," he says.

For the past fourteen years, he has brought enthusiasm, patience, and a commitment to student wellbeing to classrooms, as well as the federally funded organic chemistry research that he carries out with undergraduates. "I would like to think that I am able to anticipate their problems and I am easy to talk with," he says. His style is conversational but enthusiastic, and he uses "chalk-talk" extensively, rather than falling back on PowerPoint. Students say that this "amazing professor and really nice guy" is "extremely enthusiastic, very approachable, and ALWAYS available to help with class or just to chat."

In courses such as introductory Organic Chemistry and advanced Organic Chemistry, he tries to teach with stories, anecdotes, and humor; students claim he makes the material "bearable, and that says something." "He was a BRILLIANT teacher, and he restored my enthusiasm for chemistry," says one.

Douglas A. Vander Griend, Professor of Inorganic Chemistry, Calvin College

Calvin College chemistry professor Douglas Vander Griend wants "to see the light bulb of [students'] minds light up with new and deep understanding." A tall order, for sure, for someone who teaches one of the most difficult subjects an undergraduate can encounter. Though, as he puts it, "You should expect to be confused. If you're never confused, you're probably not learning chemistry."

"It's not uncommon for students to have had a bad experience with chemistry in high school," so he tries to structure his courses as "a combination of passion, insightful analogies, and effective class structure that avoids busywork." "Learning chemistry is very empowering, in part because there are no shortcuts to the challenge, but also because understanding the material world around us is so relevant and rewarding." Group projects are an essential part of his classes too, and students are given a lot of freedom in their choice of what to do. In pursuit of a deeper understanding, he loves to ask big/broad questions at the onset of a new topic or chapter and force students to answer by writing something down, then sharing what they write. "For example, when beginning to study chemical bonding, I will have students draw what they think a dihydrogen molecule looks like and then compare and contrast with neighbors. We always end up having quite a discussion and I am consistently reminded how many different ideas are out there on even a relatively simple molecule." He also loves analogies, as "they are amusing and often very effective tools for helping students visualize and truly understand what can otherwise be somewhat abstract concepts."

Proactivity is also encouraged, as it can be intimidating to ask questions as the material flies by. Professor Vander Griend is big on responding to feedback and evaluations, and he regularly conducts informal focus groups, in which he will ask five to ten people to join him for lunch in the dining hall, where he then asks about class policies and tactics to determine what works, and what doesn't. "Face to face, students are both more tactful and more helpful," he says.

Students says that "the notorious DVG" is "a hard grader and gives lots of homework (personally, I am not big on the homework part of the quote here, as it is not so much 'I' who gives a lot of homework, but the chemistry itself that demands it to learn it), but he does a really great job of keeping the class engaged, is willing to give help inside and outside of class, and has a great personality."

Ephraim Woods III, Associate Professor of Chemistry, Colgate University

Ephraim Woods III, a chemistry professor at Colgate University, merely tries "to keep students on course and help them over the occasional bump in the road."

"I've learned that setting a good example is a big part of my job," he says. In the classroom, he is clear, provides context, and communicates his enthusiasm to the students—when he gets excited, he tends to run across the room, "which makes class pretty interesting"—and if he can make them laugh, then it's an added bonus (one student says he "kept classes light, which isn't necessarily the easiest thing to do with chem"). "I treat them as if they're smart rather than just telling them that they're smart." Professor Woods also believes that practice makes perfect, and he says that the best students in his classes share this view. "We expect it of athletes and musicians, but it is just as important for students."

He currently teaches General Chemistry, which is an introductory course, and Statistical Mechanics, which bridges the gap between quantum mechanics and thermodynamics; he is also an active researcher in the field of atmospheric physical chemistry. "He teaches you the deep, thought-provoking chemistry instead of the boring calculations," says a student.

Marc Zimmer, Professor, Chemistry, Connecticut College

Students can identify with Marc Zimmer, a chemistry professor at Connecticut College, and "where my enthusiasm for fluorescent proteins comes from and can see why chemistry is important."

His courses include Introductory Chemistry, Environmental Chemistry, and Glow, a course about bioluminescent organisms and biotechnical applications of the proteins involved in giving off light. He is absolutely fascinated by what he teaches and researches, and he uses this fervor as a weapon against students who find chemistry boring. "Even the dentist drilling holes in my teeth seems to think that his chemistry class was torturous," he says. "I don't want my students to equate chemistry with pain, I want them to look forward to chemistry, to enjoy learning about the joys of playing with molecules."

He often visits area kindergartens to conduct fun, well-received fluorescent demonstrations using his family's two transgenic 'nude' GFP pet mice, Shine and Shimmer, who glow green when placed under a blue light. "I want my undergraduate students to be bursting with questions about chemistry and have the same enthusiasm for science as the kindergartens and elementary schools have for the mice," he says. To do this he must be a performer (a student says "he is always laughing and smiling"), make the material relevant to the students, and bring his research into the class. "He makes chemistry easy, fun, and interesting. Can't wait for next semester!" says a student.

Cinema Studies

Steve J. Wurtzler, Associate Professor, Cinema Studies, Colby College

Steve J. Wurtzler, who teaches cinema studies at Colby College, would like students to challenge their established conceptions, to take intellectual risks, and to do so confidently. "At best, we're all teachers and we're all students," he says. His excitement about the course material is infectious, making it easy for students to recognize that he's having fun in the classroom. "I get paid to read, think, write, watch films, and share ideas with students. I can't imagine a better job." "He's passionate about the subject matter and really cares about his students. This is what you want to see in a professor," says a student.

He teaches classes that include Intro to Cinema Studies ("it introduces students to new ways of thinking about a subject they often take for granted and introduces them as well to types of film they haven't seen before"), avant-garde film ("the students' critical skills and confidence change so dramatically in a single semester"), and documentary film ("students seem surprised and pleased to explore the intersection between representation and politics"). His classroom is interactive, and he keeps lectures to a minimum, instead using focused class discussions to develop ideas. "Of course, with the right students, I'm also willing to let discussion veer off into an unexpected area so as to explore students' ideas." These students return the compliment: "[He is an] amazing man in general, and I would take the class again just for enjoyment."

Classics

William Hutton, Class of 1955 Distinguished Associate Professor of Classical Studies, The College of William & Mary

Throughout twenty-four years of teaching, William Hutton, a professor of classical studies at The College of William & Mary, has learned a thing or two about how to move his students forward. "Teaching is about starting students off with some basic knowledge, then helping them to develop their own skills for learning more," he says.

He treats teaching "as something I do with them, rather than to them," following three basic tenets in his approach to the classroom: 1) always pay attention; 2) treat students as colleagues, not underlings; 3) humor is essential to teaching. He aims for a teaching style that is interactive and flexible, with an emphasis on getting students actively involved in the learning process and allowing the plan for the course to mold itself around the strengths and weaknesses of a particular group of students. For instance, in a recent class on ancient comedy he instructed students to bring to class texts or videos of modern comedy that show some parallels and differences with the ancient comedy they had been discussing. "I had no fixed plan for the class going into it, but it generated a healthy discussion of some of the more important aspects of ancient comedy which I think enhanced the students' appreciation of those concepts."

He is currently teaching Intermediate Greek ("I am so passionate about Greek that sometimes I can't believe that I'm lucky enough to get paid for the opportunity of sharing it with others") and an upper-level archaeology seminar on Roman Britain. His own interest in his field came about quite organically: "At some point when I was a teenager I decided I wanted to learn everything from the beginning, so I started with the Greeks and Romans and got stuck."

"I've had many classes with Hutton, and I'd have to say that he's my favorite professor. He's highly interested in helping students learn and has a wicked sense of humor," says a student. "He is really clear and he loves what he's teaching about."

Joshua T. Katz, Professor, Classics and Linguistics, Princeton University

Joshua T. Katz, who teaches classics and linguistics at Princeton University, wants "to teach facts, to inspire wide-ranging, interdisciplinary knowledge and approaches, and to foster good arguments," meaning "both that I want my students to appreciate a logical mode of argumentation and that I want them to engage in interesting fights, with me and with one another."

When it comes to non-factual matters, he says there is nothing better than a heated discussion among members of a captive audience, and he is happy to play neutral umpire and let matters fall as they will. He advises his students to learn from as many different kinds of top-notch scholars as they can, and then take their respective best features and combine them in the way that suits the individual. "Be yourself. Make your own style. Do not strive to be my or anyone else's clone." Students consider him to be one of those top-notch scholars himself: "Professor Katz is one of the finest professors Princeton has to offer."

In classes such as Wordplay: A Wry Plod from Babel to Scrabble, Origins and Nature of English Vocabulary, and Ancient Greek: An Intensive Introduction, he tries to get to know—and know by much more than name—every student he teaches in every class, whether big or small. "To me that's not the mark of a great professor; it's just a simple case of good practice. Why would I want to spend a semester in the company of people I don't know?" He doesn't much care for strict syllabi and actively welcomes intelligent input from students as they go. "A good teacher in any class that has leeway in the material that is covered should be able to make students see that this is *their time*, that it is to a significant extent up to them to influence what gets treated—and how," he says. "He will make the most mundane subject fascinating," says a student.

B. M. Lavelle, Professor, Classical Studies, Loyola University Chicago

B. M. Lavelle, professor of classical studies at Loyola University Chicago is bringing the dead back to life.

"I want to make the world of ancient Greece and Rome come alive to my students by helping them, through study of the classics, to see how very similar we all are and to stimulate the students to think about themselves, their lives, and their values," says the professor of twenty-eight years.

Students say that he is "awesome and eloquent" in lecture, gracious and open in accepting and addressing all questions and comments, positively fair in grading, and absolutely respectful of every student. Professor Lavelle says that he "tries to make the 'heavy' material light and the obscure lucid. Class time must be something good for both of us, teacher and students, a time to look forward to and enjoy. Ya gotta have fun!"

A breakdown of one of his "interesting and enjoyable" classes might go as follows: "Discussion topic: heroes. Discussion subjects: Herakles and James Bond. How are they alike? Why are they alike? What do they actually do? Why is the motif of 'nature vs. culture' = 'good guys vs. bad guys' so recurrent in storytelling that pleases us all?" The idea is to get students to see that, with obvious adjustments, "one hero is very much like the other and that it is important for every culture to have its own 'supermen' heroes."

In opening doors to Greece and Rome through classes such as Classical Mythology and Humanism of Antiquity, "he encourages students to speak out in class or to converse about class issues with him one-on-one during office hours." He returns to Greece frequently to renew information about sites, museums, artifacts, and art objects, and even led a class tour to Greece last summer focusing on ancient Greek art. "There is nothing—repeat, nothing—that rivals seeing the 'light' of comprehension in my students' faces, whether in class or on site."

Joseph Pucci, Associate Professor of Classics, Brown University

Joseph Pucci, a professor of classics at Brown University, sees his roles in and out of the classroom with striking clarity. In the classroom he must "communicate something of the beauty and complexity of ancient and medieval literature and also suggest the ways in which authors now long dead are still relevant to our lives." In his office hours (and in other interactions with students), he seeks "to listen to students' views and, as much as possible, affirm them and build upon them as a means of furthering their engagement with the traditions I study and love." Students simply call him a "fantastic teacher, incredible mentor, [and] gifted and original academic." "He has integrally shaped the way I think about not just classical literature but literature as a whole," says one. "If you let him, he'll change your world," says another.

Professor Pucci's classes are based on student input rather than preset outlines, and each builds organically as students and professor turn their ears to each other. Words and themes arise of their own accord and natural curiosities build as the class explores a text or an idea at its own pace, together. "One of his talents as a professor is interweaving classical texts and modern themes; the course never seemed like a tour of a dead world," says an engaged student.

His classes focus mainly on classical and medieval literature, and his most popular course is The Idea of Self, a course in literary selfhood. Students are always asked—and expected—to read a text, and then he always begins a class "by asking students their own responses to the words at hand." "I use their (usually excellent) responses as a way to interrogate the text and usually manage to get in any and all points that I wish to communicate, while making students understand that it is their class and their issues that drive things," says Professor Pucci.

Communication

Rick Bommelje, Associate Professor, Department of Communication, Rollins College

Rick Bommelje, who teaches Listening and Leadership courses at Rollins College, gives students the space to experience the learning dynamic from their own perspective, and challenges them to stretch outside of their comfort zone into the discomfort zone.

The Listening course was created by Professor Bommelje twenty years ago and comes from his own mistakes in life. "I was not listening effectively, professionally or personally. I set out on a journey to improve, and in the process, several years later was invited to develop the course at Rollins. I have learned firsthand that teaching is one of the highest forms of learning." he says. Among the many innovative practices offered in the course, he establishes listening "circles" in which four to five students have a conversation about a "third thing" for a specified period of time (a "third thing" could be a story, video clip, poem, painting—anything that could have a voice of its own). Upon conclusion of the session, other students identify specific behaviors that they observed in the dynamic dialog. "The learning comes in many different ways and to make it stick, I use a four-step system: commit, know it, do it, be it," he says.

In courses such as Listening (which is the study of the art of listening and its importance in our personal and professional lives), Self-Leadership and Communication; and Leadership, Film, and Communication, he establishes well-defined goals and creates a shared space in which multi-level teaching and learning occurs. ("He lives what he teaches," said a student). Dr. Bommelje also uses the case-in-point method the members of the group become the living case.

"This man changed my life. He's not warm and fuzzy—but he's very fair and an incredibly good, inspirational teacher. He not only teaches the course content but he gives you life lessons that will stay with you forever," comments another student.

Dara N. Byrne, PhD, Associate Professor, Rhetoric and Intercultural
Communication Specialist, John Jay College of Criminal Justice

Regardless of what course students take from Dara Byrne, a professor of rhetoric and intercultural communication at John Jay College of Criminal Justice, students can expect to learn how to read texts more carefully and judiciously, develop an understanding of the cultural context of the artifacts we examine, and strategically formulate messages for specific target audiences.

Professor Byrne teaches courses such as Public Speaking and Civic Engagement and Persuasion, and encourages students to actively engage and think about the reading material. "One cannot do well in my class simply by showing up, nor should they, quite frankly; learning is all-encompassing and it is hard work." Students must learn "the importance of the codes, conventions, and ideologies that shape our social world," and that "communication is a process that is closely linked with routine practice, performance, and criticism." "She is the best teacher; she has high standards for her students, but she works with you and helps you to meet her standards," says a student.

Classes are mix traditional lectures with roundtable discussions, to expose students to a variety of learning situations and teach them the importance of effective listening to the communication process. "I hope students see that I love ideas and possibilities and that I get excited about their ideas and their possibilities. For that semester I am there with and for them 100 percent," she says. "She wants students to learn and pushes freshmen to do exactly that," says a student.

Rachel Gans-Boriskin, Visiting Lecturer, Communication Studies,
Northeastern University

While in the classroom, Rachel Gans-Boriskin, a visiting lecturer of communication studies at Northeastern University, strives to make the complicated accessible and the accessible complicated.

As a professor of communication, it is a fairly easy task to find topics that excite students, and she considers herself lucky in that regard. She mainly wants students to question the way they interact with the world and the things they take for granted, and "to look at the ways that communication, both on the mass and interpersonal levels, has structured their lives, and help them understand these processes so that they can become better at whatever field they choose to pursue."

Both during her office hours and in her classroom (where she teaches courses including Health Communication, Principles of Organizational Communication, and Mass Communication and Culture), she wants students to "feel supported as whole human beings, so that they leave my classroom nurtured intellectually and spiritually." She is genuinely excited about what she is teaching, and that translates into a fun atmosphere in the classroom that is infectious for the students. "When you are excited they become excited too," she says. She encourages students to take away something positive from every article, book, and class, even if the lesson learned is that you would not conduct your research in that way. Students say that "she has a really great teaching style: casual, but treating students with respect and expecting respect in return."

A performer at heart, she tries to make class as entertaining and interactive as possible, and to grab her students' attention in dramatic ways. For instance, in a discussion of the theory of the magic bullet or hypodermic needle model of media effects, she will use a clip from the *South Park* movie as an illustration of how some people envision people being indoctrinated by mass media. "The students, familiar with characters and the ways in which the creators of *South Park* regularly make fun of such notions, then engage in a debate about these ideas, and we then relate that debate to the scholars who have been having these debates in more esoteric language, and discuss the merits of both Bandura and Cartman."

Students say that aside from her clear dedication to her work, she "even wears themed outfits to go along with what we're learning!" "I am extremely grateful to have had Professor Gans," says one.

Pauline Bary Khan, Lecturer, Associate Professor, College of Engineering, University of Michigan

Pauline Bary Khan is a professor in the College of Engineering at the University of Michigan. She has a strongly technical background—obviously—but her particular specialty is technical communications. As such, she also has a strong interest in writing. Her courses typically involve case studies where students approach the kinds of problems engineers have to tackle and "determine possible responses and solutions." Different students "identify problems and solutions in multiple different ways," Khan explains. "My teaching style is varied and very interactive." Her goal, she says, is to identify the specific needs and the "preferred learning style" of each of her students. Once she does that, she is able to address students in a very individualized way.

The subject matter of Professor Khan's courses is reportedly "extremely helpful" because it has such an array of "real world" applications. "I used the material in my internships," points out one student. Khan is "knowledgeable" and "down to earth" in front of her classes. Lectures and discussions are regularly "enjoyable" and they occasionally even rise to the level of "fun." Khan's "innovative worksheets" help tremendously in this regard. If you end up in a class with her, don't expect to be able to blow it off. "She definitely is not an easy grader," cautions one student, "but I think that she's fair." Her most appreciated quality is her willingness to assist them—with class material and with their lives and futures as well. "She actually tries to get to know her students," which certainly isn't typical at a big state school like Michigan. "I love Professor Khan," beams one student. "She's really helpful and cares about you personally. She always offers to write recommendation letters and will review anything before you turn it in." "She is always doing extra to help," agrees another student. "She even offered to review my résumé and cover letter." "Khan was the professor who spent the most time helping me," recalls one student. "She met with me when I didn't do well with the exam. I recommend her highly."

LisaMarie Luccioni, Adjunct Professor of Communication, Certified Etiquette Expert & Image Professional, Corporate Presenter, and *Psychology Today* Blogger, University of Cincinnati

LisaMarie Luccioni, a University of Cincinnati communication professor, loves her job. "My own work environment invigorates me. Crisp weather, striking architecture, campus greenery, students sporting jeans and sweatshirts with backpacks strapped across their bodies...now there's a workplace that keeps you humming."

She has been teaching for over twenty years and still "loves every minute; the classroom is my second home." Students have the utmost admiration for her as a teacher and a person: "Never seen a teacher who has such passion for her subject. One of the best teachers in all my years in school. Not the easiest teacher but the best." In return, all perspectives are respected in her classroom. "We may not agree, but we'll listen," she says.

Professor Luccioni positively thrives on seeing students succeed. "Get a group of A-gamers in a speech class and hear rhetorical brilliance that can eclipse paid presenters. Mention a course term we learned three weeks ago into your current class answer and watch me smile." One of her priorities is connecting course material to personal/professional futures. As a certified etiquette expert and one of fewer than one-hundred CIP's (Certified Image Professionals) in the United States, she gives students the benefits of her real-world techniques. Her course, Business Etiquette & Professional Image, is quite popular and culminates in a five-course meal at a high-end restaurant where students demonstrate what they learned in class." One student says, "She is truly concerned for her students and wants them to succeed. She makes a three-hour lecture feel like thirty minutes!"

Most of Professor Luccioni's courses are required, and she wants students leaving each term understanding that her class directly impacts their verbal, visual, and behavioral future. "If students knew how much faith I had in their ability to enrich our world, they'd be flattered, staggered, and challenged," she says. Her deep care for her students is immediately apparent, and she has each first and last name memorized by the beginning of the second class. "If someone can take the time to pronounce my Italian last name correctly (loo-CHOE-knee, by the way), I can do the same," she says. Students can even call her at her home number; she has fielded thousands of calls over the years.

Dr. Jonathan Millen, Associate Dean of Liberal Arts, Professor of Communication, Rider University

Don't hesitate to ask, ask, ask away in the classroom of Rider University communication professor Jonathan Millen. Dr. Millen believes that questions are too often seen as a sign of ignorance, and makes it very clear that there is no question too small for him to address or to put to the class for discussion. "The most important thing you can do in crafting your own education is ask good questions," he says.

Dr. Millen is well aware that most students who study communication enter the major with a very narrow focus, such as multimedia or journalism, and in turn, he challenges them to study the field from a richer and broader perspective. "My goal is to stimulate their interests and intellect. I attempt to create a climate in which students can explore the world around them from an informed and critical perspective."

He takes a collaborative and conversational approach to his teaching, delivering lectures in plain English and building upon his reputation as one of the department's funnier teachers. Still, "fun does not mean easy. They can have fun and do a lot work. I respect my students' role in the conversation and demand their respect in return." As a result, classes such as Communication Studies: Theory and Practice and the popular Social Impact of Rock and Roll are usually filled with lively discussions about important/current/relevant issues. "As opposed to a traditional lecture, I use a dialogic approach to working through course material. For example, I often will share a news story and challenge students to see how an assigned reading can be used to form a critical opinion on the topic." Group work makes up a large part of his classes, and for every group project students must assign a reading to the rest of the class. "A lot of the readings I use are coming from what I listen to on the way to work. NPR, the *New York Times*. [Students] use that as a basis to apply what we're talking about in class."

It's easy to see why Dr. Millen's classes have such a high entertainment value, as a "whole course is one long conversation." "He is an amazing teacher and brings a certain enthusiasm and lightness to all of his classes every day! If you're looking to really learn in a fun, upbeat atmosphere, Dr. Millen's your teacher," says one. "I would take any class he teaches. Every teacher at Rider could take a lesson from him," agrees another.

Eric Ronis, Assistant Dean of Communication and Creative Media, Champlain College

Eric Ronis, who teaches communication and creative media at Champlain College, thinks of the classroom as an adventure. "I want to push students beyond where they are comfortable—so they can get comfortable in that new, 'larger' place," he says.

In classes such as Public Speaking, Small Group Communication, Foundations of Human Communication, and a unique senior seminar called "Performance, Protest and Terror," Professor Ronis tries "to make students see that communication is an art that can be practiced upon and improved, as well as a science that can analyzed and understood." He has been teaching for twenty-five years, and people fascinate him; he says that "communication is power, and power is the way we change the world."

As an actor, he has worked a lot on stage and in film (students comment that he is "really open and very entertaining"); as for being a communicator, well, "I do it every day," he notes. In class, Professor Ronis will have students do a speech as badly as they possibly can to get them "performing" but without the tension of needing to "get it right." After that, "they can work on 'getting it right!'" This follows one of Professor Ronis' key tenets of teaching, which is to "have your eye on the work the students do, so that criticism can be individualized but never personalized."

One student says, "Eric is the best teacher I have had thus far at Champlain. He's so funny and makes class interesting. Time flies, and I hate when class is over."

Tony Smith, PhD, Associate Professor, Communication, St. Petersburg College

St. Petersburg College communication professor Tony Smith motivates students to want to attend class by emphasizing the importance it can have in their future careers, relationships, and daily life experiences. "A mentor once told me that all learning begins with motivation, so unless students are motivated in some way to learn, they won't. Those words of wisdom have stuck with me over the years," he says.

His classroom creates a positive learning climate that encourages students to contact him whenever they have questions or concerns (and which also aids in his public speaking courses). One student writes, "He will make you feel comfortable when you feel the most uncomfortable." Students in classes such as Intro to Speech Communication and Business and Professional Speaking are frequently struck by his passion and enthusiasm for the subject; his experience as a professional deejay and deejay business owner from 1994 to 2001 instilled in him "the importance of communication skills in working with people, and gave me valuable experience in being and speaking in front of others." "His speech critiques and pointers are helpful. If you follow all of his criteria, you will leave this class confident in giving public speeches," says a student.

He starts most topics with an in-class writing assignment for which students answer a question relating to the material to be covered, then uses this assignment as a springboard for a brief class discussion of the topic, which allows students to share their answers and hear other students' perspective on the topic. He is a stickler for providing examples to explain what he is teaching, and he loves to play devil's advocate and challenge students to defend their answers or opinions. "'Why do you think that is?'" or 'Why do you feel that way?' are questions I often ask to ensure students have valid reasons and support for their views, as opposed to believing something 'just because.'"

Students say he "takes a subject most students are nervous or uneasy about, and makes it interesting and fun by being humorous and fun."

Computer Science
David Bernstein, Professor of Computer Science, James Madison University
David Bernstein is a computer science professor with a very distinguished academic pedigree. He has degrees from the University of Pennsylvania and Princeton, and has taught at Princeton (where he received the President's Award, the highest award for teaching at that august institution) and at MIT. He is currently on the faculty of James Madison University in Virginia.

Bernstein is known as one of those professors who has different personas inside and outside the classroom. Students say that "one on one, he is very nice" and "if you go ask him questions, he really does want to help." "I e-mailed him after I graduated with a question and he answered me right away," adds a grateful alumnus. As a classroom professor, though, Bernstein is, by his own reckoning, "intimidating all the way through." You know those professors who tell you that there are no stupid questions? Bernstein is unambiguously not one of those professors. "There are stupid questions," he declares. "An important part of what I do is to teach students how to learn." Sometimes that involves "telling a student that a question is irrelevant or has not been thought-out." The material is hard, and substantial work outside of class is absolutely required. Classes move "very fast." "In the classroom, my goal is to help students understand the aspects of the material that they might have difficulty learning on their own," Bernstein says.

At the same time, Bernstein is very highly acclaimed as a professor because he has the uncanny ability to "explain anything" and because it becomes evident to students that they shouldn't mistake his intimidating presence for hardhearted indifference. "They know I care about whether they learn or not," Bernstein says. "Starting off, he seems far too cocky," relates one student, "but you soon realize he's just awesome." Bernstein is also "extremely entertaining." He describes his teaching method as a "dog-and-pony show." If too many eyes are glazing over, he'll "do something bizarre" or "manufacture some excuse" to tell a personal story that more often than not has "nothing to do with the material." These practices add nothing to anyone's body of knowledge concerning computer science, but they "help the way the lecture proceeds" and, when Bernstein gets back on topic, captures the rapt attention of the class.

Ran Libeskind-Hadas, Professor, Computer Science, Harvey Mudd College

Ran Libeskind-Hadas, who teaches computer science at Harvey Mudd College, looks to help students develop their creative problem-solving skills and to express their solutions clearly, both orally and in writing.

His classes revolve around computer science, algorithms, computability, and complexity theory, and he teaches several introductory courses. One is a novel course that explores computing concepts in the context of biology, which is "an exciting course because it shows students how computer science is important in solving some of the most challenging and important problems in biology." He also teaches a course on algorithms, which provides students with insights on "how hard problems (such as the 'Google maps' problem of finding the shortest path between two points) can be solved so quickly." These courses are "creative and full of counterintuitive surprises," and give students the tools and techniques for designing and evaluating their own algorithms for a wide variety of real-world problems. "His enthusiasm is almost inhuman! Going to class becomes an exciting experience when Ran is teaching it!"

He motivates each class with a compelling real-world problem, and tries to involve students by asking them for approaches, which he will try (and modify) in class. "Learning by 'mistakes' is key, since all hard problems are solved by trial-and-refinement." In working with students individually and in small groups, he is able to make an effort to get students to his office to work on challenging problems together. "Though the class was about ten hours of homework and ate my weekend like potato chips, I really enjoyed it, and Ran is basically the most helpful professor I've encountered," says one appreciative student.

John P. Rogate, EdS, Associate Professor, Computer Science, Champlain College

John Rogate, who teaches information technology courses at Champlain College, is constantly monitoring and assessing to ensure students are always on track to succeed (both inside and outside the classroom), and that they are obtaining the best learning experience within the realm of their personal objectives.

This "entertaining" professor takes what some perceive as a dry topic and tries to "make learning fun," sparking students to want more. In (both graduate and undergraduate) classes such as Linux System Administration I, Introduction to Data Communications, and Convergence of Telecommunications and Business, he finds it important to always make connections as to why students are learning a particular topic, and where it fits into the big picture (and the "real world"). "It is my philosophy to expand learning as much as possible. In technology courses, it is easy to use logic to get from point A to point B. But when you expand to include imagination, you can get anywhere you want," he says.

Professor Rogate has over thirty-five years of technology industry and academic experience and does a great deal of research in the area of disruptive technologies for education and specializes in virtual world environments (for education). He favors project-based assignments and finals, and makes it a point not to flood students with meaningless busywork in the name of rigor. "If you let students be responsible for their own learning as much as possible...[it] usually turns out to be more rigorous that I could ever define," he says. "John is a lot of fun—and he makes classes fun," says a student.

Andrew Russakoff, Associate Professor, Computer Information Systems and Decision Sciences, St. John's University

Andrew Russakoff teaches statistics and a couple of other subjects in the College of Business at St. John's University, a large commuter school in the nether reaches of Queens, New York. He has a doctorate from the City University of New York and two other degrees in modern history from Oxford. Students describe Russakoff as "the best prof you could imagine." He is "super helpful." Depending on who you talk to, he is either "really energetic" or "very laid-back." He is also "a really good person" and a "very interesting guy." We don't know for sure, but we are willing to venture that he is the only business professor in the United States who plays the bagpipe on St. Patrick's Day. He is very approachable, too. You can "talk to him after class for help or just to joke around."

"I am very clear about what students need to know," Professor Russakoff says. The "best teaching is from examples," he adds, and he provides them amply. "If you go to class and pay attention," students promise, "you'll do well." Exams are reportedly fair. In his statistics course, there are three tests and a final. If you ace the first three, there's a good chance you'll be able to walk away with your A without bothering with the final. Russakoff also "gives goofy extra credit on the tests to help your grade."

Students say that Russakoff runs a very well-structured class. He makes "everything completely understandable" "and repeats anything if you don't understand." He makes you "want to be in class, something that is hard to do for a stat class." Perhaps best of all, Russakoff is ridiculously efficient. "You will rarely be sitting in class for longer than thirty minutes on a given day." "He is one of those professors you must take," urges one student. "I was upset at myself for cutting," laments another student. "Why can't every prof be like him?"

Mehran Sahami, Associate Professor of Computer Science, Stanford University

Mehran Sahami, a computer science professor at Stanford University, helps students understand material by building on what they are already familiar with, which involves making sure that they are clear on conceptual issues as well as the nuts and bolts of how to apply the material. "I really care about whether they are learning, rather than just trying to get through the material in lectures," he says.

Through his methods students are able to take "real ownership over their learning" by getting involved in class discussions, asking questions when something isn't clear, and coming to office hours to review concepts. Students who succeed in answering questions correctly even get candy! "We try to make [classes] involved and relevant so students feel like they are empowered to harness technology to do a lot of things, even very early on in computer science," he says. The introductory classes often have students from across the spectrum of academic disciplines, and he tries to give them "something that resonates with students as a way they can impact the world."

Current courses include Programming Methodology, and Probability Theory for Computer Scientists, which is one of Professor Sahami's favorite courses. "I love helping students appreciate how probability is useful and applicable in ways they didn't expect and how it can change their outlook on many things they do on a daily basis." In all of his classes, he uses concrete examples to show how concepts can be employed in a real way, as well as "in-class demonstrations and a healthy dose of humor to help students remember what they've learned."

Professor Sahami also has a cult following from videos of his online lectures, which win raves from those who aren't even his students. "I have seen most of his online lectures on programming methodology and I have been blown away," says one. "I am not even taking this course yet, but was just intrigued by the lectures!" says another.

Criminal Justice

Erik Fritsvold, Assitant Professor, Criminology and Legal Studies,
University of San Diego

Erik Fritsvold, who teaches criminology and legal studies at the University of
San Diego, has a special recipe for his classroom goals: He wants to "nurture
academic excellence with a twist of practicality."

In providing the critical thinking, reading, writing, and professional skills
needed to serve students for a lifetime, he looks to give them the ability to critically evaluate policy and to understand crucial social issues that can really make
a difference in society. "I have high expectations for my students and for myself.
We are truly engaging the material together." He goes into each class expecting
that they have good systems in place to succeed, just as he tries to have good
systems in place to present the material and evaluate their work. "We are all
adult professionals working toward a common goal," he says.

Professor Fritsvold teaches a broad array of classes in the criminology and
legal studies area (such as Corrections, Criminology, Drugs & Society, Law &
Society, Social Deviance, and Social Control), and he particularly enjoys capstone
courses that allow a deeper examination of the issues. "Criminology issues are
arguably some of the most pressing issues facing modern America. We need a
sound understanding of these issues to hopefully improve public policy," he says.

Each class is approached as if the students are "experts engaging crimino-
logical policy." Using the tools of social science, he enthusiastically engages
the classroom, and students say he "knows how to give you concrete evidence."
"Classes involve a high level of discourse and, if nothing else, class is fun and
exciting," says a student. "The more input that can be incorporated from diligently prepared students, the more cooperative a classroom can be, the better
the outcome," says Professor Fritsvold.

Dr. James O'Keefe, Associate Dean & Professor of Criminal Justice, St. John's University

Dr. James O'Keefe, a former undercover vice cop who teaches criminal justice at St. John's University, imparts the following to his students: "Justice is the mother of all virtues and we all have a moral imperative to make the world a more just place with our education."

In his classes, which include Police Administration, Criminal Justice, and Principles of Leadership, he looks to inform students—in all interactions—that "nothing is more personally empowering than intelligence and a solid education," and so they must learn to think critically and to apply critical thinking skills to their life. His classroom environment is safe, academically challenging, and fun ("You live, learn, laugh, and understand every bit of information in his classes"), and he seeks to provide every student with "the time, care, and compassion I would show my own son and daughter." "Because every student I meet is someone's child, and they probably represent the hopes and dreams of their families. It is my honor to be trusted with such a sacred trust," he says. "He's a great guy, he'd go above and beyond for his students," says one.

In his courses, both undergraduate and graduate, he identifies key academic principles to be learned, and then brings them to life in class with real-world examples and/or current events. "My students are essentially involved in a mutually beneficial critical conversation in class," he says. Students are consistently encouraged and learn not to be afraid to be wrong. "If we never fail, we are simply not trying hard enough!" He tells his students that they are not studying criminal justice to be a police officer; they are studying criminal justice to be a police commissioner. Everyone is simply asked to take their studies seriously and be courteous: attend class, be on time, and be prepared. "My students have a saying about my class: 'If you're early, you're on time; if you're on time, you're late, if you're late, don't bother," he says. "You have nothing to lose but everything to gain with any class that Dr. O'Keefe teaches," says a student.

Developmental Studies

Dr. Melvin A. Jenkins, Professor/Chairperson, Department of
Developmental Studies, Indiana University of Pennsylvania

Melvin A. Jenkins, who teaches in the Department of Developmental Studies at Indiana University of Pennsylvania, believes that teaching and advising is designed "to create better people, not just better students." In this regard, he looks to impact the "entire" student in order to facilitate as many positive changes as possible within the population. "He teaches you more than book work, but also life lessons," says a student.

He values the importance of contact with the students and therefore teaches courses that maximize the amount of time he can spend interacting with his classes. His courses include Introduction to Higher Education, Learning Strategies, and Career Exploration (which helps students clarify their choices of major with an understanding of the theoretical foundations involved in career choices); in these courses, he seeks to engage students of all levels and to challenge them to become active learners. "I continually demonstrate to my students the value of staying committed to task despite any obstacles. I have made it a rule to hold students accountable for unexcused absences or tardiness and require that they do the same of me," he says.

While he insists that they strive for perfection in even the simplest of tasks, he fully understands that many of his students are slow to learn for a variety of reasons, and has developed a teaching technique that allows and understands genuine academic deficiencies without discouraging the student suffering from them. "As I teach, I try to mentor my students….My ultimate goal is to reach each of my students holistically, thus creating a better person—not just a better student." Students say it is "a great help to have Mr. Jenkins on your side as a scared freshman coming to a place you know nothing about."

Digital Forensics

Jonathan Rajewski, CCE, EnCe, CISSP, CFE, Assistant Professor of
Digital Forensics, Champlain College

"Through our faculty's ongoing connections to and work with local law enforcement and the digital forensics industry, we're able to bring the current trends of digital forensics—all those rapid evolutions that are happening outside in the field—into the classroom every day," says Jonathan Rajewski, an assistant professor of digital forensics at Champlain College in Burlington, Vermont. "And students here are benefitting tremendously from that experience."

Previously employed as a senior consultant for a global consulting firm where he traveled the world conducting and managing digital forensics investigations, Professor Rajewski is not only a faculty member at Champlain but he is also the co-director/principle investigator of the Champlain College Center for Digital Investigation (C3DI) and an examiner for the Vermont Internet Crimes Against Children Task Force. Recently named the "Digital Forensic Investigator of the Year" by Forensic 4cast, Rajewski is as passionate about teaching and empowering students to become leading-edge digital forensics professionals as he is about the exciting work of digital forensics itself.

Despite the relative complexity and unfamiliarity of most people with the field, Professor Rajewski is committed to giving his students a complete education in digital forensics from the ground up. "Incoming students don't need to be 'techie'-type people," says Professor Rajewski, "they need to be people who love to learn and apply knowledge. So you don't need to come in as a computer expert to be hugely successful in this program—our first-year foundational courses give you all the grounding you need." His students agree, saying that in his classes, "you will NEVER be confused."

Students also report that Professor Rajewski "cares about what we think of the class and makes changes accordingly," and he "goes the extra mile to make sure you understand the information being presented." Very technical topics are broken down into layman's terms, followed by him showing the class "how it actually applies to the subject." He also gives real-time demonstrations when someone asks a question, then has the students apply that topic to a hands-on activity. "This method reaches all learning styles: visual, auditory, and kinesthetic learners," Rajewski says.

Through this detailed, hands-on approach to learning, his students gain mastery-level understanding of the subject matter. "I want students to become experts," says Rajewski. "The Champlain digital forensics curriculum has been built around what the industry needs. We polled the industry and studied job descriptions to find out what skills the industry is requiring for certain positions in the field, and we've created courses to match those needs." This industry-based curriculum has been highly successful for students and grads alike: Last year, recruiters from major consulting firms and government agencies came to Champlain College for the express purpose of interviewing Champlain's digital forensics majors for summer internships and full-time positions—a high percentage of students were hired as a result of those meetings. "It's really impressive that the employers come to us seeking out our students," says Professor Rajewski.

He says that in addition to the depth of forensics course offerings, digital forensic majors get unparalleled experience in the Champlain College Center for Digital Investigations(C3DI) working in a real digital forensics investigation lab. "What our students become capable of doing is tremendous," he says. "A big part of that is the experiences they have working in C3DI conducting the digital forensics research that helps local law enforcement solve actual cases. It's also an amazing resume builder."

Professors Rajewski's teaching style is as hands-on as his students' educational experience in Champlain's digital forensics program. Each course is presented differently, and Rajewski tends to draw from experience and tell stories about why the discussion topic is important for the students to understand. By their senior year, students are well prepared to take the capstone course in which they conduct research into a "new" technology and create a presentation and report of how they would forensically analyze a device or Internet service. "This year, many of our students conducted research that hasn't been done before, making new discoveries—a number of papers they wrote have a high probability of being published in digital forensic industry publications," Rajewski reports. "Now, that's truly impressive."

It's all about the results with Professor Rajewski. And, he's proud of what his current and former students have achieved already. "Our students come from all over the world," he says. "And we've seen them land positions with local law enforcement, the federal government, the Department of Homeland security and other Department of Defense agencies as well as government contractors and consulting firms from across the country."

Economics

T. Randolph "Randy" Beard, PhD, Professor, Economics, Auburn University

Randy Beard is an economics professor at Auburn University with a "very dry wit." He teaches industrial organization, microeconomics, and public policy, and he has published a number of books and scholarly articles. He also makes appearances as an expert before federal regulatory bodies (like the Federal Trade Commission) and federal courts.

Beard tells us that he is enthralled by the "dismal science". "Nothing is more interesting to me," he insists. He describes people who like economics as "cynical nerds who find kindred spirits" in their fellow majors, and he describes the courses he teaches, particularly Microeconomics, as "a vaccination against wishful thinking." However, underneath the ostensibly gloomy veneer is a certified optimist who loves to teach and loves to get students excited about his subject. "I want them to know firsthand that they can understand economics," he says. "It is difficult but not impossible, and every one of them is capable of doing it."

According to students, Professor Beard "really cares about teaching" and his classes are "worth attending" for the sheer entertainment value alone. He is able to make even the dullest material fairly scintillating. As one student puts it, he does "a good job of taking what amounts to stereo instructions and applying it to real life." "His sense of humor is where he really shines, though." "He is funny and interesting to listen to. He gives examples that can make the material a lot easier to learn and tries to keep everybody involved." Beard also makes himself "very accessible" outside of class, which is not always the case for professors at big schools. "He cares about your grade." "Tests are tough and you have to study for them," but students seem to appreciate the challenge, and they definitely don't lack for study resources. "He gives reviews, worksheets, and answer keys to the worksheets," catalogs one student. "Whatever it is that you need, he has it." Also, "his grading is very merciful." "Dr. Beard is the magical pot of gold that leprechauns hide," gushes one happy student. "He is a two-horned unicorn. Above all, though, he is an amazing teacher that loves to teach and loves his students." "He is a true gift to Auburn and economics."

Jay Corrigan, Associate Professor, Economics, Kenyon College

Jay Corrigan, a professor of economics at Kenyon College, has two goals as an educator. "First, I want my students to learn to think like economists—to look at everyday interactions with an eye for the tradeoffs people face. And, second, I want my students to be able to clearly and persuasively communicate these economic insights to a lay audience."

In his classroom, he tries to strike a balance between lecture and hands-on learning, drawing students in by "making regular use of in-class economic experiments designed to introduce nuanced concepts like externalities or the dead-weight loss from taxation." On the first day of his Principles of Microeconomics class, he auctions off a copy of the course textbook with the proceeds going to Kenyon's scholarship fund. Not only does this teach his students something about the design of auctions (the central focus of his research), but plotting students' bids reveals the class' demand for economics textbooks. "Corrigan is energetic and interesting, loves his subject matter. He wears an I Heart Econ T-shirt on every exam day," says a student.

One of his most inspired exercises (students say he is "funny beyond belief") occurs when he asks his upper-level students to write a series of letters to the editor of the *New York Times*, applying economic reasoning to a pertinent economic issue. "The *Times* has strict guidelines for its letters. Letters must refer to an article that has appeared in the paper in the last week, they must be no longer than 150 words, and they must, of course, be written in lay language. The first time I used this exercise, it became clear within a few weeks that this was the most difficult assignment I'd ever given." Through this rite of passage, students learn that as hard as it is to say something thoughtful, it's harder to say something thoughtful and concise, and it's harder still to say something thoughtful and concise in language anyone can understand. He gives detailed feedback on both the rough draft and final draft of students' letters, and the quality of letters improves dramatically over the course of the semester. "The last time I used this assignment I was enormously pleased when the *Times* printed one of my student's letters," he beams.

Dr. W. Macy Finck, Lecturer, Economics, Auburn University

A sound believer in the Socratic method, Macy Finck, who teaches economics at Auburn University in Alabama, wants to get students to discover the answers without having to be told.

In his classroom, he has the unique ability to strike a balance between serious work and a light atmosphere; he says, "While I expect the students to know the material thoroughly, I try to maintain a low-stress classroom environment." Students appreciate that he tries to stay in tune with what is happening in their lives, and "shockingly, my sense of humor" (some have even said he should have a career as a stand-up comic; he says, "I think I'll stick to lecturing, however").

He primarily teaches the Economics of Sports and the large auditorium sections of Principles of Microeconomics, which is a core course at Auburn, so he gets a wide spectrum of majors throughout. He attempts to relate every possible topic in economics to the life experience of a typical college student. "For instance, one of my favorite lectures involves using in-state/out-of-state tuition differences and scholarships as examples of price discrimination," he says. A student says that "his tests are kinda tricky, but he's young so he tries to relate it to funny movies."

Students say that Professor Finck "keeps things interesting" and "his lectures are very clear and if you go to class, listen, and study the study guide, you'll do great!" Classes are "always interesting and he even though attendance wasn't mandatory, almost everyone showed up because they generally wanted to." Or, just take the testimonial of one student: "I hated econ, but he actually makes it fun and pretty easy."

James Hartley, Professor of Economics, Mount Holyoke College

Mount Holyoke College economics professor James Hartley's primary goal is to demonstrate the joy of learning. "The world is full of unbelievably fascinating ideas, and the more you learn about them, the richer and fuller life becomes."

He thinks that a professor should always strive to know just about everything there is to know about a subject, but that this should never be an occasion for talking down to anyone. "Students should always be talked to as if they are capable of learning everything," he says. "The most successful students realize that the point of an education is not to maximize their grade on an exam but to simply learn the material because it is fun to learn."

He's "patient, accessible, knowledgeable, and he makes students think." He is "quite original in his presentation" and, in classes such as Macroeconomic Theory, Money and Banking, and Introductory Economics, delivers lectures as riveting stories, without referring to notes; he "draws a classroom into a puzzle which we then see if we can solve." He never gives easy answers to hard questions, and is "willing to talk to students in his office about any subject in the world (and always strives to be well-read enough to talk about whatever topic is of interest to a student)." "Hartley ran an amazing class full of intelligent and groundbreaking discussions!" says a student.

Elizabeth Jensen, Christian A. Johnson Excellence in Teaching Professor of Economics, Hamilton College

Elizabeth Jensen, an economics professor from Hamilton College, tells her students that she wants them to hold onto three things: a curiosity and awareness that lets them recognize interesting issues and ask questions; an understanding of problem-solving techniques that allows them to think about how to answer questions; and a critical eye and common sense for determining whether or not evidence supports hypotheses.

It's a tall order from a woman who took her first economics course "to satisfy a distribution requirement." Now, after teaching since 1983, she loves her field and loves her students. They say that she "does a wonderful of explaining the concepts," and "always makes herself available for office hours." "I consider her the ideal Hamilton professor," says one.

Professor Jensen regularly teaches Issues in Macroeconomics, Microeconomic Theory, American Economic History, and Industrial Organization, and is "organized and clear in presenting material and in communicating expectations to students." "I try to set high standards that are achievable," she says. She varies the format of her class, sometimes presenting more technical material and making extensive use of graphs, but she is always asking a number of questions of the students, both "to keep them involved and to gauge their understanding of the material." She also incorporates consideration of material found in the business press, an antitrust case study, or a game, experiment, or demonstration. "I might, for example, assign an antitrust case to students and then have a mock 'trial' in class, with teams of students presenting the issues and with me acting as judge."

Dr. James J. Jozefowicz, Professor of Economics, Indiana University of Pennsylvania

James Jozefowicz, an economics professor at Indiana University of Pennsylvania, seeks to enable his students to make a personal connection with course material whereby they can relate course content to their daily lives.

To do so, he employs real-world relevant examples and stories in his classroom to make the course material more relevant, and weaves the current topic together with previous topics to reinforce learning. He stresses the need for students to enhance their resumes/job applications, provides numerous opportunities to prepare for their professional careers, and is always willing to go the extra mile to help them succeed not only in his courses but also in the real world. "He's fun and entertaining and really breaks the material into layman's terms," says a student.

He teaches Principles of Macroeconomics, Managerial Economics, and Introduction to Econometrics & Advanced Econometrics, the latter of which looks at the application of statistical methods to economic data, accomplished with a "learning by doing" approach. "These are the courses I most like to teach because students finish the semester with an oral presentation of their findings and a paper written like a scholarly journal article; these students have presented their research at professional conferences, won awards for their research work, and published a number of their papers in refereed journals with me." In introductory courses, he utilizes data hunt and create-your-own consumer price index assignments; in upper-level economics courses, he seeks to refine students' analytical skills and engage them with economic data. Typically, he will begin a topic by providing a definition, and then broaden the discussion to provide some real-world context. "After that, I ask my students to provide their own examples before giving them my own example/story. This way, the students take greater ownership of learning the material," he says.

His teaching style stresses application and personal connection through active learning strategies; he has great enthusiasm for teaching, and "I want to create a setting for learning where that ebullience is infectious." "This prof epitomizes what teaching at the college level is all about," says a student.

Chris Kingston, Associate Professor, Economics, Amherst College

"I think the professor's role is not just to present the material but to help each student understand how the material might be useful to them in pursuing their individual goals and interests, whatever those might be," says Chris Kingston, a "very helpful, very funny, and very engaging" professor of economics at Amherst College.

To do this effectively, he tries to get to know the students' interests and help them understand what they may be able to draw from the course. He finds it important to convey the passion he feels for the material, while also encouraging students to feel comfortable challenging it and asking questions. "It's only with a two-way flow of information that I can know how whether a student is understanding the material, what they were each hoping to get from the course, and whether they are getting what they need." "We kept him an hour over office hours the day before the last problem set was due, and he still thanked ME for coming," says a student.

His courses include Game Theory, Microeconomics, and New Institutional Economics, in which students say he "breaks down difficult concepts into easy-to-understand bits." He thinks that learning is a cumulative process of discovery; economic theory "is about telling stories to help us understand the world." As he tells those stories (using mathematical models), he encourages students to think not only about what insights they can get from a model but also what might still be missing—"which hopefully leads us to the next (better) model/theory/story."

Avi O. Liveson, JD, LLM, Professor, Economics, City University of New York—Hunter College

Avi Liveson, in the economics department at Hunter College, has an almost crystalline simplicity in his approach: "In class I try to make the material clear, logical, and interesting. Outside of class, I try to treat the students with respect."

He teaches taxation and law within the accounting program, including Income Taxation of Individuals (the federal tax system as it applies to people), Business Taxes (taxation of corporations and partnerships), and Business Law I (contracts and negotiable instruments). He's been at Hunter for all thirty years of his teaching career—"I bleed Hunter purple"—and was a practicing tax attorney for three years, and on the editorial staff of several tax publications for several years. "Do yourself a favor, take him before he retires. He's an unbelievable treat," says a former student.

To present material clearly, using words and examples, is "a great art—rarely achieved." "If you can connect with a student in that fashion, there is no limit to what can be achieved, educationally," he says. "He takes a subject that I could see being very dry if taught by someone else and makes it fun. His style of teaching is unique and he really knows his stuff," says a student. In doing so, he tries to place the student in a situation that illustrates the application of whatever principle the class is covering. "In contract law, I have Tom offering to sell a jacket to Sally and we run dozens of hypotheticals off of that simple beginning to confront and resolve problems and issues that can arise." In taxation he tries to reveal how logic and fairness underpins the system (or fails to). "If Tom is forming a corporation and contributing property in exchange for stock, how is he taxed on the exchange, and what is that tax treatment seeking to accomplish or avoid?"

N. Gregory Mankiw, Robert M. Beren Professor of Economics, Harvard University

"I teach introductory economics, and most of my students have never taken an economics course before," says N. Gregory Mankiw, an economics professor at Harvard University. "Economics gives them a new lens through which to see the world around them."

This new perspective comes courtesy of a twenty-six year teacher who long ago learned that social science can be truly scientific. "One can study human behavior from an objective vantage point using logic and data analysis," he says. He loves economics and delights in introducing others to the field. "While at times the content is a bit beyond comprehension, he brings with it a refreshing sense of relevance," says a student. Professor Mankiw tries to instill in his students a persistent, methodical, and patient approach to learning, and tailors his classes as such. "A student cannot learn well by cramming just before the exam. A successful student will spread the work out as evenly as possible throughout the semester."

He teaches a full-year course in introductory economics, which includes microeconomics in the fall and macroeconomics in the spring, and enjoys getting students when they are new to the subject, typically during their first year in college. This "born professor" (and former Chairman of the Council of Economic Advisers) is "devoted to his subject and his students," and "is a brilliant man and great professor."

Roberto Serrano, Harrison S. Kravis University Professor of Economics, Brown University; and Research Professor, Madrid Institute of Advanced Studies

Roberto Serrano, an economics professor at Brown University, has an insatiable curiosity about his discipline. "The more one learns, the more one realizes there are even more things one should learn." For his part, he challenges his students to develop the same hunger, and "fosters their critical understanding of the subject of study and the world." "I find economics an ideal discipline to use mathematical and formal models in order to study questions that are truly important for the world around us," he says.

Professor Serrano strives to provide balance in his presentation of ideas, and to infuse his teachings with a good dose of humor. "For example, when I cover the problems that the presence of environmental externalities cause to markets, I like to make fun of the two extremes, the 'Chicago school fanatic' that would tell us to do nothing at all, and the 'hippy fanatic' that would ask us to shut down any industry that pollutes, disregarding its important social benefits." Students appreciate his precision, clarity, and humor, and say that he "certainly makes Brown University a better place to be."

His advanced courses, both undergraduate and graduate, cover topics such as game theory, bargaining theory, and the economics of information and uncertainty, and students say that "he obviously cares very much about doing things right." "Economic theory is not something one learns without truly applying oneself on it."

Kevin M. Simmons, PhD, Professor of Economics, Austin College
It is Austin College economics professor Kevin Simmons' fundamental belief that teachers have an obligation to their students to maximize learning. "This is not always synonymous with being a popular teacher. Rather, learning occurs when students are propelled beyond their own expectations," Simmons, who served as a Fulbright Scholar in 2010, says.

Beginning with the awareness that economics is not a popular subject ("Perceptions of our discipline are a dull, hard class"), he uses his passion as an educator to light a spark in his students "to become excited about the 'dismal science.'" Without diluting the material, and providing the necessary rigor, his objective is for his students to truly learn the subject. "There is no greater reward in our profession than to see our students succeed."

He maintains an energy level in the classroom that keeps students engaged in the material, and designs classes that approach his subject from a fresh angle. His January-term class (Economics of the Working Poor) requires each student to volunteer ten hours per week in a setting that ministers to the working poor; Tornadonomics, which is a class that is based on a book that Simmons co-authored titled *Economic and Societal Impacts of Tornadoes*, is meant to show how social scientists can offer insight into how society should approach living with tornadoes in an efficient and cost-effective manner. In Econometrics, which introduces students to the theory and practice of empirical research, students are expected to design an empirical study of their choice, collect the data, perform the analysis and present the results to the class in a format similar to professional conferences. Students say his classes are highly math-based, so "be ready, it will come in to play very quickly and very heavily." However, if anyone has any problems, he is "always ready to help those who want to help themselves."

Cindy van Es, Senior Lecturer, Dyson School of Applied Economics and Management, Cornell University

Cindy van Es, who lectures in the Charles H. Dyson School of Applied Economics and Management at Cornell University, looks to ensure that the content provided in her courses is as relevant and up-to-date as possible, and that it is presented in a way that educates and inspires students.

Most of her classes center around statistics, including Introductory Statistics, Business Statistics, and Decision Models. She believes that if you expect the best from every student, that is what you get; she finds it her place to provide as many resources as possible and to be as accessible and helpful as she can. "I am aware of the strong impact a 'stat teacher' has on students' views about the subject. They always remember their statistics class, either for good or bad reasons, and I want to make them good," she says. "If you hold up your end by attending lecture, paying attention and doing the homework and section work, she will help you get an A!" says a student.

She tries to vary her delivery of information in the classroom and uses active learning exercises, gives lectures, has students do presentations, and has outside speakers; she also tries to vary her assessment measures, using class participation, group projects, and assignments, as well as exams. "I would say my style is basically 'enthusiastic.' I believe that the students only see me three or four hours a week for classes, and they deserve my best effort during those meetings." Students say that "she truly wants you to succeed, and there are so many opportunities to get help."

In addition to her teaching responsibilities, she also serves as the Director of the BOLD (Business Opportunities in Leadership and Diversity) Program. "It is important to me that both in and out of the classroom I respect multicultural and gender differences, and that my classroom has an inviting and inclusive climate," she says.

Akila Weerapana, Associate Professor, Wellesley College

Akila Weerapana, who teaches economics at Wellesley College, wants students to become better economists by starting with the fundamentals.

He helps students grasp the concepts that are critical to developing an awareness of the world outside of the classroom through lectures and a great deal of office hours, which he considers to be a necessary supplement to his classroom efforts. An ideal setting would be one in which he talks about a topic (such as what a currency board is], followed by a class discussion of the reasons why a country might adopt such a system, using real-world examples. A student would then read up on that country's woes or successes, and then come talk to him about the events that occurred, in order to try to understand more subtleties than could be presented in class. "Professor Weerapana is one of the most helpful, humane economics professors I have met so far. His lectures are very encouraging, he answers your questions, and he is THERE for you," says a student.

Students consider Professor Weerapana to be someone who cares about their learning. There is an implicit promise that, in exchange for making them work hard to succeed, he will work just as hard to help them succeed. "When you are passionate about knowledge and passionate about conveying knowledge, it shows," he says. His classes include Intermediate Macroeconomics and International Finance and Macroeconomics, which is an elective course dealing with issues like exchange rates, the interaction of exchange rates and macroeconomic policy, and current developments such as the situation in the EMU and China's exchange rate policy. "He's definitely challenged me to look at econ in a different way," says a student.

William C. Wood, Professor of Economics, James Madison University

"I think anyone can learn economics, and I try to help students develop their own ways of connecting with the material," says James Madison University economics professor William Wood.

One thing that he strives for is to be "brilliant on the basics." For example, when he gives a test, he returns the graded test papers the next time the class meets. He always starts class on time and ends on time, keeps his website current, and works hard preparing for class, even after thirty-three years of teaching. "In these small ways I try to signal that I take class seriously (and I hope students will too)," he says.

His recent course load includes Econometrics (the application of statistical methods in economics), Principles of Microeconomics (which he refers to as "my first love") and Principles of Macroeconomics. Though he was initially daunted when he began teaching and was faced with 500-seat lecture halls and intro classes, "not even that setting could diminish my enthusiasm for showing students how economics can change their thinking and their lives." Now, in fifty-student sections, "it's just fun." "He is both brilliant and hilarious—I never thought I would enjoy econometrics so much," says a student. Wood is the author of the web comic "Academic Mice," and he frequently draws on humorous in-class incidents for the comic.

In a nod to America's national pastime, this "very sweet man" calls his teaching style "hit and run" economics, where "you get a quick start and swing at everything." In practical terms, this means having quick interactive things to do that don't take a lot of setup time. To illustrate labor force turnover, for example, he has students come down front and pretend they're swimming in a pool. "Some swim a long time, while others just jump in and get wet before they get back to sunning with their friends. I draw the analogy with the labor force, showing how long-term unemployment interacts with larger numbers of short spells of unemployment." "He's such an educated man who lectures with realistic events which makes understanding Econ 100 percent better," says a student.

Education

Larry R. Huffman, Adjunct Instructor, Learning, Technology & Leadership Education, James Madison University

There is nothing more important to the future of academia than the teachers that we create today, and Larry R. Huffman, an adjunct professor at James Madison University is completely invested in making sure the future remains bright. Professor Huffman sees his role as helping students "to gain an understanding of the meaning of teacher effectiveness and professionalism," and stresses the need to pay attention to the classroom climate and care about students.

To talk to any of his students, he certainly practices what he preaches. "Not only did I LOVE this class, but I honestly felt that education was the perfect decision after taking him. All students who want to improve the life of children and make a difference in the field of education, then this is who you should take," says one.

By asking himself "What do I want my teachers to know?" Professor Huffman was given the basis for his course Educational Foundations, in which he "works every day to provide [students] with essential information in a creative and meaningful way, using a variety of approaches to teaching and learning and inspiring them to maximum performance." He "constantly changes things up by using videos, guest speakers, and group activities," and he calls upon his decades of experience as a former teacher, principal, and school historian to make his classes come alive. "I was a principal for thirty-one years and I hope to let my students know what it takes to become an excellent teacher."

Though universally considered to be a "sweet guy," he has strong expectations of his students (mainly sophomores seeking certification in education and teaching). "Come to class every day on time, complete all assignments, maintain a consistently positive attitude, and develop your ability to articulate your beliefs (oral and written) about what it takes to be a successful teacher."

Engineering

Lori Bassman, Associate Professor of Engineering, Harvey Mudd College

Lori Bassman, who teaches engineering at Harvey Mudd College, knows that her students are often burning the academic candle at both ends. She encourages them to be aware of the significance of what they are learning: "Of course I want them to retain as much of every topic as possible at the end of a course, but, even more importantly, when they are later faced with a problem related to course ideas, I want them to remember basic principles and know how to teach themselves the details they need." She may assign difficult work, but most students in a class will come to what they call "the most approachable teacher at Mudd" for help, giving her the chance "not just to answer the specific questions that they have, but also to be sure they have concepts straight in general and reinforce ideas when needed."

She incorporates in-class problems and active learning exercises throughout every class to keep students engaged. In nearly every lecture of every course she teaches she incorporates a physical demonstration, which helps students to see concepts behind the equations. Taking advantage of the intimacy of the school, she does her best to get to really know each of her students, and they can tell that she genuinely enjoys spending time with them. "She will help you a lot... very patient. No question is stupid for her," says a student.

Her classes include Continuum Mechanics and Rigid Body Dynamics, and she also helps supervise Engineering Clinics, which are industry-sponsored team projects that juniors and seniors are required to do as their capstone experience. She stresses the need for continuous learning and still takes courses from fellow professors at Harvey Mudd to learn new material and teaching techniques. She recently co-taught a "studio math course" for engineers with a colleague in the math department, and is continually inspired to new teaching heights by her colleagues. "I am just one part of a remarkable team of professors at Harvey Mudd," she says.

Paul Clingan, Lecturer, Engineering Education and Innovation Center, The Ohio State University

Because Paul Clingan, an instructor of engineering at The Ohio State University, teaches first-year students at a large school, his goal is to find some way to connect with students on an individual level to help make the field of engineering and the university feels a little bit smaller and more personal. "I work to make sure that I learn all of my student's names, maybe a little something about them like where they are from, things they enjoy doing when not in school, where they see themselves in the future." Not everyone wants their instructor to know them, however, and the ever-sympathetic Professor Clingan gets that, too: "I try to respect those students who would rather get through the class without speaking to me very much as well," he says.

No matter how technical his topic, he operates under the teaching maxim that if students know you have their best interests at heart, they are much more apt to be open to your suggestions. "I try, as best I can, to minimize the 'distance' between student and instructor," he says. "They get to see me as I really am (warts and all) and I try to present information to them in a genuine fashion." Students know that there aren't any questions they cannot ask him or subjects that cannot be discussed, and that Professor Clingan is willing to laugh at himself. "Initially I did not expect to be teaching more than a few months and now I'm approaching the end of my first decade. I don't know if I chose to teach these subjects as much as they chose me."

In his various engineering classes and labs, this student-proclaimed "God of a teacher" enjoys helping students develop their problem-solving skills and their ability to solve large problems by deconstructing them into smaller, more manageable ones. Students say he "kept the class lighthearted and fun even though it was stressful and a lot of work."

Phillip Cornwell, Professor of Mechanical Engineering, Rose-Hulman Institute of Technology

Phillip J. Cornwell, a professor of mechanical engineering at Rose-Hulman Institute of Technology, prepares his students to approach any problem with confidence. He teaches material with constant reference to applications of the principles, helping his students become better problem solvers in all situations. "The important part of what I teach is the process, not the answer," he says.

Active learning is an important component of Professor Cornwell's teaching style. Recent classes have included Conservation and Accounting Principles, Analysis and Design of Engineering Systems, and Mechanical Vibrations, in which his students perform a modal test of a structure of their choosing on campus. He presents the material for his classes through a mini-lecture and then demonstrates problem-solving techniques through interactive examples. "I want them to recognize that there is not a unique path to the solution. I want them to identify a system, apply principles, and keep track of equations and unknowns."

While Professor Cornwell has high expectations and difficult classes, he is always willing to help students outside of class. "It also gives me a good chance to actually get to know students better and to learn more about their lives." A student summarizes Cornwell's classes perfectly: "One of the hardest classes was made easier than almost every other class merely because he was an amazing teacher."

Ronald Gronsky, Professor, Engineering, University of California—Berkeley
If a student is left curious, then University of California—Berkeley engineering professor Ronald Gronsky has done his job.

For thirty-four years he has sought to make students' learning experiences "exciting, effective, and efficient, [and] to prepare them for solving the most technically difficult problems." Above all, students praise Professor Gronsky's availability and the simple courtesies he extends them, such as not answering the phone when students are in his office. And personal contact trumps electronic messaging for the delivery of difficult technical content, anytime. "Ever try to 'text' a partial differential equation? Don't! My office door is always open. We'll sketch images to illustrate that equation." he says.

Over the years, he has taught seven different undergraduate courses and seven different graduate courses, including Materials in Music, Electron Microscopy and Microanalysis, and Metals Processing. He preaches a lifelong commitment to learning, particularly in light of his students' chosen field. "Today's engineers work in rich hyperdisciplinary teams, facing problems that have no precedent solutions, using tools that have yet to be invented, tools that they are most likely to invent. For tomorrow's engineers, simply being facile with modern technology is not enough to invent new technology."

His classroom approach varies on the topic being covered, and whether it's a lab or a lecture. For lectures he'll begin with a motivational story, then progress through conceptual detail, asking rhetorical questions (some of which have "common" answers that are wrong, and then "asking for class responses as to why common understanding is SO wrong." No matter what the subject, he always ends by motivating the need to attend the next class. "Gronsky is clear, interesting, enthusiastic, funny, and (long list of other adjectives)," says a student. "Drop by anytime his door is open, and chat about math, science, and everything else under the sun."

Barrett Hazeltine, Professor, Engineering, Brown University

There is no passive passing in Barrett Hazeltine's engineering classes at Brown University, where students are treated as "partners in the learning process." The engineering professor looks to give students not just the tools they need to solve problems on their own, but the desire to use them. "Usually they can work out the details of the solution on their own, if they feel confident and want to," he says.

An electrical engineer by training, Professor Hazeltine long ago came to the conclusion that creating a beneficial technology was only half the battle in making engineering useful to society; the other half is the management issues of making the technology widely available, which gets into the financial and social aspects. He is a firm believer that "being sensitive about so-called 'unintended consequences' is also an important aspect of making engineering truly beneficial, and the sensitivity involves both the technology and how it is implemented."

In service of this credo, the man that one student calls "by far my most beloved professor, cross my heart," teaches all manner of engineering and entrepreneurial management courses, with a particular focus on how it applies to less industrialized areas (particularly Africa). After fifty-two years of teaching at Brown, his current course load includes Management of Industrial and Non-Profit Organizations, Managerial Decision Making, and his personal favorite, Appropriate Technology, a course intended for liberal arts students which "deals, on one hand, with basic technologies—energy, drinking water, waste, and so forth—and, on the other hand, with how useful technologies can be made available to people with few resources. Water pumps for irrigation is a commonly used example."

Papers and exams are a regular part of some of Professor Hazeltine's courses, but even those tend to have a twist. In one course, students are required to act like they were a consultant, and pick a case/problem out of the fifty that he makes available. During the semester, each student comes in a couple of times and talks about what they're doing and presents their recommendations to date, which acts as an opportunity to prepare students for the many presentations that they'll have to do in life. "I think there is a pedagogical advantage for people to concentrate on one problem and put it all together, and integrate everything they know," he says. "If the student doesn't get a chance to integrate everything in the end for a final, then we're missing something," he says.

Brad Lehman, Professor, Electrical and Computer Engineering, Northeastern University

Brad Lehman, a professor of electrical and computer engineering at Northeastern University, tries to captivate and involve students in their process of learning. "I bring in relevance to technical material and show them the path to understand aspects of engineering," he says.

Through his own education experiences as a student, he learned that a great teacher is "more of a facilitator of learning than a lecturer. An effective teacher does not drill facts but instead ignites a student's desire to learn." He does this by introducing a perspective and then attempting to guide students through difficult concepts, supplying enthusiasm and encouragement, and placing knowledge in a context where relevance is apparent. In his classroom, he uses visual aids, laboratory demonstrations, multimedia animations, videotapes, and humor, and makes great efforts to take complicated material and simplify it to understandable levels. "He excites you about learning material and becoming an electrical engineer. He shows research, such as LED lights, in his class," says a student.

Teaching at Northeastern University has provided him with opportunities to interact with students who, at times, due to co-op or full-time jobs, have more experience than he does in dealing with many technologies. "Together with my students, I grow and learn in each class that I teach. This is invigorating and challenging, but most importantly, provides me immense satisfaction," he says.

His courses include Renewable Energy, Power Electronics, and Electronics, and he enjoys teaching the latter the most, as "it is the first time that many students realize that the engineering theory they have learned in equations can be applied to build very important electronic systems, such as audio amplifiers, LED lighting systems, and solar energy systems." Classes can often be viewed as "deep technical conversations that sway back and forth between instructor and students." "The way he teaches makes it so much easier to understand what is going on," says a student.

Mark Somerville, Professor of Electrical Engineering and Physics, Franklin W. Olin College of Engineering

Mark Somerville, who teaches electrical engineering and physics at Franklin W. Olin College of Engineering, wants students to become reflective, engaged, self-directed learners. In giving students the drive to strike out independently, he simply listens to them, and tries "to make them responsible for their own progress."

His classes involve a lot of "interdisciplinary stuff" at the intersection between physics, engineering, and mathematics, including Modeling and Simulation of the Physical World (which is heavily project-based and taught in a studio), which he and his colleagues designed because they felt that "the traditional approach to mathematics, science, and computing left students solving pattern-matching problems without understanding the thought process or work process that engineers and scientists use in approaching real-world problems." His efforts are appreciated by all who he touches: "He teaches full course load despite being a dean at the same time (and having a family) and always gives 100 percent."

Engineering education has become a focus of his research, and his general rule in teaching is that he tries "to have students talking more than me." In a studio setting, this might involve his asking a particular team to explain their approach; in a class that requires more directed content delivery, it might involve quite a bit of cold-calling and having students work in groups (at the board or at group tables) on problems while he circulates and ask questions. "I went into Mark's class knowing almost nothing about the subject, and I came out feeling like I could actually keep up with kids who'd been studying for years," says a student.

Richard Stamper, Professor, Mechanical Engineering, Rose-Hulman Institute of Technology

Richard Stamper, a professor of mechanical engineering and engineering management at Rose-Hulman Institute of Technology, wants students "to see the beauty that is found in engineering."

Professor Stamper, who has been teaching for thirteen years, cares about more than just disseminating information; he cares about the impact that his students will have on society and the engineering profession. "It is important in engineering classes to show how the material (which may sometimes seem a bit sterile and dry) provides a powerful tool—once mastered—to serve the greater needs of society," he says.

His courses include Failures of Engineered Systems and Intellectual Property for Engineers and Scientists; in the former, he reviews past failures of engineered systems in order to improve an engineer's ability to anticipate, prevent, and respond to failures. Despite the scientific nature of his subjects, he learned from one of his past professors that there is no need to suppress emotion in an engineering class. "When he described the development of life-saving technologies, he beamed with pride in the biomedical engineering profession. When he talked about engineering tragedies you could sense his sincere sadness."

Students treasure his teaching; one says "He's really fast, really nice, and really cool. Dance if you get him." "He explains things well, and even cracks a few jokes here and there, which makes the class go by faster."

Monica Zima, CPA MBA, Adjunct Faculty, School of Engineering and Technology, Miami Dade College

The challenge in teaching in the sciences is that one must communicate with students at different learning levels if they are to obtain a thorough understanding of course fundamentals. Monica Zima, a professor in the School of Engineering and Technology at Miami Dade College is more than willing to devote time to each and every student that has a desire to learn." With patience and varying explanations/presentations of the same material, EVERYONE can achieve a level of understanding," she says.

A polymath by nature, she is both Certified Public Accountant and instructor in the U.S. Coast Guard Auxiliary, and has an MBA. She primarily teaches Microcomputer Usage, which focuses on the presentation of essential computer concepts and fundamentals of certain software. She strongly believes the subject is of great importance, as "anyone who acquires knowledge and skills in basic computer software applications will have an increased level of efficiency with respect to personal and professional organization." Her teaching style is "clear, concise, and at a level of understanding than anyone can comprehend."

This busy but "very responsible" teacher always answers e-mails, "gives you time to complete your work," and "gives you feedback on what you did wrong so you know how to better yourself."

English

Beverly McCullough Almond, Adjunct English Professor, University of Mary Washington

Students in the classes of Beverly McCullough Almond, who teaches English at the University of Mary Washington, engage with literature.

"Good literature provides one the opportunity to learn more about self while grappling with the universals of the human predicament," she says. Her classes are both reading and writing intensive ("the writing process is essential to clear thinking and clear communication"), but she is completely willing to give students more of her time outside of class to make sure they succeed.

Her thirty-five years of teaching have included Writing About Appalachian Lit and Folklore, Bible Lit, and Art of Literature, a general education course that emphasizes the major genres, covering Western Lit from the classical period to the present. Lit classes are "short on lectures, long on class discussions with the students"; notes are available online, and students must do their reading ahead of time. Her writing classes also include literature that will provoke thought and discussion, and students must bring in at least one working draft of assignments to be shared with their peer group, who give feedback based on guidelines Professor Almond has provided. "Those who succeed dare to think independently, and look for something in a piece of lit that is not covered in class," she says. "The essays are very open-ended with little specific-topic requirements. You can talk about what you want to talk about for the most part and she's fine with it," says a student.

Elizabeth Barnes, Professor of English and American Studies, The College of William & Mary

Elizabeth Barnes, professor of English and American studies at The College of William & Mary, tries to "facilitate an atmosphere where students are able to think their best thoughts, without fear and with curiosity, empathy, and reason."

Her lectures involve asking a lot of questions in guided discussions, in which she hopefully leads students towards a meaningful analysis of the work they are reading. "I have a sense of what ideas I want to have covered by the end of class, but how we get there very much depends on what people say. Discussion is the most important thing, and you have to respond honestly to what students think, feel, and are saying." "Don't worry if she gets quiet after you talk; she's not judging you, she's thinking about what you said," warns a student.

Professor Barnes does not shy away from an honest discussion and is not afraid of conflict; instead, she helps guide it to a place where both sides understand the other viewpoint better by the end. "I draw them out and towards a meaningful articulation of an idea, or a synthesis of ideas that we've been discussing. I don't give them answers, but I do take what they say and go somewhere substantial with it. They feel like we got there together," she says.

Her course load includes American Renaissance, Love and the Novel, Christianity and 19th Century American Literature, and a popular course on Ernest Hemingway, who "has a lot to teach about life, but since he couldn't live up to what he thought the ideal man was, it makes for good discussion." She thinks that all of her topics provide fodder for endless conversation, as "American authors are very strange and conflicted and serious. Somewhat tortured and yet sincere. It's never boring."

Students say that "she makes you think about the text in a different way. She's also really easy to talk to outside the classroom." "She is very difficult when it comes to paper grading, but it's a small price to pay for what you will learn," says another.

Jeffrey Berman, Distinguished Teaching Professor of English, State University of New York—University at Albany

University at Albany English professor Jeffrey Berman's 2001 book, *Empathic Teaching: Education for Life*, reveals his approach to teaching. "He will invoke your strongest emotions—watch out!" says a student.

In encouraging students to write about issues that they have never written about before, he tries to create an empathic classroom where students can write about the most important issues in their lives without feeling criticized or judged. Lately, he has been teaching courses and writing books on love and loss, and the ensuing recovery. "I began writing about suicide many years ago when my best friend (and mentor) committed suicide. Since then, I give students the opportunity to read literature about suicide and to write about their own experience with the subject," he says. His students find such courses valuable both from an educational and psychological point of view; he doesn't "do therapy" in the classroom, and he's not a therapist, but his students find personal writing in an empathic classroom to be therapeutic. "He dares you to confront him on any number of his claims; say he is wrong, and argue your point," says a student.

This "warm and brilliant man" also constantly checks in with students to find out how they are doing in the course and whether they need special help, and to get their suggestions for improving the course. "You might hysterically cry one day, and laugh like crazy the next...either way it's an experience not worth passing up!'

Victor L. Cahn, Professor of English, Skidmore College

Students claim that Victor L. Cahn, a professor of English at Skidmore College, "knows exactly what he wants and needs to say, and how to say it." He is also "very attentive to student needs, and brings a good mix of humor and understanding to the texts he uses."

In classes such as Shakespeare: Comedies, Histories, and Romances and The Art of Reading Plays, he uses "energy, humor, and passion," first to involve students in the material, then to invite them to respond to it through discussion, and finally to inspire them to explore it further on their own. He respects creativity in almost any form, and hopes that his writing assignments "allow students to exercise their talents in this area." One quality that students seem to enjoy is Professor Cahn's willingness to share his own feelings and experiences about a subject; they also appreciate that he treats literature as not just an academic study but a reflection of real issues that are part of the world. "For instance, when we read Shakespeare's history plays, discussion inevitably turns to contemporary politics and similar matters, and no matter which party or individuals are in power, the parallels are always striking. Individual politicians come and go, but the themes remain timeless."

He wears a suit and tie to class every day, but sits on his desk and never uses notes. "In other words, I try to be organized, so students trust that they can rely on the course structure I present, but I also try to remain flexible so that when discussion veers off in an unexpected direction, I'm ready." Students enjoy the levity he brings to serious texts, and claim that "you'll learn SO MUCH, but in a fun and stress-free way!"

Rebecca Walker Clarke, Adjunct Faculty, English, Brigham Young University

Rebecca Clarke, a professor of English at Brigham Young University, wants to help students learn to communicate clearly and take responsibility for their own learning. "Getting students engaged in learning is the mark of a good teacher," she says.

She loves writing, and mainly teaches Writing 150 Honors, a survey course in which students have the opportunity to learn about university genres and how to navigate the library. Her classroom style is interactive; she enjoys teaching personal essays and loves to have students write about small but meaningful topics they've not talked to others about (that way "the goal is fresh rather than secret"). Students begin by writing a paper focused on how a piece of writing transformed them, making this experience as powerful as possible for their audience. During that exercise students are able to focus on the power of story and detail. Then, the class moves into analysis, argument, and research, where students learn and practice critical thinking, utilizing outside sources, and the value of entering into meaningful academic conversations.

Students are encouraged to choose their own topics on all papers and to tie their research to their service learning experiences in order to be highly invested in their writing. Professor Clarke also urges students to consider a larger audience "than the person standing at the front of the classroom" by helping students consider publication and writing contests.

"I meet with students individually before every major paper is due to go over questions and look at rough drafts. Peer editing is a hallmark of my classroom as well." "She gives plenty of detailed feedback while grading papers, to the point that the grade that accompanies it feels unimportant in comparison," says a student.

"Honestly the best teacher I have ever had. She genuinely cares about the students and her fun-loving personality makes going to class always enjoyable. It was hard work, but I learned so much," says a student.

Christopher Fee, Johnson Distinguished Teaching Professor in the Humanities and Professor of English, Gettysburg College
Students in the classes of Christopher Fee, an English professor at Gettysburg College, must work hard to develop the skills he requires them to have.

"My role in this enterprise is to offer guidance and encouragement, NOT to think or to act for my students—to do so would run contrary to the liberal arts context," he says. He believes his area offers a wide variety of challenges and experiences "specifically so that my students may gain intellectual tools, individual initiative, and personal confidence which will serve them well for the rest of their lives." He always encourages his students to take charge of their own learning, and challenges them on this point: "This is YOUR life and YOUR college experience; I'm here to help you to gain the tools you need to thrive, to offer strategies for success and the benefit of experience, but NOT to tell you what to do!" "You can tell he loves the subject and has a great sense of humor," says a student.

He holds true to the ideals of his vocation and tries to weave its greater themes into his classes. He teaches a first-year seminar on homelessness that includes twenty hours of local service as well as five days working with non-profits in Washington, D.C.; History of the English Language; and Medieval Drama, at the end of which the class stages a medieval play. He is a staunch proponent of student-centered, active learning, and thus believes that students learn best when they can apply theoretical knowledge in a real-world context. Those who take his *Beowulf* and Vikings Studies courses compile multimedia research projects which ground broad research topics in the soil of specific archeological sites. His service-learning students in the Homelessness course as well as the Poverty and Rural Education course take their book-learning out into the real world and concurrently bring practical experience back into the classroom. "He once reenacted a scene in *Beowulf* by jumping on a desk and screaming. I take his classes for the sheer fun of it," says a student.

Richard Gillin, Earnest A. Howard Professor of English, Washington College
Once students have read enough that they have something intelligent to share with others, then Washington College English professor Richard Gillin feels he has accomplished something.

In shaping individuals to become critical thinkers, in both his and in other disciplines, Professor Gillin teaches his students to draw insights from English literature that can be useful in their lives. He has been teaching for thirty-eight years, and is currently teaching the History of English Literature, which is a year-long survey of the best in English Literature, and Victorian Age, which includes selections from fiction, nonfiction prose, and poetry. "I take students through a text, asking questions of them as we go. As certain topics capture the attention of the class, I dwell on them. I like to develop a give-and-take atmosphere," he says. "Gillin expects literary chitchat in class," says an appreciative student.

Students call him "extremely helpful and flexible," as well as the "best English professor and kindest soul you'll ever meet." He "validates, encourages, and inspires," and is "a model for educators…[and] a man for the ivory tower as well as the struggling student."

Jared Green, Associate Professor and Department Chair, English, Stonehill College

Whether in the classroom or out, and irrespective of the specific material of a given course, Stonehill College English professor Jared Green's intent is to encourage students to thirst for intellectual challenge and to love engaging with their world both critically and creatively. "I see my role, at its best, as helping to guide students toward the realization and further development of what their own minds are capable of achieving independently," he says.

It is his hope that students emerge from his courses with a firm grounding in literary analysis and "an appetite for pursuing an examined life." He approaches teaching not simply as the delivery of disciplinary knowledge or a particular skill set, but rather as a means of enjoining students to appreciate the broader ideals of thinking critically (they say he is "great at presenting big ideas in an accessible way for students" and that he "gives amazing feedback on all papers, your writing will improve a lot"). According to Professor Green, it is essential that students realize that "intellectual labor is not the deferral of nor mere precursor to meaningful action, but rather the key to engaging with literature and life as fully as possible."

In classes such as Iconology: Studies in Word and Image, Acts of Criticism: Literary and Cultural Theory, and Madness and Insight: Psychological Narratives Before and After Freud, he encourages students to take themselves seriously as thinkers, using an open and improvisational style that balances prepared lectures with free-form discussions that allow the class to pursue new ideas and connections as they occur. "These spontaneous flights of inquiry may take us down unexpected pathways and may even necessitate revisions to the syllabus, but this is what keeps my teaching vital and fresh."

Students say he is "an incredibly eloquent speaker, with a great reading voice that really captivates. He knows how to get everyone in the class interested in the reading no matter what it is."

Linda Hall, Associate Professor, English, Skidmore College

"Henry James urged, 'Never say you know the last word about any human heart.' I'm still learning that lesson," says Linda Hall, who teaches English at Skidmore College.

Early in her career, one of her colleagues told her a story about one of his own mentors, and this tale has stayed with her as "excellent, memorable advice: "Early in his career, the teacher feared he'd run out of material, so he came in with maybe six lessons. By the end of his career, he had only one lesson and six different ideas of how it might be received." She's aware that her students often don't realize what they're learning at the time they're learning it, but so long as they eventually come to understand it—even if this occurs once they've left her classroom—then she still counts it as a victory. One student says: "She is the most incredible English teacher I've ever had. Every class is enjoyable and fast-paced, and you'll learn without even realizing it. She will meet with you whenever you need help and will improve your writing by leaps and bounds."

She teaches nonfiction writing at all levels, including 100-level courses in expository writing as well as upper-level seminars in Cultural Criticism, realizing that "not everyone has a natural talent for it, but everyone has something worthwhile to say on some particular skinny—or large—subject." One of her main goals is to make clear the importance, for a writer, of reading. Most students who write know they should read, but I'm not sure they know that reading can lead to instant improvement—that it's a surprisingly efficient way to make yourself better." She also likes them to see how much they can learn from writing that is "merely good, not brilliant." The effects are noticed by her students: "You will become a much better writer without even realizing it."

Claude Mark Hurlbert, Professor, English, Indiana University of Pennsylvania

Claude Mark Hurlbert, a professor of English at Indiana University of Pennsylvania does everything in his power to help students write about "the most important subject matter in their lives and world, so that they might also learn as much as possible about writing as they do so."

Over the course of more than three decades spent teaching, he has designed a pedagogy that treats with respect and integrity, which a student says "prepared me for life." "[He] cares about students, and the whole class becomes friends—such a great environment for learning," says another.

He is currently teaching a doctoral class in composition theory and a first-year College Writing course, which is his favorite course. "I truly feel blessed to teach first-year writing and to be in a classroom with students as they discover what writing can do both for them and others." Typically, this "funny and flexible" professor will ask his first-year students to write short books on what they are burning to tell the world over the course of the semester; additionally, they will write a foreword to one of the books written in the class, and desktop publish them. Along the way, they continually respond (in student-centered workshops), to the evolving manuscripts of the other students in the room. "I'm not the most social person and I loved this class and got a lot out of it," says a student. "His class is like a big family and I still am close to everyone from that class."

Justin A. Jackson, Professor of English, Hillsdale College

In the classes of Justin Jackson, a Hillsdale College professor of English, everything centers on getting the students "to rub up against the literature we read and to be prepared for it to push back."

He strongly believes that writing about literature functions as one of the most crucial ways to engage it in dialogue. Professor Jackson believes that literature allows students to push themselves in intellectual directions they probably never imagined existed. "Great literature should always challenge us; if it doesn't, then we're probably doing something wrong." He assumes that each of his students possesses a keen mind and expects nothing less of them than to articulate its thoughts. "I find students will rise to our expectations, and will even do so joyfully," he says. "I hate hearing students whine about how hard he is. I'd take a D to hear the man lecture," says one admiring student. "He could teach the telephone book and make it interesting."

He teaches multiple survey courses, including Great Books I: Ancient to Medieval; Great Books II—Renaissance to Modern; and Anglo-Saxon and Medieval British Literature. A trained medievalist, Professor Jackson usually teaches seminars in Old and Middle English literature, but he also teaches a year-long seminar in Dostoevsky, which "is pretty hard to beat" in terms of his favorites. Under Professor Jackson's guidance, students are usually impressed with the sophistication and nuance of the poetic and theological insights of the Middle Ages, and are even more taken aback at just how unserious medieval poets could be. He especially loves teaching fourteenth-century literature, as "the students seem to walk away having a much deeper admiration for their mother tongue."

Even after seventeen years, he wakes up every morning and reads the assigned reading for the day, using his two-mile walk to school to think about the literature he's just reread. His lectures/discussion usually revolve around his morning meditations, and he tries not to enslave himself to the syllabus, playing off of student interest. "I want to talk about the things that have intrigued them, and if this means we fall behind or don't cover everything, then so be it." Impromptu close readings of texts are commonplace and fun, and allow students to participate in the process of close analysis—"to somewhat demystify the process, to see me offer a reading, run into a detail which negates said reading, and then go back to the drawing board (literally on the whiteboard in front of class). It sets them at ease to see me fail and to have to start over."

Though he won't give you any answers, one student notes that he is "very helpful in office hours; meaning he destroys any idea you come up with and then helps you work from there."

Dr. Thomas M. Kitts, Professor, English, St. John's University

A very useful credo Thomas M. Kitts, an English professor at St. John's University in New York, picked up from his favorite professors and teachers is that the more you expect from students, the more they will achieve.

Dr. Kitts may set the bar high for his students, but he works to make sure that it is reachable, creating a relaxed but demanding classroom environment in which students feel comfortable and stimulated. Classes are developed as a conversation on the day's topic, with a set outline of points that will be included in the discussion by the end of the class. How and when those points are covered depends on the direction the students take the topic. "I strive to develop student curiosity and increase student enthusiasm for learning. I try to make them active thinkers, or as Emerson said, 'Man thinking'," he says.

The student-proclaimed "coolest man ever" is well into his fourth decade of teaching, and is currently conducting two classes: Literature in a Global Context, a writing intensive course that introduces students to critical thinking about culture, cultural differences, and social values, and Writing About Music, an upper-level class in which students write about the music that interests them, developing a portfolio of reviews, profiles, features, and interviews. "He does try to appeal to listeners of different kinds of music; we had a lot of choice in what we wrote about," says a student who appreciated the freedom. In both courses Dr. Kitts loves watching his students develop the skills necessary to contextualize, evaluate, and then, most importantly, write about the mediums of art at hand. "I especially enjoy seeing students develop their appreciation for literature and music come to the realization that both are vital to the human experience."

As tough a grader as this "firm but fair" professor is, he is always sure to talk to students individually outside of class, and makes a personal guarantee "that they will improve their writing." "He really helped me develop quality writing skills. His comments and criticisms were always insightful…. If you want to develop and cultivate skills you will need in the marketplace, take his class," says a student.

Kim McMullen, John Crowe Ransom Professor of English, Kenyon College

Kim McMullen, a professor of English at Kenyon College, inspires students to analyze literature and culture with "sophistication, sensitivity, and subtlety," and to express their insights with "energy, lucidity, and originality."

Under her tutelage, students learn never to settle for the obvious or easy answer; she continually challenges her own assumptions and those of her students in order to complicate them and make them more nuanced. She tries to meet each student where she/he is, and to draw them into a dialogic exchange on the topic at hand. "I try to help them recognize these conversations as part of a larger discourse which engages writers, theorists, critics, and other readers across time and cultures." Through this dynamic engagement, she hopes to lead them to the skills, methods, and inspiration that will allow them "to own their own educations so fundamentally that my contributions will ultimately become unnecessary." Though she is notorious for the amount of reading she assigns, she is "incredibly clear, helpful, and willing to give it all for her students."

In classes such as Imaginary Homelands (an introduction to literature and analytic writing, thematically based in a range of postcolonial texts), 20th-Century Irish Literature, and Texting: Reading Like an English Major, she "keeps the classroom walls permeable," using conversations over coffee or (more exotically) field trips during a study abroad program, or a community-wide marathon reading of *Ulysses* (involving over 150 different readers and lasting 28 hours) to broaden and energize the discussion. For her seminar on James Joyce, she asks each student to research and compose an introduction to one of the eighteen chapters of the novel and distribute it to classmates who, in turn, use the student-generated material to guide their initial reading. "At the end of the semester, the seminar has created its own distinctive 'Introduction to Ulysses,' with each chapter representing the voice and perspective of every individual participant." When the classroom dynamic comes together as she hopes, students recognize that "they need to know exactly what I've positioned them to discover—through open-ended critical questions or close analysis of a passage of text or connections made among assigned readings—and thus they actively achieve knowledge and insight as part of a collective enterprise."

A terrific compliment comes from a student who says: "If there were stenographers in class every lecture of hers could be publishable."

Margaret Oakes, Professor of English, Furman University

Margaret Oakes, an English professor at Furman University, believes that students already come into her class with the capacity to ask good questions and explore the answers for themselves. "They don't always need me to feed them information," she says.

Operating under the belief that "an interesting class is a challenging class where the tools for learning are provided for a student, but not necessarily the answers," she tries to provide her students with information that makes the material "relevant and living to them." Her classes are taught with "humor, high expectations, and individual attention," and it is not unusual for her to come into class with a contemporary news story, piece of literature, or song. For instance, when the class discusses the frequent anonymity of early modern authors and the transition to a culture in which authors got paid for their work, she may bring in an ad for rare books showing how we place monetary value on certain authors. "For instance, a first edition of a Harry Potter book can bring in more than $13,000." "Oakes is awesome, for sure. She's fun, super-intelligent, and very flexible to your needs," says a student.

Her courses include Major Authors, The History of the Liberal Arts, and Renaissance Epic; her love for the early modern period is infectious and provides a wealth of discussion topics for her students. "Early modern Britain exploded with literature in all forms; the creative energies in this period, both using classical models and new innovations, make it endlessly fascinating for me. I also find that I am constantly surprised at the analogues to contemporary life that both the students and I are able to find in literature of the period." "It was not easy…but she cares so much about whether you understand the literature," says a student.

Elizabeth Renker, Professor, English, The Ohio State University

No matter where students start off, the goal of English professor Elizabeth Renker, who teaches at The Ohio State University, is to get them to the next level of their ability.

She accomplishes this by assigning challenging reading and creating a classroom environment in which everyone is required to participate in the process of developing, discussing, and articulating ideas. "My student evaluations consistently describe me as tough in a way that is fair and constructive," she says. She works hard to maintain the balance between challenge and support, and recognizes that "college can be a very anonymous experience," and that anything she does to genuinely attend to her students' development does not go unnoticed. "Literature draws upon many dimensions of society, self, history, philosophy, aesthetics, and so on. It provides an endlessly fascinating terrain for exploration, analysis, and self-discovery," she says. "Her clarity of communication, breadth of knowledge, and sincere interest in teaching make her an extraordinary professor," says a student.

Professor Renker teaches an array of classes focused on topics in American literature before 1900, including a class on *Moby Dick* and a class called Poetry/ Alternative, which teaches, in tandem, current song lyrics by indie bands alongside poems from the past four centuries. After spending a term building skills, students interview working musicians via videoconference to talk with them about their interpretations of the songwriters' lyrics. "We have conducted interviews with Rivers Cuomo of Weezer, Matt Berninger of The National, Peter Silberman of The Antlers, Richard Edwards of Margot and the Nuclear So and So's, and more. It's an exciting class that energizes all involved, including the musicians!"

She teaches by engaging students directly in the process of critical thinking about the evidence at hand; she trains them in how to hone their analytical skills for reading, writing, and discussion, in order to build sound, perceptive arguments based in precise uses of evidence. "Renker skillfully weaves class discussions (that include ALL of her students) to synthesize both her expertise and our understanding into vastly effective instruction," says a student.

English (Creative Writing)
Warren Rochelle, Professor of English, University of Mary Washington

Warren Rochelle, a professor of English at the University of Mary Washington, "treats students as a whole person."

Many of his classes revolve around creative writing or upper level literature classes, and hence he usually works with smaller groups. His creative writing classes cover a variety of different types of fiction, including fantasy, science fiction, and short stories, and he starts each semester by asking people their name and what it means. He emphasizes the ability to critique something constructively, and learning a technique and voice. "I work to make classes inclusive so that they don't feel overwhelmed by a strong personality in class. This is a safe place. Everything you say is valid," he says. Students commend his "good sense of humor," and the fact that he "always takes into account how everyone is coming along with assignments to decide whether the due date is fair."

Professor Rochelle and his colleagues are all active practitioners of their craft, and free-writing often takes place during classes. "Even though I am the teacher, I am also a writer with them. I think that's important." He also acts as an advisor to first-year students, where he sees his job as helping them have a successful first year, including teaching them how to approach a professor and understanding why this is so important. "He genuinely cares about the success of his students," says a student.

David Rosenwasser, Professor of English and Co-Director of the Writing Program, Muhlenberg College

"I think the goal of education is to find nothing boring, and if you do, to see that as your weakness—so I guess my goal is to get students to learn how to take an active interest in everything, to see the questions and to be skeptical of easy answers."

So says David Rosenwasser, who teaches English at Muhlenberg College. He works hard at listening and at encouraging members of the class to nominate the starting points for their discussions, and "really believes that you can say something deeply interesting and will push you if you try to hover on a surface level." "He wants his students to feel smart and think smart. He doesn't believe he owns all the good ideas, and genuinely wants to learn from his students. His classes were the highlight of my college career," says a fan. "[This was the] first (and last) class/professor that ever inspired me to read ahead, to read beyond the assignments, and to start a paper a week ahead of time."

Some of his courses include Irish Literature, Theory and Methods of English Studies, Reading *Alice in Wonderland*, and 19th-Century British Fiction: the Marriage Plot. He is devoted to "opposing the vicious binary between 'creative' and 'analytical' writing. I like to see what happens when writers move between the producing and consuming ends of narrative. It can be enlightening to learn to see one's life as a story, and the course also encourages members of the class to see how they are awash in cultural narratives that are actively scripting them, often unawares." Students are required to bring passages from the reading they wish to discuss to class, and he often begin with a few opening remarks and then calls on someone to offer the passage and talk about why it matters to the collective understanding. Often, students write in class at the beginning or end. "I ask the question 'so what?' a lot," he says. "If you want a literature class that will challenge you, make you laugh, and leave you floored after every session, his classes are what you want," says a student.

Randi Lynn Tanglen, PhD, Assistant Professor of English, Austin College

Austin College English professor Randi Lynn Tanglen wants students to know that she is merely a conduit to the greater world of literature. "I don't want students to think that the interpretation of literature or the generation of knowledge comes from me, as the professor, but rather from the individual student."

Rather than allowing them to passively absorb knowledge, she encourages them to be active participants in their own education, and she aims to provide them with the skills that will make empowered, active, and critical thinkers, all while accepting them where they are at. "She makes you feel like any contribution you make to the class is valued," says a student.

In student-centered, collaborative classes such as Expository Writing, American Origin Stories, and Canons of Nineteenth-Century American Literature (in which students are exposed to canonical authors as well as little-studied women and minority writers), she teaches students that studying colonial and nineteenth-century American literature "allows us to reflect on—and even change—our own cultural and political moment by making us aware of what has mattered to Americans in the past."

Students say, "She really knows her stuff, and really likes sharing it with her students." "I wish I could take another Randi Tanglen course."

Barton D. Thurber, PhD, Professor of English, University of San Diego

Barton Thurber, professor of English at the University of San Diego, hopes that his students come to understand how breathtaking the humanities can be.

He believes completely in the value of the material he presents to the class, and he tries to teach his students "how to interact with, occupy, and even breathe a text." He invites to students to partake in this relationship, and tries to make them feel empowered "without agreeing with them, necessarily." "I make it a point to be wrong early, because I have yet to meet a student who does not delight in proving the professor wrong," he says.

Having taught for thirty-three years, his classes include Introduction to Poetry ("Take this class if you hate poetry! It will change your perspective of poetry," says a student) and Romanticism and he has a tried-and-true formula: "I never ask a question. Instead I make a claim, which is sometimes true, sometimes false, but most often just false enough to provoke interest. Then I invite the students to evaluate my claim." This creates an immediate buy-in from the students; they're not answering questions—they're getting the better of their learned professor. In the meantime discussion takes place, and Professor Thurber is able to demonstrate that being wrong is not quite the huge sin students once thought it was, especially when it comes to poetry, and that "sometimes being wrong can provide an unexpected pathway to being right." Class discussions are "intense, but he makes you think...very rewarding."

Steven C. Walker, Professor of English, Brigham Young University

It's a tall order for Steven C. Walker, a professor of English at Brigham Young University, who wants to motivate his students to live more intensely and fully than anyone ever has. In cases where it proves too idealistic, he simply tries "to get as close to that as possible by convincing my students to read profound literature throughout their lives."

In order to fully absorb students in the stories in front of them, each class is a discussion, or the continuation of one. Using the texts as a springboard for discussions on life, Professor Walker engages students in meaningful and relevant conversation with the literature and with each other. "I hope they can feel it's not just professional with me, it's personal," he says. His classes are open and conversational, and based in a conviction that "none of us is as smart as all of us." He asks questions that are not leading or Socratic—"real questions, questions for which I don't yet know the answers"—so that he can dig into those with the students. "It's a good day for me when everyone in the class contributes, and I try to connect by interacting as unscripted as possible with those contributions," he says. Students say that "he has the ability to facilitate critical and creative thinking on almost any subject." "He, and the things I have learned in his classes have truly made me want to be a better person."

In classes such as The Bible as Literature, Modern British Literature, and Christian Fantasy: Tolkien and Lewis, he involves students in everything from class conversation to determining test formats. After forty-six years of teaching, he admits that he "can't get enough of the Bible as Literature." "I wouldn't trade Genesis for...The *Lord of the Rings*. The Bible is the best literature I could find. And it's the most relevant to students' academic lives and, more crucially, to their real lives."

Mark Walters, Professor of English, William Jewell College

Mark Walters, an English professor at William Jewell College, wishes "to know as much as can be known, and to pursue and share this knowledge with discipline and passion and pleasure."

His classes are not easy—"I demand and expect much from my students; I hold them accountable; and I'm considered a tough grader"—but he is fair and good humored and engages them in the subject matter in ways that move the students intellectually and emotionally, in large part because he himself is continuously moved by the texts in such ways. "I want to instill in students a desire for and sense of the meaningfulness of engagement with ideas—the habit of this, which can deepen their lives," he says.

His courses run the gamut, and he has recently taught a fiction workshop, a poetry workshop, a U.S. literature survey, and an introductory course in the college's core curriculum, which every student takes during the first year. The course is demanding but, according to many students, the most transformational course they've ever taken, leading them not only into the challenges and joys of rigorous academic work, but causing them to examine their own assumptions regarding reality and knowledge. "I particularly like teaching this course because the growing sophistication within students—in terms of critical thinking, reading, and writing skills—is most dramatic," says Professor Walters. "He is about three times more brilliant than any student could possibly be, which means that he is always on a completely different level," says a student of her teacher.

His teaching style is conversational, with close attention to the text; he rarely lectures, uses no notes, and has only the book in his hand. This requires that he know the text very well, and he rereads everything, even if he's taught it just the semester before, or has read it a dozen times. "Because I'm always reading a range of materials, and in conversation with my colleagues in different disciplines, I come into the classroom bearing a host of possible connections and frameworks with which to open the texts, many that occur to me, with pleasure and surprise, at any moment, and allow us to work a particular critical methodology." "I could listen to him talk all day long!" says a student.

Steve Watkins, Professor of English, University of Mary Washington
University of Mary Washington English professor Steve Watkins is just looking to have an interesting conversation. "Everyone has something interesting to say if you ask the right questions," he says.

This straight-shooting teacher of twenty-eight years, author of several award-winning and critically acclaimed works of both fiction and nonfiction, loves to find the interesting in people and to bring his own to the table. He finds sentimentality and cliché to be "vile, evil things"; once, a student made note of every cussword he used all semester long and listed them on the anonymous student course evaluation at the end of the term ("I was disappointed at my lack of variety"). Students can see through the blue and call him "the best professor I've ever had. He's positively impacted my life and my career path more than any other." He is "honest, smart, caring, hilarious, thoughtful, insightful, [and] always on point."

His favorite class, Literature of the Vietnam War, is the perfect example of the unorthodox but highly effective teaching methods he uses; he will divide the class into squads and make them do everything—"and I mean everything"—as a unit, whether they like it (or one another) or not. For the final he tells them to come prepared for field exercises, then sends them out across campus to find "The Enemy"; they then have to write about it, imitating the style of one of the writers they've been studying, and emphasizing representative themes and stereotypes from the Vietnam War literature. Other highlights include a class field trip to see *Hair* at the Kennedy Center, the singing of pro- and anti-war songs (such as the "Ballad of the Green Berets," "Feel-Like-I'm-Fixin-To-Die Rag"), and, of course, puppet shows. "He is awesome, and makes the literature seem alive through games," says a student. "We did yoga in the middle of class once."

Dr. Janice Gohm Webster, Professor, English, Champlain College

Janice Gohm Webster, an English professor from Champlain College, hopes to foster in her students a love of learning that goes beyond the classroom, and to instill a curiosity that inspires them "to widen their lenses as they take on the challenges of the world with joy and a sense of their own abilities to make a positive impact."

After nearly three decades of teaching, she has learned that enthusiasm and joy in the subject matter go a long ways toward cultivating enthusiasm and joy in students. She creates an atmosphere of mutual respect in the classroom so that all students feel comfortable joining in the conversation, and is always interested in them as individuals. "And I love what I do; this comes across to students and makes for a great classroom atmosphere," she says. "My writing improved dramatically thanks to her," says a fan.

Her classes include Rhetoric I and II, American Lit I and II, and Aesthetic Expressions, which is an interdisciplinary course that combines art, music, and literature, and Professor Webster's enthusiasm for the subject matter "has remained keen after many years of teaching." Her organization is a huge attribute, and she learns students' names immediately so that discussions can begin the second day of class. "I assign poems, stories, and/or articles, provide questions for students to answer for the next class period and ask them to add questions of their own that they can then ask of me and/or their classmates during class. I let everyone know that they all have something to contribute to class discussions, and they recognize that their contributions matter." Once a question has been answered during discussions, Professor Webster will ask another student to expand on that answer or to ask another question, which all find to be "rigorous, informative, and fun." Students say that she "has a special talent for teaching...[she is] supportive, able to motivate, [and] provides criticism without being discouraging."

Dr. Patrick White, Assistant Professor, English, University of Delaware

Patrick White, who teaches English at the University of Delaware, is what his students call "the man." He "is crystal clear and he really keeps the class entertaining by giving out hilarious examples of what not to do," says one.

His goal is total engagement—diagnostics, instruction, and hands-on assignments that provide the opportunity for students to "work the material." "The best students are the ones who don't merely want a degree as a union card, but want to excel." He describes his teaching style as "flexible," and he keeps personal politics and beliefs out of the classroom. "When you expand on a topic, you are a moderator, not a preacher," he says. Every class has a writing component, and he even teaches an entire class on technical writing, which includes several papers and then a large group project. Other courses cover the topics of the American Civil War, medical history in America, and the influence of natural disasters on local culture. "I love going to work. I was born to be a teacher because I'm a showoff. This is the job I was meant for," he says.

In his informal classes, Professor White tries to mix lecture and interactive techniques, not only to prevent monotony, but "to give the students the feeling that they are actively involved in the process." "I like my students to feel comfortable, and, at the same time, involved," he says. Emulating his favorite professor, Millersville's Gordon Symonds, his door is always open for office hours, and students are welcome to talk about academics or personal lives. "I try to treat my students as adults with serious opinions and interests. I never condescend. Sure, I know more than they do, but, at age fifty-seven, I'd better."

J.C. Ellefson, Poet-In-Residence, Professor of English,
Champlain College

Jim Ellefson has taught writing and literature at Shanghai University and at the University of the Azores (smack in the middle of the Atlantic Ocean). He is currently a creative writing professor at Champlain College, "in the middle of nowhere Vermont." He's a wonderful raconteur, and he wears many hats. In addition to the courses he teaches, Ellefson "referees" the campus literary magazine. He is Champlain's poet in residence. He runs a writers' weekend for high school students on campus as well as the Intercollegiate Writers' Exchange, which allows students from different colleges in the area to "read to each other, and the world gets delightfully smaller" for a little while. In his spare time, he and his wife own and operate the appropriately poetically named Stoney Lonesome Farm.

Students say that Ellefson is a great professor because he consistently "brings out the best in people." He's "out there" sometimes but in the best way. "His classes are never boring." "He has real heart. He gets to know you and cares about you and how you do. He keeps it light, but he's serious about his subject." "I'm using all of my electives to take anything he teaches," reveals one satisfied student. "I love him." "He truly loves what he does, and goes far out of his way for his students," adds another student. "He was helpful outside of class, and I never talk to teachers outside of class."

Professor Ellefson says that his teaching methods are pretty basic. "My job is to get kids to go forth with their ideas," he says. "I want to provide a place where students can develop their individuality on the page." He also admits that he feels amazingly fortunate. "I have a tremendously privileged job. Of all the jobs in the world, this is the one that I really wanted," Ellefson explains. "In the classroom, it's the land of the free and the home of the brave. It's the America we all signed up for. Students are asking questions like, 'what's good?' 'What am I willing to fight for?' And I'm getting paid for it. I feel like I'm getting away with murder. It's not like I'm not tired when I get home. But I have a ball. My face hurts from smiling so much."

David Walker, Professor of English and Creative Writing, Oberlin College
"In my view, teaching is much less about imparting information than about training students in intellectual habits that will last a lifetime," says Oberlin College professor of English and creative writing David Walker. "Too many students seem to learn in high school that questions have one right answer; I try to get them to appreciate that the most obvious answer may not be the most valuable one," he says.

It's a view that his students respect and eagerly adopt, calling him "an absolute genius when it comes to analyzing literature." "I think I've taken every 300-level course he teaches, so clearly I'm a groupie...but in three-and-a-half years I've never had another professor who genuinely listens to and cares about his students the way David does," says one. His "modest and understated" teaching style and thoughtful book selection are highlights of his approach, as is his clear desire for students to exhibit creativity, persistence, and a willingness to take risks in the pursuit of truth. Rather than taking his or any critic's word for it, Professor Walker wants students to build on what they can learn from others, and to think independently and to articulate ideas effectively via writing and speaking. "I learned from my college mentor how important it is to share one's passion for the material with one's students," he says.

His love of literature is infectious, and he has spent thirty-four years (all at Oberlin) passing it on to students through a wide variety of classes ranging from Contemporary British and Irish Drama to American Poets Since 1960 to Playwriting. He teaches almost exclusively by discussion; when the rare lecture takes place, it is simply to establish a frame of reference for discussion. "I see my role in class as one of focusing and moderating the discussion, but my favorite classes are the ones in which the students generate productive discussion with only minimal intervention from me. I love it when they learn to think for themselves and surprise themselves by how much they have grown intellectually in the course of a semester."

English (Linguistics)

Evelyn McClave, Professor, Linguistics and English, California, State University—Northridge

Whether on the undergraduate or graduate level, Evelyn McClave's goal is to explain linguistic concepts clearly and to train students how to think analytically and to conduct linguistic research.

This professor of linguistics and English at California State University—Northridge attempts to convey her own love of linguistics with enthusiasm and humor. Her teaching style is "highly interactive and very energetic," and she attempts to relate all concepts to students' lives. For example, students are stunned to find out that they harbor negative attitudes toward speakers of certain dialects of English. "I demonstrate that this may be the case by using a matched guise; that is, students listen to a tape on which they hear the same excerpt read in multiple dialects. Unbeknownst to the students, the same individual is 'performing' the different dialects. Inevitably, the students rate the speakers of prestige dialects of English as more intelligent, trustworthy, competent, etc. than speakers of minority dialects," she says. "This makes the following lectures on dialects all the more personally meaningful."

She regularly teaches seminars in Cognitive Linguistics, and Discourse Analysis, as well as a class called Language Differences and Language Change, and is well prepared for each and every class with a wealth of material and many examples. "The subject is not easy but she makes it fun and easy to learn," says a student. Professor McClave treats all students as "full of potential and worthy of respect" (on the first day of class she shakes everyone's hand and introduces herself) and "really gets into her lectures." "If you don't understand something she stops to make sure you do," says a student.

English (Writing)

Dr. Sri Mukherjee, Preceptor, Writing Program, Harvard University

Sri Mukherjee, who teaches writing at Harvard University, facilitates in her students a shift from descriptive thinking to critical thinking, making the moves essential to achieving such a shift as transparent as possible.

Currently, Professor Mukherjee is teaching Cross-Cultural Contact Zones, which aims at teaching students strong critical thinking and writing skills through an analysis of fiction representing encounters between Eurocentric and non-Eurocentric worlds. She adopts a "conversational" teaching style that caters to the individual strengths and needs of each student during required one-on-one conferences (which she holds frequently), instead of using a single teaching style for all students." "I try to create a classroom environment in which students don't just listen to or talk to me, but engage in an intellectual conversation with each other," she says.

For example, she might introduce a topic (such as the representation of interracial attraction in a certain text), then ask a student to offer some critical observation on that topic in regards to a particular scene/episode, and then have another student respond specifically to the first student's observation, instead of a totally different scene or episode. "I find that once I initiate this kind of conversational/relational mode, students do a pretty good job of sustaining that themselves during the rest of the class period. This results in a truly productive and deeper intellectual exchange than just my talking or students talking at tangents would generate." "She guides students rather than being authoritative, and allows us to grow as opposed to being forced in a particular direction," says a student.

Students say that this "brilliant and engaging professor" teaches students "to create strong academic arguments and guides students in the transition to scholarly writing." "Her thoughtful, thorough critiques of our work reflected her passion for teaching and her strong interest in students' growth."

Finance

Shreesh Deshpande, PhD, Associate Professor and Area Chair, Finance, University of San Diego

"I really do enjoy being in class. Maybe that gets reflected in how I teach," says Shreesh Deshpande, who teaches finance at the University of San Diego. It does, according to students: "Best professor I have ever had at USD! He has made me look at finance differently," says one.

His class, Corporate Finance (Financial Management), is taught at the undergraduate, graduate, and executive program levels, and the "rigorous content" covers financial management principles such as valuation, risk and return, capital budgeting, and options. He is "genuinely interested in students learning the subject matter," and believes he has the ability to make the subject more interesting by linking textbook financial concepts to corporate practice. "I try to make the discussion of finance concepts intuitive. Whenever possible I also relate the topics to contemporary corporate events and businesses." One such topic is capital budgeting. While most textbooks start this topic with the assumption that the manager forecasts the sales of a proposed new product as "X million" per year and go from there, Professor Deshpande spends time in class going over how to actually estimate sales of a new product by covering industry analysis, the anticipated market share, and expected competition, etc. "Many of my students have entrepreneurial aspirations and are very engaged in this discussion," he says.

One of the perks of teaching in executive programs (and his membership in professional organizations) is that it has a beneficial effect on his teaching at the other levels. "I interact with business executives, and can take that information back to my students."

Colby Wright, Assistant Professor of Finance, Central Michigan University

"All the pedagogical magic in the world won't compensate for deficient content," says Colby Wright, a finance professor at Central Michigan University, of the time and effort he puts into selecting the information he brings into his classroom.

He mainly wants students to enjoy the learning experience, and to retain the material he has carefully selected; he believes both of these are enhanced by how dynamic the presentation and discussion of the material is. "The more enthusiasm a professor can exude, and the more dynamic s/he can be in the presentation, the more the students will remember it," he says. This drives him to look for interesting, funny, exciting, and curious ways to expose students to the material, such as having them bring in a *Wall Street Journal* article, share it with the class, interpret it, and offer their own opinion on the piece. "I can see they really like being able to decipher what they are seeing on TV and in the *Journal*. It makes them feel more informed and better equipped to make decisions," he says. "Class is crazy, he explains things so well and is really funny," says a student.

He teaches courses such as Financial Statement Analysis & Equity Valuation; Investments; and Money, Banking, and Capital Markets, which "helps students make sense of the current news stories dominating the headlines —banking crises and regulation, Federal Reserve decisions and actions, asset market bubbles, the housing market, etc." His dynamic presentations incorporate interactive games and object lessons, frequent quizzes, assignments that require students to learn and demonstrate new knowledge and technical skills, and a "healthy dose of self-deprecating humor throughout." "It is not easy taking a subject like finance and making it interesting. Dr. Wright does exactly that!" says a student.

Foreign Language (French)
Joshua Landy, Associate Professor, French and Italian, Stanford University

What Stanford University French Associate Professor Joshua Landy wants to communicate is not just ideas, but also momentum; to put it another way, what he wants to transmit is enthusiasm as well as information. "My main hope is that I will give students a reason to fall in love with the great books we are reading. That is, I want my own enthusiasm to become contagious," he says.

He believes that we typically learn best what we find out for ourselves, and therefore sees a major part of his task as being that of making students eager to go off and discover more on their own. Very often, this involves students coming up with their own individual approaches to texts and questions; and he is simply there "to help them develop their ideas, to help the ideas gain more clarity and depth." Most of all, he really wants every lecture and every discussion to have been worth the students' time, to have shown them something genuinely interesting, and "even to have helped them see their own lives a little bit differently."

In his classes, there is ideally a productive give-and-take between the student's real-world concerns and the written works they are studying; every now and then, Professor Landy tries to share with his students "the magic of close reading, the ability to see what's really there." In a small seminar setting (as with The Art of Living), he finds that there is nothing more important than the group dynamic. "Having a sense of humor in the classroom is completely compatible with seriousness of engagement; it can help to revive attention, to lift conversation out of a rut in the gentlest way, to loosen the grip of a limiting position, and to foster a sense of community."

His classes vary between lectures and seminars, and he is fond of asking "truly open questions," such as what (if anything) art is good for. In seminars, he tries to establish a framework for discussion but also to allow things to emerge organically, allowing for "a sense of freedom and improvisation."

Students speak highly of their professor: "Brilliant. Articulate. Generous. Funny. Basically, Landy's everything good." "Probably the most charismatic professor I've ever had. He's funny in a witty, self-deprecating kind of way, and seems genuinely interested in what students have to say," says another.

Patrice Mothion, Associate Professor of French, Centre College

Patrice Mothion, a French professor at Centre College, wants to make learning fun and to give students the confidence that they need in order to be successful.

Through three decades of trial-and-error classroom experience, he has found that he tends to get the best results by accentuating the positive rather than by focusing on the negative. Students can sense that he genuinely cares about their progress, and indeed, Patrice often claims that he never gives up on a student. "He's fun in the classroom, assigns a manageable amount of homework, is clear about expectations and assignments, and is readily available for questions," says a student.

He teaches Intermediate French, The Francophone World, and From Napo to Sarko, and gives his students a relaxed, though challenging atmosphere in which to learn. He is fair, accessible, and "able to improvise." "I plan my lessons with the students' interest in mind, which is why I always bring culture into every class session. For example, when teaching the future tense to a beginning language class, I might play Claude Nougaro's 'Tu verras' and use this song as a way to lead into the importance of jazz music in French culture over the decades."

Students say that he has "great comments and a really good sense of what each student needs to know to be successful." "I don't know of a single person who doesn't like him."

Stephanie Ravillon, Lecturer, French Studies, Brown University

"As I see it, language learning is a way of enriching oneself and of opening up to other cultures; it is also a way of reaching beyond one's own points of reference in order to better communicate with others," says Stephanie Ravillon, who teaches French at Brown University.

As a consequence, her teaching philosophy is based on trying to create a relaxed, yet challenging learning environment that fosters risk-taking and stresses the real-world applications of foreign language learning. In giving students the necessary tools to succeed, communication is her keyword in and outside of class. "I always encourage my students to meet with me during office hours, and I schedule one-on-one appointments whenever necessary in addition to office hours. From this personal interaction, I learn about their goals and may adjust my objectives for the course accordingly" ("she takes students' interests into account while teaching").

Her courses have ranged from beginners to more advanced classes in language, culture, and translation, and she has recently developed a growing interest in translation studies, which she particularly enjoys teaching. "It seems to me that translation is a great way of increasing the students' proficiency while facilitating their passage from language to literature classes," she says. "It's also a productive way to help students refine their writing and editing skills, to expand their cultural knowledge, and to help them become more careful and critical readers."

From the first day of class, Professor Ravillon makes it clear that students and teacher are classroom collaborators, working together towards mutual goals and objectives. "She is smart, energetic, and clearly works extremely hard, which motivates the students to work hard as well," says a student.

This "truly passionate" professor primarily designs activities that build group interaction, as she has found that students "are more motivated to use their French skills when it is for authentic communication and personal interaction." Within the classroom, she strives to keep a balance between computer-assisted language tools and more traditional pedagogical tools such as stories, novels, plays, and essays.

Christopher Rivers, Professor of French, Mount Holyoke College

Christopher Rivers, a professor of French at Mount Holyoke College, tends to center his teaching around his desire to help students foster as deep and as genuine a desire to learn as possible. "I want them to want it," he says.

Professor Rivers has carefully sifted through the best traits of his former professors and discovered the importance of communicating one's own enthusiasm and passion, not only for the subject being discussed but also for the process of discussion itself. "From my colleagues in the French department at Mount Holyoke, I have learned the importance of following through on the oft-stated claim that a seminar is not a lecture course, and of insisting that students be genuinely active and engaged participants in what happens in the classroom." This principle certainly resonates with students, who note that the professor "really cares about whether or not you feel like you gained something from his class."

Students are appreciative of his intellectual nature and the fact that he "considers the academic enterprise a serious one but also a pleasurable one." Not only does he insist that students talk in class, he listens carefully to what they say and responds directly, maintaining an atmosphere of complete respect and courtesy. "I think this makes them feel confident and 'safe' about speaking their minds, which can be daunting, especially in a foreign language." Students agree: "He brought my hope back about speaking French confidently," says one. "He gave me so much confidence that I actually started speaking French," says another.

This year, Professor Rivers will be teaching a course on contemporary French media and culture (such as recent bestselling novels, movies, and popular music, in addition to more social and political topics), as well as an introduction to French literature and a seminar on the "femme fatale" in nineteenth- and twentieth-century French novels. His courses are carefully designed to be intellectually seductive, thereby "motivating both the professor and the students to share their curiosity, enthusiasm, and fascination for the subject matter." He likes to ask questions to begin a discussion and encourages students "to talk to each other as well as to me. I also like to incorporate humor where appropriate," he says.

Paul Rockwell, Professor of French, Amherst College

"Making courses easy turns students off," says Amherst College French professor Paul Rockwell. "They need a challenging, yet not a threatening, classroom environment where they are free to make mistakes."

After twenty-three years of teaching, he has it down to a science. In his "interactive lectures" he analyzes the persuasiveness of student-generated arguments to make his students realize how to support their positions. His most popular course is French 321: Amor and Metaphor, which focuses on early French medieval literature, and is conducted in French; he also teaches Intro to French Lit, an introduction to twentieth-century texts with a focus on reading and writing techniques, and has published two books and eleven or so articles on medieval French literature, usually with an Arthurian focus. He is "engaging, enthusiastic, [and] attentive to the class. For example, [he] will drop a discussion question if little interest is shown."

Students are often surprised by the level of interest they find they have for his classes, thanks to his presentation; they say that he makes "material that could have been boring and dry very entertaining," and class is a "delightful surprise!"

Foreign Language (German)

Walter Campbell, Lecturer, German, University of California—Santa Cruz

Walter Campbell, who teaches German at the University of California—Santa Cruz, looks "to advance students along the path of communicative and cultural competence in German and to advise them individually of opportunities in the U.S. and abroad to help them achieve their personal, academic, and professional goals."

He teaches primarily German language courses (as well as German Media), which he considers "skill-building classes." Classes are "well-organized and fast-paced," and he plans lessons to help students acquire active command of the German language through sequential steps, while at the same time "trying to expand students' knowledge of the culture(s) where German is spoken." "In the first year, one has the excitement of introducing students to a language that is new to most of them. In the second year, one is able to work with students at a higher level of language and do more with culture in the language. In the advanced seminar, one is able to work with the cream of the crop—students who are quite communicative in German." "I choose Herr Campbell's class hands down. He commands your attention and he's helpful!" says a student.

Each level brings its own rewards and challenges, but he stresses to his students that language learning demands extensive practice outside the classroom. "He begins to immerse you in the language from the first day of teaching using his body language to assist ones comprehension. I have never had a more competent professor and recommend him highly to anyone with an interest in the language," says a student.

Foreign Language (Hebrew)

Shalom Shoer, Senior Lecturer, Modern Hebrew Language,
Cornell University

Shalom Shoer is a professor in the Near Eastern Studies department at Cornell University with some twenty-five years of experience honing his craft (plus a lifetime of speaking Hebrew). He is a native of Israel and he landed at Cornell after teaching for several years at Binghamton University. If you take any of "the first three classes of Hebrew" at Cornell, the odds are pretty high that you'll encounter Professor Shoer. That's a good thing because, by all accounts, Shoer is a "great teacher and a great guy." "I would like the students to be able to develop the knowledge and understanding of Hebrew to a degree where they are able to live the language and gain an understanding of Hebrew culture," Shoer explains. "I would like to arouse their intellectual curiosity and appetite to further explore modern and ancient Hebrew literature, poetry, and films." He also says that his goal is to challenge students "without taking them outside their comfort zone." "I love the satisfaction the students get when they suddenly they realize that they had started with no (or sometimes very basic) knowledge of Hebrew and now they are able to communicate well in Hebrew."

Students say that Shoer is "clearly very enthusiastic about his subject material." "He's incredibly helpful and knows how to structure a language class." "Even though many come with prior knowledge," promises one student, "there really is no disadvantage if you didn't know Hebrew before taking the class." Homework is "due daily for the most part" and "doing the homework and keeping up is a must" for everybody. Students report that you don't need to sweat the format much, though. "If you do the homework, you'll get a good grade," says one. "He's not looking to give bad grades."

"I am only half way through the second semester, but I already feel like I am extremely proficient in Hebrew," says one satisfied student. "He really wants his students to learn, and takes extra strides to make sure no one is left behind to struggle with the material," says another elated student. "Class and homework are enough to adequately cover the material without being burdensome. I can't sing his praises enough."

Foreign Language (Russian)
Natalia Olshanskaya, Professor of Russian, Kenyon College

Natalia Olshanskaya, who teaches Russian at Kenyon College wants her students not just to learn more about Russian language and culture, but to also to want to learn more about many other things in the world. "I want my students to become open-minded people with a sound system of ethical and intellectual values. And I want them to be happy," she says.

She has been blessed with some wise and knowledgeable professors and colleagues in more than thirty years of teaching, and has learned that an ignorant person stops being ignorant when she/he realizes how much she/he does not know. "So I always remember how little I know, and I try to learn more." This "eclectic" and "really funny" woman teaches all levels of Russian language, as well as Russian literature and culture (she "throws Russian parties with yummy food and shows Russian movies with Papa John's"), and finds it extremely rewarding to see students who have no knowledge of the alphabet find that after a year with her, they can (or they think they can!) speak the language. "I can't even begin to describe how great Prof. Olshanskaya is. I took intro Russian with her on a whim and now I'm a major," says a believer. "She is my absolute favorite person on earth; not only is she a great teacher, she really cares about her students," says another student.

Joseph Troncale, Professor of Russian, University of Richmond

Joe Troncale is a professor of Russian literature, language, and visual studies at the University of Richmond, a medium-sized liberal arts and sciences institution located in the capital of Virginia. Troncale's "discussion-based" classes are typically composed of about a dozen students. He takes advantage of such intimate environments to create a unique classroom experience. "With a painting course, for example, students come in and I turn out the lights," he explains. "I encourage them to sit with correct posture. We sit in silence for a few minutes, which is a long time for them. It's a form of composing, centering, and becoming present to what we are doing together. Then, I put an image up in front of them and ask them to comment on it. There are no boundaries or preconceived notions about how they should see it. It is a matter of perceptual feeling. I give them information but I always expect them to interact with it."

Professor Troncale sees his role as a mentor rather than a disciplinarian, and attempts to help students cultivate an understanding of themselves through the liberal arts. "We're one of the last bastions where someone can make such demands on them," Troncale says of himself and his fellow faculty members. "I care about the process of why students are here for four years, which is to gain some kind of self-understanding. The most important thing they can do is begin to understand who they really are and how they make meaning in their lives. I could be teaching any subject," he adds. "That's just the medium. The extent to which students are willing to probe ideas is the same extent to which they are honest with themselves."

Students call Troncale a "super energetic," "interesting and provocative" professor who is "difficult at times but well worth it" and "very fair." "He's cool, down to earth, and can really connect with his students." He's "a sincere person as well." "He challenges his students to go further and look deeper," explains one student. "He is a really great person, who cares about the success of his students and is a practical joker at heart." "If you haven't thought of taking Russian before, you should," suggests one student, "just so you can get him to teach you."

Foreign Language (Slavic)

Karen von Kunes, PhD, Senior Lector, Slavic Languages, Yale University

Karen von Kunes, who teaches Slavic languages and literatures at Yale University, tries to inspire students to value knowledge above grades. In her own words, success as a teacher means having stimulated students' intellectual curiosity and love for learning, and "awakened compassion for human beings and to understand a problem under discussion at a large scale."

Professor von Kunes is also a prolific translator and the author of several Czech language textbooks. Her classes focus on the Czech language, contemporary Czech literature and film, and Czech culture, and she currently teaches Elementary, Intermediate, and Advanced Czech, as well as popular courses titled Milan Kundera: The Czech Novelist and French Thinker (which one student refers to as "the capstone of my college experience"); Milos Forman and His Films; and In Kafka's Spirit: Prague Film and Fiction. She sees her role in the classroom as helping the students bridge the intellectual connections between that which they read outright, and that which they discover themselves. "My approach is to make students think, to see the invisible and discover the unknown, to making connection at the global level, to see patterns and similarities within one system (for instance, Czech language), [and] to project the theory of literature or film not only to the text or screen but also to real life and life experience," she says. "Not only does she teach us the language effectively, she gives us a great sense of Czech culture," says a student.

Students are encouraged to see their own experience (intellectual, everyday, etc.) as a part of human condition, and to think "out loud" in class, so their ideas and concerns are viewed and discussed by the whole group. "Essentially, I encourage students to be participants while I myself retain a role of a coach," she says. Those who have taken her classes commend her for being "more interested in having her students become deeper, more thoughtful people than in drilling useless facts into them" and praise the fact that she "makes difficult Czech concepts manageable and never ceases to provide encouragement and motivation."

Foreign Language (Spanish)
David Bost, Professor of Spanish, Furman University

David Bost, who teaches at Furman University, doesn't just want to educate students in Spanish; he wants to "challenge and engage students as fully as possible with the subject matter and to help them evolve into lifelong learners."

He knows a thing or two about teaching, having done it successfully for thirty-seven years. "Teaching is ultimately relational in that it does not happen in a vacuum. It is the result of honest and open exchange between teachers and students. Teaching is not really about information exchange. Rather, teaching is dialogical in nature," he says. He listens to and respects and his students as human beings above all else, and tries to find ways to communicate clearly and meaningfully, all while seeking the balance between fairness and academic rigor. "He knows so much about the Spanish language and is able to convey it in a fun and meaningful way. His class is definitely challenging, but manageable," says a student.

His courses include Intermediate Spanish and Introduction to Reading, and he relishes the enthusiasm that students bring to class as they become more and more advanced. He attempts to have students speak as much as possible in class, so that the language becomes second nature. "In a literature class, for example, I will nearly always start the class with a short group report on the reading for the day. The students will often break into small groups to discuss a particular topic or theme. After some of the groups quickly share their work with the class, I will conclude with some comments and observations of my own," he says. "His tests can be pretty hard, but he is great to talk to and will help you understand difficult concepts," says a student.

Hector R. Campos, Associate Professor of Spanish Linguistics, Theoretical Linguistics and Modern Greek, Georgetown University

Hector Campos, who teaches Spanish linguistics, theoretical linguistics, and modern Greek at Georgetown University, hopes that he can make students feel his same passion for the study of language and its intricacies.

In trying to show how linguistics connects with other fields of study in the sciences, social sciences, and humanities, Professor Campos is always looking for "exotic languages with fun properties that will develop students' curiosity to look at other languages." He is warm and accessible, and establishes a relationship with students "where they can feel free to come talk to you about linguistics or anything else they want." He speaks ten languages, leading one student to refer to him as "a genius brain housed in a gem of a man," and another to say that "his ability to relay information is incomparable."

His list of courses includes Syntax, History of the Spanish Language, Historical Spanish Morphology, and Generative Syntax I and II, and all of them explore the generalities of language(s), while looking at the exotic properties they exhibit and seeking an explanation for the exotic features. "He is a genius and has an amazing ability to transfer his knowledge on to his students," says a student.

A student sums up her "complete and total adoration" of the man: "Consider it a privilege to study under Campos. He's brilliant."

Devon W. Hanahan, Spanish Instructor, College of Charleston

"So many people are afraid of learning languages. I want each and every student to believe that he/she is capable of learning Spanish and using it in the real world," says Devon Wray Hanahan, a Spanish professor from the College of Charleston. "I also want him/her to be excited about the prospect of speaking Spanish, because that excitement is what motivates them."

It's the belief that one can learn anything if it is broken down into simple steps that guides her teachings, and she is very strict and predictable in terms of starting and finishing on time, sticking to the syllabus, returning homework promptly, and adhering to class rules. Professor Hanahan is more creative and unpredictable during the actual teaching process, and as a member of the trial-by-fire school of thought, she insists that students can't become good at something by watching others do it: "You must plunge in and start trying while you're still bad at it! Only then will you improve."

The rewards of her career never get old, and she truly gets excited every time a student uses the language successfully. "There's a certain courage required to use a second language in front of others, and when students dominate their natural fear of using it, they do well, no matter what grades they have had in the past." Students say "her teaching is crystal clear and she will explain something until you get it."

Her classes include Spanish 201 and Spanish 202, and she finds it enthralling "to teach a skill that anyone can use, no matter what their major or discipline." She tries to incorporate many approaches into her teaching style in order to keep class interesting and to reach as many different learners as possible. "She will find fun ways to help you learn the material, including *Jeopardy* games and fashion shows," says a student. "She isn't easy—she is just a really good teacher. This makes the tests 'easy' because she has taught the material so well."

Geography

John Knox, Associate Professor, Geography, The University of Georgia

Geography professor John Knox of The University of Georgia is only too happy to wax poetic about his classroom goals, which is only appropriate since he is a published poet as well as a meteorologist and an award-winning teacher: "In the classroom, where I usually teach about weather and climate, I want students to feel 'at home' with the subject matter—with the same confidence and familiarity that they have when they flick on the light switch in the dark or locate the 'secret key' to their house in the middle of the night."

How does he know he's succeeded? "Every semester, some of my students will e-mail me and say, 'I went home for break, and I can't stop telling my parents/siblings what I've learned in class!' That's a good indicator of at-home-ness." In both small and large classes such as Atmospheric Hazards, Weather Forecasting, and Introduction to Weather and Climate, Professor Knox wants his students to be able to hear a news report of a tornado or global warming. Then, he wants them to be able to say, "I know about this! I know why they're showing that graphic, I know why it's an important issue, I even know more than the person reporting the story!"

His classes are full of exciting games and illustrations ("If you are not excited about geography after his class you are not breathing," says a student); to demonstrate wind, students will play-act different aspects of the wind (such as gravitational and Coriolis forces), and then he will lecture a little on each one. "In these ways we cover some of the hardest material in introductory meteorology, and we learn it in a variety of ways that resonate with the different types of learners in the class." Though he strives to keep his large lectures "chock-full of compelling material that keeps students interested in the subject months or years after the course has ended," he especially wants his students to find their own voices. In one-on-one discussions he tries to lead students so that they are able to discover themselves as people and as scholars, and "learn to think and do for themselves, not just think and do what others want." Students also appreciate that he "makes review sheets for every test, and he puts all of his (detailed, picture covered!) lecture notes online."

He is constantly aware that teachers often impact students' lives in unpredictable ways: "As a teacher, you'll think that you made a big impact on a particular student because of X, and instead it was some little something Y that you did or said that you don't even remember doing," he says. Students say that "he adores what he's teaching, especially weather. He's very comical and really makes an effort to get to know everyone in a big class."

Geology
Tekla A. Harms, Professor of Geology, Amherst College

Tekla A. Harms hopes to change the way students see the earth around them. The Amherst College geology professor instills in her students a level of curiosity that could kill a cat, which she hopes will stimulate them to build from the foundation of knowledge and the critical thinking skills they gain in her class.

Professor Harms' enthusiasm for her subject has never waned, and she finds it rewarding "to share the subject with students and to watch their excitement as they come to understand the earth differently." Given the breadth of what could be covered in a geology course, she elects to concentrate on material that, when integrated, "prepares the student to engage in some aspect of independent scientific reasoning, which can be very empowering." In the classroom, she strives to present the material in a logical way; to keep the atmosphere in the classroom "lively, interactive, relaxed, and still completely focused on the topic"; and to be approachable but also maintain high expectations. "She is incredibly clear and is very intent on making sure that everyone understands everything. And she is a very kind and interesting person outside of the classroom," says a student.

She has thirty years of primary research experience (including fieldwork) in the evolution of mountain belts and the interactions of plate boundaries in creating those belts. In her courses Principles of Geology, Structural Geology, and Plate Tectonics and Continental Dynamics, she always teaches "how we know what we know about earth processes" while being clear about the limits of our knowledge; still, she encourages her students to become the ones who press those boundaries forward. "I want my students to be informed citizens and good stewards of their planet," she says.

Students appreciate that she is "very clear and frank, to the point of being blunt," but know that even if she is sharp on occasion, "it's really a form of respect: she has high expectations for you, because she sees you as an adult."

Karen Harpp, Associate Professor, Geology, Colgate University/ University of Idaho

Karen Harpp, who teaches geology at Colgate University and the University of Idaho, looks to demystify science, and get her students "to embrace the creativity and imagination inherent in science, which is probably rarely the way they've had it conveyed to them in the past."

It is fitting that a geology professor should be as down-to-earth as Professor Harpp, whose accessibility and willingness to listen humanizes her to no end. "If that means going over concepts multiple times in several ways, I will. If it means listening to them talk about some personal problem, then I'll do that.

Nobody can learn well if they're not comfortable with the teacher or battling more serious personal issues," she says.

In classes such as Geochemistry and Weapons and War, she finds a way to get the students to invest and care about the topic at hand. At its simplest, this means showing its relevance to their lives in concrete ways ("solubility constants sound unapproachable but when you realize that your teeth rot or can be protected on the basis of understanding that concept, it gets more important and interesting"). This may also mean finding a way to get the students' hands on the concepts, through activities, field trips, and "anything to make it come alive and become real. The effectiveness of learning is enhanced significantly if the students are having fun and are comfortable." For example, in her Volcanology class, students monitor a volcano throughout the semester, and do background research on its eruptive history, design alert levels and evacuation plans for the area at risk from that volcano, and even are "sent" in to handle a simulated eruption crisis. "The main goal is for students to realize it's not all about the science but real-time pressure to make decisions about science, personal safety, and lots of complex political questions," she says.

Many of her classes are project-based (and all focus on understanding concepts more than just memorizing facts), so that students learn the fundamental concepts through application to something of driving interest to them, which results in "great chaos" in class sometimes, but far more engagement and learning than in canned labs and classes. "I push them intellectually but we have a blast doing it. I treat them as equals and friends, and I take lots of time to listen to them, about anything. Plus I can be a huge dork sometimes, which helps, I think," she says humbly. "If you do not take a class with her you are making a mistake. Best teacher I have ever had," says a satisfied student.

Richard Hazlett, Professor of Geology, Stephen M. Pauley Professor of Environmental Studies, Coordinator, Environmental Studies Program, Pomona College

Professor of Environmental Studies and Geology Richard Wesley Hazlett, who teaches at Pomona College, loves what he is teaching, and he sincerely hopes his students will, too. He chose to leave his strictly geological and traditional career path to develop and teach in the environmental field because "it is vital that interdisciplinary bridges be built between the humanities, social sciences, and 'pure' sciences in order to deal with pressing environmental questions."

During office hours his mission is twofold: to "help smooth the bureaucratic hurdles of completing academic work," and to "help students imagine where they can run with various ideas pertaining to theses, study abroad work, curriculum planning, etc." "Office conferencing really is the best time in which to get to know an individual student well—what makes each 'tick'," he says. Those who take his classes claim that he "goes above and beyond the call of duty to help out students."

During class, Professor Hazlett's lectures tend not to follow a strictly charted format; "the spontaneous digression sometimes is a greater teaching moment than a rigidly followed topical checklist." He teaches in areas that students call "eye-opening and important," such as environmental studies and science, agroecology and agricultural impacts on the environment, and physical volcanology; one of his courses, Food, Land, and the Environment includes a field section in which students grow and harvest their own crops, learn how to bee-keep, and engage in construction improvements (e.g., building an outdoor classroom, making biodiesel fuel, composting, etc.). "I like to be creative and bring interesting angles or case studies to class as a means of introducing students to new concepts and principles."

He also has the enviable superhero power for reproducing maps of practically any place in the world on a chalkboard. "The personally drawn figure in this way can be more interesting to a student than a PowerPoint image highlighted with a laser pointer," he says. Professor Hazlett has faith that "if a teacher can capture the interest of students in a topic, then they will remember the material more easily over time and potentially do much to teach themselves about it in future."

Rowan Lockwood, Associate Professor, Geology, The College of William & Mary

The students of Rowan Lockwood, a professor of geology at The College of William & Mary, learn to "observe the world around them and ask how it works, overcome their misconceptions and fears concerning science and math, and understand how science relates to their daily lives."

In all of her courses, she uses in-class activities, field trips, debates, simulations, role-playing activities, and discussions to create an active, dynamic learning environment. Her courses include Earth's Environmental Systems, the fantastically named Extinction is Forever, and Age of Dinosaurs, which includes a screening and scientific critique of Jurassic Park. "My students and I joke that this course gives us the opportunity to rediscover the kid in all of us who is still captivated by dinosaurs," she says.

Professor Lockwood feels strongly that, as a scientist, she has a responsibility to encourage and inspire students to gain an appreciation of how science can help them explore the world around them (one student says she will "bend over backward to help you"). Equally important to mentoring young scientists is introducing and demystifying science for students concentrating in the humanities and social sciences. "For many of the non-science majors that I teach, I am one of the few scientists that they will encounter in an academic setting and I have the opportunity to positively shape their view of science and its importance in their daily life."

In her "loud and enthusiastic" classes, this "very active and dynamic lecturer" is always moving around the room and encouraging students to participate. When she lectures on radiometric dating and half-life, she distributes pennies to the standing class and asks students to flip their coins and either sit down or stay standing, depending on whether they flipped heads or tails. After doing this multiple times, she constructs a simple graph of time versus students standing on the chalkboard, which provides a simple but memorable demonstration of how exponential decay works. "This activity also breaks up lecture by getting students up and moving around the classroom, dropping their pennies, and laughing at each other."

Paul R. Pinet, Professor of Geology and Environmental Studies, Colgate University

The goal of geology and environmental studies professor Paul R. Pinet, who teaches at Colgate University, is "to instill passion for life-long, self-motivated learning, pondering the questions that have no answers and yet lead to ever deeper queries, to ever greater humility."

His signature teaching style blends science and the humanities, and he encourages students to draw from all disciplines as they "begin to construct their meaningful lives," urging them to read fiction and nonfiction incessantly, and to relate what they "know" to what they are now learning. "My chief concern is that they confront throughout their lives their animality and their mortality," he says. He is always honest with them, including in his assessments of the quality of what they produce: "I try hard to make them realize how great their creative and intellectual potential is, provided that they take risks and are willing to fail." "I still think about something from the class nearly every single day," corroborates a student.

In the classroom, where he teaches Introductory Oceanography, Technology and the Human Prospect, and Ecology, Ethics, and Wilderness, he enables students to immerse themselves in the ideas presented, in such a way that they begin to understand their potential as self-learners. He likens his teaching style to jazz improvisation, in that he begins a class and "decides what to use to foster learning as it is emerging by student reactions and comments." For example, in Ecology, Ethics, and Wilderness, he will lecture about a complex topic that challenges students' existing knowledge, introducing pieces of art, poems, short stories from his personal life experiences as a high-altitude mountaineer, and philosophical snippets. "I do not make the direct connections for the students, and so force them to expand their creative abilities to see how everything in the world and in their minds is interlaced."

Students are certainly impressed: "We need more people like Paul Pinet in this world. You cannot, repeat, CANNOT leave Colgate without taking at least one class with this man. You'd be missing out on a life-changing experience."

Government

Matthew Carnes, SJ, Assistant Professor, Department of Government, Georgetown University

Matthew Carnes, a professor of government at Georgetown University, tries, in his own words, to "push/cajole/encourage students to confront themselves with the world, and in particular the political and economic systems that we study." This encounter forces them to think critically about the complex and unequal world and how they fit into it, and "to think about their responsibility to it—whether locally, nationally, or globally."

This is not to say that he does not drill home the facts, figures, and methodology, but he sees this skill-building always "at the service of the larger project of how they will act and serve as citizens of the world." He envisions his class and each student's college education as intertwined processes, and invites students to reflect on how his class connects to other classes, as well as to the hopes they had initially when they enrolled at Georgetown, and to how it is forming them for their future life and career. He finds that "even those who will not pursue politics or political science as a career appreciate the opportunity to set the class into the larger context of their education."

His course offerings in the field of comparative government include the lecture-based Comparative Political Systems (one of the core introductory government courses at Georgetown), as well as seminars on Social Policy Around the World, the Politics of Labor, and Comparative Political Economy. In addition to being a professor, he is a Jesuit priest, a member of the religious order that founded Georgetown. He is particularly interested in questions of inequality and distribution, and "the ways that government policies support (or undermine) opportunities for the most vulnerable members of society—the young, the old, the ill, and the unemployed." "He cares about his students and motivates them to do their best—not just in the class, but in the world," says a student.

His model for every class is a small seminar, even if that class has two hundred or more students in it, and he "wants every student to be engaged, every minute—leaning forward to participate, even!" To facilitate this, he presents students with puzzling facts, graphs, maps, events, or texts; in his lecture courses, he uses electronic "clickers" so that students get to weigh in on the questions raised. "About eight to ten times per class, I have some sort of question (factual, opinion-based, making connections across the course, etc.) about the material we're studying. Students get immediate feedback on how they're understanding the material, and we can discuss why students answered in different ways." One student says that he "made the class completely worth my time, I would take any class given by him."

David Dessler, Government Department, The College of William & Mary

David Dessler, who teaches government and international relations at The College of William & Mary, hopes to inspire in students a passion for learning and a desire to participate in the creation of new knowledge. "I want them to find their place in the conversations that define the field of study I teach, and to see that they have a great deal to contribute to these dialogues," he says.

Professor Dessler is "very thoughtful and easy to approach," and tries to encourage consistency by giving twice-a-week quizzes that are very short and simple, but serve the purpose of keeping everyone moving through the material at an even pace. Students eventually come to recognize and appreciate their own unique abilities as thinkers and writers: "Speak up in class; it makes it more interesting for everyone!" says one.

His courses include Introduction to International Politics, Theories of the International System, and Intermediate International Relations Theory, and "he makes the class interesting by bringing in current events and encouraging lots of discussion." He focuses on clarity, and tries to make his presentations as straightforward as possible. "For example, to teach the concept of the Prisoner's Dilemma, I first have the class play a simple game to illustrate the core idea. Then we carefully build a game theoretic depiction of the exercise. Finally, we consider how that depiction can be used to explain real-world events in world politics. What pulls the different parts of the class together is a consistent focus on the core idea underlying the concept," he says.

John J. Pitney Jr., Professor of Government, Claremont McKenna College

"After twenty-five years of teaching, it's still as fun, exciting, and rewarding as it was on my very first day." So says John J. Pitney Jr., a professor of government at Claremont McKenna College in California.

This lauded professor—"Prof. Pitney is one of the institutions that make CMC what it is"—comes steeped in political experience and connections, which he draws upon to "get students thinking seriously and critically about the subject matter." And it works: "I've never been so excited about going to class before," says one.

He currently teaches Introduction to American Politics, Politics of Journalism, and a class on Congress, which provides an overview of the institution, along with a four-day-long, multi-college role-playing simulation of the U.S. Senate. Largely because of the simulation, this is the course that students remember most; says one, "Take it, sweat it, live it, and learn from it. You'll never regret the time and effort." Classes are a mix of lecture and discussion in which students are legendarily called upon at random, which Professor Pitney sees as good training for both life and law school (which many students go on to attend). "They might as well get used to cold calling in a warm and nurturing atmosphere," he says. He also uses plenty of graphs, video, and audio. "For instance, when I talk about LBJ, I have my students listen to his recorded phone conversations. That's as close as you can get to the Oval Office without actually being there."

His academic writing is informed by his firsthand experience as a New York State Senate legislative fellow, staffer for the House Republican Research Committee, and deputy director of research at the Republican National Committee, among other positions, and his contacts in the political community help with research and obtaining student internships and jobs. Every semester, he places up to eighteen in the Washington Semester Program, where they take two classes and an internship. Professor Pitney also blogs for every class he teaches, which "enables students to raise questions or follow up on discussion." "It is a fact that he is 'the most quoted political science professor in the nation'," says a student. "If you ever listen to NPR news, he will most likely be quoted in it."

Health

Steve Lytle, Associate Professor, Department of Health Professions, University of Central Florida

All of the teaching and learning methods used by Steve Lytle, who teaches in the Department of Health Professions at the University of Central Florida, are focused on a singular goal: his students' success. In 2001 the United States Distance Learning Association gave Steve their award for Most Outstanding Achievement by an Individual in the Higher Education category.

He believes that communications and organization are the keys to effective teaching. "It is important to show the student what they need to learn and how they need to go about the process. I have learned that if I keep to these ideas, I can deliver the content and the students will be successful." "I wish every professor was like this guy. [The] work is straightforward, and you have two chances to do [it]," says a student.

His undergraduate students are his full-time job, as he handles approximately one-thousand students a semester in three fully online courses; he has taught more than sixty different courses in his thirty years of teaching. Over the years, he has developed a set of procedures, exercises, and skills that he emphasizes and insists upon. In teaching his various health care courses (including Introduction to Epidemiology, Issues and Trends in Public Health, and Wellness and Personal Health), he has each student develop a role in a simulated hospital environment, and then links the content of the course to their "job" at the hospital. "He is truly an angel, because he is so caring and understanding," says a student fan.

Jennifer Wegmann, Health & Wellness Studies, Binghamton University

Jennifer Wegmann, who teaches in the Health & Wellness Studies Department at Binghamton University, helps students discover how to become healthier in ways that include, yet go beyond, the physical. "She is full of confidence and has some kind of power that intrigues people right away," says a student.

The double Binghamton alumna (both undergraduate and graduate) feels that "the classroom can foster individual creativity and uniqueness if you create a classroom environment that is flexible and student-centered." Her health/wellness courses include Nutrition, Love Thy Self (a course designed to help women learn to respect their bodies, which looks at the role the media and society plays on one's body image), and Women's Wellness.

Her teaching approach is very student-centered, and she relies on the students to determine the direction of lectures. She includes music as much as possible, and is "constantly trying to find music that is relevant to the topics I am teaching." Assignments are "thought-provoking yet not too much to handle," and "she truly cares about her students and loves her job." "The way she speaks of her family with such love is so touching. I couldn't think of a better role model for women at Binghamton University," says a student.

History

Paul Christopher Anderson, Associate Professor, History, Clemson University

"I want students to understand one fundamental thing about what we've done together by the time a class is finishing up: I want them to understand that I don't teach history—I teach curiosity."

This comes from Clemson University history professor Paul Christopher Anderson, who says that "the art of learning history is the art of learning how to learn, and that is nothing but the art of pursuing questions: relentlessly, joyously, seriously pursuing questions." The good news about history is that it does have answers to share; it is, in his words, "a creative, life-enriching discipline." His goal is to teach students how to continually listen for new things within the discipline, and also to teach them to "excite in the questioning as a means of seeking history's living purpose." "You'll come away with so much knowledge. He keeps you engaged and always wanting more," says a student.

The man "will go almost anywhere in pursuit of good humor," which is his way of building the relationships he needs to teach effectively ("he's teaching more than history on a daily basis"). He operates under the belief that there's a difference between being committed to mastery of the material and being committed to the students who are trying to master the material: "I'd like to think they sense I know that difference."

In courses such Lincoln and the Carolinians and Recent Readings in the Civil War Era, he "teaches on his feet": "I have to have a lot of room in my teaching for spontaneous response and even digression, which might produce a lot of jokes or a story or two on the way to elucidation." "You don't regurgitate, you learn and analyze," says a student. No two classes on the same subject will ever be the same, even if the material covered is; his smaller classes often take the form of what he calls "flexture"—a combination of lecture and discussion, moving in and out of both according to the rhythm of the class. "History is not something that someone else, usually dead, made for us; it's what we the living make of it and its relevance to the questions we have about the world we live in."

John Beeler, Professor of History, The University of Alabama

"History matters because it is the story of us. Alone among academic disciplines it is concerned with the whole range of human thought, activity, and accomplishments," says University of Alabama history professor John Beeler.

The most poignant thing that stands out in Professor Beeler's memory is the number of students who have told him that history stood out as the most "boring" of their high school classes. "The challenge to me is to make students want to learn about how things came to be as they are," he says. His mission, therefore, is less about making students learn a slew of facts than it is convincing them to think for themselves, rather than relying on authority. "If, in so doing, they are forced to confront their own long-held beliefs, so much the better. Even if they leave my classes with no more than a superficial understanding of the past, if I have managed to convince them to question received wisdom, my efforts have not been in vain."

To this end, he thinks it vital to reach the largest possible number of students, and so often teaches large introductory classes such as Modern Western Civilization. There is a significant entertainment component in his teaching strategy—"History is, for many students, something that has to be made interesting before they will tune in"—and he tries to make students as comfortable and relaxed as possible, and to establish a good rapport. "Dr. Beeler is the most dynamic lecturer I have encountered at UA," says a former student. Even the most elementary of questions is considered, and "if a question stumps me (as often happens), I am happy to admit it (and equally happy to find the answer after class), and if my own standing as an authority is challenged, well, that's simply the price paid for encouraging intellectual autonomy."

Students say that his lectures are "loud, entertaining, and very interesting," and "he is very intelligent and is able to give an hour and fifteen minute lectures from his memory—impressive!"

Victoria Brown, Professor, History, Grinnell College

Victoria Brown, professor of history at Grinnell College, reveals her missionary zeal when she describes the guiding principle of her three-decade-long teaching career: "To persuade [students] that they have the capacity to make a well-supported argument and that the work involved with doing so is emotionally and intellectually satisfying." No wonder her students—whose "sheer grit, persistence, [and] perseverance" she applauds—refer to her as "an all-around wonderful woman, let alone an outstanding professor."

The mutual respect that abounds in Professor Brown's classroom is no doubt in part due to the culture that she fosters through high expectations of academic exploration. "She will work her butt off for you if you work your butt off for her! If you slack off, she will call you on it. She rewards hard work and active class participation," says a student. She makes it clear that students will not just be going through the motions of schoolwork, but will develop a genuine "hunger to improve their intellectual game and a willingness to shoot intellectual hoop after intellectual hoop to gain improvement." "That passionate interest in any topic is the route to a satisfying, happy life," Professor Brown says.

Her own interests in history have a special focus on women's history, but her current docket of classes includes History as Family History (a senior seminar in which students research one or two family members employing professional historical methods to create an analytical narrative), U.S. Immigration History, Art of Biography, and 1968 Around the World, a survey of youth, race, worker, and anti-war rebellions in that year. She approaches her classes with a "directed discussion" style of teaching, giving students questions to guide their reading and to help prepare them for discussion. "Those questions—and here's the HEART of the matter—do not simply ask students to regurgitate information. They create conceptual problems for them to ponder. Every class meeting has an articulated purpose and we try to walk out every day with a sense of having 'done' something. But we do it together."

Thomas Conner, Professor, History, Hillsdale College

Hillsdale College history professor Thomas Conner has a refreshingly uncomplicated view of his chosen field. "History is, after all, something with which all human beings are connected, and if I can help my students to grasp that fundamental point, their engagement with and enthusiasm for the subject normally follow quite naturally."

Students can tell that Professor Conner loves what he does, though they may not be aware that "my fondest wish is that they love it, too." He judges their work fairly, and cares about their growth and development as individuals, well beyond whatever their capacity might be to perform on academic assignments.

His courses include The Western Heritage to 1600, Russia to 1917, and Europe in the Twentieth Century, which incorporates stories and experiences from the past thirty years of his travels. "Both the goodness and the evil in man are on display during the twentieth century with a richness that I find almost uniquely compelling," he says. His style is that of a fairly traditional stand-up lecturer ("he has a talent for oratory," says a student), but he always tries to maintain a conversational approach and periodically seeks to elicit responses to questions of fact or interpretation from the students as a means of helping them to stay actively involved. If a humorous or poignant anecdote or timely reference to current events can be worked into the discussion, he likes to do that "in order to convey the intensely human character of historical events and the ongoing connectedness of them to today's situation."

Students see him as a "great lecturer with about the best baritone professor-voice on earth," and say that he is "kind, funny, self-deprecating, [and] engaging." "If you don't like him, you shouldn't bother being at Hillsdale," says another.

Light T. Cummins, Bryan Professor of History, Austin College

Enthusiasm and fervor are the keys to teaching for Light Cummins, a history professor from Austin College. "I attempt to communicate an honest zeal and an explicit excitement for my subject in every moment of my teaching," he says.

It is this act of disseminating eagerness that lies at the root of his existence as a professor, and he does his best to infect every student who enters his classroom with a similar passion ("one of the great storytellers of our time," claims a student). He uses history as a launching platform in "communicating the need for ardor of purpose and unequivocal devotion to ideals as important building blocks for everyone's success in life, no matter what that might be." "My primary task is therefore to serve as an analogous and generic model for all students as they seek to image and develop their own individual enthusiasms and passions based on their own interests," he says.

That's not to say that his areas of expertise lack for focus; he "provides a never-ending series of new hands-on approaches to the study of history" in classes such as Survey History of the United States, Texas History (a personal specialty), and a class on the Civil War. Students learn by doing, and Professor Cummins is flexible and open to change in his classroom demeanor so as to account for the individual experience. "I believe that history holds essential lessons for all of us. It is one of the common threads of experience that holds our society together. It can provide us with an analytical basis, encompassing multiple areas and time frames, for judgment and perspective on the past."

He is "absolutely and completely" committed to collaborative learning, and includes students in his own historical research (he has also redefined his own activities to synchronize with their interests). From 2009 to 2011, he served as the official State Historian of Texas—a gubernatorial appointment—and he works with students on a variety of individual and group research projects. "I attempt to serve as a model for my students in every contact I have with them."

Philip Daileader, Associate Professor, Department of History, The College of William & Mary

"I conduct all interviews by e-mail these days, so that there is a written record of what I said," says (types) the quintessential history professor Philip Daileader of The College of William & Mary.

However, it's not just dusty old tomes and archives for this "hilarious" professor who "keeps everybody interested and laughing throughout the hour." Even throughout his larger lecture classes (typically on European and global history), discussions make up a portion of each class, in accordance with Professor Daileader's belief that good professors are "more like personal trainers than like prophets handing down the truth from on high." "There's much to be said for people sitting down and talking with people who think very differently than they do—at the very least, it gives one a chance to see that those who think differently are nonetheless just as human as oneself."

In class, Professor Daileader and his students grapple with texts and issues together, and he is always looking for opportunities to push the students to think and to express themselves more clearly. Although open to new teaching technologies, he tends to gravitate toward the tried and true—he is perhaps the only professor under the age of eighty-five who prefers overhead acetates to PowerPoint. "My only advantage over the students is that I have been doing this sort of work longer than they have, so I can raise possibilities that they have not considered before. Sometimes, they raise possibilities that I had not considered before, and they push me to think and to express myself more rigorously and clearly," he says.

Energy and enthusiasm are two dynamic traits that he can call his own, along with the self-described teaching style of "manic detachment." "It is manic in the sense that I tend to teach like a person possessed, storming around the room, roaring at students, going through the material at a rapid clip. It is detached in the sense that, to the extent that it is humanly possible, I try to take each subject on its own terms." He finds it crucial to start semesters and classes off by piquing students' interest from the start. "Everything has a history: literature, science, the earth and the universe, you name it. I do not think it's possible to be bored with a subject that encompasses everything. The primary goal is to challenge students, to provide just enough resistance so that students grow stronger and more rigorous in their thinking without being overpowered." One student puts it more simply: "You will never be bored in lectures."

R.M. Douglas, Professor of History, Colgate University

Colgate University history professor R.M. Douglas aims to overcome "generational chauvinism," which is the instinctive belief that we can see further, are wiser, and make better choices than those who came before us. Basically, he wants to make his students "into the kind of people who will test their own arguments more rigorously than the most stringent external critic could ever do."

His faith in his students is great—one of them wrote recently, "You found a gear in me that I didn't know I had"—and he impresses upon them the idea that it is okay to look foolish and ask stupid questions. "Just as a quarterback learning a new playbook doesn't expect to turn in an MVP performance from his very first practice snaps, students shouldn't become discouraged by early struggles," he says.

His classes include War and Holocaust in Europe (which "draws huge crowds, largely because according to the History Channel, the Second World War is the only thing that has ever occurred in the past"), Europe Since 1945, and Introduction to Modern European History. It's his intro classes that he and the students find most difficult, as "showing a classroom full of people who know nothing about history what it is and why they should care about it takes all the skill in the world. In a properly ordered universe, only the most experienced, imaginative, and talented professors would be allowed to teach basic introductory courses."

He describes his classroom approach as "Paleolithic—chalk and talk"; he believes that true interactivity comes from engaging with students, not showing them PowerPoint presentations (he shouldn't be so modest, according to the student who says that "his lectures will blow your hair back"). Often, he will begin by telling them a story, putting them in the position of a historical personality facing a pivotal decision, and then have them construct alternatives to what actually occurred, and to prove, using evidence, that those alternatives truly existed. "To their surprise, they often find that even with the benefit of hindsight, they can't come up with a "better" course of action than the one that was ultimately pursued. And in the process they come to perceive historical figures as real people facing genuine dilemmas that they understood as well or as poorly as we do ours today, rather than simply pigeonholing them as heroes or villains."

"Douglas rocks my world. Never have I met someone who knew so much about everything. Really sickly smart," says an impressed student.

Melvin Patrick Ely, Kenan Professor of History and Africana Studies, The College of William & Mary

"Good work, good thinking, good talk, and good writing inspire us all—my students and me—to see ourselves and our world in new and different ways," says Melvin Patrick Ely, a professor of history and Africana studies at The College of William & Mary. It's an uncomplicated enough formula that he is only too happy to carry out. "As he puts it, he doesn't want to 'hide the ball'—he makes everything very clear and reasonable," says a student.

A veteran teacher told Professor Ely at the beginning of his career that, if he showed students respect and expected a lot of them, they in turn would respect him and do their best in his classes. "That approach quickly proved itself and has never failed me since." He loves the subjects he teaches, and that makes it easy to keep things lively. He tries not to act as if there were only one politically acceptable way of seeing things: "I tell students what I think, but usually only after I ask them what *they* think." Students recognize that his main goal is not only "for us to learn history; it's for us to learn how to think about history."

Professor Ely's classes include Free and Enslaved Blacks in the Old South, African American History from Emancipation to the Present, and U.S. History Since Reconstruction, which explores the question "What is American, and who are the Americans?" and emphasizes political and cultural development. Having grown up in the South during the civil rights movement, he became interested in society's frequent failure to honor the principle of liberty and justice for all. He began investigating "the ways we Americans came to be what we are as a society, especially in the realm of race," and says he has "been teaching and writing about those subjects throughout my adult life."

Professor Ely believes straight lecturing is a perfectly good way to convey information, but only in moderation. "I might spend fifteen to twenty minutes laying out crucial points about the material we're addressing on a given day," he says, "but then I try through a series of questions to elicit students' varying understandings of the readings they've done." He allows the discussion "to take whatever route seems most promising and exciting at each given moment." "I learned more from his discussions than I did from taking tons of notes on lecture last semester," says a student. Professor Ely works diligently to get to know each student and help each one individually. Students rave that he "genuinely cares about his students and makes the subject matter interesting and engaging." "Brilliant professors aren't supposed to be this funny and helpful." "He's nationally known for a reason; great prof. Great guy, too."

Timothy Fehler, Professor of History, Furman University

Timothy Fehler, a professor of history at Furman University, wants to fundamentally encourage students to recognize complexity. "When looking at historical causation there are so many layers of possible analysis; each of which can yield different, yet correct, results," he says. While it is impossible to cover everything exhaustively in a class, he hopes that his students come away with "a nuanced understanding of the complicated nature of analysis and the multiple perspectives that shape the construction of history."

Professor Fehler's classes are typically given as lectures, but the small size of Furman's classes enables many opportunities for student involvement. He tries to present a detailed narrative "that also accounts for multiple perspectives, appropriately placed disclaimers, and questions." While he requires a fairly thorough mastery of the course material, he is aware his classes and exams can be stressful and is generous with his time, always willing to meet with, talk with, and tutor students individually. "I try to act with kindness in all of my interactions," he says. Student comments recognize Professor Fehler's sincere interests both in the field of history as well as in their own personal and intellectual development. He is always open for students' questions during lectures; when he doesn't know answers, "I try to model the analytical skills of an historian: think before responding, acknowledge what I can contribute, talk about where we might find the answers and then go find them."

His myriad courses have recently included Germany and the 30 Years War: War and Peace in Early Modern Europe; Off With His Head: The Trial of King Charles I; and Life on the Margins in Early Modern Europe. In the fall of 2011, he is teaching Repression, Resistance, and Remembrance in Central Europe since 1750, which includes a five-week study abroad portion in Poland, Germany, Austria, and Czech Republic. "While I often get the most intellectual fulfillment from teaching the more advanced courses where we can delve deeper … I still find myself with more dramatically exciting teaching moments in the introductory courses for General Education credit—where a hitherto uninterested student suddenly discovers something interesting or gets excited about analyzing a complex story that was previously difficult."

Students say that "his courses are difficult, but he is unequaled as an individual and as a professor. He is essential to a complete history major." One says, "My knowledge of history skyrocketed, and so did my love of studying women in early modern Europe! He treated us with a great deal of respect. His comments on papers were very helpful, and my writing improved."

Steven W. Guerrier, Professor of History, James Madison University

Steven W. Guerrier, a history professor at James Madison University, looks "to inspire students to know the material, to use it to develop their own ideas about the material, and to see the value in having this knowledge."

In courses such as U.S. Diplomatic History (a survey of the history of American foreign relations from 1776 to the present) he brings a mix of lecture and "a degree of irreverence" to the classroom (or, as a student puts it, "Dr. Guerrier will make any other teacher look like a chimpanzee"). Largely a narrative historian, throughout his lectures he develops the story, presents interpretations, and aids students in developing their own understanding of the material, both verbally and in writing. "[He is] very passionate about history, and makes it more interesting than any other history professor I've had," says a student.

Students find that his personal stories are "both relevant and funny," and that "his voice is soothing." He gives you three options on tests, "is a fair grader," gives a list of terms at the beginning of the semester that are "very helpful for following the class," and gives an extra credit assignment to help boost your grade. "He's hilarious and chooses extremely interesting material to cover. You will not regret taking this class."

Raymond "Skip" Hyser, Professor of History, James Madison University

Some call it teaching; James Madison University history professor Raymond "Skip" Hyser sees it more as sharing his passion and enthusiasm for the subject he loves, U.S. History. "He is COMPLETELY fair, and class is very interesting (and I never thought I would say that about a history class)," says a student.

By having students read primary sources, Professor Hyser is able to help aid them in reaching their own understanding of the documents through discussion. "When students come to my office, I seek to help them as much as possible by offering advice and suggestions or placing them in contact with someone who can help," he says. Still, his classroom interactions are his favorite part of the job, and his enthusiasm for discourse ("he is so animated") allows students "to ask questions and make comments in an academic environment that promotes discussion and interaction in a collegial manner."

In courses such as U.S. History, a fast paced, one-semester survey of U.S. History from pre-colonial times to the present required of all JMU students, and a history seminar for majors (which teaches them how to conduct scholarly research, analyze primary and secondary sources, and produce an article quality paper), he tries to achieve "constant interaction between the faculty member and students." "This was NOT an easy class, but it was definitely worthwhile," says a student. "He helps you improve your research and writing skills immensely," says another.

Now in his twenty-eighth year of teaching at JMU, his classes will typically involve the assignment of readings (usually primary sources), followed by a class discussion. During the course of the discussion, students are asked to engage questions, to provide additional information, and to "try to understand the moment or topic from the perspective of the document author and understand the past."

John Majewski, Professor, History, University of California—Santa Barbara

John Majewski, a history professor at UC Santa Barbara, strives to provide an environment "where motivated students can take control of their own learning." He wants to create a supportive environment for those who want to be there, and who "happily and enthusiastically" take responsibility for their studies.

In order to accomplish this, Professor Majewski gives give clear, highly organized lectures, all while being completely transparent about his expectations. "He speaks with perfect pace and clarity, makes it interesting, and gives students plenty of time to copy the slides and take extra notes." He most often teaches a large, lower-division survey of nineteenth-century history, as he enjoys "the challenge of reaching students who are not history majors or even not that interested in the subject." On the other end of the spectrum, he also loves teaching about the Civil War in a specialized upper-division course. "Teaching that class has really influenced my research and writing," he says.

Even in his larger classes, he directly engages students. "In my survey of nineteenth-century U.S. history, for example, I have the class develop their own plan for Reconstruction. The ensuing debate and discussion is really enlightening about the possibilities and limits of a wide variety of approaches," he says. "I love history, but I guarantee if you don't you'll still enjoy this class, maybe even change your mind!" says a student.

Jeffrey W. McClurken, Associate Professor of History and American Studies, University of Mary Washington

Jeffrey W. McClurken, who teaches history and American studies at the University of Mary Washington, wants to push students out of their comfort zone, regardless of the topic at hand. "I tell students that I want them uncomfortable, but not paralyzed," he says. "Students who can get used to, even enjoy, trying new things while not being frozen or overwhelmed do well in my classes."

His approach to teaching is both classical and modernist, "grounded in the importance of historical inquiry, the multidisciplinary nature of the liberal arts, and…key related beliefs." He works to involve students in classes as participants, leaders, and fellow learners, and believes that technology can play a key role in enhancing traditional pedagogical practices. "I often integrate WordPress, Omeka, Facebook, Twitter, and web-based discussions, online research, multimedia content, digital history projects, and electronic editing of papers into my classes," he says. All of these aspects of technology are used to vary and improve communication, offer alternative forms of discussion or presentation, and "broaden the academic experience in and out of the classroom, while holding on to scholarly and intellectual rigor." As one student puts it, "He makes each class something you look forward to because it's like listening to an interesting story every day."

In striving to make students "critical consumers of knowledge," this "hilarious, innovative, and knowledgeable" professor wants to impart to his students an understanding of how knowledge is produced, but stresses that "being skeptical about one's sources also makes one a better writer and speaker." "I believe I have a responsibility to teach students to approach all primary and secondary content with a skeptical eye," he says.

Throughout many of his classes, including U.S. History in Film, American Technology and Culture, and Remembering the Civil War, he works with students to critically analyze what have become the key popular sources of information about the past, namely movies and the Internet. Students are encouraged to express themselves in various ways: formal and informal, written and oral, online and in person, skills that Professor McClurken believes "will stand students well in the post-college world, regardless of their major."

Daniel R. Miller, Professor of History, Calvin College

Much of what Calvin College history professor Daniel R. Miller does is help students develop skills—to write clear, effective essays or to summarize fairly an author's point of view—but his overarching objective is "to help students develop intellectual and moral maturity," using the subject of history.

"I don't want to produce cynics and I don't want to produce ideologues," he says. "I want my students to have enough confidence in their knowledge and convictions to act on them, and enough awareness of their limitations to remain open to new information, to criticism, and even to a change in course where indicated." Through his courses, which include History of the West and the World Since 1500, Survey of Latin American History, and The U.S. Civil War and Reconstruction, students learn that it's not all black or white: Some ideas about the past are pretty well founded, while others are very tentative. "And they learn that while no one is perfect, some historical actors and actions are worth emulating, others are cautionary tales to be avoided."

He uses a variety of teaching methods (games, film clips, small groups, etc.), and tries to infuse his classes with enthusiasm ("we even spent a few classes playing a Civil War strategy game he designed!"), but it's this "friendly, smart, and witty" professor's humble opinion that his built-in advantage is more cosmetic: "Let's be honest, I'm an old guy with a beard so many students just assume that I know a lot." He has taught, studied, and done research in the field of history (especially Latin America) for the last thirty years, and assigns frequent ("labor intensive") reading and writing assignments based on texts he has encountered, asking students to summarize various authors' arguments and critique them using other resources and information. "To become good writers, students must learn to rewrite," he says. "It's only when you write down your thoughts that you truly know what you think."

His office hours are also a hot ticket: "I love history, but was not studying it, and just being able to have conversations with him after class was a gift itself," says one student.

John Warne Monroe, Associate Professor of History, Iowa State University

"History is important, in my opinion, because the highly disciplined ability to understand others—to walk a mile in their shoes—that it teaches is a skill with considerable social value," says John Warne Monroe, a history professor at Iowa State University.

Professor Monroe is deeply invested in the idea of liberal arts education, believing that in the process of mastering a limited amount of specialized material in a disciplined way, students will develop broader intellectual skills that will come in handy in a wide array of different situations once they enter the workforce. "When you study history, for instance, if you're taught well, you learn both a particular body of knowledge about the past and a distinctive way of thinking through intellectual problems. The facts aren't an end in themselves— I fully expect my students to forget many of them within a few years of their graduation—they are a means to an end," he says. "In a way, I think of them as a kind of exercise machine, like a bench-press or treadmill, that you can use to condition your mind intensively in ways that would take longer, and be more difficult, if you didn't have the rules and practices of the discipline to push you."

For this reason, his courses focus pretty tightly on content, though he doesn't obsess about the specifics—"I strive to remember the larger intellectual goal I want students to reach, and to make it clear to them as well." His courses include European History, 1517–Present; France 1715–Present; and Modern European Intellectual and Cultural History, a class he purposefully schedules in the morning in order to make sure that the only students who enroll are those who are prepared to take it seriously. "History is obviously about facts, about analyzing evidence, seeing patterns in it, using it to construct reasoned arguments, and so on. But it's also about stories. And that's something I try to harness in order to get students involved in the material." "You'll work hard, but never feel like you're going at it alone," says a student.

As his classes can be larger, he works to make his lectures interesting by using narrative in creative ways. Some lectures tell stories of particular people and events, while others start with an element of everyday life that students take for granted, "like a packet of sugar or a department store, and use it to draw out broader historical themes." By drawing out the huge issues at stake in something as seemingly innocuous as a packet of sugar, he wants to lead students to a key insight: "that their own everyday reality is historically contingent, and that one of the purposes of history is to come to grips with this crucial fact."

Steven Noll, Senior Lecturer, Department of History, University of Florida

"Be yourself in the classroom. Understand you are teaching students, not just a content area."

So advises Steven Noll, a history professor at the University of Florida. He wants students to "understand that history is a process and not simply names, facts, and dates," and does his best to make class interesting and challenging without dumbing it down.

Professor Noll has taught in public school for twenty-eight years and has been teaching at UF since 1988, and students claim he has "so much knowledge to offer." His courses include both halves of the intro American History Survey course, Disability History, Florida History Since 1860, and Gilded Age/Progressive Era, which he loves "because students know so little about it, and also because it has significant relevance for contemporary issues." In his upper-division classes, he starts each class with something that happened on that particular day in history, then talks a bit on how that relates to the broad topics we discuss in class. He's a "great lecturer, even for those who hate lectures," says a student.

His classroom style is "informal and interactive"; he says he simply "gets to know students, and encourages them to participate." "You can tell he really cares about history and his students," says one. "He really is inspirational. He plays out history like you're right there living it."

Jeremi Suri, Mack Brown Distinguished Professor of Global Leadership, History, and Public Policy, The University of Texas at Austin

Jeremi Suri, who teaches global leadership, history, and public policy at The University of Texas at Austin, wants his students to become highly analytical and critical thinkers, who are creative, open-minded, and comfortable with challenging points of view.

His love for his job is inspiring: "Teaching is also learning. I treat each student as an adult who has something to teach me. Teaching is a two-way street." His love for preparation is legendary: "I am someone who prepares for every lecture, every meeting, every conversation." Most importantly, his love for history and foreign policy trumps all: "I believe that studying these subjects together is the best preparation for contemporary policy, business, and citizenship."

His recent classes have included History of American Foreign Relations, Grand Strategy and Foreign Policy, and American History since 1865; in all of these he likes to challenge his students to think differently and work harder than they ever have before. "I believe they are often under-challenged and that they will do more when given sufficient motivation." Says one student, "He never makes a mistake and makes his points with a forceful voice."

He requires all undergraduates to complete rigorous take-home exams that require extensive reading, analysis, and writing in only forty-eight hours, as he wishes for them to experience and learn to respond to pressure. "I want them to have the pride of fulfilling a tough and serious assignment. Most students are proud of the experience, when they are done," he says. "His lectures are amazing. Don't expect to sleep after getting his exam. Expect to learn a lot in the process though," warns a student.

Steve Voguit, Assistant Professor, History and Geography, Flagler College

Steve Voguit, who teaches history and geography at Flagler College, wants to be the type of professor he wanted his own children to have.

Professor Voguit's students are well aware that, after forty-two years of teaching, he genuinely cares about them as people, not as just as moldable minds. His high energy, high-passion teaching works well for students whose "switch is on," and they return the compliment: "He is funny, caring, smart, articulate, passionate...the list goes on and on. He loves his students and you will love him back!"

He teaches surveys in American History and Human Geography, which is a study of what humans have done on the surface of the earth, as well as Oral History, Intro to Public History, and Immigration History; these subjects have been his life's work right from his undergraduate days. He makes a sincere effort to make the material "relevant, interesting, and engaging," with lectures including technology, film, higher-order thinking assignments, and out-of-the classroom experiences. Sometimes he'll have students take a look at a historical event and then write a paper that explains what happened but alters something in the account, then speculates on how history would have been different had this change occurred. "His lectures don't feel like lectures at all," says a student. He also is linked to an art professor (who is a close friend), and the two collaborate on creative projects for their students, such as a recent silhouette project for which students created black silhouettes of individual characters from an era of history that were then placed around campus for an art walk. "He is always there for you no matter what you need help on. I can't wait to take more of his classes!" says a student.

David Wetzel, Lecturer, History, University of California—Berkeley

David Wetzel is a professor of history at the University of California—Berkeley who specializes in German history and the history of international relations between great international powers. Wetzel is a prolific author with six books and numerous articles in scholarly journals to his credit. At the same time, he is very serious about his responsibilities as a lecturer. "I rehearse each lecture I give in front of a mirror so that by the time I go before the class I can deliver it without notes," he says. "I figure I'm an actor going on stage." Students say they like his preparedness and his dedication to his craft. He "makes the classes genuinely fun to attend," they say, and "he is able to clarify complex issues." "Wetzel breathes new life into dense material," reports one student. "He is loud and passionate and it keeps you interested in the lecture." By all accounts, though, Wetzel talks a mile a minute, though, so be prepared "to have a cramped wrist at every lecture." "I do talk fast," Wetzel admits. "I try to compensate by repeating the points I make once, maybe twice."

According to students, Wetzel "stresses the importance of personalities and how the power of individuals has driven history." "I try to frame in a compelling way how states become states," he explains, "to make the past come alive, and to teach history as a drama in which the movers and shakers are human beings." The outbreak of World War I in July 1914 in particular is a subject of endless fascination for him. When he has finished the last lecture on the topic, he requires students to lay down their pens and take their hands off their laptops. "In return," he relates, "I promise never to ask them anything about what I am going to say on an exam. I read three poems and three lyrics, which I find very moving as do they."

Students say that Wetzel is "a brilliant man," and their acclaim is universal and effusive. "He is the most prepared, detailed, knowledgeable, professional and inspirational professor I have ever had," declares one student. "He truly loves his subject and his job." He "understands how interesting history is and makes the classes genuinely fun to attend," says another student. "I spend the rest of the week looking forward to his lectures." "He makes those who have no interest in history fall in love with it," adds still another student. "If that's not pure genius, I don't know what is."

Jim Whittenburg, Pullen Professor of History, Lyon G. Tyler Department of History, The College of William & Mary

Pullen Professor of History James P. Whittenburg, who teaches at The College of William & Mary, wants his students to approach history with an open mind, and to bring to the field a sense of adventure and open-ended inquiry. "Professor Whittenburg is one of my idols," says an admiring student.

His classes currently include From the Founding of Jamestown Through the American Revolution and From the American Revolution Through the American Civil War. His classes have followed the same traditional-yet-not format for some years, teaching various slices of American history through 1865 visits to historic sites. Students and teacher meet once per week, all day; during preliminary meetings in the classroom, he will typically involve video clips, music, or the Internet. The class travels by van and holds class on site at one or more of the many museums, archaeology projects, or surviving period structures in the Chesapeake region ("which might be something as grand as Thomas Jefferson's Monticello or as modest as the slave house at 'Bacon's Castle' in Surry County, VA"), and seminar discussions are conducted over lunch. "The wealth of historic sites, archaeology, and museums in the middle Atlantic is seductive. I doubt I could teach in this fashion in many other places." Readings for each class are moderately heavy, and students maintain online journals in which they bring together their thoughts about the readings, the sites, and the discussions in the form of a well-organized and expressed blog. A student says: "This is the best history class—you discuss, think, and actually learn history. I wish I could take this class over and over again."

One feature of his teaching style, developed over the past forty-plus years of his career, is to present students with a variety of "elements" that pertain to a historical pattern that he hopes they will uncover. "In the end, I hope they will sort through the often-opposed points of view they encounter in my classes and arrive at their own conclusions about the nature of the American past," he says. "I changed my major to history because of this man, and everyone I know worships the ground he walks on," says a student.

Steven E. Woodworth, Professor, History, Texas Christian University

Steven Woodworth, a professor of history at Texas Christian University, wants to connect with students personally as much as possible and help them understand and enjoy history.

Ask him why he thinks students value his teaching, and he'll modestly say "Maybe it's because I'm having so much fun with history. Maybe it's contagious." He finds his area "fascinating and fun," and has attempted to spread this enthusiasm to his students over twenty-seven years of teaching. His current course load includes two sections of a survey of United States History to 1877, and one section of the History of the Old South. He's a "great professor," according to one student. "My favorite since coming to college." "He knows his Civil War history, so don't try to play around, he will catch you on it!"

There's no magic formula to his classes or his appeal; he is "a storyteller, plain and simple. History is composed of stories, and people not only enjoy stories but also understand and remember them." "He will get up and lecture without notes for the entire class," says a student. "He was pretty funny while lecturing at times, and he does it all from memory," says another.

Samuel Yamashita, Henry E. Sheffield Professor of History, Pomona College
Samuel Yamashita, a history professor at Pomona College, spends a lot of time choosing reading material, drafting writing assignments, and commenting on students' written work. "I want students to be engaged and to think as deeply as they can about whatever topics I present in classroom lectures or raise in seminars," he says. Individual meetings during office hours are more open-ended, with students shaping the conversation by raising issues or asking questions.

Professor Yamashita is an Asian history specialist, and therefore most of his "hardcore" classes focus on Asia. Asian Traditions is a survey of the history of China, India, Japan, and Korea from prehistory to 1500, covering the most important and dramatic changes in the histories of these countries; and State, Citizen, and Subject in Modern Japan uses material that he gathered, translated and published—the diaries of a kamikaze pilot, an Army straggler on Okinawa, a Tokyo housewife, a teenage girl mobilized for war work in Kyushu, and two children evacuated from cities to the safety of the countryside. An accomplished author and researcher, he has written nearly three hundred class lectures, and he continues to give public lectures to general audiences all over the United States and Asia. Students refer to him as "absolutely brilliant, thoughtful, very tough and demanding, generous, [and] inspired."

"I try to create opportunities for students to engage in 'reading against the grain'." For example, he begins Asian Traditions with a discussion of how the power of a religious elite enabled it to write the canonical South Asian texts called the Vedas, which affirmed their high status and relegated everyone else to subordinate positions. "Five weeks into the course and after several other exercises in critical reading, I ask students to use what they have learned and to identify the many intricate manifestations of power and their sources in the eleventh-century Japanese classic *The Tale of Genji*."

A student says that he is a "great mentor to have in your corner, as he is genuinely interested in your success." It should not be surprising that he has won Pomona College's teaching award six times.

Human Development
Larry J. Nelson, PhD, Associate Professor, School of Family Life, Brigham Young University

Larry Nelson, who teaches in the School of Family Life at Brigham Young University, seeks to help students apply the course information to their own lives, and to provide them with the knowledge and skills that will benefit the lives of the children for whom they will have stewardship in life as teachers, leaders, and parents.

His passion for his subject is evident in classes such as Strengthening Marriage and Family, Advanced Issues in Human Development, and Introduction to Human Development, which he considers his "baby." "When I decided to become a professor it was my goal to teach this class and that goal kept me motivated throughout graduate school." His devotion to the field runs deep; he wanted to teach a subject that would not only have scientific application and help students prepare for their careers but would hopefully be instrumental in changing lives. "I learned SO much that actually changed and applied to my life, and always really felt the Spirit during his lectures," says a student.

He tries to bring topics to life via the use of real-world examples, and engages students in an attempt to get them to think about the topic through the use of critical thinking exercises. Students refer to it as the "best class I have ever taken up to date." "I honestly leave every lecture thinking I just had the best class ever and learned so much," says one.

Humanities

Kathleen A. Bishop, PhD, Adjunct Assistant Professor, Humanities,
New York University

Kathy Bishop is a humanities professor at New York University. Her theory on
the reasons for the rave reviews she regularly receives is pretty straightforward.
"I love what I teach and I'm fair," she says. "Almost anybody who is teaching at
a university is going to be qualified. But if you're not doing what you really love,
your coworkers can tell. So, your students can tell." Getting students interested
in the course work and keeping them interested is the primary thing, she says.
"One could be like Einstein but, if nobody's listening, nobody's learning anything." "Convey your own love of the subject in an engaging way and students
will listen and learn even if they thought they weren't interested in the subject,"
she asserts. If you do find yourself in one of Bishop's courses, be warned: She is
reportedly "a stickler for grammar in papers," which is probably an impossible
habit to break given her previous stint as a long-time editor at McGraw-Hill.
Also, "exams aren't so easy." However, "she gives lots of hints about what's on
the midterm and final."

Students recognize and value Bishop's love of the material. Her enchantment
captivates them. "She is very knowledgeable about the subject matter," explains
one student, "and knows how to convey that knowledge." "She is really passionate about the subject she teaches," adds another student, "which in turn makes
you really interested in it too." Bishop has an uncanny knack for leading "great
class discussions" and putting "ancient things in modern terms." "She's so cool
and knows how to engage a class." She makes complex literature "easy to understand." She relates "material to the students' real world." She "structures all of
her lessons and readings around what is interesting and relevant to students as
much as possible," elaborates one student. For example, she will make a point
about the *Iliad* by comparing it to *Gossip Girl* or *Glee*. Students also appreciate
the fact that Bishop also bothers to take the time to get to know the people in
her classes. "She is genuinely interested in all of her students." "I get to know
students' names," Bishop tells us. "I connect with them as people. I really want
them to do well."

Timothy Baker Shutt, Professor of Humanites, Director of the
Integrated Program in Humane Studies, Kenyon College

If Timothy Baker Shutt, a professor of the humanities at Kenyon College, can encourage his class to fall in love with the subject, and, in a broader sense, with knowledge, wisdom, and virtue, then he has had a good day.

The tremendous concern and affection for his students does not go unnoticed; one former student tells of the time that "Professor Shutt received a standing ovation after the final class of the semester. That's the first time I've even heard of something like that happening." He has been teaching for thirty-eight years in total, driven by the simple idea that he himself is deeply interested in what he professes. Despite often teaching large classes, this "relaxed and amiable" man tries to involve every student. "I genuinely like and respect my students and their lives and values."

This "Kenyon legend" teaches in the humanities, which consists of history, philosophy, literary study, political science, religious studies, history of science, and art history, and his courses include Dante's *Divine Comedy*, his personal favorite, The Odyssey of the West, and Celts and Germans, which he finds particularly valuable in that it teaches "a taciturn, steady courage and devotion to the task at hand as well as, on the Celtic side, an ineradicable sense of play." Small classes with him are "100 percent discussion; he can make the driest material fascinating." "This man embodies what Kenyon is," says a student.

Interdisciplinary Studies
Professor Kimora, PhD, John Jay College of Criminal Justice

Professor Kimora, who teaches in the Interdisciplinary Studies Department (ISP) as well as the Law, Police Science and Criminal Justice Department (LPS) at John Jay College of Criminal Justice, long ago learned that "unless we question what we are learning, we are capable of becoming an uncritical thinker who could learn to victimize others."

This "excellent mentor" finds it crucial for students to appreciate learning and develop critical thinking skills in order to be productive in a global economy, and fosters a trusting environment in her classroom so that they may do so. She teaches classes including Introduction to Criminal Justice ("I like to teach introductory courses to instill a sense of ethics") and The Law and Institutional Treatment, which gives her the opportunity to validate learning in a prison setting. Prison education is a specialty area of hers, and she has taught in prisons and jails since 1990. "Students need to realize that many people in prison have the ability and wish to change," she says.

Topics in class are expanded a by having students discuss both sides of the issue with evidence; she does not call on students, as she considers it to be shaming. "Over half of the class will be involved in the discussion" at any given time. "Professor Kimora is one of those professors that can change your life and view on topics," says a student. "It was my pleasure to take her class," says another.

Ronald Pitcock, J. Vaughn & Evelyne H. Wilson Honors Fellow, John V. Roach Honors College, Texas Christian University

Ronald L. Pitcock, who teaches honors courses at Texas Christian University, strives to create a student-professor relationship that transcends the classroom, as well as a student's four-year university experience, and can serve as "a life-long, life-changing bond for both the student and professor."

He tries to achieve this by following five principles when teaching: Be accessible and student-centered; communicate clearly and honestly as both a speaker and listener; inspire students to set and achieve goals; serve as role models for students; and create thoughtful communities excited about learning and life. Whether helping students to develop strengths or helping them to recognize areas of deficiency, "I must be trusted to tell the truth….Though at times it can be difficult for students to hear about weaknesses, the underlying relationship of trust forged over time allows me to share these truths in a constructive manner."

Being so accessible and honest, he frequently has breakfast, lunch, or dinner with students, and tries to model behaviors that students can follow, both in negative as well as in positive situations. "I hope students observe me handling difficulties with grace and learning with great passion and excitement. I hope every student can say that I respected him or her in times of success and in the face of adversity," he says.

In the interdisciplinary honors courses that he teaches (including Cultural Memory, On Human Nature, and Nature of Giving), he uses his considerable knowledge to pose questions, create excitement, and guide the discussion that students drive. "Good mentoring involves not just chatting with students about their dreams, but looking for concrete ways to help students achieve goals," he says. He does not begin discussions, but creates frameworks and asks questions that will help the students arrive at their own conclusions. "Students should leave each class feeling as if they were the significant, active learner responsible for making the class a success." "You learn a lot from a professor NOT interested in proving how much smarter he is than the students," says a student.

Students speak more than highly of Dr. Pitcock, saying that "he is by far one of the most influential people I've had the blessing to have in my life. I aspire to be a teacher like him." "His lectures are never boring, he is an incredibly nice guy, and he manages to wring interest out of materials that a person might otherwise think boring or antiquated."

International Studies

Vinnie Ferraro, Ruth Lawson Professor of International Politics, Mount Holyoke College

Vincent Ferraro, professor of international politics at Mount Holyoke College, uses the issues of world politics to help students understand the importance of knowledge and self-discipline. "Power over oneself is the one and only objective," he says.

It is no surprise that he shows such passion for what he teaches ("a teacher is always a student"), and he considers teaching to be a truly noble profession. His classes, which include World Politics, Rhetoric of Peace and War, International Political Economy, and American Foreign Policy, are "riveting" and highly dependent on current topics; his weekly quizzes are even based on news articles. He is "more interested in developing YOU as a person to be able to think intelligently in the world than in just shoveling knowledge down your throat," according to one student.

He's enthusiastic about teaching (yet "calm and wise"), and always begins a class by giving his conclusion first and then working backwards. "I also try to use a concrete historical or contemporary example for every theoretical point I make," he says. In one of his classes, "he doesn't give a final, except that you have to create a website on a topic of your choice."

"There is no way you walk away from a class with him without learning, gaining interest, and feeling it absolutely necessary to take another class with him! He is understanding, helpful, compassionate, and wicked smart!" raves one student.

Alan Karras, Associate Director and Senior Lecturer, International and Area Studies, University of California—Berkeley

Alan Karras, the associate director of international and area studies at the University of California—Berkeley, wants to get his students' critical thinking skills to the point that they can easily participate in local, national, and global society. They should leave his class with "the idea that knowledge does not come from simply absorbing what others have to say but from actively engaging with and challenging ideas that each of us encounter on a daily basis."

Professor Karras not only wants students to apply these skills as they work through course content, but also to the engagements they have with each other and the world around them. One student preaches his success: "I have used things I learned in his class in almost every other class I have taken in some form or another." Students respect him because "I provide them the toolbox that they need, but don't spoon feed them." He enjoys teaching for the same reasons he originally got into it: "It is a combination of a lucky accident and intellectual curiosity in why the world today is the way that it is."

His recent courses have included the Senior Honors Program in International Studies; World History; and Classical Political Economy, which covers the origins of political economy and which requires students to read original theorists. The last class is usually his favorite to teach, as the original theory never changes, but the application to the modern world constantly does (one student says he "challenged everyone to question the authors we were reading"). His readings are thorough, sometimes even dense, but students claim that he "will make you rethink people you thought you knew like Smith and Marx." As another student said, "In his last lecture, he nearly brought me to tears as he challenges us to change the world."

Dr. Constantine Pleshakov, Professor, Russian and Eurasian Studies and Critical Social Thought, Mount Holyoke College

Constantine Pleshakov is a self-described "academic nomad." He studied at Moscow State University and the National University of Singapore and since then he has held a slew of positions in the United States and abroad, including a stint at Amherst College. He is currently a professor of Russian and Eurasian studies and critical social thought at Mount Holyoke College, a small, historically women's school in Massachusetts. He is also a prolific fiction writer and the author of several books concerning Russia.

Students tell us that it takes no time at all to discern that Pleshakov is "clearly super brilliant"—an "entertaining, insightful, just overall an amazing professor." "Lectures are engaging." "He makes even the most boring and bland things interesting." He is "easily one of the best professors" at Mount Holyoke and, at least according to one student, no less than "the coolest man in the world." "I think it should be a requirement to take a class by Pleshakov to graduate," pronounces one student. "He's hilarious, engaging, very respectful, and loves hearing what students have to say."

Pleshakov is pretty circumspect about all this praise. While students say "he will give you priceless life lessons out of the blue," for example, Pleshakov is far more modest. "I am not sure there is such a thing as a master key to living," he reflects. "I try giving career advice." "Keeping up the dialogue in the classroom is the most challenging thing I know," he says. "It's not about taking questions and asking questions. It's more about the state of mind and mood of the audience and you reacting to it. Theater actors call this paradigm a 'magic orb.'" "It is essential to have a Plan B," he adds, in what turns out to be a pretty good life lesson for teachers everywhere. "Sometimes a neatly structured lecture turns into a complete disaster. The more you struggle to repair it, the worse it gets, so it's best to abandon the losing strategy and switch to the alternative. The most horrible thing, of course, is when the Plan B fails to work."

Journalism

Dr. Connie Fletcher, Associate Professor, Journalism, Loyola University Chicago

Connie Fletcher, a journalism professor in Loyola University Chicago's School of Communication, loves what she does. "I think that when you believe in the importance of your subject area, there's a current that runs throughout the room, from prof to student and student to student."

In this digital world, Dr. Fletcher tries to get a high degree of interaction between her students, so that "they will walk out of class with at least one person they can say hi to on campus." She eschews Facebook and online interactions, and instead encourages students to use her classroom as a place for problem-solving, openly discussing difficult topics, and meeting people. "The person you're destined to go into business with, or fall in love with, may be sitting right behind you. Don't check Facebook—check out this classroom," she tells her students.

At the same time, Fletcher tries to get students excited about learning the skills inherent in journalism: being able to observe directly, being able to talk with anyone, and being able to fully research a topic, which "can open up the whole world to you." Highly accessible—"she makes everything you need to know readily available for you," says one student—the goal of her office hours is to remove the "thorn in the foot," or whatever it is that is holding the student back. Students are also given the opportunity to do rewrites, which is a huge boon for freshmen. "Everyone pretty much flounders around at the beginning of a writing course, but the ones who succeed are the ones who recognize and confront their weaknesses," she says.

A prolific writer that has written five published books, she now teaches Reporting and Writing Across Platforms, Ethics and Communication, Narrative Nonfiction, Interviewing, and Investigative Reporting. Fletcher says she counteracts short attention spans by choreographing her classes into intriguing segments, "which give students opportunities to view supplemental materials, think and respond in class, and do actual reporting and writing." For example, if she is teaching a segment on "What Is News?" she'll start the class by airing a live broadcast from the local radio station, then ask the students what they noticed. "Without my listing the characteristics of news in a dry lecture format, the students themselves discover them," she says.

She also feels the thrill of turning students on to new books. Fletcher adds full-length nonfiction books to her regular classes: "There really is nothing like a college student who is excited by a book. They get so excited, and that is a big reward of teaching, to see them become so alive and so enthusiastic." Says one student, "She makes going to class fun. Time seems to fly by because she has great assignments prepared and she also shows great documentaries."

Mike Foley, Master Lecturer, Hugh Cunningham Professor in Journalism Excellence, University of Florida

The "tough but fair" journalism professor Mike Foley of the University of Florida spent thirty years at the *St. Petersburg Times*. Now in the pedagogical games, he grades two papers per week per student, down to the punctuation. "They learn it, or they retake the class until they do," he says.

"While you're actually in the class, it's as bad as everyone says it is. You'll fail your first assignment. You'll question your major. You won't have a social life. But once you've finished, you'll see how much you improved as a writer, and you'll know it was all worth it," agrees a former student. Professor Foley teaches courses such as Reporting (an upper-division, rigorous class in which students learn to gather information and write news and news feature stories); Professional Practice (a one-hour course on employment); and Advanced Reporting, a more sophisticated news writing class with emphasis on good writing. "I don't grade papers; I edit them and give them back for further revision. They learn that good writing means rewriting," he says.

Professor Foley loves to see how his students improve their work over the course of a semester, and is a firm believer that you cannot demand students' attention, so "I do my best to command it." In the classroom, he is "part teacher, part comedian, part philosopher, and part journalist. I dance, too." "He's funny, entertaining and knows how difficult reporting is and tries to lighten up the lectures," says a student. The course is "hard, but worth it."

In his previous job, he worked with two dozen reporters that won Pulitzer Prizes, and he shows their work to his students, telling them why it's good. "I also share with my students stories written by students their age who have won the Hearst College writing awards. It shows them they can do it if they put their minds to it." Students echo the efficacy of his trial-by-fire approach: "By the end, you'll look back at all of your F's and D's and you'll see how much better you are for it. Don't expect to pass until the fourth or fifth week."

Mary Stillwell Haupt, Lecturer, Journalism, Binghamton University

Mary Stillwell Haupt, a lecturer in journalism at Binghamton University, looks to help students "become clear communicators, people who can say or write what they meant to say or write," because "no matter what happens technologically, solid communication skills will always put them ahead of the pack."

Professor Haupt is "open to being challenged by my students," and tries to share her excitement for the topic with her students. She wants them "to find themselves in their writing—to sound like themselves, even within the boundaries of journalistic writing." She particularly values the diversity of people, backgrounds, and talents that spring up in her classes. "I love to teach editing because of the variety of skills involved. A student who struggles with rules of grammar might prove to be a brilliant headline writer or page designer," she says.

Her courses include Intro to Journalism, News Editing, and Feature Writing; for the latter course, students must create a blog on a topic about which they feel passionate. "In effect, we're creating a sort of mini-newsroom where everyone is involved in publishing stories. Many discover their writer's voice in their blog posts more easily than in the full-length stories they write for the course." Her own personal experience covers time spent as a newspaper reporter, editor, and columnist, and she tries to make her lessons as real-world-applicable as possible. "I try to mix it up. If the topic is, say, coming up with good story ideas, I'll give a brief lecture, try an interactive exercise in the classroom to encourage creative thinking, then send the students out of the classroom to see how many ideas they can come up with just by walking around the campus for half an hour."

Most importantly, "Prof. Haupt teaches you how to condense and distill your writing into something more compelling and powerful than anything before." Students say that "she is like a mom-away-from-home figure. She definitely gets to know her students on a personal level and is an asset to BU!"

Alan Schroeder, Professor, School of Journalism, Northeastern University
The laundry list of Northeastern University journalism professor Alan Schroeder's goals is thorough: He "looks to make students better consumers of journalism, to improve their ability to gather and communicate information, and to heighten their powers of visual literacy."

Students say that "professors like Schroeder are hard to find." He spent fifteen years as a print journalist and television producer before coming to teaching in 1989, so his courses such as Interpreting the Day's News, Journalism 3, and Video Newswriting are all tinged with examples and advice from real-life experience. "In teaching journalism, I rely on a lot of examples from the professional world to illustrate my points," he says. "He's such an awesome guy, keeps the class entertained with his witty and funny remarks," says a student.

Professor Schroeder stresses the visual aspects of pedagogy, and his classes enhance learning by using imagery as well as words. "I try very hard to keep my classroom presentation both educational and entertaining," he says. He incorporates current events into every course (which is doubly important in the field of journalism), and, according to a student, "the news is always interesting, hence, the class is very interesting." Through "visual storytelling," he is able to inject humor into his classroom presentation in order to make the class something students look forward to attending. Often, he will show several versions of the same news story as covered by different networks/local stations, so that students "can begin to appreciate why certain things work in this style of journalism, while others do not."

Literature

John Gordon, Professor of English Literature, Connecticut College
For John Gordon, a professor of English literature at Connecticut College, the primary objective is that every student leave the classroom knowing something they didn't know when they came in.

He finds lectures, however rousing, to be a "waste of money," as they offer nothing that a book couldn't supply far more cheaply and efficiently. "What makes teaching worthwhile is that you can interact with the teacher," he says. He begins by trying to find out what students don't know and then works to fill in the gaps. The price of admission for each class is that every student be ready to ask about a passage in the reading that they don't understand. If they don't have such a question ready, Gordon is liable to ask them something from the assignment to which they probably won't have the answer, then demand why they didn't bring it up. "This incentivizes them to come back next time with a real question. My opening line is almost always the same: 'Are there any questions?' The point is to train them to take that question seriously. If they do, everything follows."

His courses include James Joyce, Charles Dickens, Modern Poetry, Contemporary Poetry, and a Modern Literature survey, but his favorite is a course on *Finnegans Wake*, which "is bottomless—never the same book twice. In a way, my students and I start from the same point." He believes follow-through is key; he'll allow almost any number of rewrites and re-gradings, provided the student is making an effort.

"He makes class fun, but it's always intellectually exciting too. Conn College is so lucky to have someone like this on the faculty," says a student. "John Gordon, or J-Go, as we called him, was the most important teacher in my life. His classes were memorable, educational, fun, and challenging."

Joseph Lauinger, PhD, Professor of Dramatic Literature, Sarah Lawrence College

Joseph Lauinger is a member of the faculty at Sarah Lawrence College, a tiny bastion of the liberal arts and sciences a few miles north of New York City where there are no major requirements and virtually all classes are seminars that occur at a roundtable, literally. It's exactly the sort of place where you'd expect to find a slew of stellar professors but, according to students, Lauinger is peerless even here.

Lauinger teaches literature—specifically dramatic literature, and he is adept at everything from ancient Greek tragedy to contemporary theater. He also writes plays that have been produced in the United States and all over the world, so he has "very practical knowledge of what it takes to make a play come alive."

The secret to engaging students in his subject, Lauinger explains, is allowing course readings to "speak in their own terms instead of imposing on them a personal agenda." He pays "a great deal of attention to primary texts." "I try to place plays within their cultural context, which means trying to reconstruct the conditions of their production and performance," he says. "When I teach Sophocles, I teach it as a play put on by a guy who was looking for a certain audience." The discussions in his classes are by all reports profuse and free-flowing. "There's a sense of shared ownership of the material." "There are whole stretches of class where I just function as a referee," he says. At the same time, Lauinger maintains "a very clear idea of the material that has to be conveyed from class to class." "If I find the conversation straying," he says, "I bring it back by providing background and focus."

Students tell us that taking one of Lauinger's courses is "an absolute must" if you attend Sarah Lawrence. "Not only is he insanely well-read, well-spoken, and hilarious, he's also immensely concerned with every student's progress and welfare." He is "thoroughly supportive," too, and "an expert in many disciplines who can bring them all together rather neatly." "Joe is a brilliant, extraordinary, life-changing professor," beams one student. "He is also one of the most kind-hearted human beings I have ever met." "Joe is one of the most amazing people in my life," adds another student. "He's like my other dad," adds another student, "but in a non-creepy, non-stifling sort of way."

Mark Sibley-Jones, PhD, Literature, University of South Carolina

Mark Sibley-Jones has had a multitude of careers in his day. "I've done so many things," he says. "I was a minister. I keep failing at writing novels." Currently, he teaches English at the Governor's School, a residential public high school for extraordinary artists. He also teaches British Literature—from *Beowulf* to Milton—at the University of South Carolina. His views on why he receives such outstanding reviews as a professor are unpretentious to say the least. "I think the suggestion that I'm a great professor is preposterous," he asserts. "Who comes up with these ridiculous assessments?"

In spite of—or maybe because of—his modesty, students love Sibley-Jones. He is "hugely intelligent, but immensely personable" and "his lectures are interesting and often funny." "He makes those long reading assignments feel like nothing." "If you have no sense of humor, don't bother," advises one student. "But if you are up for a good laugh and learning some new, interesting stuff, I'd definitely suggest taking any class of his you can get into." "Sibley-Jones is quite possibly the best instructor I have had at any institution," proclaims one student. "He picks books that he sometimes doesn't like. That says a lot about him. He focuses on understanding and critiquing literature, and wants you to do so properly as well." "He helped me improve my writing skills beyond words," lauds another student. He is "a really great teacher who actually cares about you."

The courses Sibley-Jones teaches at South Carolina don't involve much in the way of discussion. "Classes are a little too big for that." Nevertheless, he says, he manages to connect with students. "I have a lot of energy. I am fairly animated. What students say to me is that it's obvious that I have a love of the material and I am able to communicate that to them." "The best teachers love their students and are genuinely interested in them as human beings," he adds. "Interest in what people say and do is reciprocated." After talking to Sibley-Jones and after hearing from students, we're going to go out on a limb here and say that, above all, it's this obvious concern for his students that has caused them to "ridiculously" assess him as a great professor.

Karen Sullivan, Asher B. Edelman Professor of Literature, Bard College

Students often come into a class with certain preconceptions about the Middle Ages; it is the job of Karen Sullivan, a professor of literature at Bard College, to dispel these ideas, and get students to connect to medieval literature. "I have a theory that every student knows something that no one else in the world knows and that it is my job to enable him or her to articulate that insight. I want to teach my students, but I want to get them to teach me as well," she says.

In general, she encourages students to identify what is most strange, most foreign, and most "medieval" about medieval literature and then asks them to consider whether they can't find this quality in modern culture. "While I obviously teach texts I know a great deal about, we occasionally come across a passage that I find puzzling or difficult to interpret. It can be empowering for students, I find, if I acknowledge the difficulty I find with this passage and ask them for their insights into it," she says. She thinks the most important trait in a professor is being able to listen to what students are saying, and wants not only to answer a student's question, but also "to figure out where that question is coming from and to respond to that latent agenda." "She has a little cult following among the students, and you can totally see why," says a student.

She specializes in medieval literature (in courses such as Scholasticism vs. Humanism and The Literature of the Crusades), but is also teaching First-Year Seminar, which is a required course that introduces all first-years to the great works of the Bible, Plato, Virgil, Augustine, Dante, Shakespeare, and Galileo. In class, she tends to make two columns on the blackboard, contrasting two topics under discussion (such as the characteristics of epic versus those of romance). Once there is a series of opposing concepts on the blackboard, the class can step back and generalize about the larger patterns at work. "These two columns enable us to visualize, clearly and specifically, what is at stake in what we are talking about." "You can always tell that she's leading you to some conclusion, but she's very open to that conclusion being challenged, and letting the class talk it out," says one student. "I sort of want to be her when I grow up, drinking tea and having a giant sword in my office," says another.

Management

Paul Bracken, Professor of Management & Political Science, Yale University

"Education is not about the transfer of information," says Paul Bracken, who is a professor of management and political science at Yale University. "Students must learn to think critically."

In classes such as Problem Framing (an MBA core class that focuses on redefining hard problems) and Strategy, Technology, and War (which looks at sources of international order and disorder), he encourages students "to think beyond the usual stovepipes of academic disciplines." Very few professors cover these important topics, and he tries to give serious, real examples of the key points in the class, and emphasizes creativity and practicality. "They focus on opportunities rather than problems," he says.

The man that some call the "best teacher at Yale, hands down" has taught for over twenty-five years, including in many executive education programs, and his classes are highly interactive, particularly his trademark use of business war games in classes. "If you can take a course from him, do it. Very interesting." This "very straightforward professor" is "very approachable and helpful if you have questions." "I definitely recommend this class!" says a student.

Gerard Callanan, Professor, Management Department, West Chester University

"Students are my customers and I treat them that way," says Gerard Callanan, who teaches in the Management Department at West Chester University. "My goal is to ensure that my students have the knowledge and the critical thinking skills to be successful in work and in life."

His rules for being a good teacher are straightforward: "Be on time, stay true to the syllabus, return assignments promptly, establish a relaxed atmosphere in the classroom, encourage participation, make sure to quickly learn every student's name, have fair tests that are directly related to the material that was covered in class, and be available to the students to answer their questions." In following these simple tenets of decorum, he establishes a fun, relaxed, and informative atmosphere that students "look forward to going to."

His courses include Business and Society and Career Management, and he teaches "old school" style: chalk to the blackboard. The classroom environment is fast-paced with a constant dialogue between Professor Callanan and the students, and he tries to make sure that he uses the most current real-world example to underscore the points that he is making. Professor Callanan is a big proponent of using humor to keep the students engaged, and always tries to relate whatever material he is teaching to a current or well-known fictional event, even using TV and movie references to make a point. "He has the funniest stories. I took him…at 8:00 in the morning, and it was still a very exciting class," says a student.

Marketing

Regis Clifford, Adjunct Professor, Management, Marketing, and
Economics, St. John's University

Regis Clifford, an adjunct professor or management, marketing, and economics
at St. John's University in Queens, shares his forty-plus years of business experience in order to demonstrate the application of the academic subject in the "real
world." A former military man, he has been teaching at St. John's since 1993,
but is still involved in the financial services industry (not to mention volunteer
firefighting). "It's not that I don't use the book as a guide, but I have to include
real-life experience and how it is applicable," he says. "He always gives helpful
tips on how to 'market yourself'," says a student.

Professor Clifford is currently teaching economics, where he has the students
put together a business plan. "That is the foundation for all of the subjects. The
business plan enables the student to research what are the essential components
of running a business." His laid-back classroom demeanor inspires the students
to call him "so down-to-earth and a great speaker"; one even gives him the highest honor: "Even though attendance isn't mandatory, I would actually WANT
to go to class." "The more I can get them to participate, the more I can keep
their attention," he says. "We have a common goal which is for the student to
learn the material and be in a position to utilize it," he explains. To accomplish
this, he has his own personal formula: K-A-S-H. "It means we have a fifty-fifty
arrangement. I will share my Knowledge, the student will have an Attitude
to learn, I will teach them the Skills, and they will show good work Habits. It
should be a win-win situation."

A polymath, he loves studying the teachers of other disciplines to learn what
he can do to become a better one himself; he has studied martial arts, anatomy,
and physiology in service of this. "It's a learning process for teachers too. The
minute you stop learning, you become stale and ineffective."

Aric Rindfleisch, McManus-Bascom Professor in Marketing, University
of Wisconsin—Madison

Aric Rindfleisch "worked in both advertising and marketing research" prior to
getting his doctorate and he is now a professor of marketing in the business

school at the University of Wisconsin—Madison. Students call Rindfleisch the "best professor in the business school" and quite possibly the best professor at UW—Madison, period. He's "brilliant" and a "refreshing breath of fresh air from the oftentimes bottom-line-oriented outlook of the business world." One reason students love Rindfleisch is that he talks "about things that are actually happening in the world of business today, a rarity in most classes." His courses are the kind where you have to be "prepared to be flexible and take risks" in order to get a good grade, though. "He likes you to be creative." He "spends a lot of time designing a class that will actually help you learn" and his very unique "democratic grading structure allows students to tailor their grades based on their strengths and weaknesses."

"My teaching philosophy is pretty basic," Rindfleisch says. "I hope students learn something interesting, do something important, and share what they learn with others." His passion is what he calls user-based innovation, and his courses are "very hands-on." You will definitely "learn by doing" and in extraordinarily novel ways. For example, while most college professors demand that students spurn Wikipedia at all costs, one of his assignments is to create or extensively edit a real, live Wikipedia entry. You will also leave his courses "with new ways to think about things." Rindfleisch's courses transcend mere marketing. It's not hyperbole to say that he is a kind of prophet. Listening to him is like catching a glimpse into the future. Imagine learning how to use Google—or the laptop computer, or the wheel—long before virtually anyone else. That's exactly what happens during his 3D printing assignment. Students find a design they like and load it into a 3D program. With the addition of a little manufacturing-grade plastic—voila!—Rindfleisch's students have an actual bottle opener, or a toothpaste squeezer, or a whistle that makes real sound. That's totally cool in itself, but Rindfleisch insists that it's much more significant: This sort of democratized manufacturing that his students use to create objects is nothing less than the next logical step in the Industrial Revolution. In our lifetimes, he says, we'll be making the stuff we want to buy right in our own homes.

Robert D. Winsor, PhD, Professor of Marketing, Loyola Marymount University

"Every professor thinks he or she is a great teacher. Few likely are," says marketing professor Robert Winsor, who teaches at Loyola Marymount University. This disconnect, he argues, results because many teachers are not willing or able to put themselves in the shoes of the students. In order to meet this standard, he busies himself with three main goals: be prepared before class, be enthusiastic during class, and be empathetic and have integrity outside of class.

Professor Winsor always considers that different students have different abilities and different learning styles, and makes sure that he never takes anything for granted when teaching. "Students are not dumb. And, if students appear lazy, it is probably the professor's fault for not motivating them properly," he says.

His courses include Price Strategy and Marketing and Consumption in Contemporary Society; no matter the topic, he relishes the reliability of his chosen field. "Everyone is a consumer. In my particular classes, I want to provide my students with unique perspectives that both create value for their future lives and careers, but that also makes them really rethink their assumptions about many topics (and about life in general)." "I can say without a doubt that he has been my favorite professor at LMU. He made me think, question what I believed in, and really learn to love learning," says a student.

His intriguing teaching style is that of "shock and awe," and he tries to truly overwhelm students in his class by providing a very entertaining, but also very content-rich class experience. His model for teaching is that of a very riveting documentary movie or television program; he uses a wide variety of approaches, material, and media (lecture, movie clips, advertisements, pictures, articles, etc.), but keeps each segment limited to no more than five minutes. "By mixing things up this way, student interest levels are kept high, and every learning style is accommodated." This approach requires extensive preparation before class, and he is happy to invest the time. "You can tell he spends a ton of time preparing to make class great," notices a student.

Mathematics

Soha Abdeljaber, Mathematics Instructor, New Jersey Institute of Technology

Soha Abdeljaber, who teaches mathematics at New Jersey Institute of Technology, just wants her students to love learning.

She is continuously improving the curriculum and instructions she uses, and vows "to never remain in status quo but change for the better." Students can see and feel that she deeply cares about their learning, and she gives each one the time they need to learn, and pushes them to excel.

Professor Abdeljaber's love of mathematics stems from her teenage years, when she used to tutor. "The satisfaction from seeing them understand the subject and doing well on exams afterwards inspired me to continue teaching more students better understand mathematics. I like to show students that mathematics is not as hard as they think and can even be easy when you understand it," she says. One student recommends her: "She is so kind, sweet, and such a great professor that you'll love math."

She has been teaching for twelve years; her courses include Algebra, Precalculus, Trigonometry, and Calculus. She likes to take the best of traditional and constructivist teaching styles, where she lectures when she needs to introduce a new topic, and then allows the students work together and construct their own knowledge through collaboration and practice. "She made calculus easy to understand and actually interesting. I didn't mind going to class at all," says a student. She may make you work a lot in class and lots of homework, but "it's worth it in the end when you see your grade."

Sarah Spence Adams, Professor of Mathematics and Electrical and Computer Engineering, Franklin W. Olin College of Engineering

"I love, love, love it when a student figures out how to solve a hard problem," says Sarah Spence Adams, a professor of mathematics and electrical and computer engineering at Franklin W. Olin College of Engineering. "I love seeing the excitement in a student's eyes when he or she pulls all of the pieces together and makes a great argument for how to solve a problem."

Easy problems require easy solutions, and this goes against the teaching of Professor Adams; she wants her students to challenge themselves, and learn from their mistakes. "I want every student in my class to have an opportunity to really stretch their limits, which sometimes means getting a wrong answer in a math class for the first time in their lives," she says. In giving them "hard but fun hurdles to climb over," students can tell that "she loves discrete and is amazing at making you understand it and have fun at the same time." She may not make things easy, but she "gives you every opportunity to learn."

Her classes such as Discrete Mathematics and Death Claw(!) vary from day to day; sometimes students do something "normal" like taking a quiz, sometimes they present their ideas on certain problems, and sometimes they work on the open-ended projects that Professor Adams assigns. "I want them to know that math is alive, math research adds to our knowledge every day, and that there are still many unanswered questions in the math world." During her office hours, her goals are the same as in class: She tries to build confidence by asking small questions, celebrating the small successes, and then helping them make bigger leaps. Her hope is that every question elicits multiple answers and can eventually lead to a brainstorm, or a discussion of a harder concept or proof. "These are the hard questions to answer, but the critical questions to ask. I love students who ask good, hard questions because they get the whole class thinking on a deeper level."

Dr. Vittorio Addona, Assistant Professor, Mathematics, Statistics, and Computer Science, Macalester College

Ultimately, good teaching requires careful preparation: of the way concepts will be explained, of ideal examples to present, and for anticipated questions. Vittorio Addona, who teaches statistics at Macalester College, has always aspired "to be a teacher who is clear, concise, and organized, but also one who establishes a jovial environment, where no one should feel intimidated to speak out." "Vittorio is an amazing teacher who is very energetic, even during his 9:00 A.M. courses," says a student.

To him, an ideal classroom atmosphere is one that feels like a conversation between a group of people, so he strives to achieve as much student participation as possible. He gets to know students outside of the classroom and keeps the mood relatively light in the classroom, never shying away from a good (or a bad) joke. "Even if students seem to understand material, there is always room for improvement and it is important to keep examples and exercises current and fresh," he says.

Professor Addona has abandoned almost all notation, "as it serves only to confuse students." Essentially, everything is introduced via an example, which he works through with the students before letting them tackle a variation on their own. A student thanks him: "He made every aspect of statistical analysis crystal-clear; he simplifies things enough so that you understand them without dumbing down the material."

Paul Anderson, Professor of Mathematics, Albion College
"I try to get them to dig math—try it, you'll like it."

That's the straightforward, call-it-like-it-is approach that Albion College mathematics professor Paul Anderson takes when winning over his students to the side of mathematics. "I make fun of the material and by doing so I disarm the material and make it friendly. Math is easy if you can cop the right attitude."

His course load includes Calculus I—"I teach this class because it's usually the students' first math class at Albion, and I want the experience to be a good one, if I may say so"—and Math Stats I and II. The self-proclaimed "designated driver," as far as the classroom dynamic is concerned, is purely a lecturer. "The class is welcome to join in, but I'm definitely the engine driving the whole works," he says. In doing so, he makes mathematics more like a story with meaning and less like "solving a bunch of weird and seemingly unrelated problems." His dry sense of humor makes students want to come to class every day, not to mention the fact that "he's a really nice guy and is willing to help you out as long as you just ask him some questions."

"Math is like a novel if you approach it correctly—there's a beginning, a middle with all sorts of interesting paths to take, and there is an end where we tie it all together and reflect on what we've learned," he says. "The mathematically challenged will be amazed at what they can do!" says a converted student.

Denis Auroux, Professor, Mathematics, University of California—Berkeley

Denis Auroux, who teaches mathematics at the University of California—Berkeley, simply looks to communicate the material as clearly, efficiently, and engagingly as possible.

His understanding of the challenges of large lecture courses such as Multivariable Calculus helps him effectively approach speaking to several hundreds of students at once, and he always maintains the appropriate levels of energy and organization. Multiple students cite him as being otherworldly; "Auroux is GOD! He is the most awesome professor you'll ever have!" says one. He himself admits that he is probably most well-received for being "not scary," which can be a challenge considering the complex material, and students agree that his approachability is key to his appeal: "He's the nicest guy and amazing at explaining one-on-one."

Students say that he succeeds in explaining otherwise difficult material in a manner that is clear and easy to grasp, and that "his tests were very reasonable and accurately reflected the material he taught in class." He makes classes enjoyable "by adding a bit of his own humor," and "he is extremely thorough, never leaving a stone unturned." "I was not enrolled in the course, but I was blown away watching the [MIT Open Courseware] lectures—how clear they are yet how much he packs into them. Not to mention he is the king of speed erasing!"

Arthur Benjamin, Professor of Mathematics, Harvey Mudd College

Harvey Mudd College mathematics professor Arthur Benjamin wants all of his students to appreciate the beauty and power of mathematics. "The goal is not for them to see how smart I am, but how smart they can be," he says.

This is a fittingly noble aspiration for a man that believes that "teaching is a conversation, not a monologue." Lucky students don't just leave the classroom having learned; they leave having been entertained. Ever since high school, Professor Benjamin has worked as a part-time professional magician (he has given hundreds of math talks and thousands of "mathemagics" shows to audiences around the world), and the habits that he acquired entertaining audiences also work well in the classroom. "In every lecture, I strive to include some humor, lots of audience participation, and at least one 'wow, that's cool' moment." "The 'how to win at blackjack' subject the day before fall break was a great idea, and you can't beat his square-six-digit-numbers-in-his-head-faster-than-a-calculator trick or singing pi to 35 digits…I still remember!" says a student.

He is currently teaching a new course, The Mathematics of Games and Puzzles (which is also being developed as a DVD course for The Great Courses lecture series), along with Probability and Statistics. "All my life, I have found the theory and applications of mathematics to be great fun, and I love sharing my passions with others," he says.

Students describe his teaching style as "enthusiastic, interactive, and entertaining"; he memorizes the names and faces of all of his students before the semester even begins, so that he can start calling on them by name from the first day. Students also are impressed by the fluidity of his "performance": "The way he can write on the board, legibly, at a normal speaking pace is bizarrely amazing."

Dr. Curtis Bennett, Professor of Mathematics, Loyola Marymount University

Through the instruction and guidance of Curtis Bennett, a mathematics professor from Loyola Marymount University, students can "become independent in their ability to use mathematics to analyze problems and topics from the world around them."

Now teaching for twenty-four years, he stresses that professors must "listen to what the real questions and problems are for students, not just what they think to tell you." He tries very hard to hear every question and to consider it from the students' points of view, and puts in incredible amounts of time to work with students individually and in groups. "I care deeply about their success," he says. He has a clear passion for the subject that is contagious, and "you will learn a lot and have fun doing so in Bennett's classes."

He loves teaching "just about any math class," from Quantitative Skills for the Modern World to Advanced Linear Algebra, and he particularly loves teaching group theory, where he will teach the students about groups, often applying the subject to solving the Rubik's cube or other puzzles. "Before this math class, I have never understood mathematical concepts or enjoyed any prior math class.

His Quantitative Skills for the Modern World introduced applicable concepts like the tax code, loans, and savings plans formulas," says a student. His teaching style is very student-oriented; whether lecturing or giving out worksheets or running group work, "I always try to look at the material from the perspective of what is the best approach for learning."

Diane Evans, Associate Professor, Mathematics, Rose-Hulman Institute of Technology

Diane Evans is at home teaching pretty much any kind of math you can think up, but these days she primarily teaches statistics and probability. "Almost everybody takes statistics" at Rose-Hulman Institute of Technology and, if they are lucky, they get Evans as their professor. The reason is uncomplicated: she is exceptionally good at getting people to understand mathematical concepts. "I really, really work hard at" teaching, she says. "I really see myself as a teacher more than a researcher." "I encourage collaborative learning, in which students can draw upon their collective knowledge base, and expect students to take an active role in their education. I want students to think mathematically and do more than manipulate algebraic symbols." "I'm pretty approachable and easy to talk to," she adds. "Students feel comfortable asking me questions they maybe wouldn't ask other professors."

Professor Evans honed her craft at a handful of universities before landing at Rose-Hulman—finding out what works and what doesn't. One thing she has found that works is creating handouts full of facts and basic definitions for each class. Once she passes them out, she can get past the terminology quickly and spend valuable class time on "lots of examples." "Class is a conversation" that way, which keeps students involved. Evans also involves her students in all manner of games that illustrate statistical probability. "I stress applying mathematical concepts to real-life situations," she says. Evans will "do something with cards," for example, or "bring a big die and throw it around the room." She also gets a lot of learning mileage out of making bets with her students, risking a soda or something similar. The birthday problem is a good example. This is where Evans offers to wager that two or more students sitting in the class will share the same date of birth. It's probably always a bad idea to indulge in games of chance against a statistics professor, but our advice is to avoid this bet in particular. "The odds are going to be in my favor if there are at least twenty-three students," she explains.

Students say that Evans makes "simple boring things fun and exciting." She is "excited about the material" and "very enthusiastic about teaching," and her enthusiasm rubs off on students. She is also "super helpful." "If making sure that each and every student totally understands concepts before moving on makes her easy," suggests one student, "well, she must be guilty." "I had her for 8:00 A.M. stats and she woke me up every day," adds another student. "She's all over the place and says awkward things that are completely hilarious. If you have the chance to take her for stats, take her! You will not regret it."

John B. Geddes, Professor of Mathematics, Franklin W. Olin College of Engineering

To put it straight, John Geddes, who teaches mathematics at Franklin W. Olin College of Engineering, is "humble, friendly, smart, and interested in the students."

In fifteen years of teaching (he "makes math concepts crystal clear"), he has introduced numerous students to his field, many of whom had never seen the subject before. His flagship course Modeling and Simulation provides an introduction to mathematical modeling and computer simulation of physical systems. In working collaboratively with a broad range of examples, students practice the steps in modeling and analyzing a physical system, learn the role of models in explaining and predicting the behavior of the physical world, and develop skills with the programming and computational tools necessary for simulation. "Students work in a studio environment on increasingly open-ended projects, and learn how to present their results, with an emphasis on visual and oral communication," he says.

"John is one of those professors who can look at you, realize you're not understanding and find another way to make you understand something. I've had him beg me to understand something a few times," says a student. He is so approachable and willing to spend lots of time helping students. What a guy!" says another student.

Mary Glaser, Senior Lecturer, Mathematics, Tufts University

Tufts University mathematics professor Mary Glaser believes that the key to her success is to give her students clear, accessible explanations and to create a comfortable atmosphere for learning. "I respect them and really want them to learn the material," she says.

At the same time, she challenges them and demands the requisite rigor needed to do the work properly. "Success comes to those who give the subject matter the time it needs and who start their assignments early enough so they can process the harder concepts and have time to ask questions if necessary." On her end, she is totally prepared so that "the lesson is more like a dialogue than a lecture," and she keeps her classroom at high energy (students say she has a "great presence" and a "breath of fresh air"). At the same time relaxed and confident. "I enjoy using props in class. I chop a butternut squash with a cleaver in my lesson on volumes of revolution. I use different colored birthday hats to form human graphs for graph coloring," she says. "She's down-to-earth and makes class fly by," says a student.

Her courses include Discrete Mathematics and Calculus II; the former is a "real smorgasbord of fun topics," the latter involves sequences and series—two of the most challenging topics in calculus. "I especially like the counting problems—so easy to describe but often insidiously hard. It's a real thrill to see students learn how to analyze and solve hard problems as well as write great proofs," she says. Students describe her as an "extra-mile kind of teacher, who follows up on students outside of class and is quick to give extensions or mid-class breaks when needed."

John Goulet, PhD, Professor of Mathematics, Worcester Polytechnic Institute

"I want them to succeed and will work with them as individuals to achieve this," says Worcester Polytechnic Institute mathematics John Goulet of his students.

In classes such as Calculus I and II and Linear Algebra, he teaches a range of students that throw up all manner of obstacles to overcome, and strengths to develop further. "The Calculus courses for weak freshmen are the most challenging. They have had poor experiences in math in addition to weak backgrounds, so getting them through calculus is a big challenge in some cases." However, his thirty-five years of teaching experience have taught him how to "build some confidence"; he will introduce a concept and carefully show the techniques and applications involved, and then he'll have the students cooperatively try it out to get them actively involved. In overseeing their work, he will listen to the students and identify key weak points in their understanding or thinking, and will try, when possible, to "relate the material to future courses and their majors as specifically as possible so as to foster credibility."

"I was so awful at math and hated every math class I had before I took Calc with Goulet...his structure and teaching style really helps anyone do well." Says another student, "His class is set up to motivate students and make it very possible to pass, while still ensuring that there's a firm grasp of the curriculum."

Megan M. Granich, M.A.T. Visiting Assistant Professor, Loyola Marymount University

Megan Granich, who teaches mathematics at Loyola Marymount University, looks to the number of comments such as, "when you do it in class it makes sense, but when I get home, I can't do it alone." "My goal is to the bridge the gap between class and home," she says. She thinks her role as a teacher is to "motivate and mentor students and make them want to go further than they ever thought they could," which she accomplishes by using her "knowledge, creativity, patience, love, and enthusiasm for the subject of mathematics."

Her classroom environment is dynamic, and the daily instruction is simple to understand, while at the same time pushing students to their educational limit. Whether it is face to face in office hours, or via e-mail and phone, her students feel comfortable reaching out for help, and she uses that rapport to motivate students to do well in the course. She likes to collaborate with her colleagues, which she finds to be one of the best resources to better understand appropriate and meaningful ways to be a better teacher. "As an example, we collaborated on one of the most effective projects that I have done to date. It was a group project that asked students to film a video showing how related rates can be found in real-life situations. My students found it not only to be fun and creative, but very successful in getting them to fully understand the concept."

In classes such as Math Analysis for Business, she is very organized and runs a tight ship when it comes to the schedule, which is supplied on day one. Her comprehensive course lecture notes are distributed in the first week, and contain all of the definitions, theorems, steps and helpful tips already written out, with blank examples for students to fill in during the lecture. "This allows them to concentrate more on what I am saying and pointing to and less on furiously writing everything down." She tries to keep things light in order "to take away as much of the 'math anxiety' as possible," and group work plays a focal part in her teaching. "A tremendous amount of mathematics can be learned once you are able to explain it to someone else." Students say "she doesn't go off on tangents and is a very structured and precise teacher. She takes her time when explaining a concept."

Elton Graves, Associate Professor, Mathematics, Rose-Hulman Institute of Technology

It's not an easy thing that Elton Graves, does. Day in and day out for the past thirty-four years, this mathematics professor at Rose-Hulman Insititue of Technology has attempted to make his subject "clear, relevant, and interesting" for the students that pass through his classroom. Best of all, he "makes sure that EVERYONE understands whatever he is saying."

In doing so, he emulates his college calculus professor, whose "lectures were so clear that he could teach a rock how to integrate." He gives students precise notes on what he is doing when presenting material on the blackboard or computer, allowing them "to pay attention to the lecture, watch any calculations being made, and to type any computer example on their own computer without having to worry about writing down all the details." "He was so spirited about [fast track calculus] that we couldn't help but get excited with him," says a former student.

He regularly teaches calculus, fast track calculus, differential equations, boundary value problems, and applied linear algebra, using computer animation, real-world applications (i.e., electrical circuits, GPS systems, global warming), and physical demonstrations to reinforce mathematical points. "An example would be to take a calculus class outside on the side of a hill and demonstrate the concepts of the gradient vector, direction derivatives, and the method of Lagrange Multipliers. These mathematical concepts are demonstrated by having the students walk around on the hill. After the students understand the physical concept, we go back into the classroom and show how the mathematics ties in with what they have just experienced outside," he says.

Jon Jacobsen, Associate Professor of Mathematics and Associate Dean for Academic Affairs, Harvey Mudd College
The directives of mathematics professor Jon "Jakes" Jacobsen, who teaches at Harvey Mudd College, are clear. "Excite them about the power and beauty of mathematics. Challenge them to go beyond their current comfort zone and reexamine their notion of what it means to 'know' something. Help them learn how to learn, believe in themselves, and defend their ideas."

In gratitude and emulation of many of his own great professors, he similarly tries to encourage every student—who makes the effort—to continue to work hard and develop his or her mathematical abilities. Students like his enthusiasm and clear intuitive approach for presenting mathematical concepts, as well as the fact that he "has a little fun in class." He sees math as a language and believes that anyone can learn this (or any) new language with enough time, practice, and conversations. "Most people who 'do not like' mathematics will pinpoint some teacher along the way that really turned them off. Similarly, most people that love mathematics can pinpoint some teacher along the way that really encouraged them and/or turned them on to mathematics. I want to be one of the latter teachers," he says. It's working: "I was all set to hate [the class], and Jakes made me see the light," says a student.

His courses include Differential Equations, Complex Analysis, and an Advanced Calculus course that is designed for students who have already had at least a year of calculus, changing their perspective from "how" to "why." "That is, they already know 'how' to do many of the common calculations but they often lack an understanding of 'why' and the goal of this course is to focus on the 'why' and help them develop an even deeper appreciation for the subject and how it all fits together." He views each class as an "improvisational jam session." "The score is there; there are rules and certain themes will emerge, but in a given class the dynamic can drift and sway wherever the rhythm takes it."

Students say that homework problems are interesting and often challenging. But they also appreciate that Jakes is approachable and "very friendly and helpful in office hours!"

Martin Jones, Professor, Mathematics, College of Charleston

College of Charleston mathematics professor Martin Jones long ago learned that academic subject matter and our common humanity cannot really be separated, nor should they be. "These things must reinforce each other for learning to take place," he says.

He is realistic about students' perceptions of math (even if they are only superficial), and he uses this awareness in his teaching approach, which is "very animated, high-energy, but quite informal and relaxed." "I think that they relate to the fact that I am trying to share some interesting ideas with them while understanding that they may not be as excited about the material as I am," he says. "Even at 8 A.M. you won't fall asleep and you will learn easily. He explains things in an elementary way so you will ace the tests. He is always available for extra help," says a student. His courses center on probability and statistics, and he is currently teaching an interdisciplinary course with biology. "I find the material incredibly fascinating, both mathematically and for what it can tell us about the world around us."

Students say he "really wants his students to be able to apply statistics outside of class. He teaches it to apply it."

Panayotis Kevrekidis, Professor, Mathematics & Statistics, University of Massachusetts—Amherst

Panayotis Kevrekidis, who teaches mathematics and statistics at the University of Massachusetts—Amherst, is just looking to make his students comfortable. No matter how much effort needs to be expended, he will ensure that his students are interested in and engaged with the material. He is a continuous presence in and out of the classroom; he listens to his students (especially in office hours) so he can understand what they know and build on it; and he brings the highest possible energy in the classroom, day in and day out. "He loves teaching and math. He learns everyone's names. I'm looking at what other classes he teaches just to take another one of his classes," says a student.

He has most recently taught Introduction to Partial Differential Equations but happily teaches across the field of mathematics: "One has to be equally excited for any single course one teaches, even Calculus! If I am not excited about it, why should the students be?" Classes are very hands-on; he starts each class by getting there early and posting both a "review board" on what they did in the previous class, and a "what to remember" board from what they are going to do in the upcoming class. "I often try to complement the latter with computer notes or graphics or some inclusion of some application prepared by me or available on the Web. I try to involve the students in this segment by asking questions, having them ask questions, etc." Once the new topic has been completed, he "interrupts" the class for a "practice problems" session, where the students try to solve (pre-prepared) problems on the new material on their own, with Professor Kevrekidis hopping around to assist them to digest the details. This "dynamic" guy also "makes everyone understand math, and actually shows that he is invested in each student's success."

Stephen Pennell, Professor of Mathematical Sciences, University of Massachusetts—Lowell

"To learn math you have to do math," says Stephen Pennell, who teaches mathematical sciences at the University of Massachusetts—Lowell. His straight-forward pedagogical approach is as old as the science itself: convey the main ideas, give examples, and answer the questions. "Dr. Pennell made some pretty complicated material very easy to understand. One of the most considerate professors I have ever encountered. I don't think I could have passed this class with another professor," says a student.

Outside of the classroom, students praise Dr. Pennell's availability, his "crystal" explanations, and his ability to make difficult material seem easy. When working with individual students, he will "try to understand how s/he is thinking about the topic at hand, correct any misconceptions, and ask leading questions to help the student figure things out for himself or herself." He has been teaching such complex fodder as Introductory Differential Equations and Engineering Differential Equations for more than twenty-nine years, using a combination of lecture and discussion; in any given class, he spends at least a third of it going over the homework, and the rest introducing new material. "I try to convey ideas by means of specific examples whenever possible," he says.

High praise comes from one student: "Literally the greatest teacher I have had. Believe me, he should be teaching a course on how to teach to all the other professors."

Laurie Poe, Senior Lecturer, Mathematics, Santa Clara University

Laurie Poe, who teaches mathematics at Santa Clara University, works to get students past the idea that math is all about formulas to memorize and helps them see "how cool it is and how logically it all fits together."

"Math is your friend," according to this teacher of twenty-two years, who places the strongest importance on explaining the material as clearly as possible. "Their learning is my number one concern," she says. She's "very old school" in her approach to teaching, using only chalk and a chalkboard to convey information to students. If the energy in the room is low, though, she will share humorous stories to keep the students' attention. She "provides students with a plethora of examples, goes over handouts she puts together herself in class, and makes herself available for questions all the time and especially before midterms."

Her recent courses have included Calculus I & II, Business Calculus, Statistics, and Finite Mathematics. She finds it fun to get students to rise to the challenge of the material and surprise themselves with how well they can do. Her style is to teach the material as precisely and clearly as possible, following any explanations with examples and guided practice. To expand topics in class, she usually draws on personal experience. "When teaching statistics, for example, it is super easy to reference a story from the evening news or some horrible use of statistics in advertising," she says. She grades her own homework, which students find "really helpful because she makes sure you see exactly what you're doing wrong so you can fix it for the tests."

Dan Saracino, Neil R. Grabois Professor of Mathematics, Colgate University

When Dan Saracino, who teaches mathematics at Colgate University, can communicate the fundamental ideas of his field as clearly as possible, then he has achieved his basic objective; but what he ultimately wants to do is "to help my students to see the beauty of mathematics and to experience the exhilaration of mathematical discovery." "He teaches you how to think about math problems, not just how to do them," says a student.

He tries "to be a good example of someone who loves the subject" and upholds the standards of the discipline. Students say that it is obvious that he loves teaching, and he also loves "the rigor and precision of the subject." Former students say that "he went over problems very clearly and never made assumptions about what we know, instead going through all the steps," and "he was also a great mentor on life in general."

He is now in his fortieth year of teaching, and he has published a couple of books and over three dozen research articles. His classes include Mathematical Logic, Number Theory and Mathematical Reasoning, and Abstract Algebra I and II, which he loves "because the proofs in these classes are so pretty." He teaches in an informal lecture style, with plenty of room for interaction, and never uses notes (as a student puts is, "he teaches the class directly from his own head"), because "I want to talk with my students, not read to them." He often tries to give more than one way of establishing a result, because "it frequently happens that there's one way that's straightforward and perfectly fine, but not exciting, and then there's another way that takes your breath away, by its cleverness."

Sergei Shabanov, Associate Professor, Mathematics, University of Florida

University of Florida mathematics professor Sergei Shabanov tries to get his students "to reach a crystal clarity of concepts versus a mindless use of formulas."

He is "extremely respectful and fair," and does everything possible to make students comfortable asking questions, always stressing a general concept when answering students, and students say that "his knowledge of the material is astounding, and he is extremely effective at imparting this knowledge to students."

In classes such as Calculus, Multivariable Calculus, Differential Equations, and Mathematical Physics (graduate level), Professor Shabanov very much appreciates the applications of mathematics to real-life phenomena, and he always emphasizes this with examples. While discussing possible ways to solve problems, a mathematical (abstract) problem is formulated to model these real-life examples, and then theorems needed to solve the abstract problem are formulated. "I used to conduct the discussion by asking students questions to motivate them to think about ways to solve the real-life problem, and how it can be converted into a mathematical problem," he says. After he explains the concept he introduces a "trick" question (a question would have a simple answer if the concept is understood, whereas a use of formulas would make it difficult, if not impossible, to answer it), which is used to gauge the level of understanding of the audience. "Understand the proofs he gives, and everything else will be easy," advises a student. Professor Shabanov recieved a Teacher of the Year Award from the University of Florida in 2009 and a similar award from the College of Liberal Arts and Sciences (University of Florida). His research achievements have been recognized by V.A. Fock Prize in Mathematical Physics, awarded by the Russian Academy of Sciences in 2010.

Yosi Shibberu, Associate Professor, Mathematics, Rose-Hulman Institue of Technology

Yosi Shibberu, who teaches mathematics at Rose-Hulman Institute of Technology, inspires students to set ambitious goals and work hard to achieve them. "Shibberu is the nicest and considerate professor I have had at Rose so far! No exaggeration! He makes learning come naturally too," says a student.

Despite the number-driven nature of his field, his approach to teaching is more humanities-inspired: "Teaching is really storytelling. Like a story, a course should be consistent, have interesting characters, have mystery and suspense, be inspiring and have a satisfying conclusion." He tries to maintain an informal atmosphere in class to encourage as much class participation as possible, believes in active learning, and keeps his lectures as short as possible in favor of having students work during class on carefully prepared problems which illustrate key concepts. Summers are spent doing research on the application of mathematics to problems in biology and chemistry, often with undergraduates when funding is available. "The amazing utility of mathematics is often underappreciated," he says.

He is currently teaching Differential Equations, as well as Probability Theory, and he uses problem-based learning to reach students. "Problem: How much runway does an airplane need to take off? I ask students to solve this problem several times during the first week of differential equations, each time using fewer and more realistic assumptions." "He forces understanding, and is simply one of the best teachers at RHIT," says a student.

Erl Sorensen, Senior Lecturer, Mathematical Sciences, Bentley University
For more than thirty-five years, Bentley University mathematical sciences professor Erl Sorensen has been facilitating students' learning, understanding, and love for mathematics and statistics.

His classroom is populated with real data and applications that students can relate to, creating a casual, fun, and nonthreatening environment in which inquisitive students can, well, inquire. His classes Business Statistics and Discrete Probability often even help to transform students' opinions of the larger field of math itself. "It is really fun seeing students enter the Business Statistics class with a negative bias toward the course, then end the course admitting how much they enjoy the subject and related activities once they understand it," he says.

He likes to introduce a topic with a simple but thought-provoking example; in order to introduce a general probability unit, he will challenge the students to estimate the probability that at least two people in the class have the same birthday. "This brings lively discussion and even a betting mood before we determine if there is a match, and what the real probabilities are." "This guy is the man! If you do not get a good grade in his class, shame on you; make sure to go to each class and do all the work," says a student. There is no final for students that do well on the quizzes, projects and homework, and "he can help you with anything" that you're having problems with, which is unsurprising for this "funny/adorable grandfather figure [that] will do anything he can to help you out. TAKE HIM and you will fall in love with this man!"

Zvezdelina Stankova, Professor of Mathematics, Mills College, and Visiting Professor of Mathematics, University of California—Berkeley
If Zvezdelina Stankova, who teaches mathematics at Mills College and the University of California—Berkeley, can make her students as passionate about math as she is, then something's gone well. "I wish to give everything I have to teach them what I know about the subject," she says.

She is extremely organized and disciplined, and prepares her lectures and class structure thoroughly, which shows in class and in office hours. "She expects the best from each student, pushing them to reach their potential and expand their skills, enabling them "to solve mathematical problems with self-confidence and maturity."

In making students "walk the extra mile" in her various algebra and calculus courses, this "wonderful professor with a sparkling personality" uses a problem-solving approach. Whenever the topic and class set-up allow it, she starts with a problem that intrigues students into figuring out how to solve it. "She makes class fun," says a student. After she has motivated them, she'll introduce the necessary theory and work the students through problems with an increasing level of difficulty/depth until the class reaches the solution to the initial problem. In the end, "the students are mesmerized by the applicability of the learnt mathematical theory to a problem they would have loved to do." Students say that "you can practically copy down her notes from the board, word for word and number-for-number because her explanations and examples are so effective."

Martin Sternstein, Professor of Mathematics, Ithaca College
If all goes according to plan, students that leave the classroom of Ithaca College mathematics professor Martin Sternstein are hungry for more.

His main concern is that "each and every student masters the material, feels challenged to the utmost of his/her abilities and beyond, and is drawn in to share in my enthusiasm for the subject." With forty-one years of teaching (all at Ithaca College), he almost never lectures; "My classrooms are interactive with my working with and helping students to come up with insightful questions and answers, to see relationships and make connections, and to apply their results and ideas."

His work in mentoring inner city high school teachers has instilled in him a strong interest in national educational and social issues concerning equal access to math education for all, and he is constantly working hard to make some contribution in this critical area. This "infinitely patient and kind" professor has taught all undergraduate-level math classes, and sincerely tries to make every one of these classes "a worthy intellectual endeavor for every student." He especially enjoys teaching Math in Non-Western Societies, where students view the development of mathematics not only from throughout history, but especially from across cultures. One student gives him the highest praise: "I can't say enough about this man. He is one of the best teachers I have ever had."

"Ask him about all the places he's taught at, he's amazing! He even wrote an AP stats book," says a student. "Marty is a mentor of multitudes." Other students mention that "Marty is my role model. He has never-ending patience, and is ALWAYS willing to help students—best math prof at IC!" "So patient, so generous with his time and talent, and he loves what he does and cares about his students."

Allen Strand, Professor, Mathematics, Colgate University

Students are encouraged to think critically and carefully in the classes of Allen Strand, a mathematics professor at Colgate University, and to pay very close attention to the presentation in a word problem. They also learn not to hesitate when presenting a solution to a problem, as "one may learn more if an (honest) incorrect attempt at a solution is given by the student."

"As a teacher of mathematics one should try to 'crawl inside the skull of each student' to carefully examine the technique being employed to solve a problem and to gently advise the student where an error has occurred," he says. He sincerely wants each student to succeed and is willing to meet to assist students at any reasonable time. Students say this "funny, engaging, patient, [and] helpful" professor "has office hours at least three days a week, and is more than happy to explain whatever you want during those hours."

Even after forty-eight years of teaching, he believes that "the precision in mathematics is intriguing, and it is a challenge to pass this precision on to the students." His courses (which include Elementary Calculus and Linear Algebra) usually meet one more class day per week than similar courses taught in the department, and he teaches a special section of Calculus I to students who have been identified, via a readiness test, to need additional support in pre-calculus mathematics. Presentations are very carefully prepared and well presented, and he takes a casual lecture approach with open access to student questions throughout each session. The one-on-one approach during office hours and evening problems sessions are also "very important as a learning tool for the students who take advantage of my presence."

Students agree: "Dr. Strand is perhaps the most thorough, clear, helpful math professor in the department." "I would highly recommend Strand to anyone, whether a math major or someone who's taking Calculus just for distributions," says another.

Gary Towsley, Distinguished Teaching Professor, Mathematics, State University of New York at Geneseo

Gary Towsley, a SUNY Geneseo professor of mathematics, wants his students "to be able to see where what they are learning fits into larger contexts." "Mathematics fits into everything else they are learning—as far away as poetry and painting," he says.

Through his education and in his team teaching with other faculty—he is now in his thirty-eighth year at Geneseo—he has learned the power of responding to student questions with other questions. "While my questions may redirect their thoughts or open new channels for them, I am not taking away from them the joy of resolving something by themselves." He accounts for the varying levels of skill and understanding in his classes by trying to challenge those who already understand the material, while simultaneously being patient and supportive with those that feel they are lost. In a true classical approach, homework assignments are not only given, but collected and graded. "Opening the textbook every day is a good habit. Learning mathematics becomes a continuous rather than an episodic process."

Professor Towsley often relies on narrative math to get his points across. "I want to tell a story about calculus or algebra or geometry. Of course, while I am doing this, I am constantly asking questions so that the students can participate in the story and clear up misunderstandings." His current course load includes History of Mathematics, Real Analysis (the toughest course required in the math major), and Poetry and Cosmology in the Middle Ages, which he co-teaches with a professor in the English department. "We read Ancient and Medieval Science and Mathematics texts and then apply this to a reading of Dante's *Paradiso*, the third Canticle of his comedy, the part that is least often read," he says.

This "nice," "kind-hearted" professor is "like Santa Claus...but better!" according to students. "His notes are very straightforward and he is always willing to help you outside of class," says one.

Steve C. Wang, Associate Professor of Statistics, Swarthmore College

Students are often intimidated when they begin learning statistics. Thus, statistics professor Steve C. Wang of Swarthmore College always strives to impart an intuitive understanding of difficult concepts and help students see the common sense behind the formulas. "I always encourage students to focus not just on finding the answer, but also on what that answer means, and what further questions may be inspired. Numbers can tell a story, and I try to show students how statistical methods can be used as important tool in discovering those stories."

In classes such as Introduction to Statistics and Quantitative Paleontology, he strives to inspire students to see statistics as a process of reasoning and thinking critically about data, and he challenges students not simply to calculate answers but also continually ask questions. "How were the data collected? What potential sources of bias exist? My goal is for my students to be as comfortable critiquing a quantitative argument as they would an argument by Plato, Kant, or Foucault," he says. Students find his lectures "superb" and say that "he has mastery both of the material and the art of teaching."

In the classroom, he shows how statistical principles are used to answer a wide variety of real-life questions, from discovering why the dinosaurs went extinct to which country has the world's happiest people, to testing whether low-carb diets work. Students are required to do final projects in which they apply statistics to a topic they themselves choose; for instance, a group of students on the lacrosse team conducted an experiment on the best angle for taking shots on goal, in which they actually went out on a lacrosse field and made hundreds of shots, and then analyzed the results. "I want my students to have fun and create a piece of work that they will be proud of and that is meaningful to their lives," he says.

"I'm ready to join the ever-growing Steve Wang fan club: He makes statistics really fun by putting the concepts into interesting and funny real-world contexts (often with short and entertaining video clips)," says a student.

Paul Warne, Professor, Mathematics, James Madison University

Paul Warne, a professor of mathematics at James Madison University, believes that helping students grow both personally and academically requires a delicate balance between challenging them beyond what they believe they are capable of and providing a safety net for their self-esteem.

His goal is "to force them to recognize that success requires them to leave their comfort zone and push beyond perceived boundaries so that they can learn to rely on their own analytical skills and creative ideas." He strives to keep his classroom alive and believes that active student participation and interaction is crucial; he also makes "a concerted effort to keep time spent in the classroom fresh, incorporating what I view as a kaleidoscope of pedagogy.'"

In each class, he deliberately moves from the front of the room out into the desks, moving among his students, having them turn and spin, letting them know that there is no separate "teacher space" or "student space" in the classroom. "I have found that physical communication can be as important as verbal communication and rely on my background in theater to help me with this type of communication." He succeeds in creating an environment that is "disarming, inviting, and comfortable, one which encourages open and honest interaction between all involved." Vanity is not an issue; he is more than willing to trade letting himself look silly for getting students to be willing to open up and be honest, even if it means exposing fragility. "My worst enemy in the classroom (next to a lack of prerequisite skills) is boredom."

One technique that has worked exceptionally well in the classroom is for Professor Warne to incorporate brief stories from his life into lectures (these stories usually make the students laugh, and appear on the surface to be unrelated to the course). "But right after they finish smiling is when I hit them with the moral of the story, which is a mathematical moral that relates directly to the topic I am trying to teach. This I have found gives students a non-mathematical visual image on which they can hang the topic and thus better retain the ideas. When I revisit the topic one of the first things I try to do is refer back to that picture." "He'll wear desks, stand on tables, and yell at people outside, whatever it takes to make you understand the material."

Stephen R. Wassell, Professor of Mathematical Sciences, Sweet Briar College

Sweet Briar College mathematics professor Steve Wassell's overall professional aim is "to explore and extol the mathematics of beauty and the beauty of mathematics."

Much of Professor Wassell's research is done on the math/art interface (especially the relationships between architecture and mathematics), and he tries to give examples of the beauty of mathematics whenever possible so that his students might develop more appreciation for math. "I have always loved math, and I feel that I have a pretty good gift for helping others to see the beauty of this often underappreciated subject," he says. Students can indeed tell that he cares not just about trying to convey topics as clearly (and as entertainingly) as possible, but about them as individuals. "Before this class I absolutely hated math and found it barely comprehensible. Wassell is a wonderful teacher who has made the idea of taking more math not only tolerable but actually interesting," says one.

He works hard to help his students, "even holding homework help sessions at 10:00 P.M." His courses include all levels of calculus, as well as various classes designed for those who will go on to teach math at some level themselves. While it is admittedly hard to avoid the "lecture" style in math, he tries to keep as lively and interactive an atmosphere as possible. And if a student's question or comment can lead to an interesting side discussion, "I'll run with it. I'm not averse to going off on tangents on my own as well, especially if I can demonstrate the beauty of mathematics while doing so." Students agree that "his classes are fun... you will always come out of there with some kinda great quote."

Susan M. Young, Senior Lecturer, Mathematics, The University of Akron

Susan Young is a mathematics professor at The University of Akron who primarily teaches calculus. "Her classes fill up fast" because, well, she's certainly "the best calc teacher on the campus" and possibly "the best math teacher ever." What's her secret? In a word: patience. "My students tell me all the time that I am very patient with them," Young says. "Students feel free to ask questions. They feel at ease." Her methods are also very straightforward. "I teach the old-fashioned way—chalkboard—with the occasional use of technology," she explains. "I introduce the topic and then do many examples of increasing difficulty to reinforce the topic. During this presentation I always ask students for questions so that each student has a thorough understanding of the topic. I also give them insight as to how they will use the concept in future courses." Young also reflects on her efforts at the end of each semester in order to make herself a better teacher. "I change my courses every semester," she says. "I find things that work and discard things that don't work."

Students laud Young to the stratosphere. She is an "amazing teacher" who is "very helpful" outside of class. "She is articulate, explains concepts well, and her teaching style engages the student as she frequently poses questions and solicits for students' responses and feedback as she gives a lecture." Of course, Young's classes aren't easy. It is calculus, after all. There are "lots of quizzes and homework." Tests can be "a little rough." "The content is actually over stuff she taught," though, and students insist that there is really no excuse if you don't master the material. "I want all my students to succeed," Young says. And a very high number do succeed, in what are high-casualty courses at most schools. "I highly recommend taking her for any math class, as she is very clear in explaining the subject matter and has no problem fielding questions," advises one student. Even—perhaps especially—students who describe themselves as "terrible at any form of math" love Professor Young. "I had to drop this class last time I took it with another prof because I was failing so bad," relates one grateful student. "This time around she explained everything so perfectly clearly it was like I barely had to try."

Joseph Yukich, Professor, Mathematics, Lehigh University

Lehigh University mathematics professor Joseph Yukich's enthusiasm can't help but draw students in. Although his courses are not easy, one student explains that "he makes the class fun and knows exactly how to teach math the right way so the students understand it."

This vigor, together with well-crafted lectures, makes a perfect classroom environment for students in classes such as multivariate calculus. To start, Professor Yukich learns the names of almost all the students in his large lecture hall classes. He favors chalkboard presentations, shies away from PowerPoint, and, to facilitate mastery of lecture material, assigns daily homework.

All of Professor Yukich's students report it is evident that "he loves what he does and shows that as he teaches." He lectures on each topic with a freshness that makes it seem as though he is speaking for the first time on the subject. "When I teach a topic in calculus I strive to make it rigorous and relevant, I try to put it in proper historical perspective (telling a story if necessary), and I give plenty of examples illustrating the main concepts." Students say that "his love for calculus is contagious," and that "his enthusiasm inspires and reinforces the same spirit in all of us."

This "very funny and sociable" man very much wants his students to succeed, and makes a point of regularly reviewing difficult concepts and hard homework problems, explaining mathematics rigorously and systematically. "His love of teaching (and calculus) is one of a kind. I absolutely love his class," marvels one student. "He is crystal clear in lectures and his stories are priceless," adds another. For his part, Professor Yukich recognizes the contributions of his students, remarking that "Lehigh students bring out the best in me and it is a real privilege to teach and interact with them in the classroom."

Nizar Zaarour, Professor of Mathematics, Northeastern University

"You have to like what you're doing to be good at it," says Nizar Zaarour, and what he likes—and what students say he is really good at—is probability and statistics. Zaarour is a math professor at Northeastern University, a large private school in Boston. While he also teaches calculus, it seems fair to say that probability and statistics is his true love. "Statistics is everywhere," he says, and he takes great pleasure in telling students all about it. His goal, he says, is "to not only get students to understand the material, but also to get them motivated to see the usefulness of it." The fact that students report that they can relate to Zaarour is "the biggest compliment" he says he receives.

Students say they "absolutely love" Professor Zaarour. He is the embodiment of "how teachers should be" and "what you hope for when you get to college." Zaarour "doesn't bog you down with things you don't need, but makes sure you learn everything you need to" "and won't bore you with other nonsense." "He teaches really well," says one student. "You don't even have to read the textbook any more after you get home." "You also get to use cheat sheets on every test so there is no excuse for doing bad in the class." He is "clear, understanding, extremely intelligent, extremely helpful, and extremely fun." On top of all that, "he is a really nice guy" to boot. "Zaarour is by far the best math teacher I've ever had," swears one student. He "always explains everything and never just leaves you hanging." "Thank God I waited until this semester to take stats," agrees one grateful student. "I never thought anyone can make this class interesting, but I was wrong." "You have to take him if you want to learn and do well."

Music

Rosalind Hall, Associate Professor, Music, Brigham Young University

Musical excellence comes at a high price, and those who achieve it understand this and are willing to pay the price. This is the challenge laid down by Brigham Young University music professor Rosalind Hall.

She teaches Choral Literature (a graduate-evel survey of choral repertoire) and Choral Conducting. She also conducts the BYU Concert Choir and Men's

Chorus. She is "passionately and profoundly interested" in in both her students and her subject matter. "My goals are to lead my students to excellence, to help them both appreciate its value and understand its price, and to motivate them to want to achieve it," she says. Professor Hall believes that the positive experience students have in her classroom can be mostly attributed to the music alone; she is simply the facilitator who leads them to that experience as best as she can. "When a course is over, students may not remember the details of what they have been taught. But what they do remember is the way in which their encounter with the subject matter has changed them," she says. "If you ever get the chance to take choir from her do it. You will become a better singer and a better person," says a student.

She aims to teach students to know what real musicians know and to do what real musicians do, and to do it as excellently as possible. "This is all I can do, but I trust that music itself will do the rest." "Professor Hall is one of my favorite people in the world. Rehearsals are so productive and spiritual. She will never settle for anything but your best," says a student.

Neuroscience

Kevin T. Strang, Department of Neuroscience/Physiology, University of Wisconsin—Madison

Ask Kevin Strang, professor of neuroscience and physiology at the University of Wisconsin—Madison how he sees his role as a teacher, and he'll invoke the words of Maya Angelou: "I've learned that people will forget what you said, people will forget what you did, but people will never forget how you made them feel."

He cares about his students and respects them as people, but his designation as a Best Professor comes because "I can't contain my enthusiasm for the most interesting subject on earth to teach and study—human physiology!" This eagerness is contagious, and "he keeps class fun and upbeat."

His main class, Human Physiology, is a large undergraduate class for allied health majors, who say that "you will only come out of the class better prepared for a career in the health care field." Professor Strang is big on helping students to understand how our bodies are designed and how they work, which he says "has a fundamental importance to me that approaches the spiritual questions of who we are and where we came from."

His expertise is deep—he literally wrote the book on the subject (as a co-author of the *Vander's Human Physiology* textbook). But he's quick to explain where else his inspiration comes from. "I own and operate a human body every day!" He tries to engage students by stimulating multiple senses, by showing them how information relates to their lives, by making them feel a sense of community in the class, and by making them laugh. "For example, when teaching about lung function I might use a YouTube animation that shows the anatomical structures and how they function, then have students draw a frame-by-frame cartoon of what happens in a patient with a stab wound to the chest, then ask them to hold their breath and see how their pulse rate changes, then have them discuss with each other what happens when a person tries to breathe at high altitude, and finish with a *Far Side* cartoon showing the last cilium in a smoker's lung playing solitaire."

Nicole Y. Weekes, Professor, Neuroscience, Pomona College

Students that take classes with Nicole Weekes, professor of neuroscience at California's Pomona College, join her on a path. "I want them to feel excited about the adventure they have started themselves on. AND I want them to know that it is lifelong," she says.

She makes her humanity and fallibility known to students, as she wants them to feel like they can ask her anything, so that she can share with them what she knows, or they can find the answer together. "There is nothing more contagious than passion," she says. "I think they know how hard I work to be good at my job, and what this says about my respect for them as well as for my chosen career." One student is definitely aware: "She's absolutely hysterical! What other profs tell jokes and do impressions? Plus there is that other little fact: She seems to know EVERYTHING."

She teaches Intro to Psychology, Human Brain, and a seminar in Biological Basis of Psychopathology, which she loves because she gets to take a truly "liberal arts" approach to psychopathology, investigating scientific, legal, philosophical and first-person narrative approaches. "I teach all my courses from the perspective that all psychological functioning reduces to neurological functioning. What could be cooler than that?" Her classes are raucous, high energy, and high impact—"I have been known to do aerobics and yoga in class," she says. "I had my first morning class with her...it was like an early morning news show," says one student.

Philosophy

Erik Anderson, Professor of Philosophy, Drew University

Students must arrive at their own answers when they attend a class given by Drew University philosophy professor Erik Anderson.

He emphasizes the development of logic by way of encouraging students to use their own rational processes and their own common sense, as "intuition is a source of evidence—a fundamental source." His courses, which include Introduction to Philosophy, Introduction to Logic, The Philosophy of Mind, and a seminar on Personal Identity, all concern "the most important and fundamental issues that now face us, have faced us, and will face us in the future." "I took his logic class. Hardest class I have taken in my life, but he also was the most helpful professor I have ever had, so it worked out," says a student. He particularly enjoys The Philosophy of Mind, which is exciting "because it has implications for and draws upon knowledge of personal identity, causation, free will, and the meaning of life."

His classes are all interactive; he doesn't really like to lecture, preferring instead to guide students in engaging with one another. "I like to have students consider a philosophical problem or question, such as the question of whether the existence of an omnibenevolent God is consistent with the existence of evil, in the context of a small group discussion. I then like to have the groups come together for a larger discussion in which we attempt to come to some kind of resolution of the problem or answer to the question." This requires considerable flexibility and patience on the part of everyone, "and that is the beauty of it."

Students praise him for his enormously accessible and sweet nature. Says one, "I practically lived in his office and he was always very helpful, understanding, and willing to lend an ear.

Scott Campbell, Associate Professor, Philosophy Department, Nazareth College

The primary goal of Scott Campbell, who teaches philosophy at Nazareth College, is to show students how they can read challenging texts and think for themselves about complex philosophical concepts. "Basically, I believe in truth, beauty, and goodness. Of course, these are all complicated matters, but as a culture, we should not give up the pursuit of truth, the appreciation of beauty, and the attempt to live a good life simply because the concepts involved in doing so are complex and difficult," he says.

He is a true devotee to the idea of a liberal arts education, believing it essential to balance one's professional training with liberal learning in the arts and sciences. "Liberal arts are not practiced for the sake of utility or specifically for the sake of getting a job. The liberal arts are exercised strictly for the sake of knowledge, itself. Learning is valuable in itself and for its own sake," he says.

In classes such as Logic & Inquiry, Ethics, and Contemporary Philosophy, he tries to meet students where they are, talking to them about how philosophical concepts relate to their own lives. "In this way, I can introduce them, gradually, to higher order thinking about philosophical ideas." His "very dry sense of humor...makes it so class is never boring," and he uses the Socratic method, asking his students lots of questions, then soliciting discussion and encouraging them to ask questions and to challenge what he is saying. "He makes the material easy to understand, because it definitely is not easy to understand on your own. You have to write a lot, and follow a lot of his rules, but he is more than willing to help outline and throw out ideas," says a student.

Richard Capobianco, Professor and Chair, Philosophy, Stonehill College
Richard Capobianco, a philosophy professor at Stonehill College, helps students to recognize and own their freedom to think for themselves. "I deeply respect each student's intelligence and desire to know," he says. But there's another key to good teaching: "If you are engaged by what you are saying, students will be, too," he adds.

He has been teaching for over twenty-five years, and his classes include Ethics and the Arts; Aesthetics; Philosophy of Architecture; Existentialism; Hermeneutics; and Heidegger and His Influence. "Philosophy asks the kinds of questions that have always interested me the most," he says. He is a longstanding member of several philosophical associations, and has published numerous articles and reviews, as well as a recently published book: *Engaging Heidegger*. His classroom is lively and engaged, which is understandable in that he is "searching along with students for understanding." Oftentimes, a current event, an everyday situation, or a work of art helps to open up a philosophical problem for discussion. "[We had] amazing discussions that got me really interested in philosophy, and I talked with him a lot outside of class too," says a student.

Students say that "the most thought-provoking classes I've taken here have been with Capo. The ideas can be difficult but fascinating and class discussions are awesome, plus he's a great guy and really helpful with everything." "He's a great man who loves his students and the subject."

Kevin Corcoran, Professor of Philosophy, Calvin College
Kevin Corcoran is a philosophy professor at Calvin College, a smaller liberal arts school in Grand Rapids, Michigan with a distinctively Christian bent. He teaches introduction to philosophy, metaphysics, and philosophy of mind. "Some of my colleagues do not desire to teach intro," he says. "I love teaching it." His strategy, he says, is to teach the course as though it is the last philosophy course his students will take, "instead of teaching it assuming it is the first philosophy course they will ever take."

Corcoran describes himself as an "open and seeking" person. "I don't think I'm really all that different from my students." "I wasn't groomed for what I do," he elaborates. "I'm from a blue-collar, Irish Catholic family in Baltimore.

A hundred years from now, no one is going to know who Kevin Corcoran is, but the people we read and discuss will be around long after we're gone." One very cool thing Corcoran is famous for is that he provides "music to start class." "When I first started teaching, I was given all 8:00 A.M. classes," he explains. "Walking into them was like walking into a morgue and it drove me nuts to walk into a classroom that was so deathly quiet. I started putting on music before the students came in and the change was honest-to-God amazing." It's a practice he's maintained ever since. Regarding his choices as a deejay, Corcoran says he finds a lot of music thanks to tips from students. "A lot of my students have great taste in music," he says.

"Calvin is a Christian college and there are certain expectations students have" but, at the same time, "as a major, philosophy attracts more skeptical students." Corcoran is adept at making students think regardless of their religious beliefs. "He loves to get the class riled up." "He is a wonderful philosophy prof and really knows his stuff," enthuses one student. He is "hilarious, clear, and helpful." "He is very good at making philosophy easy to understand and enjoyable." "He really puts the subject into simple terms" and is "very willing to help" outside the classroom, "He loves what he teaches and is passionate about his students." "I was never bored for one moment," testifies one student. "Best. Class. Ever."

David Denby, Senior Lecturer, Tufts University

David Denby is a philosophy professor at Tufts University in the suburbs of Boston. Given his field, it shouldn't come as much of a surprise to learn that he's "a little eccentric." At the same time, he's very demanding and his unique teaching style is incredibly thoughtful. "I try to strip down the material, so nearly all the class time is spent explaining theories or, more usually, discussing arguments. Rather than working through the readings, I simply extract arguments from them, put them on the board, explain them, and invite the students to attack them, while I play defense," he says. "I spend about 75 percent of the time discussing arguments. And I insist on a certain procedure every time. First, the argument must be stated in full with no missing premises; second, every technical term must be defined and a full rationale must be stated for every premise;

finally, the argument must be evaluated for its logical structure, and the truth of its premises and some objection must be discussed. I allow no exceptions to this procedure. It sounds pedantic at first, but quickly—by about the third week of semester—becomes second nature to the students."

The result of Denby's method is that students "are actively involved. They have to use their imaginations to dream up ways to attack, and they get to gang up on me and catch me out. They enjoy that. And they remember the discussions and learn how to think philosophically." "Helping students learn to think critically is a specific aim—perhaps the most important one—of all in lower-level courses," Denby adds. "Without that, the students might learn about philosophy, but they wouldn't be doing philosophy, which is a lot more fun."

Denby's methods are definitely a hit with students at Tufts. "He's all about covering less ground thoroughly," notes one student, "as opposed to the shotgun approach to intro courses, which can be frustrating." "He is completely and only interested in his students' education." He "presents arguments and topics clearly." He's generally "funny and awesome," which is especially refreshing because, according to students, class material is often "rather dry." "If you want to learn how to think critically," students say, "you owe it to yourself to take a class with him if you're at all interested in philosophy."

Richard Fleming, Professor of Philosophy, Bucknell University

Richard Fleming, a Bucknell University philosophy professor, seeks to instill a rigor in student learning that will encourage his students to go on their own in thinking and reasoning. "One tries to teach careful self-reflective thinking that allows students to move ahead on their own. A good teacher knows when to stop teaching!" "He teaches philosophy by getting you to think," agrees a student.

This "gem" of a professor has been teaching at Bucknell since 1983; following extensive pre-class preparation, his spontaneous "lectures" involve him essentially thinking out loud, without notes. Whilst pacing back and forth, thinking about the subjects and texts of the day, he encourages questions and possible solutions to the concerns at hand. "He's STRAIGHTFORWARD. What you see is what you get—pure and simple," says a student. Using (at most) chalk and blackboard, he takes the students through the materials of the day by "reflecting first on what we previously did and then posing concerns about moving forward in that thinking and enhancing and deepening what we have already learned."

Every class and every semester is new and different for Professor Fleming, and he is flexible in his approach to each one. He is constantly finding different ways to master the materials in classes such as Introduction to Logic, Symbolic Logic, and an advanced seminar on Wittgenstein. A leading proponent and author of several books of ordinary language philosophy (Wittgenstein, Austin, Cavell) and philosophy of music (Cage, Bernstein), he enjoys the far-reaching nature of logic, his preferred topic of teaching, and tries to inspire a passion for inferential reasoning in his students at all levels. "Logic is about proper formal arrangements of thinking, so it applies to any content since it asks how to organize correctly that content in order to produce a good argument. No matter the content, logic gives an insight into how to think about it, so all students and all majors benefit strongly from the study of logic."

John Lachs, Centennial Professor of Philosophy, Vanderbilt University

Vanderbilt University philosophy professor John Lachs does more than teach classes; he expands imaginations. "I am fascinated by the grand problems of life, to which we don't know the answers," says the professor of fifty-two years (and also "quite simply the most entertaining professor at Vanderbilt"). "He is one of the most thoughtful people out there, and really is passionate about what he teaches," says a student.

He specializes in ethics, and teaches a large lecture-style class on the subject, as well as 19th Century Philosophy, in which he tries to show that the problems of that century are the very problems we struggle with. "The point is to help students see how many different ways even simple problems can be viewed," he says.

Each class is similar; he starts talking to stimulate a conversation (bringing in current events as illustrations of ancient principles), and then he and students converse. "He really challenges students to think critically and have fun, lively discussion as they do so." Though the material in the class can be daunting if not learned properly, "his teaching makes it crystal clear," and he encourages rewrites of papers.

One former student considers his life debt to Professor Lachs: "I went to him for advice when I was on the verge of leaving Vanderbilt and taking a dead-end service job. Expecting him to tell me what to do, he used his knowledge to philosophically help me figure it out on my own. He kept me from making a grave mistake."

Sam Mitchell, Associate Professor of Philosophy, Mount Holyoke College

Sam Mitchell, a professor of philosophy at Mount Holyoke College, has three goals that are all equally important to him. He wants students to learn the skills associated with his subject: clear thoughts, convincing arguments, and articulate writing; he'd like them to find philosophy fascinating; and mainly, he wants them to have fun. "Do NOT leave Mount Holyoke without taking a class with Sam. One of the best professors ever!" says a student.

His classes cover a wide spectrum of his field, and include Logic, Introduction to Philosophy, and Metaphysics and Epistemology, and his classroom approach intentionally lacks gravitas. "I don't have a lot of respect for the conventions of public morality or the dignity of my position. For example, I'll expand decision theory by looking at the odds of a young woman meeting a jerk versus finding love if she decides to flirt," he says. Lectures are both "clear and fun," with plenty of time for taking notes and asking as many questions as possible. Every homework counts, but "he will make sure you can handle it."

Students say that he always gives you everything you need to know, but more specifically, "talks about why we ought to care too, which is amazing and really helps put everything in perspective." "He dives into more complex material at times, but he also covers the basics from A–Z," says another.

Joel Richeimer, Professor, Philosophy, Kenyon College

Kenyon College philosophy professor Joel Richeimer has an agenda: "By the time students come to college, they have been in school for over twelve years. They know the game. They know the ropes. I try to break them out of their zombie mode."

Them's fighting words from an "animated" professor that "makes everything exciting." Which, as another student rightly points out, is "amazing, for a topic that is thousands of years old!" His classes are meant to keep students on their toes, so they "can't be on automatic." Students are expected to know all of the material all of the time. "I don't allow students to be lackadaisical and then cram for exams," he says. Surprise midterms, putting them on the spot…all this, and the students still love him. "He presents such difficult concepts so clearly, and literally knows everything. He could easily be in multiple departments at Kenyon. Every day I leave class, I feel like my world has been shattered," says one.

Professor Richeimer believes that part of his job is to "convince the students that this is a once-in-a-lifetime opportunity," and he feels obligated to teach "only that which is truly important." "You have to find meaningful material that resonates with the students," he says. To this end, he never teaches a class twice the same way, using new readings, class structures, and material each time. "This is not a repeatable event. Be totally awake or you will miss what is happening," he says.

One of his current classes is being taught with a neuroscientist, and involves "deep disagreements" occurring in front of the class. "He tries to show I am wrong. I try to show that he is wrong. Sometimes I have to modify my position or totally back down. What students learn—hopefully—is that real learning is not reading from textbooks and memorizing. It is learning to accept vulnerability, being open, and being corrected." This elaborate approach ideally demonstrates to students that "true research involves vulnerability," and gives students "a feeling—which is real—that we are doing this together."

Students respond to the fact that the course is not like other courses, and applaud Professor Richeimer's accessibility and willingness to continue the conversation outside of the classroom, whether during office hours or just running into him at the market." I randomly decided to take his Ancient Philosophy class and years later I still think this course was the best one I took in college," says a student.

Jacqueline Scott, Associate Professor of Philosophy, Loyola University Chicago

"I want my students to appreciate philosophy as a good in itself, but even those who don't should be able to find enrichment in my classes," says Jacqueline Scott, professor of philosophy at Loyola University Chicago. "I emphasize active learning over passive learning (discussion over lecture). Dialogue among students and the professor fueled by the classroom materials is the engine that drives the course."

For more than sixteen years, Professor Scott has treated her role as guiding her students towards not just mastery of the content, but more importantly, towards the development of "skills and an attitude towards learning that will spark their intellectual engagement and further their critical thinking and writing abilities." She seeks to accomplish this by requiring close and active textual analysis, which she reinforces through classroom and one-on-one discussions and frequent writing assignments. Further, she "endeavors to demystify philosophy and help students make connections between its theories and the practices of our everyday lives, particularly in terms of ethical, social, and political practices."

Her courses cover four main areas: Ethics, 19th Century Philosophy (often with a focus on Nietzsche), Race Theory, and Chinese Philosophy, and given the broad range of backgrounds and abilities in the Loyola student body, she goes to great lengths "to aid all students (whether they are struggling, excelling, or verging on apathy) by meeting with them outside of class to discuss the class materials and assignments, and by providing detailed comments on drafts to assist them in improving their critical thinking and writing." "I want my students not only to appreciate the importance of the subject matter but also to develop a facility in reading, analyzing, discussing, and writing about it," she says.

Though an admittedly hard grader, Professor Scott's tough love approach is valued by students, who are well aware that "she wants you to do well, and challenges you to do better than you think you can." She tries to be very clear about her expectations from the outset, and then does her best to help students meet them. "I don't go crazy with the red pen, but I ask questions in the margins of their papers to challenge their thinking, and I detail their strengths and areas for improvement on future assignments," says Professor Scott. "You learn so much. It's actually worth your time being there, whether or not you end up with an A. There was never a time I didn't look forward to going to class," says a student.

Brad Elliott Stone, Associate Professor of Philosophy and Director of the University Honors Program, Loyola Marymount University

The mind is like a muscle that must be exercised, and through the teaching of Brad Elliott Stone, a philosophy professor at Loyola Marymount University, students attempt to become stronger thinkers. "My successful students are clear writers who bring their 'A' game to whatever comes their way," he says.

Professor Stone fell in love with philosophy after his very first philosophy class, and he looks to show students the subject that truly captured his imagination. His high expectations are matched with a willingness to help students reach those expectations. "I do not give hard assignments and then expect students to sink or swim; I help them while fully acknowledging that the assignment is hard. He learned from a colleague that it is okay to not show all of one's cards or immediately answer any question posed, and that sometimes "it is important for students to figure something out instead of proving how much one knows as a professor." "He has strong viewpoints/opinions/beliefs about things (be prepared), but he is also very open minded and interested in different ideas," says a student.

His courses include Heidegger, Ethics, Philosophy of Human Nature, and Symbolic Logic (a course he likes teaching "because students clearly show that they understand it"), and his teaching style is a mixture of "lecture, storytelling, comedy, and true seriousness." He believes that we all have stories to tell, and that everyone can and should participate in class, and he loves soliciting examples (and counterexamples) from students in response to the reading. "For example, when discussing Ortega y Gasset's notion of the castaway, I have students tell of times they themselves felt 'lost at sea.' This allows students to learn more about each other while also demonstrating their understanding of Ortega's claims." "He challenges you to think in ways you never would have before, as well as ask yourself why you hold the beliefs that you do. It's the most enlightening, self-revealing class you can take," says a student.

Chris W. Surprenant, Visiting Assistant Professor, Philosophy, Tulane University

"Philosophy provides students with the ability to think critically about the world in which they live. Acquiring this ability is an essential life skill," says Chris Surprenant, who teaches philosophy at Tulane University.

By showing enthusiasm both for course material and for the students themselves, Professor Surprenant encourages his students to develop this skill and, therefore, develop the ability to examine their own lives more completely. "When the professor enters a course with high expectations for his students, the students will rise to meet those expectations," he says. "He genuinely wants every student to do well and will help you until you understand the material," says a student.

His courses include Logic, Plato and Rousseau, Aristotle and Kant, and Law, Liberty, and Morality. Upper-level courses are discussion-based, as he'd rather have the students work through the issues in the texts with his guidance "than me tell them what I think is being said in those texts." Grading is "clear and upfront," he lays out the difficult subject matter "plain and simple," and "he makes a dull subject fun and useful." "Chris spends a lot of time working with everyone individually to help improve their writing. Take something with him if you can, but be prepared to work hard and show up to every class or he'll be on you."

Bryan William Van Norden, Professor, Philosophy, Vassar College

The courses of Bryan William Van Norden, a philosophy professor at Vassar College, are designed to help students avoid shallow or superficial readings of great texts. He claims "Classic texts are classics for a reason. They deserve and repay thoughtful and repeated reading." His belief is that successful students are motivated not by grades but by being invested in the importance of the topics they are studying. "Students learn best when they care about the subject. One of my students told me that she was shouting at the paper I assigned her to read, because it made her so angry. I said, 'That's good. You can agree or disagree, as long as you care.'"

Most importantly, he listens to his students and takes the time to meet them where they are in their understanding of philosophy, taking great effort to grasp the perspective and presuppositions of the students in order to communicate with them and inspire them. "This might seem like an obvious thing to do, but I've talked to many professors who have dogmatic assumptions about what their students think that have no basis in what the students are actually saying."

Professor Van Norden was part of the wave of students who got interested in China when it opened up after the death of Mao; however, Van Norden was perplexed by the paucity of scholars teaching Chinese philosophy. After earning a PhD from Stanford, Van Norden dedicated himself to giving Western students a chance to learn about this great tradition. His teaching load spans all levels and now includes classes such as Introduction to Classical Chinese Philosophy, Problems of Philosophy, and Introduction to Chinese and Japanese Literature. Although his class style is very free form, he almost always assign primary texts and always has some notion of what key facts, claims or concepts he want students to walk away from the class knowing. "Although I want them to read the whole work, I will give them a list of passages that are especially important to focus on, so that they don't get lost in the details," he says.

This incredible passion for the original sources shows, and students think that he "makes difficult philosophers easy to understand." In fact, he's so beloved, one student even remarks: "I'm sad that, for the rest of my philosophy major, pretty much all other classes are taught by 'non Van-Nordens'."

Physics

Dr. David Baker, Associate Professor and Chair, Physics, Austin College

Austin College physics professor David Baker wants students to "explore, question, make connections, generate new ideas, try new things, fail, learn from their mistakes...and ultimately succeed."

It's a journey that he and his students take together, perhaps "with me leading in the beginning but eventually with the student carving the path." He learned early in his studies that teachers who take risks make impacts, and "I want my students to take risks." This "cool but hard professor" is very approachable and enthusiastic, but at the same time "very demanding." His innovative teaching style never relies on traditional methods, and "even 'lectures' sometimes don't seem like lectures." The conversation, which takes its cue from student questions, is often so natural and so relevant that students don't even realize it is a lecture. "I've had to tell them to take notes. Learning doesn't even seem like work, but rather a natural part of their lives," he says.

He teaches courses at all levels, including The Day After Tomorrow: Global Climate and Extreme Weather, a course for non-science majors in which they watch "the campy Hollywood movie *The Day After Tomorrow*" during the first week. The syllabus is then designed around student questions from the movie, and each class begins with a briefing of that day's weather. His ongoing research—often conducted with undergraduates—explores extreme weather and planetary science. One undergraduate researcher pored over thousands of images taken from the Mars Global Surveyor spacecraft to find evidence of dangerous dust devils at four potential landing sites for the Phoenix Mars Lander and became the first author listed on a paper in a top-tier scientific journal. Most recently, Professor Baker co-authored *The 50 Most Extreme Places in Our Solar System*, a popular science book that reports new scientific discoveries in a fresh, unique style. "It's a cool book, and I've used it in a freshman seminar class with EXTREME success," he says.

Sung Kyu Kim, Professor of Physics, Macalester College

Sung Kyu Kim is a physics professor at Macalester College in Saint Paul, Minnesota. Though he certainly knows his way around pretty much any aspect of physics, he has become legendary for teaching the subject to students who don't major in it. His most popular class is a physics course for non-science students who need to fulfill a natural science requirement. He also runs Macalester's Summer Physics Institute for premed students, which brings in some sixty students from almost two dozen colleges and universities.

Professor Kim calls physics an "intrinsically interesting" subject. "Most students are kept away by what they hear," he says, "or maybe because of the math involved." He resolves this problem by steering mostly clear of the math when he's teaching liberal arts majors. There's the occasional equation—it's physics, after all—but "you won't learn too much about the mathematical underpinnings" of the discipline in his class for non-science majors. Instead, Kim focuses on pure ideas. He starts his students off with Einstein's theory of relativity. "I show them how Einstein arrived at these revolutionary ideas," he says, "and emphasize the reasoning." The process takes about four weeks and, "by that time, students are in love with physics and can get onto more abstract theories like anti-matter" as well as quarks and neutrinos, which Kim drolly calls "Italian particles." "I try to develop a single topic in each lecture, and end on a thought-provoking note," he explains.

"Students respond to my enthusiasm, clarity of presentation, and personal interest in them," Professor Kim speculates. "They know that I really care about them and think of them as friends." Students wholeheartedly agree. They love his "old-school humor and wit." "You'll be excited to go to class every day and watch more of the story of the universe unfold," promises one student. "Professor Kim truly enjoys doing what he does," adds another. "He comes into class every day smiling." "His talk on the last day is so great" and, according to students, it is not to be missed under any circumstances. In this concluding lecture, Kim explains to students "their cosmic heritage"—how "they are special" because, after all, we are all "made of star stuff." He summarizes nothing less than the universe itself and, in the words of Isaac Newton, "all that order and beauty which we see in the world."

Walter Lewin, Professor Emeritus of Physics, Massachusetts Institute of Technology

Walter Lewin, who has been lecturing at MIT for forty-three years, creates rainbows and sunsets in his lecture halls to make students see "the beauty of physics." "I make a rainbow in lectures with ONLY one water drop. This is one of my best well-known demos." He wants students to "see through the equations," he says, and to "look at their own world in a way they never have." Students call his lectures "brilliant," and they love that he "emphasizes the physical reasons behind various phenomena, rather than just using the math as a proof."

In addition to changing the perspectives of some of the greatest minds in the country in courses like Newtonian Mechanics, Electricity and Magnetism, and the Physics of Waves and Vibrations, he also wows an online audience of a few million every year with lectures and demonstrations, sometimes acting as a replacement to other physics professors who take a more traditional approach. One student says, "I don't even go to MIT, but his video lectures from the website helped me pass physics at my university!" Another student calls Lewin a "legend on screen."

"Where possible, I stay away from the traditional demonstrations," Lewin says, and he admits that he is "somewhat eccentric," which may be why he can dream up these creative lectures. "There is no one silver bullet that makes a great lecture; it's a combination of many, many things." He says great lectures come from "imagination, preparation, some humor, some challenges, and surprises." He generally spends forty to fifty hours preparing a single lecture. "After my lectures, their lives will never be the same," he promises.

"I demonstrate Rayleigh scattering using cigarette smoke, and I show that the blue light scattered into the lecture hall (over a 90 degree angle) is linearly polarized. I then show that when I hold the smoke in my lungs for a minute or two that the smoke I exhale is white—the moisture in my lungs has increased the size of the smoke particles—no more Rayleigh scattering; we now see Mie scattering."

When discussing standing waves, he asks students to bring musical instruments to "show them (using an oscilloscope) the different harmonics from different instruments: violin, trumpet, flute, trombone, viola, cello, French horn, and oboe." When he presents the topic of weightlessness he jumps off of a table holding a scale and a gallon of cranberry juice to show that, for half of a second, the cranberry juice weighs nothing.

Because of his "ability to make difficult topics relatively easy," he receives dozens of e-mails every day from online viewers all over the world. One student calls the lectures "thrilling." Another student says, "If you start this class hating physics, you will end up loving it by the end." He truly strives to make students love physics. "I integrate physics into their own lives." A few students even consider coming back for more; one student says, "I may take physics again just to be in his lectures."

Douglass Schumacher, Associate Professor, Physics, The Ohio State University

"Lecture is often best when it's a conversation," and that is exactly what Douglass Schumacher, a physics professor at The Ohio State University, tries to do in his classes.

A practicing physicist for most of his life, he has been teaching for fourteen years, adapting his teaching style to the content and the students in front of him. For most subjects, he is simply struggling to keep students from getting confused: "When starting special relativity, if a student isn't confused, I know he or she isn't following lecture," he says. He succeeds and then some, as students say that "he gets concepts across in a very clear and understandable manner. He likes to joke and move around to keep class lively." Tests and quizzes may be difficult, but "he's crystal clear with new concepts and material and he makes sure the class understands the material clearly before moving on."

He's "incredibly dedicated" to helping his students in classes such as Introduction to Mechanics, Introduction to Waves and Modern Physics, and Ultrafast Lasers. Once he figures out what is currently not making sense to his students, he immediately knows how to help, and "there's no way you'll leave that class not understanding the concepts," according to students.

Political Science

Fred Baumann, Professor of Political Science, Kenyon College

"A love of the questions more than their own answers." That's what Fred Baumann, a political science professor, wants for his students at Kenyon College. He instills in his students a desire to see how delightful it is to go ever deeper into the problems" and "to see how every solution has its own difficulties."

He teaches a section of the school's great books introductory course, The Quest for Justice, as well as Politics of the Bible, and Politics and Literature (on the subject of tyranny), alternating his classroom style between "argumentative and humorous." Discussions are conducted with "the idea is that everything is on the table and nothing is personal"—"we just keep chasing the question like a beach ball"—and plenty of papers are assigned to help develop the proper technique. "What they don't get is that when you make an argument, you have to make best argument for the opposing side," he says.

In the first class of the introductory course, this "no-nonsense" professor will usually ask the students if the "self-evident truths" of the Declaration of Independence are indeed true. "They mostly agree that slavery, for example, is wrong." Next, he'll ask them if it is true that all ideas are culturally conditioned products of historical change, which most also agree with. "Then I ask them that if that's true, doesn't it follow that their belief that slavery is wrong is just a product of culture and so therefore not true. And for those who still think the Declaration's claims are true, I ask them how they know they're not just smug cultural imperialists. Having two pieties contradict themselves tends to bother them and so we go from there."

His approach is quite simple. "We read books and talk about them." Students say that he "gives every author his or her due," and "blows you away with his historical knowledge" (he was trained as a historian, leading one student to call say that he "possesses knowledge sufficient to qualify him as a 'scholar's scholar'"). "A class with him will make you a better/smarter person," says one.

Peter Burns, Professor, Political Science, Loyola University New Orleans
Peter Burns, a professor of political science at Loyola University New Orleans, is a believer in the art of bringing individual personalities and experiences to teaching. "I subscribe to Ted Lowi's theory: Teach what you research, research what you teach." Similarly, he treats students as individuals, with individual goals and problems.

This "smart, funny, and energetic" professor believes that one of the most important things a teacher can do for students is develop some kind of a trust with them and tell them how to do certain things. "I am completely convinced that those who want to do well in college will. I have never seen anyone try really hard in my class and not do well." He emphasizes focus and concentration on one's studies, and even recommends (sometimes requires) students to take notes longhand and leave the laptops at home. "Class time is the most important. Sit in front. Take notes. Listen to prof. It's simple, but hard," he says. "Professor Burns is a very hard professor, but he knows his stuff," says a student.

In terms of urban politics, Professor Burns believes "that cities have the potential to solve many of our country's problems," and the already published author currently is authoring a book about rebuilding New Orleans. "Had his class on September 11th and he made the most eloquent comments on that tragedy that I ever heard," says a student.

All of his classes are taught through an engaging discussion or lecture, and outlines of that day's class are always written on the board ahead of time so students can follow along. His current courses include Introduction to American Government, Urban Politics, and Rebuilding New Orleans, in which he solicits policy projects from elected officials in New Orleans for students to complete— some of whom even testify before city council or present their findings to elected or city officials. His classes also emphasize papers: "That's my gift to students, to make them better writers. I absolutely line edit, give them tips. I tell them what I'm looking for. I make marks on every page. And I try not to write in red."

Ralph G. Carter, Professor of Political Science, Texas Christian University

It is unsurprising that Ralph Carter, a political science professor at Texas Christian University, find politics—both domestic and international—"endlessly fascinating," and wants this to rub off on his students. His thirty-three career has seen him holding numerous positions in the academic world, including president of the International Studies Association's (ISA) Foreign Policy Analysis Section and president of ISA's Midwest Region, and he was the first recipient of ISA's Quincy Wright Distinguished Scholar Award to come from a solely undergraduate department.

The recipient of multiple teaching awards and recognitions, he believes that "you can be friendly, approachable, and caring and still maintain high academic standards and expectations." His courses include International Politics, Contemporary U.S. Foreign Policy, U.S. Foreign Policy Making, U.S. Foreign Policy in Film, Russian Foreign Policy, Mideast Conflicts, and Intro to Political Science, which Professor Carter teaches every semester. "I enjoy it for two reasons:

because there's no political subject that is off-limits and because I can try to help students make the academic transition from high school to a very selective four year university." One of his favorite classroom techniques is to ask students to role play; he will make them the policy maker and ask what they would do in a situation and why (he also employs this method during some open-ended essay exams). Quizzes often involve current events, and "you have to read your textbook and keep up with current events to do well."

He "wants the best for his students," and "knows exactly what he's talking about and makes the class interesting!" A student puts it simply: "TAKE HIM!"

Javier Corrales, Professor of Political Science, Amherst College

Javier Corrales, who teaches political science at Amherst College, wants his students to see things in a new light. "That's why they pay to have someone in front of them who has read more on the subject than they have," he says. I don't teach a class where "anything goes." Students are free to explore new and original ideas, of course, but comments have to be grounded on the material that they have read.

He tailors said lectures using evidence to illuminate or challenge theoretical arguments; he never embarrasses or calls on them but simply asks them to consider alternative arguments. "I make students think of the readings as arguments about bigger themes in life, and show them how one might either raise some doubts or at least generate new research questions. I try to connect what we are reading with themes that are connected to what they already know."

His courses include Democracy in Latin America, Politics of Extremism, and Political Economy of Development, and his classroom utilizes a mixture of lectures and discussions, with "occasional humor" and lots of media. Students say he is an "engaging lecturer who really knows how to structure a class: friendly banter, followed by a clear and prepared lecture, followed by discussion." "He was awesome! His class was the one that helped me decide my major," says one. "Corrales' classes will be some of the most useful and most memorable classes of your time here at Amherst."

Robert Devigne, Professor of Political Science, Tufts University

"What is the proper relationship between philosophy, religion, and politics?" asks Tufts University political science professor Robert Devigne, whose classes look to promote thought and discussion on fundamental questions such as the nature of liberty, nature, justice, and the best life.

He believes that thinking is what distinguishes us from other species and challenges his students with difficult philosophic texts, and the insistence that they take the authors thoughts' very seriously (a process that provides an opportunity for contemplation and discussion of difficult subjects). "He is a complete genius, a complete nut, and one of the most interesting teachers I've ever had," says a student.

He teaches intro classes to Western political philosophy (ancients and moderns) that explain how these thinkers have helped shape the way that we look at the world, as well as upper-level classes on thinkers such as Jean Jacques Rousseau, Frederich Nietzsche, John Stuart Mill, Alexis de Tocqueville, Leo Strauss, and others. "They all give us the opportunity to weigh the advantages and disadvantages of the modern way of life that the West has built," he says. In the intro classes, he focuses directly on the reading material, explaining "the intentions of this or that political philosopher and how it has helped create this world (for better or worse) and our understanding of it." Both lectures and readings "challenge your world view in a way that will make you a different person when you finish the class," according to a student. "Devigne is one of the most interesting and intriguing professors I have ever encountered," says another.

Del Dickson, Professor, Political Science, University of San Diego

University of San Diego political science professor Del Dickson wants students to get excited not just about his classes but about liberal arts education in general. "I like to follow my students' paths through school and help prepare them for their next step—whether it is school or a career— and I think students appreciate my personal interest in them," he says.

Now in his twenty-fourth year of teaching, he believes that if you challenge students, they will meet you at least halfway. "If you (the professor) are excited about your subject and having fun with it, students will be excited about learning and have fun right along with you." His thoroughness and tendency to call randomly on students is a trial by fire, and one student refers to him as "one of the few teachers I've had that really earned my respect." Another says that he is "the greatest teacher I have ever had, but also the hardest."

Students admit that his classes are "not for the easily discouraged." In his overview course Introduction to Political Science, he teaches students with the assumption that they may never take another political science course, so "I try to jam in all the essential ideas that I think everyone needs to know about political science." He teaches courses such as Constitutional Law and Judicial Behavior using a modified Socratic method, that challenges students through guided questions and offers "more guidance, more hints, and more positive feedback" than the traditional method. "I always know where I want the discussion to go, so I try to guide the conversation subtly to cover the points that students need to know to make the topic of the day gel and make sense to them. There are always more questions to ask and issues to explore, and at the end of the day I think that students—regardless of where they come down on the topic personally—have a better appreciation for the issues and, hopefully, have a better understanding of the arguments on ALL sides, not just 'their' side."

Audrey Haynes, Associate Professor and Senior Teaching Fellow, Political Science, The University of Georgia

In order to make students think, Dr. Audrey Haynes, a professor of political science at The University of Georgia, first has to get their attention. Once she gets them to want to hear what she has to say, then encouraging them to go beyond is the easy part.

Her courses include Intro to American Government (an intro-level course required of all undergraduates), American Political Parties, and Mass Media and American Politics, and she tailors her approach based on the class: "I try to respond to the interaction of the content, the venue, and the audience." "She is always telling us to ask questions and that we control the lecture. If we think it is boring then we are supposed to ask a good question!" says a student.

Larger classes require a different approach than smaller classes; but what does remain constant is that she never assumes that students already know something, and always reads their faces throughout to gauge the levels of understanding and engagement. "I would say that in every situation a common thread is that I like to provide organized information to students in a way that they can follow and then have them begin to connect it both to other content, to their own lives, and to the world. The more connections I can make them see, the more the implications are meaningful to them, and the more likely they will remember the information, whether factual or conceptual, and apply it," she says.

Students say that "she displays a true passion for her subject that is hard to find," and "lectures were light and lively and she has a WEALTH of knowledge to pull from." "I will never watch TV or read the paper the same way," says a student.

Pamela Jensen, Professor of Political Science, Kenyon College

Pamela K. Jensen, who teaches political science at Kenyon College, starts where the students are: She gets the big picture first, and then hones in on the details. She encourages them not to fear academic challenges, and is always willing to spend time with them to overcome any apprehension or confusion they might have. "She's the most helpful professor I've encountered at Kenyon," says a student.

Professor Jensen wants to help connect the students to what they are reading, by helping them to read and speak about, and eventually, to evaluate, the texts: "Above all, I want them to see that the philosophic and literary texts are about real life." Her courses include Quest for Justice, Modern Political Philosophy, African-American Political Thought, and seminars on Montesquieu and Tocqueville. The Quest for Justice is a signature course for the college, a year-long, discussion-based course on the fundamental questions of politics, taken only by first-year students; she has the most love for this course "because first-year students take risks, because I get to know the students and their work well, and because we discuss primary materials in a way that sparks the most interesting conversations and can change students' lives." Her classes are either discussion or lecture-discussion (in larger classes); for example, on the first day of Quest for Justice, the class reads part of the Declaration of Independence, and then she asks students if they think it's true. Students say she has a "great sense of humor," and "keeps her teaching unbiased politically," on top of being "extremely kind and intelligent."

David Leibowitz, Assistant Professor, Political Science, Kenyon College
Kenyon College political science professor David Leibowitz's chief goal, in class and out, is "to encourage students to think more deeply and rigorously about the handful of questions that really matter: questions about such things as love, justice, friendship, death, and God." Oh, and along the way, he also tries to get students to see the wisdom that can be found in books by great philosophers from Plato to Nietzsche. "His class has the potential to change the rest of your life," says an impressed student. "For me, it matched the idealistic image I had for what a college class could potentially be."

He grabs students' attention using colorful thought experiments and lines of argument, in the hope that students will eventually come to see the possibility of achieving a deeper knowledge (including self-knowledge) than they had previously imagined existed. Leibowitz said that in his own education "I learned that many of what we today call 'values' or mere 'preferences' are in fact 'opinions' that can be rationally examined, and thereby bolstered, modified, or even refuted."

He's been teaching for more than three decades, and his courses include Classical Quest and Quest for Justice, a year-long freshman seminar that introduces students to deep thinkers from Plato and Sophocles to Marx and Nietzsche. His classes are a combination of lecture and discussion, and he uses his lectures "to raise puzzles about, or problems in, our ordinary thinking about moral, political, and philosophic issues, and then stops so that the class as a whole can try to think out what the solution or solutions might be, if there are any." "A perfect lecturer and a brilliant man…like his Socrates, he's looking for 'potential philosophers'," says a student. "If you want a challenge and you want to question basically everything you've ever believed, take this course," says another.

Richard Leitch, Associate Professor, Political Science, Gustavus Adolphus College

"What we experience during these four years of our lives matters," says Richard Leitch, a political science professor at Gustavus Adolphus College.

Throughout more than two decades of teaching, he has never stopped believing in the intellectual potential of all of his students, maintaining the highest of standards. He is willing to develop nontraditional assignments to achieve learning outcomes and is consistent and fair in his assessment of student performance; he says, "I am not afraid to use humor and take myself less than seriously during class time if I can sense that doing so will help students understand something" (one student says of him: "the most hilarious person ever") He is always thoroughly prepared for the day's interactions yet "prepared to stray wildly from the plan if situations merit a different learning style is more appropriate." "He teaches a lot of information every lecture, but he makes learning VERY fun," says a student.

His current course load includes a first-year seminar entitled The Politics of Homelessness, in which he and the students spend three days and three nights in November living outside to get at least a sense of what it must be like to be truly homeless. "For those days and nights, students and I maintain our normal commitments (work, classes, extracurricular activities, meetings), go without showers and a secure source of food and, like homeless people, have to confront the occasionally overly compassionate, often dispassionate, and sometimes rude attitudes of others who are not participants in this experience."

Stephen Long, Assistant Professor, Political Science and International Studies, University of Richmond

"My goal as a teacher and mentor is to awaken the inner 'nerd' in each of my students," says Stephen Long, a University of Richmond professor of political science and international studies. "'Nerdy' interest is what drives humanity forward. It is disinterest and apathy that are uncool." Students are drawn to this Stephen Colbert–lookalike professor, who is "so awkwardly funny [that it] makes class really enjoyable!"

His clear passion for his discipline was developed through years of study under much-admired teachers. He learned from those teachers not to impose specific career paths or long-term goals on his students, and to listen to them to understand who they are and who they want to be. "I try to put equal effort and enthusiasm into mentoring a future landscape architect, lawyer, or software engineer as I put into mentoring a future diplomat or college professor," he says. His courses include Introduction to International Relations, Ethics in International Politics, and Conflict Processes. Humor, personal anecdotes, and dialogue with students set the tone for every class. "I follow the approach of the great philosopher of teaching, Parker Palmer, by trying to bring my whole and undivided self into the classroom." He also brings intelligence officers, policy makers, and diplomats into his classroom via Skype, and employs multiple-path slides to allow students to choose specific sub-topics that they want to explore, meaning "every group can customize what they explore with me in class." Students must be willing to tackle questions and think out loud, rather than dismissing the questions that seem too challenging or intractable. "It takes some intellectual bravery to really engage with the professor and other students in class. Part of my job is to convince students that they are in a space that is safe for those willing to put in that effort."

He is never afraid to try new approaches or change direction if something isn't working, and doesn't worry about being embarrassed; once, he even acted out the assassination of Archduke Franz Ferdinand in front of the class. "Prof. Long explains everything really well and seems to really want his students to understand the information and love the topic as much as he does. He is also very funny—he puts in these hilarious slides or tells funny stories almost every class. DEFINITELY take from Professor Long if you can—he's awesome!"

Nina Moore, Associate Professor, Political Science, Colgate University
Nina Moore, a political science professor from Colgate University, has a clear goal in mind: "My central goal is to encourage students to ask smart questions and to interpret what they find." "In doing so, they learn to think independently, to find the small 't' truth on their own and, hopefully, capital 'T' truth at some point in their future."

Her courses "aim to promote informed, civil discourse on often difficult topics," and her current course load includes Beneath the Black Robes: Courts as Political Institutions; Politics of Race; and America as a Democracy. Classes are very interactive, in that she presents reading and lecture information, invites students to react, and pushes them to dig deeper. "I take my students and their academic pursuits seriously, and I insist that they do the same," she says. She also adds humor intermittently, because "we usually pore over tons of information and because I want students to feel comfortable exploring and testing ideas."

Professor Moore sees her classes as helping to shape students as learners, and early on helps them to figure out how to ask a question, what a researchable question is, how to gather data, and what a reliable source is. Through this process, students learn to "become serious scholars and serious thinkers." "She has high standards but is very clear what those standards are," says a student. Professor Moore makes a point of emphasizing her availability on the first day of class. She says, "Because I demand much, I make an effort to ensure students know I'm available." One student attests to her helpfulness: "She is extremely helpful during the research process. [She] holds an entire session with the library folks to help you find stuff you need. She even sits down with you to go over outline after outline after outline. I'm better at papers now than ever!"

She currently sits on the New York State Commission on Judicial Conduct (she was appointed by the governor in 2009), which allows her to view the handling of cases from the judge's perspective and to share that experience with her students. "TAKE THIS CLASS if you want to understand more about political science," says a student.

Psychology
Kenn Barron, Professor, Psychology, James Madison University

James Madison University psychology professor Kenn Barron has some very specific goals for the educational climate he hopes to foster in his classroom. He wants students to believe they can learn, to see value and purpose in what they are learning, to take an active role in shaping their learning, and to leave with experiences and skills that they can apply and use to make their daily lives better.

Students appreciate how his classes are structured to promote these goals, as well as his awareness of the tremendous impact that a teacher can have on a student. His teaching style centers on working through case studies and real-world examples of any given topic, and he blends in a combination of lecture, discussion, and some form of hands-on activity. Another student raves that "Kenn is the best teacher that I've had—ever. He not only cares about his students' understanding of the material, he also cares about his students' well-being. Such a great guy. The best choice for a teacher for Research Methods and Psych Stats for sure."

His courses include Motivation, Social Psychology, and Research Methods and Statistics, and he is most interested in "what causes some people to lead more meaningful lives than others and how we can create environments that promote optimal human experiences." He has recently begun engaging in outreach and public service activities to help practitioners apply motivation theories and principles to real-world contexts, and he is the coordinator of JMU's Motivation Research Institute. "Kenn is the most amazing professor I have ever had. He explains things fully, he's interesting and fun. TAKE HIM! DON'T PASS HIM UP!" encourages a student. Another calls him an "amazing professor and advisor. Does everything he possibly can to help you succeed. He is easily reachable and makes class fun by adding real-world experiences and examples. Best teach at JMU. If you ever have a chance to take one of his classes do not turn it down!"

Charles L. Brewer, Kenan Professor of Psychology, Furman University

Charles L. Brewer is beyond legendary at Furman University, where he has been teaching psychology since the Lyndon Johnson administration. By his own count, he has had a hand in producing over two hundred eventual recipients of doctoral degrees. He has collected more national awards by himself than most entire faculties receive in a century and, in fact, the American Psychological Association just named its lifetime teaching award the Charles L. Brewer Distinguished Teaching of Psychology Award. Professor Brewer is such a fixture at Furman and within the department that his students long ago began a collection of Brewerisms. "Things always take longer than they do" is one of our favorites. Another: "Facts fade fast, so learn concepts and principles."

How does a professor become so popular for so long among finicky undergrads? Must be an easy A, right? Not at all, actually. Brewer's tests are notoriously "difficult" and even downright "tricky." He gives some of the lowest grades at Furman yet he routinely receives the highest student ratings. The key to pulling off such a feat, Brewer tells us, is enthusiasm. "Passion is the overarching theme," he says. "It's the critical thing." Evenhandedness is also tremendously important. Brewer grades anonymously in all of his courses and he is very upfront about what he requires. "You can demand what you want to demand if you set out your expectations from day one," Brewer explains, "and if you are impeccably fair in evaluating your students." If you do find yourself in one of Professor Brewer's classes, don't expect to be subjected to the latest classroom gadgetry. He's decidedly "old school." He'll use the occasional slide but you'll find absolutely no PowerPoint in his classroom, just for example. "It has a lot of power," he declares, "no point."

Students call Professor Brewer's courses "a challenging (but totally-worth-it) experience." "Dr. Brewer is by far the best teacher at Furman," gushes one typical student. "Yes, he is ancient and looks like he might croak at any moment but he is more energetic than any teacher I have ever had." "I have taken many Brewer classes while at Furman. The toll on GPA is well worth it," adds another student. "Take a bunch of easy classes while you slave over his courses." Perhaps the ultimate compliment was paid by a student—now a successful clinical psychologist—who sent Brewer a note recently reminding him to "leave no academic butt un-kicked."

Lisa Cravens-Brown, PhD, Senior Lecturer, Department of Psychology, The Ohio State University

In teaching students to think critically about the world, Lisa Cravens-Brown, a senior lecturer in the Department of Psychology at The Ohio State University, wants them to use empirically based knowledge to inform their ideas and hypotheses. "I also want them to see the humor and laughter in life and to greatly enjoy the process of learning," she says. "You can tell she loves her job and that's what makes a great teacher!" says a student.

"Any topic can be exciting to students if the instructor is excited about it," and Dr. Cravens-Brown certainly brings that requisite enthusiasm to her classroom. She is easy to approach and likes to include laughter in every class meeting: "I share enough personal information that they feel they know me well enough to come to me with questions and ideas."

A licensed clinical psychologist with a child specialty, she teaches classes that include Human Sexuality, honors Quantitative Analysis, and Health Psychology, each of which "has some really exciting material to share with students." In the classroom, she likes to spark discussion of the topics at hand; she will present a research question, ask for ideas about possible answers, and then present the research data. She incorporates "a lot of interesting media," and all tests are online; she is also "in the process of 'hybridizing' my classes to include more interactive and hands-on components to interrupt lecture." "Her lectures are fun and never a dull moment," says a student.

Susan Croll, Associate Professor of Psychology, Neuropsychology, and Neuroscience, City University of New York—Queens College

Intellectual arousal is the name of the game for Susan Croll, a psychology professor at Queens College, and students are more than happy to rise to the challenge of reasoning on their own. "I learned from others that it is more powerful to give students the ability to synthesize ideas on their own than to passively feed them the ideas of others," she says.

Statistics, Neuroscience, Contemporary Issues in Science, and Experimental Design are some of her courses; she chooses to teach subjects that facilitate broad, controversial thinking while providing the tools for critically evaluating the controversies and arriving at sound conclusions. She believes in a three-step approach to teaching a topic: Generate, Teach, and Use. "In Step 1, I provide students with the concepts and information that will lead them to generate a concept on their own. Once the concept has been generated by most students in the class, I teach and explain the concept. Finally, I give the class a real-life scenario or problem to which the concept can be applied, which gives the 'quicker' students a chance to apply the idea that they just generated to a problem, and the "'slower' students a second chance to fully generate the idea on their own."

In all cases, examples are drawn from everyday life, and she uses humor and controversy to maintain interest in her examples. Students are not shy about professing their love for her methods: "Scientists need to perfect the art of cloning. This way they can clone Professor Croll so she can teach every class at every learning institution on earth."

Furthermore, the sweetness of her personality does not go unheralded. "Not only is she the most wonderful human I ever met, but she is nothing beyond perfect when it comes to teaching."

David B. Daniel, Professor, Psychology, James Madison University

"My primary goal is for students to understand that they are in charge of their own learning and responsible for their actions, in addition to the resulting consequences," says David Daniel, a professor of psychology at James Madison University. "Students who realize that they can be active contributors to their own learning and development are then in a position to make improvements and appreciate their accomplishments. The goal is freedom, intellectual and otherwise."

Professor Daniel loves his field because "psychology is relevant in economics, education, health, engineering… and just about everything that you can think of, from individual academic disciplines like history to current events. Even last night's TV shows. It is a great thing to be able to teach. Connecting my discipline to the world is an ever-changing target."

In his classes, which include Introductory Psychology, Developmental Psych, and Learning and Cognition for STEM Disciplines, he tries to model enthusiasm and an ability to play with ideas. His classroom style is focused but relaxed, more than a bit irreverent, and his pedagogical strategies are informed by evidence. "I try to be genuine and not fake in terms of my teaching persona," he says. His presentations (which students say "show off how interesting psych is") strive to be relevant to students and memorably demonstrate the concepts to be learned in the most dynamic way that he can, often using multimedia and vivid examples mapped to learning objectives. "I hate to waste time and resources, mine or my students'," he says. "His examples are so vivid and memorable that you just get it...and he likes it when the students ask questions," says a student. He compares enrolling in a class to joining a gym: "You get access to all of the material and may even get a good trainer. But, if you don't do the workouts the right way, you don't get the benefits." One student says that "he really wants the students who care to learn and succeed and doesn't ride the other ones. That's the way it should be and he's really great and hilarious."

Kimberly D.R. DuVall, Lecturer, Department of Psychology, James Madison University

"Don't settle for mediocre in life," says Kimberly D.R. DuVall, who teaches psychology at James Madison University. "Find your talents and use them!"

She tries to motivate her students to follow this advice, making it clear that it is okay to "Take calculated risks. Speaking your mind in a college class is one of those safe risks. Usually it works and it enhances the class, on rare occasions it doesn't, but it is not a disaster. Doing so builds confidence." She realizes that students succeed in her classes when they can make the material personally meaningful, and, in classes such as Life-Span Human Development, tries to reach them using stories, which she believes serve multiple functions in the classroom: sparking interest, aiding the flow of lectures, making material memorable, and building rapport between the instructor and the students. "It helps to make the material come alive to students and assists them in making the topics meaningful to them on a personal level," she says.

Students love both Professor DuVall and the class they affectionately nickname "Womb to Tomb." "This class is amazing. I would recommend it to everyone at JMU. I wish I was still in this class and that all of my classes were run like this." "I never wanted to miss class. She also has a very positive attitude and always put everyone in a good mood," says one. "If you don't walk away loving her and this class, there is something wrong with you," warns another.

Fredrick P. Frieden, PhD, ABPP, Adjunct Associate Professor of Psychology, The College of William & Mary

Fredrick P. Frieden, an adjunct professor of psychology at The College of William & Mary, looks to offer a positive classroom/learning experience by creating "an atmosphere of mutual respect, inquiry, and creativity." "I want my classes to feel like an intelligent conversation," he says. He hopes to be a part of what inspires students to pursue and achieve their academic goals.

Professor Frieden's teaching approach is to get students to think beyond the textbooks and integrate what they have learned from other areas of academics and their experiences. "I want the learning process to feel collaborative," he says. When he asks questions, he is looking to draw out multiple answers and start a discussion, rather than get a simple response. "I also want to take the risk to acknowledge what I don't know and allow students to see the limitations of my knowledge. I think that this 'frees them up' to take similar risks and participate."

"I tell a mix of personal and professional stories… I try to make the concepts real, and something that students can understand in a vivid and practical way." In addition to teaching, he is a practicing clinical psychologist with more than twenty years of experience, and he brings this perspective to his classes, which have included Abnormal Psychology, Social Psychology, Personality Theories, History of Psychology, and his personal favorite, Human Sexuality. "I want students to have a broad, cross-cultural understanding of sexuality and to be able to understand diverse behaviors and motivations. The course does not change their core values about sex but in the end I think that they have a richer and more nuanced understanding of themselves and others."

In fact, students so appreciate his mix of videos, lectures, activities, and personal stories, that they don't mind his penchant for early classes. "I got out of bed at 8:00 A.M. looking forward to class," says one.

Douglas Gentile, Associate Professor, Psychology, Iowa State University
Douglas A. Gentile, who teaches psychology at Iowa State University, wants to help his students separate the wheat from the chaff, and to "figure out what are the really important things to know rather than to study everything."

How does he manage to do it? "Be a performer," he says. "If I don't keep their attention, it doesn't matter how good my content is. It's all about attention." He presents material in several different ways, allowing students to incorporate it via the learning style that works best for them, and making it "so easy to understand that I barely had to study for his test," says one student.

His course load includes Intro to Psychology, Focus Group Methodology, and Media Psychology. Even in the stadium-style seating of his large Intro to Psych class, he loves performing and trying to keep his students awake at 8:00 A.M. "I also like helping them to see why the material is interesting and how to apply what is learned to their own lives," he says. He uses many teaching styles to fit with students' varied learning styles. He uses traditional lecture, videos, active learning techniques where the students work together in groups, and will even "conduct demonstrations in the front of the class where I bring students down and usually embarrass them in some way." To demonstrate Piagetian egocentrism, for example, he has two students sit back to back in front of the class, each with ten Legos. One of them builds something, describing it aloud as he/she builds it, while the other tries to build the same thing just by listening to the instructions. "They NEVER build the same thing. It's a simple task—only ten pieces, all of different shapes and colors, easy to differentiate. But they never build the same thing, demonstrating that it is really hard (if not impossible) to see things from someone else's point of view."

Students love his magnetic classroom demeanor: "Dr. Gentile is nuts (but in a good way). He's zany and rather protean with what he does during lectures, but it's entirely interesting—demonstrations, videos, examples, and he dances around."

Bryan Hendricks, Senior Lecturer, Psychology Department, University of Wisconsin—Madison

University of Wisconsin—Madison psychology instructor Bryan Hendricks can be found when needed: inside the classroom, outside the classroom, even long after a student's time in the classroom is over. "I am nearly always available for student meetings and eagerly provide extensive support for student work. I always try to listen carefully, and to encourage and support students," he says. "This man goes above and beyond what any another professor has ever gone close to. He'll meet with you one-on-one at least five times to help with this class," vouches a student.

This "nearly unlimited assistance" is necessary, as he teaches "challenging" core classes such as Intro to Psychology, Statistics, and his favorite course, Research Methods, in which he works with each student as a major individual research project evolves encompassing the entire semester. "Students often approach Statistics and Research Methods with a negative attitude or at least one of apprehension. I love the challenge of confronting those attitudes and turning them around during the semester," he says. "There are times when you will want to break down and tear your hair out, but Bryan keeps you going," says a student.

He also likes to help students explore their professional goals and options beyond their undergraduate years. He is always willing to help students in any aspect of their lives, and is a firm believer in reciprocity: "If I provide help and encouragement to students, they almost always reward me with hard work, accomplishments, and further contact." "He is one of the finest professors one can ever encounter in life," says a student.

Douglas Johnson, Associate Professor, Psychology, Colgate University
"Students know when a professor is excited about teaching and feed off of that," says Dr. Douglas Johnson, a psychology professor at Colgate University "I love teaching, I care about my students inside and outside of the classroom, and I let them know this through both words and actions."

Professor Johnson recognizes that individual students learn very differently from each other, and one of a teacher's main jobs is to convey information in a variety of ways to reach as many learners as possible. He tries to maintain the attention and focus of all students through the use of a high-energy teaching style and "easy to understand explanations of complicated topics."

His courses include Intro to Psych, Psych Stats, Human Cognition, and the Psychology of Sport and Exercise, and he tailors his class structure accordingly. Intro levels use concrete and memorable examples, while higher-level courses allow for a more graduate-seminar approach to the material, with guided discussion based on student understanding and challenges. "I want students to learn how to think like a scientist; how to think quantitatively; how to judge arguments; and how to maximize their learning and personal growth."

Students say that this "amazing" professor "makes you want to come to every class. He is hilarious and connects everything you learn to both relatable information and the big picture." "Everyone should take a class with him to see how a real teacher does their job," says another.

Spencer Kelly, Associate Professor, Psychology Department, Neuroscience Program, Colgate University

Spencer Kelly, who teaches psychology at Colgate University, wants his students to be producers, not just consumers, of knowledge. "I want my students to learn enough to think independently and ask original questions. Once they do that, I teach them how to answer those questions themselves."

His focus is neuroscience, and his course load includes Cognitive Neuroscience and How to Build a Baby, a class for non-science majors that explores the nature/nurture debate in the context of understanding how children develop, and aims to teach students that science connects to their lives in important and pervasive ways. "All roads lead to the brain," he says. He is a leading expert on how the brain processes hand gestures that accompany speech, and he has published over thirty papers on the topic; much of his research involves students as collaborators and co-authors.

Professor Kelly is a strong believer that when students learn the habit of asking good questions, they "are ready to create knowledge." In his How to Build a Baby class, he starts the course by asking students to imagine that they are extraterrestrial scientists whose task is to "build" a human baby from scratch. "This forces students to consider what they would build in versus what they would leave to the environment to provide. This group exercise hooks students on a fundamental and ancient debate in philosophy: nature versus nurture," he says.

Students think that he "may be the coolest professor on campus." He "explains everything to you in a way that is simple but not condescending" and "pushes you to think in new ways." "In a large lecture hall, he manages to keep things fun and interesting, and students engaged," says another.

Robin Kowalski, Professor of Psychology, Clemson University

Robin Kowalski, a professor of psychology at Clemson University, looks to be an effective mentor and role model. "Quite honestly, I want students to look back and feel that I made a difference in their life. I want students to feel that I not only taught them about psychology and how it applies to their daily life, but that I provided them with encouragement and support along the way," she says.

As much as she would like to believe that they will remember the content of her courses ten years from now, she knows this is probably not the case. "What they will remember is the kind of relationship I had with them. I try to nurture that relationship by being accessible to them in and out of the classroom." One student will be left with a good memory: "Dr. K is extremely nice, loves it when you show an interest, [and is] enthusiastic about the course." It is important to her to make students feel that she has time for them, and that students don't just simply learn the material, they engage with it. "Students who are engaged in the class also demonstrate a greater ability to integrate material from other courses, which I think helps them to remember the material."

Her classes include Social Psychology, Health Psychology, and Psychology of Women, though she holds a special place in her heart for Introductory Psychology, which is many students' first exposure to the field of psychology. "It is so much fun to open their eyes to all of the many ways in which psychology applies to their daily lives," she says. She is very much a storyteller within the classroom, believing that stories help students remember the constructs to which the stories are linked. "This also allows me to take a laid-back approach within the classroom, and it facilitates class discussions as students can contribute their own illustrations of the constructs being discussed." For example, when she lectures on how we form impressions of others, she will use information from a book that discusses what our possessions say about our personality. "So I will present them with pictures of offices, houses, etc., and ask them to describe the people who occupy these spaces. Through this, I hope to not only teach them about impression formation but also encourage them to read the book."

Gary W. Lewandowski Jr., Associate Professor, Psychology, Monmouth University

In laying out his curriculum, Gary Lewandowski Jr, a psychology professor at Monmouth University, sets challenging but achievable goals; he is "tough but fair," and students know that "they'll learn things in my courses and that I'm not going to waste their time." "You need to remember is that since Dr. L tries very hard, he expects you to do the same and you need to in order to do well," says a student.

He's approachable, always willing to help, and best of all, he tries to be funny in class "so that students feel comfortable taking chances and expressing their viewpoints." "Dr. L is probably the best teacher I have ever had in my entire school career. He's funny and makes class enjoyable." The information in his classes is always organized, but it is presented in a variety of ways. Primarily, he puts complex ideas into his own words in order to simplify them; to expand a topic, he asks students for their own examples and ideas, or poses critical thinking questions that they then work through as a group. "Just go to class and you'll learn everything. His examples will make sure you know the material," says a student.

His courses include Experimental Methods and Intimate Relationships, which is his own research specialty, and the class he considers to be the one most likely to have a direct impact on students' lives. "Students can improve existing relationships, avoid bad relationships, or leave failing relationships. So many students from that class have told me how it changed their lives that I've lost count."

Miriam Liss, Associate Professor, Psychology, University of Mary Washington

Miriam Liss, a professor of psychology at the University of Mary Washington, says she "loves all my classes for different reasons." "She's really pumped about what she teaches and is always energetic in her lectures," agrees a student.

Professor Liss, a licensed clinical psychologist, teaches a range of courses including General Psychology, which "is a chance to share the best and greatest in psychology and to introduce a range of subjects to the most possible students"; Clinical Psychology, for which students interview local clinicians; Personality, in which students must analyze a famous person or a literary character; and Psychology of Women, which is a writing and speaking intensive course that is completely discussion-based, and involves community service learning. Before class, she posts "Questions to Consider for Class" and students come to class prepared to discuss the issues of the day; she is "always willing to clarify anything you are unsure about." "I also combine small group activities and role plays to get students engaged in learning. For example, in my Personality class, students act out defense mechanisms in skits and then other students guess what defense mechanism they are doing. They also act out each of Erikson's developmental stages dramatizing positive and negative adaptations to each stage."

She is widely published author, and has published with many undergraduate students who have worked with her on individual research projects, one of her proudest achievements. The department has a meeting in the spring semester where professors talk about research they are interested in "and the students can pick and choose the projects that they are interested in." "It's clear that she loves what she does and has a lot of interest in the material she teaches," one student says. Another student calls Professor Liss "very passionate and engaging," and adds that she is "excellent at making the material interesting and understandable."

Thad Polk, Arthur F. Thurnau Professor, Psychology & EECS, University of Michigan

Thad Polk is a professor at the University of Michigan who specializes in cognitive neuroscience. He has published over thirty articles and two books on the subject. The two undergraduate courses that he teaches are The Human Mind and Brain, a small freshman seminar, and Introduction to Cognitive Psychology, a gargantuan lecture course.

Students say they like Polk because he does everything he can to help students. He "truly cares about his students and goes out of his way to help" in a number of ways. "What most distinguishes my teaching is my effort to connect with students personally, both in the classroom and outside it," Polk says. "After each exam, I e-mail students who did really well or maybe improved a lot and mention that I noticed. I also e-mail students who did poorly. I express concern and invite them to office hours." "Anyone can teach the students who are doing well," he adds. "The real challenge is helping a struggling student turn things around."

Professor Polk "explains things very well" and he is adept at making "lectures engaging even if the topic is boring or complex." His large lecture course is pretty long (around eighty minutes), and one way he combats student fatigue is by providing "an intermission in the middle of class." He shows a "video clip of the day" that is totally unrelated to the topic of the class—like, just for example, the legendary "More Cowbell" skit from *Saturday Night Live*. "Initially, I just did it as a break for me," Polk tells us, "but it turns out that students are sort of revived after the intermission and able to concentrate better for the rest of the class."

Another cool thing that Polk does is to throw weekly dinner parties. "He goes above and beyond to get to know his students by inviting groups of them to his house" for a fairly lavish banquet. "My wife and I host weekly dinner parties of about ten students at a time," Polk says. "That's a way to get to know people and they get to know me. Instead of being a talking head in front of a room, I'm someone they've shared a meal with." Dinners are reportedly "first come, first served" and, naturally, with some 450 students in the class, "you can only sign up for one." "Make sure you go," counsels one student.

Gilda Werner Reed, PhD, Psychology, University of New Orleans

Gilda Werner Reed is a professor of psychology at the University of New Orleans, a self-described "public-school advocate," and one of the most energetic and remarkable people you are likely to run across. She and her husband have seven children (including two adoptees with disabilities), and over a dozen grandchildren. She won a Democratic primary for the United States House of Representatives (subsequently losing the general election). She never stopped teaching in the aftermath of Hurricane Katrina. She is also an honorary member of the Jefferson Firefighters Association Local #1374, a distinction she received for her work supporting the firefighters in a political dispute.

Reed teaches eight different courses both on campus and online and they are all very popular. "I get so many sad stories and I don't like to tell anybody no," she tells us. "I usually max out what the seating is. If I'm in a 120-seat classroom, that's how many students I have. If I am online, where there is no fire code, there wouldn't be a limit if it were up to me." When asked why she is such a popular professor, Reed's answer is decidedly modest. "I just put the students first," she says. "The students pay the money." She does admit that she has a surplus of enthusiasm. "I learned passion in the trenches raising my seven children and many grandchildren," she says. "It's easy to teach child development and educational psychology when I see it all around me."

Students describe Reed as "extremely helpful and unbelievably nice." "She knows what she's talking about and definitely has a passion for it," they say. "Make sure you take notes fast," though, because Reed tends to talk very rapidly. "She really is an inspiration. She is the reason I changed my major to psychology," says one satisfied student. "I have completed four of her classes. I am taking two now and plan to take as many as I can before graduation." "She has an overwhelming love to see her students succeed," concludes another student. "She will go beyond the limits to help her students and make sure they understand. I would most definitely take her a million times."

Catherine Sanderson, Professor of Psychology, Amherst College

Catherine Sanderson, a psychology professor at Amherst College, wants to help her students understand how psychology can help explain what they see in the real world, while building the crucial skills that will benefit them not only as students but also in their personal and professional lives ahead.

"I remember vividly the fabulous professors I had as an undergraduate student, and in particular the vivid way in which they described their own field—their love of F. Scott Fitzgerald, or American politics, or infant language acquisition. And I try to bring that type of enthusiasm into my own teaching."

Students say time flies in Professor Sanderson's classroom, where she is "smart, witty, quick and entertaining to the last degree" in teaching a slew of classes including Sports Psychology, Close Relationships, Health Psychology, Intro to Psychology ("the 'best hits' of the entire field of psychology"), and Social Psychology. She packs lots of information into each class, but adds many vivid examples from daily life and research to capture students' attention. "I love learning about (and teaching about) why people feel, think, and act the way that they do. I see the relevance of psychology in everything in the world, from understanding the goal behind advertising on TV, to teaching my toddler how to use the toilet, to preventing bullying in high schools," she says. "She keeps a large lecture class interesting and engaging, which is hard to do," says one student. "I listened so closely my jaw actually dropped," says another.

Shelly Schreier, PhD, Lecturer III, Department of Psychology, University of Michigan

Dr. Shelly Schreier, who teaches psychology at the University of Michigan, wants students to "find the true pleasures in the learning process and to define what it means for them to make the most of their time at the University, both in the classroom setting and in all the other opportunities available to them on campus."

She aims to help students connect with the class material as well as guide them in their own educational journey, and often encourages students to take a three-tiered approach to their educational process: to find meaningful courses which allow for the breadth and depth of inquiry, to participate in the experiential learning programs available to them, and to engage in the research which helps inform understanding. "I also encourage them to have fun along the way," she adds.

In classes such as Introductory Psychology and Social Development, Dr. Schreier is prepared for each class and presents the material in a meaningful and relevant way. "I tell my students it is their job to come to class, and it is my job to make sure that it is worth their time. I expect and receive excellent work from my students, because I demand no less from myself." Her style is one in which she actively engages the students in the material and makes it relevant for their lives; she tries to develop assignments which help students apply the material they are learning to real-life applications, "whether it is their understanding of the ethical challenges of conducting research on human subjects, defining intelligence from the perspective of the strengths and challenges of a child with Down Syndrome, or identifying the coping strategies illustrated by children who experienced the trauma of 9/11."

Students say that "she is incredibly animated and enthusiastic about teaching, and she cares about her students and tries to make lecture as interesting as possible." "Schreier is pretty awesome. Her classes were always upbeat."

Rebecca Shiner, Associate Professor and Chair, Psychology, Colgate University

Rebecca Shiner, who has taught psychology at Colgate University for twelve years, is most interested in the features that make people different from one another, specifically personality differences and psychological disorders. "I love introducing students to research on these topics because these issues are inherently interesting (who doesn't want to understand people better?) and also relevant to students' daily lives." She works hard to make sure that students engage deeply with the things that they learn, and encourages them to move from being passive recipients of information to active, critical evaluators of what they read and hear. "I also do my best to help students discover that learning is a great joy and privilege, and I encourage them to make connections between issues raised in class and their own lives and commitments."

While crafting lectures, assignments, and tests, Professor Shiner tries to put herself in her students' shoes, coming up with ways to present material in a way that is challenging but still organized and clear. In almost all of her classes, she uses a variety of teaching styles to maximize the students' learning, blending lectures with discussions and current examples, videoclips, debates, and case studies to bring the material to life. She helps students tackle Freud by introducing his original ideas as well contemporary research investigating his claims, and then asks students to apply what they have learned by discussing the question, "How would Freud explain the tendency of some college students to drink to excess?" She also shows a portion of a documentary that checks in on the lives of individuals once every seven years to illustrate the ways that early relationship experiences influence later relationships.

Students agree that she "truly cares about her work and it shines through in her classroom discussions and willingness to help outside of class." They find her to be entirely kind, approachable, and helpful, even "despite concerted efforts on my part to become more intimidating," says Professor Shiner. "I was lucky to attend a small liberal arts college [Haverford College] where the professors set high standards and committed themselves to helping students become better thinkers, writers, and speakers. They got to know their students as people. I still try to follow my professors' examples of strong commitment to my students' learning."

Dr. Melinda Shoemaker, Professor of Psychology, Broward College

Dr. Melinda Anne Shoemaker, a psychology professor at Broward College teaches her students to apply the information they learn in her classes to real-life situations that have meaning and relevance. "I loved her class, and also her acting skills when demonstrating different mental illnesses," says a student.

She believes that cooperative learning equals cooperative teaching, and shares her passion for people and psychology with her students and colleagues alike. Her courses include General Psychology, Advanced Psychology, Marriage & Family, and a human sexuality course known as Sex in the Summer. She brings the experiences from the twenty years she has spent in private practice as a psychologist to her classroom, where her teaching style is all about application of the material to life. "We define psychology, and explore how we apply behavior and mental processes to our lives every day," she says. "This is one of the best professors I've had in my life. She gives you detailed notes, her tests are easy, and you barely use the book. She knows her stuff and she's good at what she does!" says a student. "She is absolutely amazing teacher. You will never be bored in her class, ever," says another.

Sheldon Solomon, Professor of Psychology, Skidmore College

Students love the collegial manner of Skidmore College psychology professor Sheldon Solomon, a "modest, slightly crazed, genius with a wicked sense of humor," who "loves talking to students about anything." "I guarantee you'll wet your pants in his class," says a fan of his hilarity.

He "professes" with clarity and conviction, and conveys his enthusiasm "for the course material and for the virtue of learning, in general." A true scholar of psychology, his teaching style echoes Vygotsky's notion of the zone of proximal development, in that he engages students at their current level and in a fashion that conveys to them a sense that he respects them, expects them to succeed, and will hold them to the highest standards. His style is eclectic, and he admits that "sometimes my presentations are very typical and pedestrian (although

I look like a homeless janitor, which takes some people time to get used to; I decided early in my career that it was important for students to learn that you should never judge that quality of an idea by the appearance of the person who conveys it)"; other times he will have ten-minute polemics instead of lectures, or use music and film to convey psychological principles. Any way you look at it, students agree that he has no problem being able "to engage an auditorium full of over one-hundred students."

His current courses include Introductory Psychology, Evolutionary Psychology, and Human Dilemmas, an interdisciplinary first-year seminar based on fundamental questions about what it means to be a human being. Professor Solomon is a great believer in feedback (particularly for underclassmen), and some students who submit three page papers may find themselves with five pages of microscopically detailed notes. "I don't think it's appropriate to have a young student have vague feedback," he explains. A bastion of fairness, papers are graded anonymously so as to avoid any unintentional subjectivity on his part, and he encourages students to collaborate and cooperate, as long as their work is their own.

Howard A. Starr, PhD, Professor, Psychology and Education, Austin College

The image of the stuffy professor has no place in the classroom of Dr. Howard A. Starr, who teaches psychology at Austin College.

Having taught for more than forty-seven years (all at Austin College!) and having racked up numerous credentials in the psychology field (including Diplomate status in the American Association of Psychotherapy and a license in clinical hypnosis from the American Association of Clinical Hypnosis), Dr. Starr works to make his classroom relate to real life, and to "avoid being overly abstract." He vows to be "open and real and to model excitement for the class I am teaching," and his courses include Psychology of Gender and Dynamics of Counseling and Psychology of Death and Dying. He uses a local funeral home for the experiential portion of the class, and "he founded a (HOME) hospice and trained in the UK for hospice care and in Egypt and Israel for grief and bereavement work, experiences he calls upon to "give the class a global perspective on death and grief."

His classes call upon movies and related case studies heavily, and he uses an open lecture/discussion format; they quite pointedly involve "NO PowerPoint!" "I have taken all the classes he offers. His classes are very interesting, and he is very funny," says a student.

Peter M. Vishton, Associate Professor, Psychology, The College of William & Mary
Critical thinking is key for Peter M. Vishton, a psychology professor at The College of William & Mary: he wants students to learn where the information came from as well as what it means.

He teaches by discussing as much as by lecturing: "I rarely talk for more than about ten minutes before I am involved in asking students questions and engaging them in discussion to probe their understanding of the material as well as extend it." His courses include Sensation and Perception, Introduction to Psychology as a Natural Science, and Developmental Psychology; he says that "most people strongly associate psychology with psychotherapy and experiments with rats pressing levers, but there is so much more than that. Psychological science is a topic that has become increasingly broad and rigorous in recent decades."

His style of teaching varies tremendously depending on the topic and the size of the class, but in most cases, he seeks to engage the class in discussion. "I describe material to the students and then talk with them to derive what the meaning of that information really is—and why." His notes are all provided on PowerPoint, and his relaxed classroom manner is appealing to undergrads. "From YouTube videos to class polls and experiments, Vishton reinforces the material with activities," says one student.

Lawrence Wichlinski, PhD, Associate Professor of Psychology, Carleton College
Carleton College psychology professor knows how to play the game: First you pique the students' interest and curiosity, then you get your knowledge out there.

"I genuinely like students. I like to tell people about new things I've learned. And I do funny, original things in the classroom," he says. In order to get his students "to think about things they haven't thought about before in ways they haven't thought before," he connects with them at both emotional and intellectual levels, and takes what they tell him seriously. In return, they know he respects them and that he can (and will) learn from them. Says one: "His teaching style and enthusiasm, as well as his helpfulness, are truly unparalleled."

His classes include Behavioral Neuroscience, Psychopharmacology, and Sleep and Dreaming; in lecture classes, he teaches in a traditional style, peppered with videos, handouts, and odd, off-the-cuff digressions, using what students refer to as his "fantastic humor." For discussions, he'll usually have prepared questions, and relies heavily on small group and large group work. "Sometimes I have small student groups lead discussion. I get involved when the class is off topic or stuck," he says. "He is one prof who truly cares about his students and goes out of his way to help all students, even if they aren't psych majors," says a student.

Religion

Rick Axtell, Associate Professor, Religion, Centre College

"In 1976, while working in Bangladesh, I looked into the eyes of fellow human beings who were starving to death. Haunted by the suffering I saw that summer, I embarked on a quest that has remained with me for the rest of my life," says Rick Axtell, professor of religion at Centre College. "Experience of a new and disturbing reality raised questions that became my own, fueling a lifetime of teaching and research on issues of poverty, development, and revolutionary violence."

As his students have played with children of the municipal dump in Managua, Nicaragua, joined the harvest in a mountain coffee cooperative, interviewed victims of a massacre in Chiapas, Mexico, or stayed overnight in Louisville homeless shelters, he has known that the resulting questions would fuel lifelong quests for knowledge, and ongoing commitments to put knowledge to use making a difference in the world. "Teaching is transformative, and it can develop students with a critical consciousness who are more likely to be involved in creative social change as informed and responsible citizens," he says. His students call his courses "incredibly enlightening about real-world issues," which "will inspire you to do what you can to effect positive change and to critically analyze social structures."

A main value that motivates his teaching is a commitment to integrative studies, and he tries to blend theoretical and practical knowledge at every level. In his class Studies in Ethics: Poverty and Homelessness, which is a study of poverty and homelessness in light of six major philosophical and theological approaches to economic justice, pairs of students stay overnight in Louisville shelters and interview addicts, single moms, and low-wage laborers (numerous students in the class have gone on to find careers in homeless assistance agencies, demonstrating "that they have embarked on a lifelong journey"). Professor Axtell's other courses similarly overlay theory with application, and include Religion and Violence and Liberation Theologies in Historical and Political Context. "The subject of religious social ethics allows for a wide variety of courses that are eye-opening, relevant, integrative, and often personally transformative, with a real-world experiential dimension. They have the capacity to raise questions about what kind of people students really want to be in a world of seemingly intractable problems," he says. "You'll be shocked at the end of the year about how much you've learned about the world and yourself," says a student.

Jane F. Crosthwaite, Professor of Religion, Mount Holyoke College

Religion professor Jane Crosthwaite helps students to think in creative ways about interesting issues; to know basic information so that creativity is possible; and to find gentle ways to deal with painful and difficult issues. "You will learn so much—you won't want to part with her!" says a student.

The Mount Holyoke College professor listens to her students and encourages them "to see the paradoxes and inevitable ironies in our human ventures." She encourages students to find a place and time to study, and to take an interest in outside activities, whether sports or music or theater, as it all contributes to the holistic individual. Classes play out pretty generally: "Students read; we talk; they correct me; I tease them; they listen to one another; they write papers; we talk more." She is "delightful, supportive, brilliant, an intriguing mind, and FUN! She shines," according to one student.

She has been teaching since 1962, and currently teaches a seminar on American Shakers and Introduction to Ethics. Speaking highly of Mount Holyoke students, she says that they "usually come to class well prepared so that ANYTHING we read together can receive serious (and humorous) discussion; Religious topics cover everything human (and beyond?) so we are able to learn about what it means to seek understanding and meaning in a complex world." This question, of course, "remains an open one."

Sociology

Arnie Arluke, Professor, Sociology and Anthropology, Northeastern University

"I want to get students to think about and apply sociology to their lives and the world around them," says Arnie Arluke, who teaches sociology and anthropology at Northeastern University. "By the end of the class, I want all students to take with them not only a solid grounding in sociological thinking and method, which they get, but also some of my own excitement about seeing our social world from a new, and at times critical, perspective."

In doing so, he has learned never to overestimate a group's attention span or underestimate its intelligence and motivation. He is happy to show vulnerability in class by talking about problems he has encountered and mistakes he has made in his research, and talks about how his research has affected his personal life both positively and negatively. "Arluke has made my mornings much brighter with his sincere and lighthearted stories of his adventures during sociological research," says a student. He tries to make himself available: "I quadruple the required three hours of office time per week, and I routinely arrive early and leave late for all my classes to conduct impromptu office hours right in the classroom."

The core of his teaching approach in his main course, Introductory Sociology, is built around the presentation of approximately twenty-two case studies, which are usually based on research that he has conducted or is conducting. For example, he lectures about "whether animal cruelty is linked to violence toward humans, what social forces are behind the emergence of cults, and how cadaver dissection affects medical students' moral and ethical outlook."

Whenever possible, this "very fascinating storyteller" directly ties these case studies to recent or current events, giving students a behind-the-scene look at how sociological research is actually conducted, and even gives them two research exercises that allow them "to get wet in the field." "I like to teach introductory sociology because it is an important pedagogical tool to attract new majors and minors, inspire others to take more courses in the area, and impart knowledge and perspective to those who may never take another course in this field," he says. "Arnie is full of life and is a great public speaker. Seems more like a friend than a professor," says a student.

Catherine Marrone, Professor of Sociology, Director of Undergraduate Studies, State University of New York—Stony Brook University

Working at a midsize to large state school, Catherine Marrone, who teaches sociology courses at SUNY Stony Brook and also acts as the director of under-graduate studies, begins each semester by attempting to assuage students' fear of big classes. "I try to make a large class seem much smaller and more intimate. I like my classes to feel interactive, and I truly want to hear what they have to say. My students say the most amazing things and I usually leave class thinking I learned something from them."

It's no surprise that Professor Marrone's classes are on the larger side, given her reputation for being "extremely articulate and brilliant" and a course load that includes such titillating classes as The Sociology of Drugs and Alcohol and the brand new Perverts, Pimps, and Pills, which gets students to see that "we are the ones who actually turn out to be those who can fall into these categories," and that "while we tend to see others as deviant and behaving outside of normal behavior expectations, technological media and technological communication apparatus have turned those of us who like to think of ourselves as 'normal,' sometimes, into something else." In lieu of PowerPoints and Overheads, she carefully prepares lectures that allow for the class to "lead, in some ways, where we're going to go." Current themes are par for any given course, and hot topics in her Winter Class include the growth of online dating as well as shifts in our expectations for privacy, our fascination with the "exposure" that comes with mediated culture, and the growth of a new "peep" culture.

Provocative titles aside, Professor Marrone's goal is to broaden the student's perspective on understanding human behavior by using the social sciences, all while learning about and connecting to them as individuals. "I really enjoy learning about my students, and love to hear about their ideas and thoughts and it is one of the best things about working on such a diverse campus," she says. Her classroom is a no-judgment zone, and she makes it clear from the start that students are welcome to come talk to her about anything; they can even interrupt her in the middle of a lecture if they feel it necessary. "She's like a mom to her students, always willing to help and really passionate about her subject," says a student.

Michallene McDaniel, PhD, Associate Professor of Sociology, Gainesville State College

"My goal is not to fill students' heads with facts, although I suspect (and hope) that ends up being a side effect of my teaching," says Michallene McDaniel, a Gainesville State College sociology professor. Rather, her primary goal is to encourage students to think about the things most familiar to them in new ways. "I tell students that I'm not trying to change their beliefs, but trying to expand their capacity to think critically about society and their place in it."

She does this by meeting the students where they are, intellectually and culturally, and demystifying the knowledge-attainment process, so they feel secure enough to consider new ideas and perspectives. Everything boils down to the fact that Dr. McDaniel considers her job to be a privilege: "As I tell students, being in a classroom talking about ideas with people who are engaged in thinking is about the most fun way I can spend my days."

She is not too concerned with formality in the classroom (teaching such classes as Marriage & Family, Introduction to Sociology, and Contemporary Global Issues: The Biological, Social and Cultural Dimensions of HIV/AIDS), and tries to remain flexible with course content and time management; she attempts to personalize just about anything she teaches by sharing examples of concepts from her personal life and encouraging the students to do the same, which leads to a discussion. "This usually achieves the goal of moving students away from their preconceived notions in a nonthreatening way, so that they may consider issues from new perspectives," she says. Students say "she tells funny stories that correlate with what you're learning," and always "leaves room for discussion among the students." "I loved this class and even at 8:00 A.M. I still found a way to get out of bed and come! Take her if you want a good experience with sociology."

Todd Schoepflin, Associate Professor, Sociology, Niagara University

Todd Schoepflin, a Niagara University sociology professor, "strives to offer material that is neither dumbed down nor over [students'] heads." "I try to offer material that intrigues them and makes them curious to learn more about the subject matter. I encourage them to engage with the material and provide examples of their own," he says. "I believe that I give them a lot to think about, and that I help to develop their critical thinking skills and their ability to see things from a variety of perspectives."

His courses include Race & Ethnicity, Social Psychology, and Introduction to Sociology; he particularly loves teaching the latter class, as he greatly enjoys teaching new students, and being the first person to teach them about the field of sociology. "I am interested in everything sociology has to offer: race, social class, gender, sexuality, culture, subcultures, deviance, marriage, family, and much more!" he says.

In his classes, Professor Schoepflin conveys an enthusiasm for his subject, and he works hard to involve students in every class session so it will catch on. "[Students] often say how I love my job. They are correct in saying so." Classes are discussion-based, and he often challenges students on their points or asks for examples to encourage them to defend their positions. He also uses media to expand a topic in class: "For example, if we're talking about the sociology of relationships, I will play a song with lyrics about relationships. That expands the conversation and provides another way to engage with the theory or concept we're discussing in class."

Students think that "he really makes you interested in what he's discussing, and makes it easy for you to understand." "You will love this class even if you are not required to take it," says one.

Alan Stracke, Professor of Sociology, Champlain College. Master Teacher (Association of Vermont Independent Colleges), Recipient of Champlain College's Lyman Award for Most Outstanding Professor (2001–2003).

Alan Stracke, began his teaching career in 1968 at the age of twenty-one, taught at Northern Michigan University and the University of Arizona before arriving at Champlain in 1973. Professor Stracke inspires his students to think critically and creatively about their place in the world and how they might have a positive influence on others through mindful interaction and self-reflection.

He is patient, creative, and engaging, and most importantly, he always "remembers that college students are young adults, responsible and open-minded when presented with information in a relevant manner." He has taught for more than forty-three years, mainly bringing students into his field through Introduction to Sociology, the major goal of which is to better understand the way in which our world of human interactions work. "Deconstructing our societies' mechanics provides us with our only opportunity to begin to better understand our place in our environments and global community. This leads to a better understand of ourselves," he says. Professor Stracke uses a methodology he calls, Collaborative Engagement Through Narrative, which is student-centered and inquiry-based; focusing on a self-reflective collaborative learning process. His extensive studies and time spent in the Caribbean have resulted in his writing of three "story" textbooks, filled with brief metaphorical anecdotes, embedded with sociological concepts that recount his personal Caribbean interactions. "The courses themselves are a cycle, beginning and ending with the personal." Students say that "because of his real-life process of teaching, learning is extremely interesting. You just really WANT to be in class!"

His favorite thing about teaching is "a young adult's willingness to risk old patterns of thinking and explore, adapt, and critically think about themselves and their culture in a different way." Specifically, he loves being the one who gets to expose the students to a new "awareness of being"—personally, culturally, and interculturally. Students warn others not to miss his class, as "the man is amazing, brilliant, welcoming, fresh, bright and fun. He will connect with everyone in his class, whether they know it or not."

Eleanor Townsley, Professor of Sociology, Mount Holyoke College

A curiosity about the world around her and a passion for sharing it with students is what drives Eleanor Townsley, who teaches sociology at Mount Holyoke College. "In general, my goal is to help students see further," says Professor Townsley. "One way we say this in sociology, following C. Wright Mills, is that we want students to develop their sociological imaginations. I hope students know that I have their best interests at heart and believe they can do great things."

These words of wisdom come from a woman who is described by students as "incredibly witty, thoughtful, and BRILLIANT in sociology," extremely dedicated to her work, and "from her lectures alone you can see how much she loves what she studies." Another student said, "I was not particularly interested in media or in sociology, and after taking her class, I've decided to major in sociology."

Though her preferred topic is theory because, as Townsley says, "big ideas are important," "she also enjoys introductory classes that allow her to act as the gateway to the field of sociology, as well as topics courses such as Intellectuals, Media and the Public Sphere, Sociology of Media, and Contemporary Theory and Cultural Sociology.

"I have always been fascinated by how intellectuals and ideas affect social change," Professor Townsley says. "It seemed to me—and it still does—that sociology can provide both the theories and empirical tools to address these questions."

Professor Townsley's classes are a combination of lecture and discussion, and she likes to pose questions that students will keep thinking about after class. "One of my favorite exercises is to introduce the idea of small-scale social structure, that is, the idea that social interaction is structured," she says. To illustrate the concept, she'll break a mundane rule of social interaction to reveal how it works. "For instance, I will offer to shake someone's hand and then quickly take my hand away when the student moves to return the handshake. Students typically laugh or say I'm mean. I then push them to elaborate why, and to describe what occurred more precisely. The goal is to get students to see how the operation of these small-scale social structures produce social order and support social institutions."

Ken Tucker, Professor of Sociology, Mount Holyoke College
"My goals are to have students understand the readings and concepts, learn to criticize them, and develop their own arguments about the readings and issues," says Mount Holyoke College sociology professor Kenneth H. Tucker Jr.

He is not a "flaky teacher"; his students consider him to be well organized, knowledgeable, and in possession of a terrific sense of humor. "He was always clear on his requirements, stuck to the syllabus, made himself available outside class and CONSISTENTLY advertised his office hours and reminded us to come," says a student. "He is such a nice guy; willing to talk anytime about career, grad school, assignments, and life. [He] makes lectures really interesting."

His classes include his yearly Classical and Contemporary Social Theory courses, which he enjoys "because the complex readings challenge the students, and they learn to understand and criticize important and substantive arguments." He's been bringing his "organized but relaxed" teaching style to students for twenty-five years; typically, he'll lecture for a bit, and then ask the students questions on the readings. "I use personal stories, humor, and occasionally videos to spark discussion. I try to incorporate what my students say into the discussion, so that they feel ownership for the class and the material," he says. "You can tell he's brilliant, but he never flaunts it, and he makes everything easy to understand," says a student.

Sport Management
Dr. Robert Kostelnik, Associate Professor, Sport Management, Indiana University of Pennsylvania
Dr. Robert Kostelnik, who teaches Sport Management in the Health & Physical Education Department at Indiana University of Pennsylvania, treats students as he would want professors to treat his own children while they are in college.

He tries to make them comfortable in the classroom and makes it clear that he has time for their academic needs and personal concerns. While he understands that they have interests other than his courses, he is upfront about the need for them to complete a professional product with papers, projects, and assignments in a timely fashion. A student from his general Health and Wellness course said: "He cares about his students and understands that your major might not be what he is teaching." Another student remarked: "You have to go to class but he makes it so you want to be there."

"Dr. Bob's" courses include Sport Facilities Management, Health and Wellness, Seminar in Sport Management, and he also serves as the Sport Management Internship Coordinator. He draws upon his past experience managing sport facilities to provide real-world examples and a practical application of concepts needed to be successful in the sport industry. "I have students complete real work assignments in class. I also use a variety of techniques to connect with students. Each week I use toy raffles, 'penny candy' giveaways, 'name that tune' for a prize, etc. It helps students relax, laugh, and connect with each other," he says. "He crams a lot into a small time but he does it well," says a student.

Theatre

Susan Daniels, Visiting Instructor in Theatre Arts, Mount Holyoke College
Susan Daniels, who teaches Theatre Arts at her alma mater Mount Holyoke College, wants to encourage curiosity, inspire courage, and empower students to use their bodies, minds, and spirit when connecting with others.

The nature of her job requires flexibility in her teaching; this means being "open to what the students need, and sometimes it means pushing your planned agenda to the side and just 'showing up' for your students." Her passion for her teaching and her compassion for her students is obvious, and students can tell that she is invested in their success. "I enjoy helping students reach a new level of understanding when they are onstage, backstage, or part of an audience."

She currently teaches two classes at Mount Holyoke: Acting I and Public Speaking: Leadership Presence. Both draw on her professional theatre background and expertise (she has been an Actors Equity Association member for twenty-five years, and has also directed). The first class introduces the students to performance through a variety of improvisational exercises designed for developing basic acting techniques (and includes two performance projects); the second uses the same techniques that professional actors use to relax, focus their message, and connect with their audience, in order to explore the art and craft of public speaking. "My Public Speaking class is especially rewarding, as I teach women from all over the world how to powerfully and persuasively connect with their audience," she says. One student says "her acting class should be the first one you should consider…no matter what your major."

Her approach to teaching is "dynamic, supportive, and inclusive." After she introduces a topic in class, students are encouraged to experience what they've learned and practice it, and are required to participate actively in each class and learn to give constructive feedback and effectively evaluate others. "We had so much fun in class while learning so much about acting and about ourselves. We juggled with different tactics, analyzed, observed other actors, and had a FANTASTIC TIME," says a student.

Gregg Stull, Professor of Theatre, University of Mary Washington
"Listening is fundamental and often undervalued. It takes a great deal of courage to be a student…to be vulnerable to what you do not know, and to be patient with yourself in the journey of learning and mastering a subject." Or so says Gregg Stull, who teaches theatre at the University of Mary Washington.

His greater plan for students is to imbue them with a curiosity about the world, so that they will be "willing to wrestle with the challenging questions that are a part of being alive." Students may initially be surprised by his candor and the honesty of his critique, but "many come to appreciate that facing challenging critique is the key." "This course taught me about acting, about life and about myself," confirms a student.

In courses such as Acting, Directing, and Theatre Management, he teaches beginning and advanced students the theory and practice of the crafts. He enjoys the variety of what he teaches and finds that each offers a different and satisfying experience for both his students, and himself. "I believe that theatre has the power to change lives and I relish the opportunity of working in this field helping emerging professionals hone their skills and thinking about the discipline," he says.

He has worked in the professional theatre (a student says he has "more wisdom and passion in his little finger than most professors have in their entire bodies"), served as a consultant to it, and maintains a close relationship with the business, so his teaching is deeply connected to his professional life; he believes that teaching is "an extraordinary opportunity to explore the world with my students." He prefers "to learn as they do, to lecture less and to engage conversation more, and to connect what we are learning to what is happening in the world beyond the classroom." Students may consider him "demanding," but they know that he is "approachable and expects everyone to work hard."

Writing

Karen Gocsik, Adjunct Associate Professor & Executive Director, Writing and Rhetoric Courses, Institute for Writing and Rhetoric, Dartmouth College

Karen Gocsik, who teaches courses for the Institute of Writing and Rhetoric at Dartmouth College, is committed to inspiring her students to think more critically, to write more inventively, and to work with more focus and intensity than ever before.

Professor Gocsik begins each class or office hour with the assumption that her students are capable of producing something astonishing. She then works to tease that something out by listening carefully, asking tough questions, and requiring students to consider perspectives that they haven't yet considered. In short, she challenges her students. Her classes are known for being difficult; students call her first-year composition class "the hardest class you'll ever love." Her knowledge of culture is "phenomenal," according to students, and she is willing to debate ideas "until she has beat the living daylight out of all the angles."

Nevertheless, Professor Gocsik believes that hard work and high standards do not, by themselves, create a great learning experience for students. "It's necessary to balance the more difficult aspects of the class with close and careful attention. And so I support my students, from starting block to finish line," she says. She gets to know the way students' minds work: what they think about, what they're scared of intellectually, and what they need to do in order to leapfrog their fears. She makes herself available to her students, in her office and over e-mail, even rather late at night. "I care about their success, and they know that—every step of the way."

After twenty years of teaching, Professor Gocsik has committed herself very strongly to the principles of active and engaged learning. In her classroom, student papers, films, and presentations are among the texts of study: "We spend as much energy—and have as much fun—discussing student work as we do Dostoevsky *et al.*" Students are entrusted with the responsibility for their own learning; they co-direct the teaching process "by shaping discussion, defining course questions, developing their own research agenda, and even collaborating with me to develop grading rubrics." Students seem to find these methods successful. "Karen has taken…my nonsensical writing, and made it make sense." She is the best professor I have ever had," says a student. "Her classes promote an intellectual curiosity that continues to serve her students even after her class."

Melinda D. Papaccio, Writing Instructor, Seton Hall University

The aim of Melinda Papaccio, who teaches writing at Seton Hall University, is to "help students to become better writers not only be developing basic essential writing skills but also, and perhaps more importantly, by developing their critical thinking skills."

One of her favorite professors always prompted her to keep in mind the question "What have you forgotten?" Remembering this lesson, she integrates new material with what has already been learned, in order to get students to reflect on their development as learners. Writing is a skill crucially fundamental to students' success in college, and she relishes being able to interact with students at this stage in their academic development. "I enjoy learning from them as well as teaching them," she says.

She teaches Core English I and II, which are freshman composition courses that focus on essay writing and researched writing; she uses a coaching style of teaching in which she provides students with instructions and examples of the work she wants them to do, then guides them as they work through the process on their own. "Whenever possible I allow them to choose the topics they write about so that they feel greater personal investment in the subject."

"She is the most respectful and caring teacher I have had in college and when it comes to her students she cares a lot!" says a student. Not only does she let students do papers over if they are not happy with their grades, she "is a very friendly woman and an extremely approachable teacher, willing to answer any questions students might have."

School Profiles

Albion College

611 East Porter
Albion, MI 49224
Admissions: 517-629-0321
www.albion.edu
admissions@albion.edu
Fax: 517-629-0569

Type of school: private
Environment: village
Total undergrad enrollment: 1,587
Student/faculty ratio: 13:1
Most common regular class size: 10–19

Range SAT Critical Reading: 540–600
Range SAT Math: 610–630
Range SAT Writing: 510–590
Range ACT Composite: 25–28

Annual tuition: $32,662
Average cumulative indebtedness: $34,282

% students graduating in 4 years: 64%
% students graduating in 6 years: 74%

Paul Anderson, Mathematics

Michigan's private Albion College aims to blend a traditional education with professional development to ensure that students are prepared to succeed in the workforce. The proof is in the pudding at this college, which places 95 percent of its graduates in prestigious law, medical, and dental schools around the country.

While emphasizing a classical foundation, Albion also requires students to take advantage of gender, ethnic, global, and environmental studies courses. Students enjoy the school's "amazing ability to provide 'small school' intimacy that they are able to build with their peers and instructors while delivering world-class education that competes with major universities."

Albion scholars praise their teachers as well, claiming the college employs "professors that would make many bigger schools drool." They say, "Since it's strictly an undergraduate institution, Albion's services are all geared toward the students."

Better yet, "the entire faculty and staff always make time for students and even acknowledge you by name when you walk past them on campus." "The professors seem to genuinely envision a greater academic career for all students and strongly encourage further schooling after attaining the four-year degree."

Amherst College

Campus Box 2231
P.O. Box 5000
Amherst, MA 01002
Admissions: 413-542-2328
www.amherst.edu
admission@amherst.edu
Fax: 413-542-2040

Type of school: private
Environment: town
Total undergrad enrollment: 490
Student/faculty ratio: 8:1
Most common regular class size: 10–19

Range SAT Critical Reading: 670–770
Range SAT Math: 670–770
Range SAT Writing: 680–770
Range ACT Composite: 30–34
Annual tuition: $40,160
Average cumulative indebtedness: $12,843

% students graduating in 4 years: 89%
% students graduating in 6 years: 94%

Javier Corrales, Political Science
Tekla Harms, Geology
Chris Kingston, Economics
Paul Rockwell, French
Catherine Sanderson, Psychology

An academic powerhouse, Amherst is one the country's premier liberal arts colleges. Situated in bucolic western Massachusetts, the school provides a "strong sense of community" and is brimming with a student body that's "open minded, intellectually passionate, and socially conscious." Add to that mix a "club or organization for every [possible] interest" and dorms that are as "luxurious as many five-star hotels" and you have a recipe for success. Of course, education is the number-one priority here, and Amherst undergrads truly appreciate their time in the classroom. Indeed, students are quick to praise their "fantastic" professors who clearly "come here to teach…not just to do research." The faculty is truly "dedicated" and "easily accessible." One happy undergrad expounds, "I'm amazed at how easy it is to sit down for a casual lunch with anyone in the administration without there having to be a problem that needs to be discussed." What more could a student ask for?

Auburn University

108 Mary Martin Hall
Auburn, AL 36849-5149
Admissions: 334-844-4080
www.auburn.edu
admissions@auburn.edu
Fax: 334-844-6436

Type of school: public
Environment: town
Total undergrad enrollment: 20,209
Student/faculty ratio: 18:1
Most common regular class size: 20-29

Range SAT Critical Reading: 535-650
Range SAT Math: 560-660
Range SAT Writing: 530-640
Range ACT Composite: 24-30

Annual in-state tuition: $7,008
Annual out-of-state tuition: $21,024
Average cumulative indebtedness: $23,491

% students graduating in 4 years: 36%
% students graduating in 6 years: 66%

Thomas Beard, Economics
Macy Finck, Economics

Auburn University, students agree, "provides excellence in academics, athletics, and social experiences, all in one of the friendliest towns in the country." One student says, "I chose Auburn because of its people. The Auburn community is so kind and supportive, and the level of passion the teachers and faculty have for Auburn is heartwarming." This sense of community helps make Auburn "a large school with a small feel" that "offers amenities only a large school has to offer" without forsaking the personal touches. "I feel that the faculty and administration genuinely care about us," says a student. Professors are "willing to bend over backwards to make sure [you] get everything out of the learning experience that [you] want."

Academics are "challenging and rewarding," with Auburn's "great engineering program" receiving especially high marks. The school's many business undergrads appreciate "the real-world aspect that many teachers try to bring into the classroom." With all these assets, it's no wonder Auburn students brag that "Auburn prepares you for life and any educational aspirations after [the] undergraduate [years], such as a graduate program, medical school, or law school."

Austin College

900 North Grand Avenue, Suite 6N
Sherman, TX 75090-4400
Admissions: 903-813-3000
www.austincollege.edu
admission@austincollege.edu
Fax: 903-813-3198

Type of school: private
Environment: town
Total undergrad enrollment: 1,328
Student/faculty ratio: 12:1
Most common regular class size: 10-19
Range SAT Critical Reading: 560-680
Range SAT Math: 570-670
Range SAT Writing: 540-650
Range ACT Composite: 24-28

Annual tuition: $29,075

% students graduating in 4 years: 67%
% students graduating in 6 years: 74%

David Baker, Physics
Light T. Cummins, History
Stephanie Gould, Chemistry
Kevin M. Simmons, Economics
Howard A. Starr PhD, Psychology and Education
Randi Lynn Tanglen, English

A "small school with a huge amount of opportunities," Austin College "is about active learning and creating unique experiences for each student" through "unsurpassed opportunities for internships, studying abroad, and a personalized learning experience," students tell us. "A strong premed program" attracts many undergraduates to this campus; psychology, political science, international relations, environmental studies, language programs featuring "the Jordan Family Language House, the language tables in the cafeteria, conversation classes, and incredibly easy access to study abroad," and an education program "where one can get a [master's degree in teaching]" also earn students' accolades. Students are especially enthusiastic about AC's "JanTerm," "where for the month of January students take one intensive course," and "many students take the opportunity to go abroad or do internships or directed studies of their choice." Best of all, students benefit from "matched tuition when abroad," which means that "all scholarships and loans remain in place for your tuition abroad." Academics entail "a well-rounded and difficult curriculum that really gives students...bang for their buck," combined with "tough classes, hard work, and great people." The end result, undergraduates explain, is "a fun yet academically challenging place that is more home than school."

Students "really enjoy the one-on-one attention" and the "close relationship with professors." "I came from a huge high school and I wanted personal attention and the ability to see my work make a difference." "Professors are extremely easy to access and have been more than willing to put in the extra time to help me reach my true potential." Many students agree. "The professors are the greatest strength. They honestly care about each student." Professors are "accessible" and "fun and intelligent." "I wanted to go to a small school where I could have good relations with my professors. Austin College is perfect for that." "The small atmosphere makes the learning experience very personal. I love being able to get to know my professors." "The professors truly care about their fields of study, and crave to teach their inquiring minds." "The faculty and staff seemed to care about students as individuals." "Professors know students by name, and grade their papers without the aid of a TA. When a student declares his/her major, the professors in that department instantly become his/her best friends, and help form connections for internships and jobs in the future." "The faculty works with you and helps you grow to make sure that you get everything you wanted out of your college experience."

Bard College

Office of Admissions
Annandale-on-Hudson, NY 12504
Admissions: 845-758-7472
www.bard.edu
admission@bard.edu
Fax: 845-758-5208

Tucked away in New York's Hudson Valley, Bard College can sometimes seem like an educational utopia. For students who have a strong interest in learning beyond grades and a passion for political and social activism, this could be the campus for them. "Bard is a place for free-thinkers, regardless of what type or

Type of school: private
Environment: rural
Total undergrad enrollment: 1,928
Student/faculty ratio: 10:1
Most common regular class size: 10–19
Range SAT Critical Reading: 680–740
Range SAT Math: 650–680

Annual tuition: $43,306
Average cumulative indebtedness: $24,311

% students graduating in 4 years: 66%
% students graduating in 6 years: 76%

Diana DePardo-Minsky, Art and
Architectural History
Karen Sullivan, Literature

affiliation of 'thinking' they subscribe to, to join together for a strong educational experience with outstanding professors," one student says.

Incoming freshman begin building their educational foundation immediately, starting with a three-week orientation and a rigorous communication and research workshop. All first-year students are also required to enroll in a year-long seminar focusing on the survey of history's "great ideas," setting them up to prepare for their senior project during their final year.

An abundance of support is easy to find at Bard. Students rave that "the administration and professors are amazingly accessible. A simple e-mail can get you an appointment with the dean of students, and the professors encourage students to ask for help or to discuss any ideas they may have." At the same time, it is made clear that "all the students must put some effort into their work to get the real payoff. It's a bit like real life in that manner."

Bentley University

175 Forest Street
Waltham, MA 02452
Admissions: 781-891-2244
www.bentley.edu
ugadmission@bentley.edu
Fax: 781-891-3414

"If you're looking to work in business in the Boston area, desire a beautiful campus, state-of-the-art trading room, and technologically advanced university, Bentley University is the place for you," one student assures us. Bentley is known for its business program, and many students cite the program's excellent reputation as their reason for choosing to attend college here, as well as strong career services and professional internship opportunities. Students are pleased with

Type of school: private
Environment: town
Total undergrad enrollment: 4,196
Student/faculty ratio: 14:1
Most common regular class size: 20-29
Range SAT Critical Reading: 530-630
Range SAT Math: 590-670
Range SAT Writing: 540-630
Range ACT Composite: 25-28

Annual tuition: $35,580
Average cumulative indebtedness: $32,710

% students graduating in 4 years: 79%
% students graduating in 6 years: 88%

Erl Sorensen, Mathematical Sciences

Bentley's abilities to create a "career-bound student while instilling the importance of liberal studies," and to "prepare you and help you earn a job with all the technical and educational background you need." They also "love that most of the professors have worked outside of academia and can bring...real-world experience and examples to the classroom." Professors are "great role models and have had a lot of experience in the business world," and "all professors hold office hours, and they are all responsive to e-mail and phone messages." "The professors are amazing, and the learn-by-doing culture that is the trademark of Bentley produces students with superior skills. Bentley students, faculty, and high level administrators care deeply for the school, and have enormous pride in our community." "Class sizes are capped at thirty-five, which gives students a solid relationship with each professor," and "a lot of classes are discussion-based and force you to think about real-world applications." Some students note that classes can be challenging but that "many of the departments have tutoring labs available for students at all levels."

Brigham Young University

A-153 ASB
Provo, UT 84602-1110
Admissions: 801-422-2507
www.byu.edu
admissions@byu.edu
Fax: 801-422-0005

Type of school: private
Environment: city
Total undergrad enrollment: 30,409
Student/faculty ratio: 21:1
Most common regular class size: 20-29
Range SAT Critical Reading: 570-680
Range SAT Math: 580-690
Range ACT Composite: 26-30

Annual tuition: $4,560
Average cumulative indebtedness: $13,354

% students graduating in 4 years: 31%
% students graduating in 6 years: 78%

John D. Bell, Physiology & Developmental
Biology
Rebecca Clarke, English
Rosalind Hall, Music
Kerry Muhlestein, Ancient Scripture and
Ancient Near Eastern Studies
Larry J. Nelson, School of Family Life
Steven C. Walker, English

Brigham Young University is a school that marries together education and faith. Affiliated with the Mormon Church, BYU provides an opportunity to learn "about secular objects through spiritual eyes." The university offers a wide array of majors and undergrads are especially quick to the highlight the phenomenal education, business, mathematics, and language programs. Importantly, "hands-on experience, internships, and study abroad are highly encouraged." The strongest praise, however, is reserved for that of the beloved BYU professors. A "very intelligent" group, faculty here are "all extremely passionate about what they teach, so even if the course work is boring, their excitement about the subject rubs off onto you." "Most professors are just as excited about the courses that they teach as they are about the research that they are conducting." While the "work here is really challenging," most undergrads agree that professors "know how to push you to your limit without pushing too far." Indeed, "every single teacher has a lot of concern for your welfare as a student and wants to see you succeed." Another ecstatic undergrad summarizes it thusly: "My professors have all been extremely accessible and very interested in getting to know their students."

Brown University

Box 1876
45 Prospect Street
Providence, RI 02912
Admissions: 401-863-2378
www.brown.edu
admission_undergraduate@brown.edu
Fax: 401-863-9300

Type of school: private
Environment: city
Total undergrad enrollment: 6,102
Student/faculty ratio: 9:1
Most common regular class size: 10–19
Range SAT Critical Reading: 660–760
Range SAT Math: 670–770
Range SAT Writing: 670–770
Range ACT Composite: 29–33

Annual tuition: $42,230
Average cumulative indebtedness: $22,468

% students graduating in 4 years: 86%
% students graduating in 6 years: 96%

Barrett Hazeltine, Engineering
Joseph Pucci, Classics
Stephanie Ravillon, French
Roberto Serrano, Economics
Daniel Stupar, Visual Arts

Brown University, unique among Ivy League schools, is home to the first engineering school of the elite group. The Rhode Island campus hosts over six thousand undergraduate students with more than eighty degree programs to choose from. While biology, history, and international relations are among the most popular, students have a wealth of intellectual paths to choose from including a rare undergraduate concentration in Egyptology.

Though no grades are given at the university there's no doubt that excellence is in abundance with five professors and two alumni having been named Nobel laureates. Brown University prides itself on encouraging freedom over one's education, and students have the opportunity to rate their courses in the annual university publication, the *Critical Review*.

Brown is the institution for the student that has a passion for the exploration of knowledge beyond their transcript. "My professors, with few exceptions, are excited to have us in their class, and so are we. Every student in a class wants to be there, and this fact makes our professors that much more enthusiastic," one student says.

Bucknell University

Freas Hall Bucknell University
Lewisburg, PA 17837
Admissions: 570-577-1101
www.bucknell.edu
admissions@bucknell.edu
Fax: 570-577-3538

Type of school: private
Environment: village
Total undergrad enrollment: 3,487
Student/faculty ratio: 10:1
Most common regular class size: 10-19
Range SAT Critical Reading: 590-670
Range SAT Math: 630-710
Range SAT Writing: 600-690
Range ACT Composite: 27-31

Annual tuition: $43,268
Average cumulative indebtedness: $18,900

% students graduating in 4 years: 89%
% students graduating in 6 years: 91%

Richard Fleming, Philosophy

A top-ranked university nestled in rural Pennsylvania, Bucknell provides a comprehensive liberal arts education. Though the academics are challenging, undergrads are laid back and noncompetitive. And with a beautiful campus and bustling social scene, it is easy to understand why students at Bucknell are so enamored of their school. Notably, undergrads are quick to highlight their beloved professors who are "always willing to engage in discussions and debate in or out of the classroom." Moreover, "personal attention" from the faculty is the rule, not the exception, and professors "go out of their way to ensure that all of their students are happy and healthy." One lucky undergrad expounds, "During my freshman year, I was sick a lot and missed my first-year seminar frequently as a result. My professor regularly sent my roommate back from class with tea for me and notes encouraging me to take as much time as I needed to get back on my feet, and then was more than willing to help me catch up with my course work once I got better. This type of behavior is not unusual at all from Bucknell professors, and was definitely one of the things that helped me to feel most comfortable upon arriving here." Indeed, the university truly "fosters an environment in which students can learn and grow on their own terms and become well-rounded individuals." And certainly that is due in no small part to professors always ready to go the extra mile.

California State University—Long Beach

1250 Bellflower Boulevard
Long Beach, CA 90840
Admissions: 562-985-5411
www.csulb.edu
eslb@csulb.edu
Fax: 562-985-4973

Type of school: public
Environment: metropolis
Total undergrad enrollment: 27,436
Student/faculty ratio: 21:1
Most common regular class size: 20–29
Range SAT Critical Reading: 450–570
Range SAT Math: 470–590
Range ACT Composite: 18–24

Annual in-state tuition: $5,464
Annual out-of-state tuition: $11,160
Average cumulative indebtedness: $10,787

% students graduating in 4 years: 12%
% students graduating in 6 years: 42%

Tom Gufrey, Chemistry

Lots of excellent, career-oriented academic options and a fabulous location are a few of the features that make California State University—Long Beach an attractive destination. There are eight colleges and tons of majors. There's a strong arts education presence here—CSULB's College of the Arts has more art and design majors than any other public university in America. Engineering is particularly strong, and the nursing program has an excellent reputation. The faculty gets stellar reviews from students, especially relative to other schools of CSULB's size.

Students enjoy a wealth of big-school opportunities, like exposure to famous guest speakers and a host of career, research, and volunteer prospects. If none of this appeals to you, the beach is just five minutes away, and the campus is situated about thirty minutes south of Los Angeles (on a good traffic day).

"Long Beach State is a big commuter school" and many students lament that "there is no real sense of community." Others disagree. "There's plenty of campus life, culture, and activities—you just have to look," counters a senior. "When walking from class to class, it's pleasant to see the juggling club on the lawn, a reggae band playing near the dining hall, and the Filipino American Club discussing Justice for Filipino-American veterans."

Calvin College

3201 Burton Street SE
Grand Rapids, MI 49546
Admissions: 616-526-6106
www.calvin.edu
admissions@calvin.edu
Fax: 616-526-6777

Type of school: private
Environment: metropolis
Total undergrad enrollment: 3,839
Student/faculty ratio: 11:1
Most common regular class size: 20–29
Range SAT Critical Reading: 510–650
Range SAT Math: 540–670
Range ACT Composite: 23–29

Annual tuition: $24,645
Average cumulative indebtedness: $27,700

% students graduating in 4 years: 58%
% students graduating in 6 years: 77%

Kevin Corcoran, Philosophy
Larry Louters, Chemistry
Dan Miller, History
Doug Vander Griend, Inorganic Chemistry

Tucked away in Grand Rapids, Michigan, Calvin College is a Christian school that strives to challenge its students intellectually and simultaneously strengthen their faith. With a demanding workload, undergrads here must be diligent and willing to hit the books. Fortunately, the passion of their "amazing" professors is palpable and students are eager to learn. Indeed, undergrads at Calvin truly appreciate that "professors are not only focused on teaching the material but [also on] engaging [their] students in meaningful discussion at all levels." Moreover, they are all "very knowledgeable and are able to bring the material to life." Perhaps most important, the faculty here really have "a desire [to see] students succeed." As one pleased undergrad gushes, "[They] are always available and willing to explain anything, even if it's unrelated to class." A fellow student agrees, adding, "You can talk to them about your assignments, bring questions about the lecture, or just chat." Certainly, you're "[not] just a face" at Calvin. And while professors "aren't afraid to challenge students," they are quick to "provide support for students to overcome the challenges." One delighted undergrad shares, "Overall, my academic experience at Calvin has been eye opening and thought provoking. I've grown intellectually and matured spiritually. [And] the more I learn, the more questions I have." And another undergrad simply sums up her professors by concluding, "They are really what made my Calvin experience wonderful."

Carleton College

100 South College Street
Northfield, MN 55057
Admissions: 507-222-4190
www.carleton.edu
admissions@carleton.edu
Fax: 507-222-4526

Type of school: private
Environment: village
Total undergrad enrollment: 1,991
Student/faculty ratio: 9:1
Most common regular class size: 10–19
Range SAT Critical Reading: 660–750
Range SAT Math: 650–740
Range SAT Writing: 650–750
Range ACT Composite: 29–33

Annual tuition: $42,690
Average cumulative indebtedness: $19,436

% students graduating in 4 years: 89%
% students graduating in 6 years: 93%

Lawrence Wichlinski, Psychology

Carleton College offers a unique opportunity: students can receive a strong liberal arts education without forfeiting a solid science curriculum. The college gives students the choice to explore before making their decision on what path to choose. "I could truly explore what I wanted to do without feeling as though I would have to have a sub-par education in science, if that was what I chose to major in," one student confirms.

The workload is known to be challenging but students agree that the professors are more than helpful. "The teachers here may not always be hired for their research qualifications, although we do have quite the research department in the sciences. On the most part Carleton is known for the teachers who go the extra mile to teach the students, and take away any barriers to self-efficacy in their students."

It's not all about in-class learning, though. A reported two-thirds of the student body chooses to spend time learning off campus and even out of the country. Carleton provides programs around the globe in Asia (Thailand in particular), Africa and Spain, to name a few.

The campus itself is located in the sleepy town of Northfield, but students don't seem to mind, boasting that the many campus events and activities more than occupy their time. "An evening doesn't go by without some kind of event, whether it be musical, artistic, theatrical, or political," a student says.

Centre College

600 West Walnut Street
Danville, KY 40422
Admissions: 859-238-5350
www.centre.edu
admission@centre.edu
Fax: 859-238-5373

Type of school: private
Environment: village
Total undergrad enrollment: 1,214
Student/faculty ratio: 11:1
Most common regular class size: 10–19
Range SAT Critical Reading: 550–670
Range SAT Math: 570–670
Range SAT Writing: 530–670
Range ACT Composite: 26–30

Comprehensive fee: $39,000
Average cumulative indebtedness: $17,190

% students graduating in 4 years: 79%
% students graduating in 6 years: 81%

Rick Axtell, Religion
Mr. Patrice Mothion, French

Centre College offers students the promise of a practical and challenging education in a genuine and caring atmosphere. Indeed, tucked away in bucolic Danville, Kentucky, Centre provides a close-knit community where undergrads can truly focus on their studies. Though many students find that they "work harder here than [they] ever thought possible," they are quick to assure us that they feel "[incredibly] accomplished at the end of each semester." This is due in no small part to the "extremely passionate and dedicated professors," who continually prove themselves to be "kind, supportive [and] caring." Moreover, they make "an effort to work one-on-one with you if necessary" and encourage students to look beyond the confines of the classroom. In fact, one of Centre's goals is "preparing students to be actively engaged global citizens," and there's a "big movement on getting out of the classroom with community-based learning." Even if "a professor doesn't require that kind of learning," a student explains, "then they almost always will still make connections outside the classroom whether to real life or to other classes." With such dedication and focus, it's no wonder that Centre students graduate ready to tackle their goals.

Champlain College

163 South Willard Street
P.O. Box 670
Burlington, VT 05402-0670
Admissions: 802-860-2727
www.champlain.edu
admission@champlain.edu
Fax: 802-860-2767

Type of school: private
Environment: town
Total undergrad enrollment: 2,067
Student/faculty ratio: 14:1
Most common regular class size: 10–19
Range SAT Critical Reading: 500–610
Range SAT Math: 490–590
Range ACT Composite: 20–25

Annual tuition: $28,490
Average cumulative
indebtedness: $34,658

% students graduating in 4 years: 52%
% students graduating in 6 years: 65%

J.C. Ellefson, Creative Writing
Jonathan Rajewski, Digital Forensics
John Rogate, Computer Science
Eric Ronis, Communication and Creative Media
Alan Stracke, Sociology
Janice Gohm Webster, English

With highly ranked programs in professional majors such as game design and digital forensics, Champlain College "is a hands-on, professionally focused college aimed at creating well-rounded global citizens that excel in critical, interdisciplinary thinking." The school offers "one of the best, most innovative systems around to prepare students for the real world after college by implementing requirements throughout the program that help shape college students into professional 'job hunters.'" It also has campuses in Montreal and Dublin, and studying abroad is popular. Students love the "Upside-Down Curriculum in which students take major-related classes in their first year." Major classes are complemented by the LEAD program, which helps students develop community-building skills and awareness, and the Core program, which emphasizes interdisciplinary studies and critical thinking. The classes are small—"a class of thirty is rare and considered large"—and this "allows the students and teachers to get to know one another exceptionally well." "The relationship between students and professors is more like a partnership. The professors at Champlain believe the process of learning never stops and that students have just as much to offer as they do." At a school with such strong digital and design programs, it's no surprise that "professors and their class materials [and] structures are constantly updated and mirror many current real-life situations."

City University of New York—Brooklyn College

2900 Bedford Avenue
Brooklyn, NY 11210
Admissions: 718-951-5001
www.brooklyn.cuny.edu
Fax: 718-951-4506

Type of school: public
Environment: metropolis
Total undergrad enrollment: 11,740
Student/faculty ratio: 15:1
Most common regular class size: 20–29

Range SAT Critical Reading: 490–580
Range SAT Math: 520–610

Annual in-state tuition: $4,830
Annual out-of-state tuition: $13,050
Average cumulative indebtedness: $9,500

% students graduating in 4 years: 23%
% students graduating in 6 years: 48%

Jennifer Basil, Biology

Arguably one of the best schools in the City University of New York System, Brooklyn College is an academic epicenter that houses an average of sixteen thousand students. While the college offers a traditional liberal arts education, students find it to be "an academically challenging and rigorous school" that "feels a lot more competitive than one would anticipate."

For students seeking an additional challenge Brooklyn College's Honors Academy boasts six advanced programs and a nationally recognized core curriculum. Its well-known School of Education, named among the top twenty in the country, turns out some of the best teachers in New York City. It's this caliber of curriculum that has attracted its celebrated staff of educators.

Despite being winners of Pulitzers, Guggenheims, Fulbrights, and many National Institutes of Health grants, professors remain accessible. "All of my professors, in the two semesters I have been there, have gone above and beyond to make sure the class understands the materials, and that they are available outside the classroom. They all have worked to make sure the class is engaged in the topic and discussions, while also enforcing a strict respect and tolerance of all the opinions of their students. My academic experience here has been more than I expected and asked for."

City University of New York—Hunter College

695 Park Avenue, Room N203
New York, NY 10065
Admissions: 212-772-4490
www.hunter.cuny.edu
admissions@hunter.cuny.edu
Fax: 212-650-3472

Type of school: public
Environment: metropolis
Total undergrad enrollment: 14,609
Student/faculty ratio: 14:1
Most common regular class size: 20–29
Range SAT Critical Reading: 520–620
Range SAT Math: 530–630

Annual in-state tuition: $4,830
Annual out-of-state tuition: $13,050
Average cumulative indebtedness: $7,500

% students graduating in 4 years: 17%
% students graduating in 6 years: 46%

Avi Liveson, Economics

New Yorkers seeking "a superb learning environment for the independent and self-motivated" should check out Hunter College, a school that offers "a great education at an affordable price." A "serious academic environment" where "learning is taken very seriously" and "most people know exactly what they want and are going for it with full determination" creates "an amazing energy" at Hunter, an energy that feeds off the diverse New York student body.

Students report choosing Hunter "because of its diversity, affordability, and great professors." "Hunter is all about faculty members who are experts in their fields, teaching students everything they know." "It's about diversity within the students, within the classes, and within the teachers."

"Hunter is all about bringing people from all different parts of the world together in one place to learn from one another and to be exposed to almost every subject imaginable to help one find their true calling in life," one student reports. The New York location also gives Hunter access to many top academics; many professors here "teach at other, more expensive, universities. Throughout my Hunter career, I have had professors who also teach at NYU, Hofstra, Cooper Union, and Yale! So it really is quite the bargain." "Crowded" classes mean students need to "take matters in their own hands" if they "want to succeed and graduate in four years," but those who seek connections tell us that "despite the heavy loads they take on, professors are always available for individual attention, and they help you through anything you ask."

City University of New York— Queens College

6530 Kissena Boulevard

Jefferson 117

Flushing, NY 11367

Admissions: 718-997-5600

www.qc.cuny.edu

vincent.angrisani@qc.cuny.edu

Fax: 718-997-5617

Type of school: public

Environment: metropolis

Total undergrad enrollment: 15,337

Student/faculty ratio: 16:1

Most common regular class size: 20-29

Range SAT Critical Reading: 490-590

Range SAT Math: 530-610

Annual in-state tuition: $4,600

Annual out-of-state tuition: $9,960

Average cumulative indebtedness: $14,000

% students graduating in 4 years: 26%

% students graduating in 6 years: 51%

Susan Croll, Psychology

Affordable tuition, "challenging academic curriculum," and excellent scholarships—not to mention its location in New York City—make Queens College one of the most desirable schools in the City University of New York (CUNY) system. "The majority of professors are well educated, approachable, and interesting to listen to," reports one student, and the "good student-to-teacher ratio" counters one's expectations of the school's urban setting. This school may be located in one of the largest cities in the world, but educators here "are solely interested in you." These "top-notch professors" form the backbone of the "amazingly high levels of education" provided at Queens.

Queens College helps students to "achieve their career and educational goals by hiring outstanding faculty." That translates to a good classroom experience, with students finding their classes to be "enjoyable, with the majority of my professors proving to be competent instructors and passionate about their subject material." The "academic excellence" and "meaningful education" students look for at Queens comes via the efforts of those "economical, great professors" who "will nourish you and turn your dreams into reality."

The "dedicated" and "enthusiastic" faculty at this city college focus on "stressing academic studies while simultaneously developing cultural knowledge," giving students an education that "can be shaped to suit the needs and wants of a wide student body." Professors "are always there to help; they really care for their students." They are "so open and warm that they help you out if you need assistance or guidance." When they realize they have professors who are "willing to meet with students outside of the classroom to discuss anything and everything," some students feel like they are "around close relatives."

Thanks to its New York City location, there are "a plethora of extracurricular activities and diversity which can appeal to any student's interests," a perfect complement to the "qualified professors" who work toward "facilitating cross-cultural and multidisciplinary dialogue." With a school that is "all about bringing all different types of people together into a warm and open-minded learning environment," it should come as no surprise that educators here help foster a "diverse atmosphere where you are constantly learning from different cultures and beliefs." The school may be located in New York, but Queens College feels "relaxed" and "more suburban" than students expect.

This school "provides the support and knowledge for each student to achieve their goals," nurturing a "helpful environment without being overbearing" in order to "push you to reach your full potential." Students are thankful to "learn from professors with pretty admirable credentials," secure in the knowledge that their educators "know what you will need to use in your career." All in all, "Queens College is about learning from an accomplished faculty alongside a diverse student body while taking advantage of one of the greatest cities in the world that is right outside your doorstep."

Claremont McKenna College

890 Columbia Avenue
Claremont, CA 91711
Admissions: 909-621-8088
www.claremontmckenna.edu
admission@claremontmckenna.edu
Fax: 909-621-8516

Nestled in sunny Southern California, Claremont McKenna is one of the West Coast's premier liberal arts colleges. The school manages to provide an intellectually demanding curriculum while simultaneously maintaining a relaxed atmosphere. Students on this friendly campus are fortunate to have access to a wide variety of academic and social opportunities. Moreover, as a member of the five Claremont colleges, undergrads here can experience the intimacy of a small school while sharing the resources of a larger system.

Of course, one area where Claremont McKenna is unparalleled is their phenomenal faculty. Students are practically unanimous in their praise, sharing that their professors are "passionate about their [chosen] subject and want you to succeed." They understand how to cultivate an "academic experience that is intellectually stimulating [within] an environment that fosters learning." Importantly, they have "invaluable 'real world' experience from years in industry as opposed to a purely academic background, which fits in very well with CMC's practical approach to education and adds considerably to the learning experience." Moreover, they are "extremely accessible outside the classroom and often go the extra mile." Indeed, professors at Claremont McKenna "see themselves [not only as] teachers but also mentors." As one supremely content student sums up, "This sounds corny, but CMC really is a place where professors become like family. I have spent a good deal of out-of-classroom time with most of my professors, including eating dinner at numerous professors' homes, international travel with my Arabic professor, and participating in an extracurricular reading group with my philosophy professor."

Clemson University

105 Sikes Hall
Box 345124
Clemson, SC 29634-5124
Admissions: 864-656-2287
www.clemson.edu
cuadmissions@clemson.edu
Fax: 864-656-2464

Type of school: public
Environment: village
Total undergrad enrollment: 15,379
Student/faculty ratio: 16:1
Most common regular class size: 10–19
Range SAT Critical Reading: 550–650
Range SAT Math: 580–680
Range SAT Writing: 500–600
Range ACT Composite: 25–31

Annual in-state tuition: $12,319
Annual out-of-state tuition: $27,858
Average cumulative indebtedness: $17,882

% students graduating in 4 years: 50%
% students graduating in 6 years: 76%

Paul Christopher Anderson, History
Robert J. Kosinski, Biological Sciences
Robin Kowalski, Psychology
Karen A. Pressprich, Chemistry
Stephen Schvaneveld, Chemistry

Located in sunny South Carolina, Clemson University is "the total package: challenging academics, beautiful campus, sports, a thriving Greek life, Southern edge, and that extra something that just makes me excited to be here every morning when I wake up." "Nowhere else feels more like home," says another student. Clemson University is a science- and engineering-oriented research university that maintains a strong commitment to teaching and student success. Clemson's enrollment is about nineteen thousand, and the campus population is carefully managed to maintain small classes and a student-to-faculty ratio more common to private colleges. For students who are making the transition from high school to college, Clemson has developed student success programs to help meet the academic challenges. Students say that "the value is unbeatable," and have high opinions of the Clemson faculty. "I feel like my academic experience is extremely dynamic, and I truly enjoy going to class." "Even the two or three [professors who] are not effective teachers still do their best to make sure the students get the information they need to be successful." "Forget Walt Disney World. This is the happiest place on earth," one student brags. "Clemson's greatest strength lies in the sense of community it fosters and the opportunities for development that it offers to its students." A finance major sums up his experience: "At Clemson,

I'm earning a respected degree working alongside the leading researcher in my field, gaining valuable leadership experience while serving the community, and having the time of my life with my best friends. What's not to love?" "Honestly, as long as you wear orange on Fridays and love your Tigers, you'll fit in just fine." Students at the school take both their social and academic life seriously. "For the most part, Clemson students go out looking preppy on Saturday night, dress up for church on Sunday, and roll into class wearing sweats on Monday morning."

Colby College

4000 Mayflower Hill
Waterville, ME 04901-8848
Admissions: 207-859-4800
www.colby.edu
admissions@colby.edu
Fax: 207-859-4828

Type of school: private
Environment: town
Total undergrad enrollment: 1,825
Student/faculty ratio: 10:1
Most common regular class size: 10–19
Range SAT Critical Reading: 630–710
Range SAT Math: 620–710
Range SAT Writing: 620–715
Range ACT Composite: 28–31

Comprehensive fee: $51,990
Average cumulative indebtedness: $24,600

% students graduating in 4 years: 86%
% students graduating in 6 years: 89%

Dasan M. Thamattoor, Chemistry
Steve J. Wurtzler, Cinema Studies

This small, close-knit liberal arts college draws praise from students for its rigorous but caring approach to academics. The popular "Jan Plan" allows students to pursue focused course work, independent study, or internships during an intensive four-week term in January. Students must not only complete their major requirements but also fulfill a hefty load of distribution requirements to graduate. This dedication to academics can make Colby an intense place to go to school, and students here aren't "afraid to work hard and study."

Small classes are one of Colby's biggest draws: "I wanted smaller classes so that I could really get to know my professors and that is exactly what I got at Colby." "Colby has one of the most dedicated and intelligent group of faculty out of any college I visited. They are truly in a class of their own." "Professors are always willing to go the extra mile," one student says. A senior adds, "Over the course of my time at Colby I've been to at least six different professors' houses for departmental events, class dinners, and group discussions." Professors get high grades for their teaching and accessibility, which together foster a "love for learning" in undergraduates. As one student dryly notes, "Waterville, Maine is not the country's academic capital, so the professors that choose to be at Colby are here to teach, not to use the facilities."

"Colby's greatest strengths lie in its people. From the administrators to the faculty, staff, students, and alumni, Colby's community is one that is genuinely caring, genuinely smart, and genuinely engaging." A student notes, "The size of the school is perfect: On any given day, I could see five friends or acquaintances (and countless familiar faces!) on my way to class." This makes for a friendly atmosphere, as "it's easy to start up a conversation with pretty much anyone." And "there are professors that you want to visit even after you take their course, and most likely these professors will remember your name. Even in the large lecture halls (large being around sixty students), the professor will know everyone's name."

Colgate University

13 Oak Drive
Hamilton, NY 13346
Admissions: 315-228-7401
www.colgate.edu
admission@colgate.edu
Fax: 315-228-7544

Type of school: private
Environment: rural
Total undergrad enrollment: 2,868
Student/faculty ratio: 10:1
Most common regular class size: 10–19
Range SAT Critical Reading: 630–720
Range SAT Math: 640–740
Range ACT Composite: 29–32

Annual tuition: $42,920
Average cumulative indebtedness: $18,629

% students graduating in 4 years: 83%
% students graduating in 6 years: 88%

R.M. Douglas, History
Karen Harpp, Geology
Doug Johnson, Psychology
Spencer Kelly, Psychology
Nina Moore, Political Science
Paul Pinet, Geology and Environmental Studies
Dan Saracino, Mathematics
Rebecca Shiner, Psychology
Allen R. Strand, Mathematics
Ephraim Woods, Chemistry

Situated in Hamilton, New York, Colgate University stands out among its peers because of its "intimate nature" and its "breathtaking, beautiful" campus. The school has just under three thousand students enrolled and its community is tight knit, with one student noting that "you can't walk two hundred feet without a professor, student, or faculty member acknowledging you by name." Colgate boasts an alumni network that "makes the Colgate connection a truly valuable resource" when it comes to building a post-college career. The school also offers a strong study-abroad program where students can spend semesters in Australia, China, Japan, and several Western European countries.

Although the school is described as "being in the middle of nowhere," the location is seen as a plus because "everything revolves around the campus." Indeed, with more than one hundred student groups and organizations, as well as strong Division I athletics (Colgate is part of the Patriot League), students are hardly at a loss to find activities to be a part of. One science major remarks, "When you're stranded in Hamilton, New York, for four years you'll inevitably end up fitting in regardless [of] whether you are the typical student or not."

Professors are distinguished as being "incredibly enthusiastic" and they "sincerely want their students to succeed academically." There is a close relationship established between students and faculty; one student says that "these relationships start as early as freshman year. Students do not have to wait until their senior year to build fantastic relationships with the faculty." All in all, Colgate is seen as a "challenging school, but at the end of the day, the challenge is all about the student's development."

College of Charleston

66 George Street
Charleston, SC 29424
Admissions: 843-953-5670
www.cofc.edu
admissions@cofc.edu
Fax: 843-953-6322

Type of school: public
Environment: city
Total undergrad enrollment: 10,132
Student/faculty ratio: 16:1
Most common regular class size: 20–29
Range SAT Critical Reading: 560–650
Range SAT Math: 550–640
Range ACT Composite: 23–27

Annual in-state tuition: $9,616
Annual out-of-state tuition: $24,330
Average cumulative indebtedness: $20,541

% students graduating in 4 years: 52%
% students graduating in 6 years: 63%

Devon Wray Hanahan, Spanish
Martin Jones, Mathematics

The College of Charleston provides "huge university opportunities with a small college, personalized atmosphere." "It's actually a fairly large school (ten thousand students), but it feels much smaller in the historic Charleston setting," explains one student. Even though it's not the small-est university, it "offers great classes in a smaller, one-on-one environment." Located "right in the heart of downtown Charleston," the university is "a Southern secret that welcomes diversity with warm arms." Students can't say enough good things about the location. "The city of Charleston is fun and inviting, the weather is a million times better than the North, and the beach is close by!" "I'm from Charleston, and I couldn't imagine living anywhere else!" one student boasts. "The weather is great, the city is beautiful, you get a great education for a reasonable price, and of course the people from here are amazing...why not choose College of Charleston?"

The College of Charleston "exemplifies 'progressive traditionalism'" and "is all about liberal arts; the education is well-rounded and intriguing." One student chose the College of Charleston because "it just had the right feel. I talked to a professor for hours before I applied, and he was sincerely interested in me and my academic goals." Many students give professors high marks. The "professors really do care about you." "The professors I've encountered in the history department truly love their field and have greatly shaped my own research," one student testifies. The faculty "go above and beyond for their students." "I have found my professors to be extremely intelligent, open to new ideas, encouraging, supportive and kind." Many students share this high opinion. "The professors that I have had for my major and minor courses have been outstanding!" "My professors are fabulous, at least the ones I have in the humanities. All work hard on knowing your name and really do care about students (a professor e-mailed me after I had missed two classes just to check in on me, not lecture me for missing class). Most professors are genuinely interested in the subject they are teaching (most have worked outside the profession of teaching and directly in the field of the subject they teach, for example, an art professor that worked on the archaeologic dig of Pompeii) and want to see you succeed." "The professors I've encountered in the history department truly love their field and have greatly shaped my own research." "Most professors are enthusiastic about their field and truly want their students to share their passion." "I see my professors out in the city often, and they're extremely accessible. They're engaging, and I feel lucky—I've never had a professor that didn't absolutely love what he or she taught." "I have found that many of my professors encourage student participation and appreciate input from students. Overall, the quality of professors is excellent and few disappoint."

The College of William & Mary

Office of Admissions, P.O. Box 8795
Williamsburg, VA 23187-8795
Admissions: 757-221-4223
www.wm.edu
admission@wm.edu
Fax: 757-221-1242

Type of school: public
Environment: village
Total undergrad enrollment: 5,862
Student/faculty ratio: 12:1
Most common regular class size: 10–19 students
Range SAT Critical Reading: 640–730
Range SAT Math: 620–710
Range SAT Writing: 620–720
Range ACT Composite: 28–32

Annual in-state tuition: $13,132
Annual out-of-state tuition: $35,409
Average cumulative indebtedness: $21,367

% students graduating in 4 years: 83%
% students graduating in 6 years: 91%

Elizabeth Barnes, English and American Studies
Philip Daileader, History
David Dessler, Government
Melvin Ely, History and Africana Studies
Fredrick P. Frieden, PhD, Psychology
William Hutton, Classical Studies
Rowan Lockwood, Geology
Beverly Sher, Biology
Peter M. Vishton, Psychology
James P. Whittenburg, History

Located in Williamsburg, Virginia, The College of William & Mary has its share of notable alumni. Thomas Jefferson, John Tyler and Comedy Central's Jon Stewart all attended the prestigious school. The second oldest school in the country also boasts a rich academic life full of challenging course work, an amiable student body and caring professors.

Perhaps The College of William & Mary is so pedigreed because it seeks exceptional faculty. Says one student, "The academics are very challenging, but working closely with professors helps to alleviate the pressure and fine-tune our reading, writing and analytical skills." Its faculty is also well-versed in their areas of expertise. "I have had some great professors who are not just knowledgeable in their fields, but are still active in them, to the extent that I've had classes cancelled so that the professor could fly to Turkey for a conference," a student commented. "This is typical of my overall academics; even the TAs are extremely well-versed in the topics they are teaching and can answer any question." Students like that professors focus "on the real-world implications of what they teach" and that they are "open to having students set up other times for them to meet with them" if they're needing help. "It is uncommon to go through all four years here without being extended an invitation to a professor's home," said one student. "Professors want to get to know their students and if you are working hard they will notice and help out," said another.

Connecticut College

270 Mohegan Avenue
New London, CT 06320
Admissions: 860-439-2200
www.conncoll.edu
admission@conncoll.edu
Fax: 860-439-4301

Type of school: private
Environment: town
Total undergrad enrollment: 1,777
Student/faculty ratio: 9:1
Most common regular class size: 10–19
Range SAT Critical Reading: 610–700
Range SAT Math: 610–690
Range SAT Writing: 620–710
Range ACT Composite: 25–30

Annual tuition: $53,110
Average cumulative indebtedness: $22,038

% students graduating in 4 years: 83%
% students graduating in 6 years: 85%

John W. Burton, Anthropology
John Gordon, English Literature
Marc Zimmer, Chemistry

Connecticut College is a tight-knit private school in peaceful New London, Connecticut. Students are privy to "a large variety of academic opportunities" and exceptionally small class sizes. The college boasts a writing center, language lab, a career services office, internship and study abroad programs, and a variety of certificate programs. There are forty-three majors and minors to compliment nearly all academic paths.

Students find their classes to be "engaging and interesting," and their "professors are available inside and outside of the classroom." Most say they are afforded "more than just a teacher-student relationship, but rather a person-person relationship" with their professors. Many teachers go by their first names, and are "down-to-earth people who place themselves at the same level as their students."

The college encourages social responsibility and lifelong service to the community; it is among the top schools for turning out entrances to Teach for America and The Peace Corps. "In the past four years, eighteen Connecticut

College students have been awarded Fulbright Scholarships and three students have been awarded Goldwater Scholarships."

Originally founded as a women's college in 1911, Connecticut College is a selective, co-ed liberal arts school that offers a "warm environment." Because of the school's small size, students are able to get well acquainted with each other, and the faculty and undergrads don't feel like a mere statistic. The college boasts a strong history of supporting undergraduate research and encourages students to "prepare themselves for life in the real world as a grad."

All students strictly adhere to the honor code, which "instills a sense of self-awareness and self-governance among the student body." Many students attribute the personal touch that professors apply to their teaching method as a major factor in Connecticut College's quality education. "I am constantly learning and enthralled in class," says a senior art history major.

Cornell University

Undergraduate Admissions
410 Thurston Avenue
Ithaca, NY 14850
Admissions: 607-255-5241
www.cornell.edu
admissions@cornell.edu
Fax: 607-255-0659

A powerhouse university, Cornell is an intellectual and academic dream. The school is structured around seven different undergraduate colleges, allowing students to "receive all the benefits of a smaller college with the access, excitement, and opportunity provided by a larger university." Importantly, undergrads can study

Type of school: private
Environment: town
Total undergrad enrollment: 13,885
Student/faculty ratio: 9:1
Most common regular class size: 10–19
Range SAT Critical Reading: 640–730
Range SAT Math: 670–770
Range ACT Composite: 29–33

Annual tuition: $41,541
Average cumulative indebtedness: $20,648

% students graduating in 4 years: 86%
% students graduating in 6 years: 93%

Gerald W. Feigenson, Biochemistry
George Hudler, Agriculture and Life Sciences
Karl Niklas, Plant Biology
Shalom Shoer, Near Eastern Studies
Cindy van Es, Economics

everything from hotel management to agricultural sciences (and everything in between). Regardless of major, academics here are "rigorous," and it "takes a lot of hard work to succeed." Fortunately, the university provides the resources you need to accomplish your goals. Though classes can definitely range in size, professors remain "incredible" across the board. However, though they are attentive, students must be proactive about seeking help and/or advice. Thankfully, we're assured that "if you show genuine interest, [faculty] are more than excited to help you." While a large number of professors are focused on their research, this does provide undergrads with a number of opportunities to work with some academic heavyweights. One ecstatic undergrad shares, "Just the other day in one of my biology classes, my professor was going over a very important topic and just added in, 'Yeah, I came up with this.'" Now that's an educational experience that's difficult to beat!

Dartmouth College

6016 McNutt Hall
Hanover, NH 03755
Admissions: 603-646-2875
www.dartmouth.edu
admissions.office@dartmouth.edu
Fax: 603-646-1216

Dartmouth's approximately forty-one hundred undergraduate students enjoy the college's strong reputation as a member of the Ivy League, as well as its high-quality academics in twenty-nine departments and ten multidisciplinary programs. Academics at New Hampshire's preeminent college, comparable with other Ivy League schools, are demanding, but Dartmouth students feel they are up to the challenge. Unlike many of the other Ivies, though, the student-faculty ratio of

Type of school: private
Environment: village
Total undergrad enrollment: 4,135
Student/faculty ratio: 8:1
Most common regular class size: 10–19
Range SAT Critical Reading: 670–780
Range SAT Math: 690–790
Range SAT Writing: 690–790
Range ACT Composite: 30–34

Annual tuition: $38,445
Average cumulative indebtedness: $19,051

% students graduating in 4 years: 88%
% students graduating in 6 years: 95%

Karen Gocsik, Writing and Rhetoric

8:1 favors the undergrads, who find graduate assistants in their classes to have the same open willingness to help them learn as the regular professors do.

Dartmouth's unique D-Plan calendar system "where students take about three classes at a time for ten weeks," gives students the opportunity to pursue internships year-round. Students love it, telling us, "It gives you great flexibility to go abroad and secure fantastic off-term internships and volunteer opportunities." Students typically take advantage of the opportunities; as one explains, "Dartmouth is really big on the 'Dartmouth experience,' which basically means trying to do the most awesome things that you can fit into four years as an undergrad. This means that about two-thirds of undergrads, regardless of major, study abroad at least once. Everyone uses their 'off terms' to either try to save the world by volunteering or doing research if they're not doing some high-profile internship."

"The binding element of the typical Dartmouth student is passion," one student tells us. "Whether it is academics or the environment, students are committed to an area of interest and try to contribute to that field." For those wondering, "Yes, Dartmouth is the school upon which Animal House was based…we do party a lot, but the mentality is definitely work hard, play hard." Students like to stay active: "We throw a Frisbee on the green, hike through the mountains, play hockey on Occom Pond, play tennis, ski at the Skiway," and "sled on cafeteria trays" to burn off extra energy. No matter what they're into, "no one leaves campus on weekends because no one wants to miss a weekend at Dartmouth."

Drew University

Office of College Admissions
Madison, NJ 07940-1493
Admissions: 973-408-3739
www.drew.edu
cadm@drew.edu
Fax: 973-408-3068

Type of school: private
Environment: village
Total undergrad enrollment: 1,715
Student/faculty ratio: 11:1
Most common regular class size: 10–19
Range SAT Critical Reading: 510–630
Range SAT Math: 490–610
Range SAT Writing: 510–630
Range ACT Composite: 22–26

Annual tuition: $41,304
Average cumulative indebtedness: $19,634

Erik Anderson, Philosophy

Situated in sparkling suburban New Jersey, Drew University is a small school that features stellar academics, intimate classes, and a bustling campus life. Undergrads also frequently take advantage of the culture and career opportunities of nearby New York City. Of course, the campus itself offers plenty of things to take advantage of, most notably the Drew faculty. Certainly, students are quick to rave about professors whom they deem "very approachable, accommodating and enthusiastic about what they teach." Indeed, many undergrads find their professors have a facility for fostering engaging discussions and a love of learning that's infectious. Additionally, the vast majority "have PhDs in the field that that they teach." Most important, as a satisfied student shares, they "seem genuinely interested in helping us improve." Another pleased student chimes in: "They're always there when students want extra help and are very understanding." The Drew faculty is also concerned with shaping the lives of students outside the classroom. They help undergrads seek opportunities to pursue their passions. One impressed English major gushes, "My professors have really encouraged me to pursue the most out of my education here. One provided me with the opportunity to read my original poetry in NYC with distinguished poets. Another has influenced my decision to write a senior thesis. Within my major, I feel like part of a family. All of my professors know me, and I think they truly care about my performance."

Flagler College

74 King Street
St. Augustine, FL 32085-1027
Admissions: 800-304-4208
www.flagler.edu
admiss@flagler.edu
Fax: 904-826-0094

Type of school: private
Environment: town
Total undergrad enrollment: 2,747
Student/faculty ratio: 18:1
Most common regular class size: 20-29
Range SAT Critical Reading: 510-590
Range SAT Math: 500-580
Range SAT Writing: 500-580
Range ACT Composite: 21-25

Annual tuition: $14,510
Average cumulative indebtedness: $20,895

% students graduating in 4 years: 48%
% students graduating in 6 years: 64%

Steve Voguit, History and Geography

One of Florida's premier institutions, Flagler is a small liberal arts college that offers students big opportunity. From its renowned deaf education program to solid business, English, communication and graphic design departments, the educational possibilities are endless. Or, as a supremely happy undergrad puts it, "Flagler College is about going somewhere and doing something with your future, challenging yourself academically, growing as an individual, and making lifelong friends and memories." Of course, this all begins in the classroom with professors that "truly take a vested interest in their students." Indeed, the small class size helps to establish a "personal atmosphere with teachers who actually know your name and care about your success." Professors go out of their way to be "friendly" and are "always there to lend a helping hand." Further, they strive to make their classes "interactive" as well as "practical and relatable to the real world." And they certainly bring their own professional experiences into the classroom. A business major brags, "I have professors who work for the FBI teaching us about criminal justice, major CEOs giving business lessons, and a retired judge teaching me about law and society. I have the best of all worlds." Finally, another undergrad succinctly states, "Flagler College is like a family more than a school, students and professors can be friends and the environment is perfect for study." You can't really ask for more from an institution of higher learning can you?

Florida State University

P.O. Box 3062400
Tallahassee, FL 32306-2400
Admissions: 850-644-6200
www.fsu.edu
admissions@admin.fsu.edu
Fax: 850-644-0197

Type of school: public
Environment: city
Total undergrad enrollment: 30,830
Student/faculty ratio: 22:1
Most common regular class size: 20–29
Range SAT Critical Reading: 550–640
Range SAT Math: 560–650
Range SAT Writing: 550–630
Range ACT Composite: 24–28

Annual in-state tuition: $3,156
Annual out-of-state tuition: $17,691
Average cumulative indebtedness: $20,993

% students graduating in 4 years: 47%
% students graduating in 6 years: 71%

Trisha Spears, Biological Sciences

Florida State University is "a large, sports-oriented, research-intensive state school that has a niche for everybody, as long as you are willing to search." In addition to its strong academics, students tended to choose FSU for its "sports teams"—the Florida State Seminoles—the "great weather," and the fact that it's "a place with great traditions." FSU has a reputation as a party school, and "many students go out on the weekend or even sometimes during the week." While a university as large as FSU—the population is forty thousand plus—has students of many types, athletics and "school spirit" are what "bring everyone together" at FSU.

Students have a lot to say about their school's "academic excellence, [and] approachability of professors." "Professors are engaging and are there for any and all students who need extra help or would like to further discuss a topic." They are "creative and interesting," "hardworking and supportive," "with tons of open office hours." "Every one of my professors throughout my experience at FSU have been readily available to help their students. They have effective teaching styles inside the classroom, as well as effective means of communication with students outside the classroom. If I ever had a question for my professors, they would get back to me in a timely fashion via e-mail. It is easy to schedule a meeting with professors outside of their office hours, as well." "I've never come across a professor or a TA who was not willing to sit down and talk about class, grades, or even just day to day things." "My professors have become my friends and they're truly intelligent, thoughtful, and invested in teaching." "They know their stuff and the way they teach makes my overall academic experience great." "FSU offers one of the top accounting programs in the country, and … many opportunities in the academic community, in the business world, and in other areas in interest." "The faculty and academic programs are of great quality." One student says, "I have had wonderful professors that have eyes, ears, and heart to a world beyond my own, and have shown me that anything is achievable if I try hard enough." As with most large universities, "Some professors are great, some are dull. If you do your research on professors you will be fine."

Franklin W. Olin College of Engineering

1000 Olin Way
Needham, MA 02492-1245
Admissions: 781-292-2222
www.olin.edu
info@olin.edu
Fax: 781-292-2210

Revered for its "tight-knit community, rigorous academics, project-based learning, and ingenuous approach to education," Franklin W. Olin College of Engineering "bridges the gap between a traditional engineering education and [the] real world." On this campus of three hundred undergraduates where "smart" and "quirky" are the norm, "students [are] eager to be challenged academically and faculty gladly deliver that challenge." "Learning is doing" at Olin, and students laud the "innovative curriculum" for

Type of school: private
Environment: town
Total undergrad enrollment: 339
Student/faculty ratio: 9:1
Most common regular class size: 20-29
Range SAT Critical Reading: 670-750
Range SAT Math: 710-780
Range SAT Writing: 650-730
Range ACT Composite: 33-35

Annual tuition: Current tuition is $39,000 (but every student is guaranteed a half-tuition merit scholarship).
Average cumulative indebtedness: $13,200

% students graduating in 4 years: 84%
% students graduating in 6 years: 90%

John B. Geddes, Mathematics
Mark Somerville, Electrical Engineering and Physics
Sarah Spence Adams, Mathematics and Electrical and Computer Engineering

its "small classes," "hands-on approach," and "group-focused learning." "Olin believes in Renaissance engineers," and allows "students to pursue passions beyond engineering." Though classes are "wickedly challenging," students say they "bond around the difficulty." The focus on "experiential education" and "entrepreneurial implementation" provides students with "the ability to help design the curriculum and the school culture." Professors are "one of the best—if not the best—part of Olin," and are frequently described as "always available, always knowledgeable, [and] always approachable." Students add that they are on a first-name basis with even the higher-ups: "You can regularly chat with the president at lunch." The kicker? Every enrolled student receives a half-tuition scholarship. Students with additional demonstrated need are awarded grants.

Furman University

3300 Poinsett Highway
Greenville, SC 29613
Admissions: 864-294-2034
www.furman.edu
admissions@furman.edu
Fax: 864-294-2018

Furman University is highly regarded for its "beautiful campus" and "warm, but challenging, academic community." Furman holds the distinction of being one of the oldest liberal arts colleges in South Carolina, and its students enjoy the "thriving, small-town feel" of Greenville. "There are tons of bars, restaurants, and clubs for people to go to" in Greenville, but for students who choose to stay on campus for recreation there are a wide variety of events, "from music concerts to improv shows to sports games." Indeed Furman has a strong athletics program, and its teams compete

Type of school: private
Environment: city
Total undergrad enrollment: 2,724
Student/faculty ratio: 11:1
Most common regular class size: 10–19
Range SAT Critical Reading: 580–690
Range SAT Math: 600–680
Range SAT Writing: 580–680
Range ACT Composite: 25–30

Annual tuition: $39,560

Average cumulative indebtedness: $27,373
% students graduating in 4 years: 81%
% students graduating in 6 years: 86%

David Bost, Spanish
Charles L. Brewer, Psychology
Timothy Fehler, History
Margaret Oakes, English

in the NCAA Division I. Although the majority of the student body is characterized as "socially conservative," one undergrad notes, "The longer I stay at Furman, the more I realize that many students don't fit the stereotype" of being "wealthy, white, and preppy."

Furman is renowned for its quality academics, and one student takes pride in knowing that "you're receiving a great education that will help you after you graduate." Indeed, many students see Furman as "an ideal choice," and believe that between the "small class sizes" and professors "who love to teach and enjoy getting to know their students," the school offers a valuable learning experience.

Furman's professors are noted for being "very qualified (sometimes over-qualified), passionate about what they teach, and are not easy graders." One student enjoys that that the classes are "taught by instructors with PhDs, rather than TAs" and that "it is great having your professor know you personally." Furman's science programs have been singled out as "challenging." While some students believe that "Furman is not for the academically faint of heart," there is no denying that the school maintains a key focus on cultivating "academic excellence through engaged learning."

Georgetown University

37th and O Streets, NW
103 White-Graven
Washington, DC 20057
Admissions: 202-687-3600
www.georgetown.edu
Fax: 202-687-5084

"Georgetown is a highly ranked school with down-to-earth students in the heart of the nation's capital." This moderately

Type of school: private
Environment: metropolis
Total undergrad enrollment: 7,092
Student/faculty ratio: 10:1

Range SAT Critical Reading: 650–750
Range SAT Math: 660–750
Range ACT Composite: 27–33

Annual tuition: $38,616
Average cumulative indebtedness: $23,333

% students graduating in 4 years: 85%
% students graduating in 6 years: 93%

Hector R. Campos, Spanish/Linguistics
Matthew Carnes, Government
Sam Potolicchio, American Politics and Public Affairs
Barrett Tilney, Art and Art History

sized elite academic establishment stays true to its Jesuit foundations by educating its students with the idea of "*cura personalis*," or "care for the whole person." The "well-informed" student body creates an atmosphere full of vibrant intellectual life that is "balanced with extracurricular learning and development." "Georgetown is…a place where people work very, very hard without feeling like they are in direct competition," says an international politics major. Located in Washington, D.C., there's a noted School of Foreign Service here, and the access to internships is a huge perk for those in political or government programs. In addition, the proximity to the nation's capital fetches "high-profile guest speakers," with many of the most powerful people in global politics speaking regularly, as well as a large number of adjunct professors who either are currently working in government or have retired from high-level positions.

Georgetown offers a "great selection of very knowledgeable professors, split with a good proportion of those who are experienced in realms outside of academia (such as former government officials) and career academics," though there are a few superstars who might be "somewhat less than totally collegial." Professors tend to be "fantastic scholars and teachers" and are "generally available to students," as well as often being "interested in getting to know you as a person (if you put forth the effort to talk to them and go to office hours)." Though Georgetown has a policy of grade deflation, meaning "A's are hard to come by," there are "a ton of interesting courses available," and TAs are used only for optional discussion sessions and help with grading.

Georgetown "challenges its students to change themselves so they can improve the world. A refusal to introspect, as well as apathy, will not be tolerated here." "People know the importance of connections and spend time making sure they get to know the people here. We all are going to run the world someday; people want to make sure they have enough contacts when they do so." Another student put it this way: "Georgetown students want to change the world and have fun while doing so."

Gettysburg College

Admissions Office, Eisenhower House
Gettysburg, PA 17325-1484
Admissions: 717-337-6100
www.gettysburg.edu
admiss@gettysburg.edu
Fax: 717-337-6145

Type of school: private
Environment: village
Total undergrad enrollment: 2,472
Student/faculty ratio: 10:1
Most common regular class size: 10–19
Range SAT Critical Reading: 610–690
Range SAT Math: 620–680
Range ACT Composite: 27–30

Annual tuition: $41,070
Average cumulative indebtedness: $24,981

% students graduating in 4 years: 96%
% students graduating in 6 years: 85%

Christopher Fee, English

Personal and intellectual growth is at the heart of the Gettysburg College experience. Students eagerly praise the school's "friendly, community-oriented atmosphere," and competent, caring professors. "The faculty takes a developed interest in the students' academics and successes, [and] the campus offers countless opportunities for leadership, self-discovery, and the like." In fact, first-year students are surprised to find that "by the first day, the professor knows each student by name and why they're taking the class." With uniformly small class sizes and an emphasis on discussion in the classroom, "Professors at Gettysburg make sure that students understand why they are learning the things that they are, and there is a lot of emphasis put on putting 'theory into practice' outside of the classroom." "Many professors go above and beyond, making themselves available to aid students." A current student shares, "My Intro to Chemistry professor would be at the Science Center until 11:00 P.M. before an exam, helping everyone study." Academic opportunities—such as the "amazing study abroad program"—are ample at Gettysburg. Plus, as an exclusively undergraduate institution, Gettysburg "allows for opportunities (i.e., research, publications) that many do not get" at larger universities. In this "nurturing environment," the "administration knows students by name" and even the "registrar, transportation services, off-campus studies, and library staff are lovely and do everything they can to help you."

Grinnell College

1103 Park Street
Grinnell, IA 50112-1690
Admissions: 641-269-3600
www.grinnell.edu
askgrin@grinnell.edu
Fax: 641-269-4800

Type of school: private
Environment: village
Total undergrad enrollment: 1,603
Student/faculty ratio: 9:1
Most common regular class size: 10–19
Range SAT Critical Reading: 610–740
Range SAT Math: 610–730
Range ACT Composite: 28–32

Annual tuition: $36,948
Average cumulative indebtedness: $18,578

% students graduating in 4 years: 84%
% students graduating in 6 years: 87%

Victoria Brown, History

Located in a small town in Iowa, Grinnell College is a private liberal arts college recognized for its social activism and strong academics. Grinnell has a "fun community" comprising "crazy and weird" students. A major emphasis is placed on individuality, with a student noting that "Grinnell is about becoming an independent person and learning how to take responsibility for your actions and studies." Indeed, the focus is placed on self-governance. As part of the self-governance policy, the administration does not actively police campus events, and student security is present at school-sponsored parties.

Grinnell is also notable for its Scholars' Convocations, which enriches the college's academic community by bringing notable speakers to campus. Over the course of each academic semester, there are six Convocations. Scholars' Convocations provide a unique opportunity for students, faculty, staff and community members to encounter a diverse array of scholarly perspectives. One student raves about these speakers, many of whom hail from a "variety of disciplines." Grinnell is notable for bringing in bands and musical performance groups of all genres, which adds variety to its numerous extracurricular events. There are more than one hundred student organizations and more than five hundred events a year.

The academics here are rigorous, but students are delighted with the "freedom of choice" offered. In fact, the curriculum is completely open, and the only required class is a writing-intensive freshman seminar that introduces academic thinking and research. Beyond that, there are no subject matter requirements for obtaining a degree. Because of the small student body, the professors are very easily accessible and the low faculty-to-student ratio facilitates strong bonds between students and their professors. One student summed Grinnell up best as "a creative, vibrant campus where the student body, faculty, and staff work together to foster critical thinking and turn ideas into reality."

Gustavus Adolphus College

800 West College Avenue
Saint Peter, MN 56082
Admissions: 507-933-7676
www.gustavus.edu
admission@gustavus.edu
Fax: 507-933-7474

If you are looking for a "small, close-knit community" with a "very welcoming environment," a "good student-to-faculty ratio" and "accessible professors," this may be the college for you! Gustavus Adolphus College, "a school that fosters a close community between the students, staff, and faculty and strives to prepare the students academically and vocationally for the post-college world," gets high marks from undergrads for its "demanding, yet encouraging" professors who are "there to help you learn, not just to give you a grade." One student explains, "Each year, I become more and more impressed with how devoted members of the faculty and administration are to the students. My professors always bend over backward to meet with students who have questions and work with them on problems related and unrelated to course material." Many students agree. "The faculty members are committed to helping students succeed in all aspects of their lives."

Type of school: private
Environment: village
Total undergrad enrollment: 2,471
Student/faculty ratio: 11:1
Most common regular class size: 10–19

Range SAT Critical Reading: 555–690
Range SAT Math: 580–690
Range ACT Composite: 25–30

Annual tuition: $35,100
Average cumulative indebtedness: $26,000

% students graduating in 4 years: 81%
% students graduating in 6 years: 83%

John M. Lammert, Biology
Richard Leitch, Political Science

Although professors have "high expectations," the "extra guidance" that is offered helps students achieve "far beyond graduation." Expect to be challenged by classes that are "rigorous and discussion-based." Small class sizes allow for "great interaction with professors" but will leave your "empty chair sticking out like a neon sign" if you are absent.

Gustavus Adolphus College "fosters a close community between the students, staff, and faculty and strives to prepare the students academically and vocationally for the post-college world." Unique opportunities here include the Curriculum II general-education program, an integrated series of courses that, together, provide a survey of Western civilization, with supplemental study of non-Western cultures for context and comparison. Enrollment is limited to sixty students and typically attracts some of the college's brightest undergrads. The college is also "known for our athletics, specifically tennis, hockey, and soccer." Students "attend a lot of sporting events" as well as "parties and social events on campus and off."

Hamilton College

Office of Admission
198 College Hill Road
Clinton, NY 13323
Admissions: 315-859-4421
www.hamilton.edu
admission@hamilton.edu
Fax: 315-859-4457

Hamilton is the quintessential liberal arts college, with "strong academics in a low-stress environment." With a beautiful campus and a rigorous yet supportive academic environment, it "runs smoothly" with "top-notch" professors who are "very committed, passionate,

Type of school: private
Environment: rural
Total undergrad enrollment: 1,843
Student/faculty ratio: 9:1
Most common regular class size: 10-19
Range SAT Critical Reading: 650-740
Range SAT Math: 650-730
Range SAT Writing: 650-730
Range ACT Composite: 27-31

Annual tuition: $42,640
Average cumulative indebtedness: $16,982

% students graduating in 4 years: 84%
% students graduating in 6 years: 88%

Elizabeth Jensen, Economics

and genuinely caring." "Professors at Hamilton, though extremely demanding, know when to recognize success and hard work."

The close student-faculty relationships are a distinguishing characteristic of Hamilton. One junior who chose Hamilton for its "small class size and opportunity to really establish a relationship with the professors" described the accessibility of the professors as "amazing." A graduating senior tells us, "My professors have inspired me to take on my education as a truly personal and important aspect of my life, even after I complete my formal education."

In addition to top professors and a broad range of courses, Hamilton also offers study abroad programs and undergraduate research opportunities with professors. Students also love Hamilton's open curriculum. The "lack of distribution requirements" gives students the freedom to make their own educational choices and to select classes that reflect their unique interests.

Students are enthusiastic about the "tight-knit community" of students and professors on campus. The following is what some of them had to say about why they chose Hamilton and how they feel about their school.

"On my visit I saw how much attention professors paid to their students and I was sold."

"During my visit to campus I met with a professor who described the differences between Hamilton and other liberal arts colleges. He told me that the professors at Hamilton cater to the needs of the students in a particular class to ensure each student is challenged and pushed to reach their potential. He also mentioned that the professors want to see the students succeed and they do everything in their power to make that happen. That is exactly what I found as a student at Hamilton."

"I feel the greatest part of the Hamilton experience is the lifelong relationships that are forged between students, their peers, and their professors. One thing that surprised me when I arrived on campus was the acceptance of freshman by the entire campus. I have great friends four years older than me and expect to have great friends four years younger than me."

"Academics come first, without a doubt. However, once all homework assignments are done, there is room to let loose and relax. There are plenty of clubs and groups to join that have many activities and field trips. The fraternities and sororities hold all-campus activities as well."

"The faculty are outstanding—they are professionals in their field and are passionate about teaching. You never have to ask them to go the extra mile—they do it automatically."

Harvard College

86 Brattle Street
Cambridge, MA 02138
Admissions: 617-495-1551
www.college.harvard.edu
college@fas.harvard.edu
Fax: 617-495-8821

Harvard needs no introduction. This legendary Massachusetts school is known the world over, making it one of the most desirable, elite, and competitive schools not just in the United States, but in the world.

When the accolades are piled so high, it comes as no surprise that the professors at this leading school are among "the brightest minds in the world." After all, you are unlikely to offer much to the country's best students unless you are in turn among the country's best professors. Such is the case here. Among Harvard professors, reported to be "incredible" and, "every so often, fantastic," "the level of achievement is unbelievable." These are the best of the best.

Unlike many schools, Harvard educators expect their students to navigate their own way through a "very difficult" maze, endure an "amazing, irresistible hell," and find a way to succeed on their own. Vast amounts of one-on-one time should not be expected. Many of the larger introductory classes are taught by teaching fellows (TFs), so students "have to go to office hours to get to know your big lecture class professors on a personal level."

Type of school: private
Environment: city
Total undergrad enrollment: 6,641
Student/faculty ratio: 7:1
Most common regular class size: fewer than 10 students
Range SAT Critical Reading: 690–800
Range SAT Math: 700–790
Range SAT Writing: 710–800
Range ACT Composite: 31–34

Annual tuition: $34,976
Average cumulative indebtedness: $10,102

% students graduating in 4 years: 87%
% students graduating in 6 years: 97%

N. Gregory Mankiw, Economics
Sri Mukherjee, Writing

Academics may be the star of the show at Harvard, but education is not the only thing happening there. When not tackling the latest challenge offered up by their professors, students here enjoy a vast array of things to do. "Boredom does not exist here. There are endless opportunities and endless passionate people to do them with," one student notes. The school has "a vibrant social atmosphere on campus and between students and the local community." Another student says, "Basically, if you want to do it, Harvard either has it or has the money to give to you so you can start it."

Getting into this "beautiful, fun, historic, and academically alive place" is just the start of the challenge. What follows at Harvard is a relentless, difficult academic program led by highly intelligent professors who are not afraid to challenge their students. But as one student notes, the experience is "rewarding beyond anything else I've ever done."

Harvey Mudd College

301 Platt Boulevard
Claremont, CA 91711-5990
Admissions: 909-621-8011
www.hmc.edu
admission@hmc.edu
Fax: 909-621-8360

Type of school: private
Environment: town
Total undergrad enrollment: 771
Student/faculty ratio: 9:1
Most common regular class size: 10-19
Range SAT Critical Reading: 670-760
Range SAT Math: 740-800
Range SAT Writing: 668-760
Range ACT Composite: 32-35

Annual tuition: $40,133
Average cumulative indebtedness: $21,806

% students graduating in 4 years: 80%
% students graduating in 6 years: 87%

Lori Bassman, Engineering
Arthur Benjamin, Mathematics
Jon Jacobsen, Mathematics
Ran "RON" Libeskind-Hadas, Computer Science

Harvey Mudd, located in beautiful, sunny Southern California, makes up one-fifth of the prestigious Claremont Colleges. Armed with a focus in math, science, and engineering, Harvey Mudd provides a "quirky community that is the perfect fit for those who are serious about their technical studies and having an indefinably strange yet amazing time." The school offers unparalleled research opportunities and a number of students continue on to graduate programs. Though the workload is intense and classes are extremely rigorous, students "act cooperatively rather than competitively [and] conquer the material rather than each other." Additionally, undergrads are happy to put in the time and effort because, simply put, they "love their professors." Indeed, the Harvey Mudd faculty is "brilliant and extremely accessible." One appreciative student adds, "Most of them know my name and will stop and talk any time!" And perhaps just as important, "lectures and office hours are both amazing! Professors really want you to understand the material." It should also be noted that the college maintains an honor code, a policy that students respect and appreciate. One proud undergrad shares, "The trust the faculty has for the students gives us a sense of responsibility, and thus everyone lives up to expectations." Overall, Harvey Mudd offers students the opportunity to mix work and play and to graduate with a number of rich and worthwhile experiences.

Hillsdale College

33 East College Street
Hillsdale, MI 49242
Admissions: 517-607-2327
www.hillsdale.edu
admissions@hillsdale.edu
Fax: 517-607-2223

"Tiny" Hillsdale College "provides a classic liberal arts education" that is "deeply rooted in our country's Greco-Roman and Christian Heritage," and includes mandatory courses on the Constitution, Western civilization, and the "great books" (like the *Odyssey* and Dante's *Inferno*).

Type of school: private
Environment: village
Total undergrad enrollment: 1,326
Student/faculty ratio: 10:1
Most common regular class size: 10–19
Range SAT Critical Reading: 640–720
Range SAT Math: 570–660
Range SAT Writing: 610–690
Range ACT Composite: 25–30

Annual tuition: $19,960
Average cumulative indebtedness: $17,500

% students graduating in 4 years: 67%
% students graduating in 6 years: 76%

Thomas Conner: History
Justin A. Jackson, English

"The typical student is religious and conservative," relates a sophomore. "That's the nature of the college." Like any college, Hillsdale has cliques, but "there is a general feeling of respect and friendship between all students." "Everyone who chooses to come to Hillsdale buys into and lives by its Mission and its Honor Code, and that's a neat thing. It's not what we learn here, but instead being taught how to learn so that we can do so even after we graduate."

There's "no grade inflation" whatsoever, cautions a Spanish major, and there certainly "aren't any fluff classes at Hillsdale." While professors "demand a lot," they "have a genuine love for the things they study and the students they teach." The "extremely accessible" faculty is reportedly full of "profoundly enlightening, deep thinkers" who have "made the Hillsdale experience what it is, period." "Academics at Hillsdale are hard, that's no myth. But what you gain from it and the personal instruction is gratifying enough to do it." "Hillsdale professors are here for their students first and foremost. They are experts in their field and they do publish, but not at the expense of sitting down with their students to answer questions or extend classroom discussion." "The professors at Hillsdale College take seriously the intent of each student to be here, and they understand the responsibility that they have in serving this intent. Not only do they wish to teach students about subjects of interest, but they also genuinely desire to teach students how to think; this is what makes Hillsdale College so outstanding." "My professors are all talented teachers as well as being academically knowledgeable and are committed to their students both in and out of the classroom. They work very hard to be available to students one on one outside of class time and are very invested in their subjects. They are tough but ready to help any willing student. My overall academic experience has been exceptional."

"An education at Hillsdale College gives students the tools necessary to learn and to keep learning how to think, not what to think, preparing them not only for a career but for the rest of their lives." "It seemed to me the kind of place where getting a degree actually signifies more than having simply managed to attend classes and not fail them for four years." "At Hillsdale, you never have to be afraid to try something new and learn something different. Your professors will help to guide you the whole way, not doing the work for you, but standing along side you, looking over your shoulder, to make sure that you're exceeding." One student summed it up this way: "Professors expect us to work hard, and we do."

Indiana University of Pennsylvania

1011 South Drive
Suite 117 Sutton Hall
Indiana, PA 15705
Admissions: 724-357-2230
www.iup.edu
admissions-inquiry@iup.edu
Fax: 724-357-6281

Type of school: public
Environment: village
Total undergrad enrollment: 11,821
Student/faculty ratio: 18:1
Most common regular class size: 20–29
Range SAT Critical Reading: 450–530
Range SAT Math: 450–540
Range SAT Writing: 440–530

Annual in-state tuition: $5,804
Annual out-of-state tuition: $14,510
Average cumulative indebtedness: $25,224

Claude Mark Hurlbert, English
Melvin A. Jenkins, Developmental Studies
James Jozefowicz, Economics
Dr. Robert Kostelnik, Sport Management

Just an hour's drive outside of Pittsburgh, Indiana University of Pennsylvania offers an affordable education in a small-town setting. The straightforward curriculum prepares students for the workforce while providing an intellectual challenge along the way.

For the student looking for a more intellectually based plan of study there's the Robert E. Cook Honors College, boasting class sizes of less than one hundred for most freshman classes, and even more personal attention from professors. Students say "we can have very small classes. Our professors know who we are and are able to give us more individual attention than would be possible with a larger group."

The tight-knit community of students come mostly from surrounding towns and is peppered with the diversity that nearby Pittsburgh has to offer. Greek life and small class sizes make it easy to socialize on this public university's campus.

Students enjoy personal attention from their professors who are often easily available and "concerned with [students'] welfare and academic growth." Outside of the classroom, the surrounding environs offer simple pleasures such as "malls, skating rinks, restaurants, movie theaters, ice hockey rinks, sports events, and campus events keep most of the students busy." Surrounding towns offer additional activities including "movies and games," and "outdoor activities when the weather is nice."

Iowa State University

100 Enrollment Services Center
Ames, IA 50011-2011
Admissions: 515-294-5836
www.iastate.edu
admissions@iastate.edu
Fax: 515-294-2592

Type of school: public
Environment: town
Total undergrad enrollment: 22,577
Student/faculty ratio: 18:1
Most common regular class size: 20-29
Range SAT Critical Reading: 460-640
Range SAT Math: 530-670
Range ACT Composite: 22-28

Annual in-state tuition: $7,486
Annual out-of-state tuition: $17,668
Average cumulative indebtedness: $30,062

% students graduating in 4 years: 37%
% students graduating in 6 years: 67%

Anne Clem, Accounting
Douglas Gentile, Psychology
John Monroe, History

Iowa State University holds true to its initial mission of providing affordable, practical education with a special focus on agriculture. Today, the school remains "a great agriculture school" with "a great food science program" and a strong pre-veterinary program. Students also proudly tout its status as "one of the top engineering schools" in the region (offering noteworthy support for women engineers) and its "strong architecture program."
Students praise this "large university with a small-town feel," telling us that "I felt like I could find a home here and be exposed to almost limitless opportunities." The curriculum offers "a lot of opportunities for student research and 'hands on' learning;" so many, in fact, that some students claim ISU is "the best 'outside of class' university in the nation." Undergrads also appreciate a strong support network; one explains, "There are so many services on campus to help students, it is almost unreal. From tutoring to study sessions and counseling

to mock interviews and resumé building, ISU offers a wide variety of services to students." Career services "are excellent" and offer such pluses as "one of the largest engineering career fairs." "We have some great advisors and professors who care about students and help us achieve our goals of great internships, leadership opportunities, or graduate schools."

Professors are "friendly, approachable, [and] understanding." They "make an effort to know you" and "are generally great lecturers." Others agree. The faculty "is one of ISU's strengths. If students take a chance and get to know their professors and other staff members, they make a great professional connection [with someone who] will bend over backwards, whether it be as a professional reference or helping fund a trip. The faculty really is here for students." "I feel the professors and staff on campus have great relationships and really care for students."

Ithaca College

Ithaca College—Office of Admissions
Ithaca, NY 14850-7020
Admissions: 607-274-3124
www.ithaca.edu
admission@ithaca.edu
Fax: 607-274-1900

Type of school: private
Environment: town
Total undergrad enrollment: 6,382
Student/faculty ratio: 12:1
Most common regular class size: 10–19
Range SAT Critical Reading: 530–640
Range SAT Math: 530–630
Range SAT Writing: 530–630

Annual tuition: $33,630

% students graduating in 4 years: 69%
% students graduating in 6 years: 77%

Michael Haaf, Chemistry
Martin Sternstein, Mathematics

"Small class sizes" that afford plenty of "personal atten-tion," "outstanding" scholarships, and cross-registration with nearby Cornell University are a few great reasons to choose Ithaca College, a smallish school in central New York that offers many of the resources you would expect to find at a much larger university. "You are able to be a part of a community and get the chance to pursue interests that are not necessarily a part of your chosen course of study," relates an English major. "We have loads of opportunities to do and try a wide variety of things." The vast multitude of academic offerings includes "one of the best communication schools in the country." Also notable are "strong" majors in music, business, and drama; a "highly competitive" six-year doctorate program in physical therapy; and the cinema and photography program.

"If you're an outdoorsy person," the wooded and rocky surrounding area is a wonderland of activity. "I love being outside in nature and needed a college in which nature played a role, and here it plays an important role both inside and outside of the classroom." "The hiking here is unbelievable," and few other schools offer the opportunity to "go cliff jumping on a hot Saturday."

Professors are "really engaging and understand how to present the material so that it is relevant and meaningful." On the whole, faculty members are "really passionate about their fields and have a genuine interest in getting students excited about their passions." "Every professor I have had has cared about me as an individual and goes out of their way to help me learn the material." "Professors all know your name, even if you're in a large lecture, and they really care about the individual students. They are readily accessible, and want to be your friend as much as your instructor."

James Madison University

Sonner Hall, MSC 0101
Harrisonburg, VA 22807
Admissions: 540-568-5681
www.jmu.edu
admissions@jmu.edu
Fax: 540-568-3332

Type of school: public
Environment: town
Total undergrad enrollment: 17,900
Student/faculty ratio: 16:1
Most common regular class size: 20–29
Range SAT Critical Reading: 540–640
Range SAT Math: 550–650
Range SAT Writing: 540–640
Range ACT Composite: 23–27

Annual in-state tuition: $8,448
Annual out-of-state tuition: $21,738
Average cumulative indebtedness: $20,417

% students graduating in 4 years: 67%
% students graduating in 6 years: 82%

Kenn Barron, Psychology
David Bernstein, Computer Science
David Daniel, Psychology
Kimberly D.R. DuVall, Psychology
Dr. Stephen W. Guerrier, History
Larry R. Huffman, Learning, Technology
& Leadership Education
Raymond "Skip" Hyser, History
David Jaynes, Biology
Scott Lewis, Chemistry
Paul Warne, Applied Mathematics
William Wood, Economics

James Madison University is located in Virginia's picturesque Shenandoah Valley. The intimate, public university is a part of the state's school system offering sixty-nine majors from six undergraduate colleges, including business, arts and letters, education, integrated science and technology, science and mathematics, and visual and performing arts.

In addition to receiving a strong liberal arts education, students at James Madison have multiple opportunities to be of service to their community not limited to programs like Alternative Spring Break as well as volunteer opportunities overseas. When students are not studying or giving back they also have four hundred clubs and organizations to choose from. Almost 80 percent of the school's undergraduates participate in research, internship programs, teaching, or semesters abroad.

Students agree that James Madison University is "a school that values education, respect, and integrity," while providing "a positive, enriching, and supportive learning environment," "filled with students striving to be productive members of society." The "classrooms and facilities are always well kept and very up-to-date with all the best teaching technology."

One student says "on the weekends, students can go to downtown Harrisonburg to the various restaurants and shops," While nature enthusiasts indulge in the "great places to hike and spend time outdoors" and JMU's proximity to a variety of ski resorts.

Kenyon College

Admissions Office
Ransom Hall
Gambier, OH 43022-9623
Admissions: 740-427-5776
www.kenyon.edu
admissions@kenyon.edu
Fax: 740-427-5770

Type of school: private
Environment: rural
Total undergrad enrollment: 1,616
Student/faculty ratio: 10:1
Most common regular class size: 10–19
Range SAT Critical Reading: 630–720
Range SAT Math: 600–680
Range SAT Writing: 620–730
Range ACT Composite: 28–32

Annual tuition: $39,420
Average cumulative indebtedness: $19,934

% students graduating in 4 years: 85%
% students graduating in 6 years: 89%

Fred Baumann, Political Science
Jay Corrigan, Economics
Pamela K. Jensen, Political Science
David Leibowitz, Political Science
Kim McMullen, English
Natalia Olshanskaya, Russian
Joel Richeimer, Philosophy
Timothy Shutt, Humanities
David N. Suggs, Anthropology

There may not be much in Gambier, Ohio, where Kenyon College is located, but this allows life to revolve around Kenyon's campus. Though the work can be challenging, the friendly academic environment is ideal for fostering cooperative learning opportunities amongst students. Its interdisciplinary programs also make for a more complete learning experience across different fields.

These things are all underscored by Kenyon's exceptional faculty. "You won't get more attention from your professors anywhere," one student says. "The education here is top-notch." The school's professors "genuinely want us to succeed in myriad ways" offering a "close-knit teaching atmosphere." Kenyon's "preservation of a true liberal arts curriculum" is one of the many reasons that students continue to excel at the college, and its small size and rural location offers "lots of opportunities for academic help, tutoring, time with professors." Overall, Kenyon has created a "learning environment that is rigorous but not competitive" and that allows students to work towards their degree but still enjoy their time at the college. "The professors are very interested in you as a student," a student intimates. "They are available for meetings, and they really seem to care about your well-being." As one student says, "Our professors are the greatest strength of the college; personable, available, and always willing to give guidance, they are the ones who make Kenyon what it is."

Lehigh University

27 Memorial Drive West
Bethlehem, PA 18015
Admissions: 610-758-3100
www.lehigh.edu
admissions@lehigh.edu
Fax: 610-758-4361

Type of school: private
Environment: city
Total undergrad enrollment: 4,766
Student/faculty ratio: 10:1
Most common regular class size: 10–19
Range SAT Critical Reading: 580–670
Range SAT Math: 640–720
Range ACT Composite: 27–31

Annual tuition: $39,480
Average cumulative indebtedness: $31,922

% students graduating in 4 years: 77%
% students graduating in 6 years: 88%

Joseph Yukich, Mathematics

A modest-sized university set on a beautiful, hilly campus, Lehigh provides a "friendly, community-oriented atmosphere." Academics take top billing here, and the school manages to attract students who "genuinely care about their education." As one content undergrad expounds, "Lehigh expects a lot out of you, which in turn allows you to push and challenge yourself." Fortunately, "students are driven but not competitive with one another." Therefore, it's no surprise that alumni connections are especially strong at this university. This is particularly advantageous when it comes to potential employment opportunities. However, and perhaps even more importantly, Lehigh maintains an arsenal of fantastic professors who are "extremely qualified in their fields." While they "expect a lot from their students…they do everything they can to help to us." And that's what makes a Lehigh education both rigorous and rewarding!

Loyola Marymount University

One LMU Drive, Suite 100
Los Angeles, CA 90045-8350
Admissions: 310-338-2750
www.lmu.edu
admissions@lmu.edu
Fax: 310-338-2797

Type of school: private
Environment: metropolis
Total undergrad enrollment: 5,797
Student/faculty ratio: :1

Range SAT Critical Reading: 550–640
Range SAT Math: 560–660
Range SAT Writing: 560–660
Range ACT Composite: 25–29

Annual tuition: $33,901
Average cumulative indebtedness: $29,906

% students graduating in 4 years: 71%
% students graduating in 6 years: 79%

Curtis Bennett, Mathematics
Megan Granich, Mathematics
Arthur Gross-Schaefer, Marketing &
Business Law Development
Brad Elliott Stone, Philosophy
Robert D. Winsor, Marketing

Founded in 1911 and located in sunny Los Angeles, California, Loyola Marymount University is one of only five Marymount institutions. Having the distinction of being one of the largest Roman Catholic universities on the West Coast, it still manages to maintain smaller class sizes, making education a more intimate experience for its more than nine thousand students in its undergraduate, graduate, and law programs.

One of the Loyola Marymount's key features is its knowledgeable professors. "The fact that every teacher I have had thus far has a doctorate in their specific field makes me feel like I am learning from the best of the best," one student gushed. Many of its students agree that faculty. "are approachable and passionate" about what they do. One student found that the professors "contributed to my ability to go out and apply my education to the real world." Another student chimed in, saying that "discussions are lively and our thoughts are welcomed and encouraged; we have [professors] who are passionate about what they teach and how it affects our lives." Students also agreed that its small class-sizes "allows for a very intimate teaching and learning experience." "I have always felt very supported by my professors," another says, "I feel like I can always go to them for help and they have made my overall experience great!" Ultimately, the professors have contributed to the student body's work ethic at Loyola Marymount. One of the students says, "I attribute my success at LMU to my professors taking a personal interest in me which inspired me to work harder for them."

Loyola University New Orleans

6363 St. Charles Avenue, Box 18
New Orleans, LA 70118-6195
Admissions: 504-865-3240
www.loyno.edu
admit@loyno.edu
Fax: 504-865-3383

Following Jesuit tradition, Loyola University seeks to turn out "well-rounded students" who strive "to serve the world around them." Liberal arts and the sciences are the school's crown jewels, but arguably the most important aspect of all is the university's focus on self-discovery, exploration of values, personal initiative, and critical thinking. These ideas are fostered through special programs to fit every student's needs, including First-Year Experience, learning communities, research, service learning, study abroad, and internships.

Small classes allow professors to "take a genuine interest in every student" and "make a firm decision to learn your name and what type of person you are." Even the administration is known to be "friendly and very approachable." Students rave that they are always "very open to students and their suggestions," and "you can see them working to make our school a better place."

Type of school: private
Environment: city
Total undergrad enrollment: 2,859
Student/faculty ratio: 10:1
Most common regular class size: 10–19
Range SAT Critical Reading: 570–670
Range SAT Math: 540–650
Range SAT Writing: 550–660
Range ACT Composite: 24–29

Annual tuition: $32,266
Average cumulative indebtedness: $22,320

% students graduating in 4 years: 47%
% students graduating in 6 years: 59%

Peter Burns, Political Science

Student life is also a strength; students have nothing but good things to say about their peers. Most are "creative," "imaginative," and "really down-to-earth." Further, they are a "driven" group, motivated "to do well academically" and "participate in a wide range of activities." "We consist of such a diverse group of people that I couldn't put my finger on just one type of person. But then again, that's one of my favorite things about being here. You can be anyone and do anything you want. Everyone fits in here. I have made friends with such a vast variety of people and that is something I never thought possible for me until I came here." All in all, a biology major says, "we all just mesh well."

One student says, "Going to school in New Orleans means that you will never be bored. Ever. There is never a shortage of good food, good times, or good music." There's plenty of access to "great opportunities for theater, music, and art," or to "go out and listen to live music on the weekends."

Loyola University Chicago

820 North Michigan Avenue
Chicago, IL 60611
Admissions: 312-915-6500
www.luc.edu
admission@luc.edu
Fax: 312-915-7216

Students often enjoy Loyola University Chicago's convenient location, taking advantage of the sights and sounds the city has to offer. On-campus activities aren't to be overlooked, though, as Loyola boasts a wealth of activities on that front as well. Division I basketball games, comedy shows, concerts, and even drag shows are just a few of the activities there to help occupy your time. They also take

Type of school: private
Environment: metropolis
Total undergrad enrollment: 9,386
Student/faculty ratio: 15:1
Most common regular class size: 20-29
Range SAT Critical Reading: 540-650
Range SAT Math: 540-640
Range SAT Writing: 540-650
Range ACT Composite: 25-29

Annual tuition: $32,200

% students graduating in 4 years: 48%
% students graduating in 6 years: 68%

Connie Fletcher, Journalism
Kathleen Adams, Anthropology
John M. Janiga, Accounting
B.M. Lavelle, Classical Studies
Jacqueline Scott, Philosophy

advantage of Loyola's small classes and helpful professors who make the academic life there that much more enjoyable.

"The faculty is amazing," one student gushes. The professors not only focus on "learning in class" but also on "giving to the world." Students agree that professors are "committed to being helpful, friendly, and informative" and "teaching students to be well rounded and ethical." Students also feel that the school is on its way to being "first tier" due to its "excellent teachers who have knowledge not only of their topics, but real-world experience" and also promote "ideas and realities of acceptance" amongst their students. One student adds, "I think we have a really strong emphasis on preparing the individual to leave college and start a career."

Macalester College

1600 Grand Avenue
St. Paul, MN 55105
Admissions: 651-696-6357
www.macalester.edu
admissions@macalester.edu
Fax: 651-696-6724

With an undergraduate base of three thousand students, Macalester College may seem like a typical liberal arts college, but its multicultural and academic atmosphere set it apart from its peers. Students from over ninety countries are represented on campus, and Macalester has one of the highest percentages of international student enrollment of any U.S. college. The curriculum is designed to include international perspectives and offers a multitude of semester-long study abroad programs. The school's St. Paul, Minnesota location may be a bit chilly, but the metropolitan city

Type of school: private
Environment: metropolis
Total undergrad enrollment: 2,005
Student/faculty ratio: 11:1
Most common regular class size: 10–19
Range SAT Critical Reading: 640–740
Range SAT Math: 620–710
Range SAT Writing: 630–730
Range ACT Composite: 28–32

Annual tuition: $42,021
Average cumulative indebtedness: $13,704

% students graduating in 4 years: 82%
% students graduating in 6 years: 86%

Vittorio Addona, Mathematics
Sung Kyu Kim, Physics

has a lot to offer for students looking to have fun off campus. In addition to a vibrant music and arts scene, St. Paul is also a great center for students seeking internships in business, finance, medicine, science, government, law, and more.

One student classifies the student body as "nerds and proud of it." Students are required to live on campus for their first two years, contributing to a robust campus scene. Conversations between peers can revolve around a variety of topics; one student notes: "A typical conversation at lunch might start with the weather, then touch briefly on physics, then classical opera, then study abroad options in Africa, then world politics, then Sherlock Holmes, then that TV show we all saw last night, and finish with 'Guess who's going to the Super Bowl, guys!'"

Macalester is notable for its rich math and science department, and the professors are very active in research. The college has garnered high rankings among U.S. liberal arts colleges for active National Science Foundation (NSF) grants relative to faculty size. Because of this, many student take advantage of the opportunity to work with professors on cutting-edge research projects. In addition, many professors stress the importance of students to apply course work to real-world events, moving studies away from the theoretical college bubble and more to the tangible applications of knowledge.

Massachusetts Institute of Technology

77 Massachusetts Avenue

Room 3-108

Cambridge, MA 02139

Admissions: 617-253-3400

web.mit.edu

admissions@mit.edu

Fax: 617-258-8304

Type of school: private

Environment: city

Total undergrad enrollment: 4,285

Student/faculty ratio: 8:1

Most common regular class size: fewer than 10 students

Range SAT Critical Reading: 670–760

Range SAT Math: 740–800

Range SAT Writing: 670–770

Range ACT Composite: 32–35

Annual tuition: $38,940

Average cumulative indebtedness: $15,228

% students graduating in 4 years: 84%

% students graduating in 6 years: 93%

Walter Lewin, Physics

Massachusetts Institute of Technology, or MIT in shorthand, is arguably the nation's premier university for science, engineering and mathematics. Located in vibrant Cambridge, Massachusetts, MIT promises endless possibility and a multitude of opportunities to expand your horizons. Though the workload is known to push undergrads "beyond [their] comfort level," they also wholeheartedly appreciate that the university's "goal is not to teach you specific facts in each subject. [Rather] MIT teaches you how to think, not about opinions but about problem solving. Facts and memorization are useless unless you know how to approach a tough problem." What's more, undergrads here learn how to think from a bevy of world-renowned professors, including a handful of Nobel laureates. Most students cite the faculty as being "excellent teachers who make lectures fun and exciting." Indeed, many MIT professors "make a serious effort to make the material they teach interesting by throwing in jokes and cool demonstrations." They also highly value the myriad "research opportunities for undergrads with some of the nation's leading professors." In the end, the "amazing collection of creative minds," the fantastic academic and recreational resources and the rock-solid alumni network render MIT an unbeatable university.

Mills College

Office of Undergraduate Admission
5000 MacArthur Boulevard
Oakland, CA 94613
Admissions: 800-87-MILLS
www.mills.edu
admission@mills.edu
Fax: 510-430-3298

Mills College is a "socially aware, progressive, academically serious, community-based, and diverse" women's institution located in Oakland, California. This small school offers more than forty major programs to fewer than one thousand undergraduates, distinguished by uniformly "small class sizes and caring professors." Across the board, students say that "academics are exceptional" at Mills, with passionate instructors, ample class discussion, and plenty of homework. Despite the challenges, "all academic expectations are reasonable and clearly stated, and professors are available to help with any questions." One student reports, "I felt immediately comfortable when I visited campus, and I was looking for a highly personal, small liberal arts college with an emphasis on political and social activism." While a majority of students feel right at home in Mills' unique environment, it is important for prospective students to take note of the school's distinctive flavor, which leans toward the left politically and values quirkiness and experimentation. A senior explains, "Mills may not be for everyone, but if it's the right place for you, you'll know."

Mills students describe their classmates as studious, serious, quirky, diverse, and atypical, and many mention that Mills has "a large population of lesbian, queer, bisexual, gender-curious, and transgender students." Acceptance is the rule. As one senior testifies, "I have yet to see any kind of prejudice or intolerance

Type of school: private
Environment: metropolis
Total undergrad enrollment: 941
Student/faculty ratio: 11:1
Most common regular class size: 14

Range SAT Critical Reading: 530-660
Range SAT Math: 520-620
Range SAT Writing: 520-630
Range ACT Composite: 24-29

Annual tuition: $38,066
Average cumulative indebtedness: $24,255

% students graduating in 4 years: 50%
% students graduating in 6 years: 59%

Robert Anderson, Anthropology

of another person's beliefs. Everyone is polite and courteous when faced with another's points of view."

Mills has "a legacy of producing strong, successful, independent women" and "empowering women." "The Mills education philosophy is very holistic, making sure that its women graduate as well-rounded individuals, and that is really important to me. Another big part of my decision to come to Mills was the obvious accessibility of all of the Mills faculty and staff."

Mills is definitely "not a party school," but this green oasis in the middle of urban Oakland is a relaxing, quiet, and studious environment that will make a good fit for serious students. "I love Mills. It's beautiful, the people are great, and I've met professors whom I'll know forever. I will leave Mills with increased confidence, skill, and lifetime networks."

Monmouth University

Admission, Monmouth University
400 Cedar Avenue
West Long Branch, NJ 07764-1898
Admissions: 732-571-3456
www.monmouth.edu
admission@monmouth.edu
Fax: 732-263-5166

Monmouth University is a small school with a close-knit community. Indeed, the campus is awash with friendly vibes and happy, engaged students. And with over thirty majors available, undergrads are able to study everything from criminal justice to speech communication. Moreover, both Philadelphia and New York City are fairly accessible, and students can easily trade in their suburban idyll for the fast pace of the city. Importantly, one area where the university

Type of school: private
Environment: suburban
Total undergrad enrollment: 4,599
Student/faculty ratio: 15:1
Most common regular class size: 20–29

Range SAT Critical Reading: 490–570
Range SAT Math: 500–590
Range SAT Writing: 490–580
Range ACT Composite: 22–26

Annual tuition: $28,000
Average cumulative indebtedness: $29,921

% students graduating in 4 years: 41%
% students graduating in 6 years: 66%

Gary Lewandowski Jr., Psychology

stands out is their fantastic faculty. Monmouth manages to attract professors that are "extremely passionate about their subjects" and undergrads stress that their excitement for learning quickly becomes contagious. And while they are "brilliant" and "insightful," Monmouth professors are also truly "interested in the opinions and questions [their] students [pose]." One undergrad adds, "They can really make a class fun and interesting by having students talk about their perspectives." Further, professors really want students to "learn rather than memorize." Ultimately, that makes "class harder but more beneficial." Undergrads at Monmouth are continually impressed with how caring and committed their professors are. Another student shares, "My professors are very helpful and are willing to get to know you to make you feel more comfortable." They are quick to "make themselves available in and out of the classroom." Or, as one content student so eloquently brags, "The professors who make Monmouth University enjoyable, they become your guiding hand and often a friend to count on in your studies throughout your time [in college]."

Mount Holyoke College

Newhall Center
50 College Street
South Hadley, MA 01075
Admissions: 413-538-2023
www.mtholyoke.edu
admission@mtholyoke.edu
Fax: 413-538-2409

Type of school: private
Environment: town
Total undergrad enrollment: 2,287
Student/faculty ratio: 9:1
Most common regular class size: 10–19
Range SAT Critical Reading: 510–700
Range SAT Math: 580–690
Range SAT Writing: 620–710
Range ACT Composite: 27–31

Annual tuition: $40,070
Average cumulative indebtedness: $22,499

% students graduating in 4 years: 74%
% students graduating in 6 years: 82%

Sue Barry, Biological Sciences
Jane F. Crosthwaite, Religion
Susan Daniels, Theatre Arts
Vincent Ferraro, International Politics
Rachel Fink, Biological Sciences
Amy Frary, Biology
James Hartley, Economics
Sam Mitchell, Philosophy
Constantine Pleshakov, Russian and
Eurasian Studies and Critical Social
Thought
Stan Rachootin, Biological Sciences
Christopher Rivers, French
Eleanor Townsley, Sociology
Kenneth H. Tucker Jr., Sociology
Craig Woodard, Biological Sciences

Although Mount Holyoke College is a women's school, it still offers a diverse experience. Not only will you meet students of different ethnicities, religions, and political viewpoints, but you'll also be able to participate in the Five College Consortium with other area colleges. Though the faculty have high expectations of students, they are also there to support as well.

The professors at Mount Holyoke "have nothing but the best to offer students" and "[work] hard to create a great academic experience." Students will find that faculty members are "extremely dedicated to their subject" and that they "really enjoy teaching" and "make sure every student is getting the most out of their class." That hard work extends beyond their regular class hours as well. "From your first year to senior year," a student says, "you feel very supported by the faculty, and they are genuinely interested in getting to know students on a personal level." Students say that their professors are "always available outside of the classroom" and are prone to "frequently extend their office hours to accommodate [student] schedules." Faculty are also willing to take student's voices and opinions into consideration as well. "We have the opportunity to disagree (respectfully) and to voice our opinions with other students as well as professors while learning about new and different perspectives," says one student. "I've heard many professors talk about how they've changed a class or a teaching style as a result of student surveys," says another. Overall, students who attend Mount Holyoke feel that their professors are "incredible" and "challenge you to be your best."

Muhlenberg College

2400 West Chew Street
Allentown, PA 18104-5596
Admissions: 484-664-3200
www.muhlenberg.edu
admission@muhlenberg.edu
Fax: 484-664-3234

Type of school: private
Environment: city
Total undergrad enrollment: 2,406
Student/faculty ratio: 12:1
Most common regular class size: 10–19
Range SAT Critical Reading: 560–670
Range SAT Math: 560–670
Range SAT Writing: 560–670
Range ACT Composite: 24–30

Annual tuition: $39,915
Average cumulative indebtedness: $23,004

% students graduating in 4 years: 82%
% students graduating in 6 years: 86%

David Rosenwasser, English

With a reputation for fostering a strong and vibrant sense of community among its students and faculty, this small liberal arts college in Pennsylvania strikes a "healthy balance between both the social and academic cultures on campus." Muhlenberg College is renowned for its "beautiful campus" and the high quality of its programs particularly in science, theater, dance and premedicine. According to one student, the school is focused on "expanding one's breadth of experiences and encouraging independent thinking in a small, friendly environment."

Muhlenberg offers a cozy academic setting that is both rigorous and supportive and "a caring environment where interdisciplinary learning is extremely important." One student enthuses, "I liked the comfort of the campus: The classrooms have intimate discussions and up-to-date technology. The professors are very astute and open-minded, but they still push the students to perform as well as they can." Other students highlight that the school goes beyond academics and that "Muhlenberg is devoted to preparing students for lives of leadership and service."

Another feature of the school that consistently garners praise from the students is the small size of the classes. Students rave that "the amount of attention professors can provide students is unmatched by many." Because of the constant accessibility to their professors, "this not only helps the students by giving them an edge, but it also allows professors to bring students in to work more closely on projects outside of the lecture. There is a lot more potential for development." Students not only appreciate the individualized attention from their professors but they also point out that "teachers are very passionate about their work." According to one student, "Professors are extremely knowledgeable, but, more importantly, they tend to be good teachers." Moreover, "Muhlenberg is a place where the professors are here to help you grow, not only intellectually but also as a person." Students seem to universally agree that their school's many accolades for being a "caring community" are well deserved.

Nazareth College

4245 East Avenue
Rochester, NY 14618-3790
Admissions: 585-389-2860
www.naz.edu
admissions@naz.edu
Fax: 585-389-2826

As a private, comprehensive college in Rochester, Nazareth College offers a "tight knit community which values a liberal education curriculum and fully supports all students in their endeavors." Referred to affectionately as "Naz" by its students, the college is particularly well known for its excellent programs in health and human services, music, and education. Many students

Type of school: private
Environment: village
Total undergrad enrollment: 2,144
Student/faculty ratio: 12:1
Most common regular class size: 10–19
Range SAT Critical Reading: 530–630
Range SAT Math: 530–630
Range SAT Writing: 510–610
Range ACT Composite: 23–27

Annual tuition: $25,046
Average cumulative indebtedness: $26,711

% students graduating in 4 years: 62%
% students graduating in 6 years: 72%

Scott M. Campbell, Philosophy

agree that "Nazareth has small class sizes and a fantastic faculty which allows for great classroom atmosphere and high levels of academic success." Some students heap praise on the school's ability to provide "an education for diverse learners that allows students to think critically while constructing meaning through hands-on learning opportunities." It's not just about academics though. The college also makes sure that "civic engagement and service learning are emphasized" and that students focus on "care, compassion, and nurture for others—and transferring those qualities to the real world."

The students are generally impressed with their professors at Nazareth who are "brilliant," "outstanding," "passionate," and "funny," and who "provide an interesting view on otherwise boring topics." The professors come from diverse backgrounds and "range from a retired substitute high school science teacher to a member of the Rochester Philharmonic Orchestra or sisters of St. Joseph." Many students feel supported and nurtured by the faculty and note that "the professors make a lot of time for the students in a way that is probably quite unusual" and "encourage participation and active learning." In addition, "Nazareth professors are very much about integrating different ways of learning into their classes, especially with technology and media." Outside of the classroom, the professors are "easily accessible," "genuinely devoted to the well-being of their students" and "take time to get to know the educational needs of individual students." According to one student, "It is evident how much my professors love the topics they teach and how much they enjoy sharing it with us. It's a great feeling to see a professor so excited about your progress."

New Jersey Institute of Technology

Office of University Admissions
University Heights
Newark, NJ 07102
Admissions: 973-596-3300
www.njit.edu
admissions@njit.edu
Fax: 973-596-3461

Type of school: public

Environment: metropolis

Total undergrad enrollment: 5,737

Student/faculty ratio: 15:1

Most common regular class size: 20-29

Range SAT Critical Reading: 470-590

Range SAT Math: 540-650

Range SAT Writing: 460-570

Annual in-state tuition: $13,974

Annual out-of-state tuition: $25,334

Average cumulative indebtedness: $24,543

% students graduating in 4 years: 19%

% students graduating in 6 years: 55%

Soha Abdeljaber, Mathematics

New Jersey Institute of Technology is one of the premier academic institutions of the mid-Atlantic region. Though the workload is quite heavy, undergrads agree that they graduate feeling prepared to tackle the "real world." Additionally, they truly appreciate an education that comes with a very affordable price tag. Above all, they walk away with a profound gratitude for their experiences within the classroom. Indeed, from the architecture program to the engineering school, students at NJIT are quick to sing the praises of their "highly dedicated" professors. As a result of "small class sizes" and a low student-faculty ratio, "[truly strong] relationships...between students and their professors [prevail]." And though faculty expectations are high and their classes demanding, undergrads here wouldn't have it any other way. This sentiment can be (at least partially) attributed to the fact that NJIT "professors care about the students and go out of their way to make sure [they] can be successful." An architecture major explains, "The greatest strengths of my school are some of the professional connections within the architecture department. I have made strong connections with professors that have led to internship positions in New York City." Undeniably, whether it's a one-on-one tutorial, research collaboration, or career advice, the faculty here is always willing to lend a hand. As one ecstatic student succinctly sums up, "We have great faculty. I think the teachers at our school are the best in the nation."

New York University

665 Broadway, 11th Floor
New York, NY 10012
Admissions: 212-998-4500
www.nyu.edu
admissions@nyu.edu
Fax: 212-995-4902

Type of school: private
Environment: metropolis
Total undergrad enrollment: 21,646
Student/faculty ratio: 11:1
Most common regular class size: 10-19
Range SAT Critical Reading: 610-710
Range SAT Math: 630-740
Range SAT Writing: 620-720
Range ACT Composite: 28-31

Annual tuition: $41,606

% students graduating in 4 years: 78%
% students graduating in 6 years: 85%

Kathleen A. Bishop, Humanities

It's no secret: New York University (NYU in collegiate jargon) is located in the heart of one of the most vivid and dazzling cities in the world. Though it doesn't offer the traditional campus experience, it's a fantastic school for independent and motivated undergrads. From a wide range of academic programs (there are over 230 areas of study) to its international student body, diversity is the name of the game here. And since New York City is headquarters to numerous industries, internship and research opportunities abound. Fortunately, though NYU features a healthy student population (over twenty thousand strong), undergrads are pleasantly surprised to find that both the faculty and administration are quite "accessible." Indeed, professors here take an active interest in their students. One pleased student remarks, "It is so easy to meet with [professors] outside of class, and I still get e-mails from professors about internships, jobs, and scholarship recommendations." In other words, NYU "attracts some amazing professors." And, as one content undergrad sums up, the university provides "students the knowledge they need to succeed in today's world."

Niagara University

Bailo Hall
P.O. Box 2011
Niagara University, NY 14109
Admissions: 716-286-8700
www.niagara.edu
admissions@niagara.edu
Fax: 716-286-8710

Type of school: private
Environment: town
Total undergrad enrollment: 3,267
Student/faculty ratio: 12:1
Most common regular class size: 20–29
Range SAT Critical Reading: 490–580
Range SAT Math: 470–570
Range ACT Composite: 20–25

Annual tuition: $25,300
Average cumulative indebtedness: $27,813

% students graduating in 4 years: 54%
% students graduating in 6 years: 62%

Todd Schoepflin, Sociology

The Niagara Falls may be the biggest and most powerful in North America, but "big" is not a word often used to describe Niagara University, a medium-sized Catholic college in the Vincentian tradition. Student after student praise the small class sizes that "made me feel a part of something" and which offer "a more intimate learning experience." Those class sizes "allow for students to build strong relationships with the faculty and community" and afford professors the ability to "provide personal attention." "Class sizes are small enough where the teacher knows you by your name," one student says, while another notes they "loved the idea of a school where I could be treated as an individual instead of just a number."

Niagara's goal is "providing good education through great teachers that want everyone to perform at their best, and prepare them for the future." One excited student testifies, "Academically it provided so many opportunities for me," opportunities that come via "highly qualified staff who are always ready to offer their support."

That proves a draw for many prospective students. One student chose this school for "the interest that the teachers truly took in the students." The thought was echoed by many others. The "highly esteemed" professors here "are there if you need them" and "genuinely care about their students." Teachers "make you feel comfortable and will help you any way possible," offering "support for the students academically, athletically, as well as on a…person-to-person basis." They "not only teach class material but life lessons as well." The goal is not merely "helping you achieve your goals," it is also "teaching (students) how to better serve others and to become leaders in their communities."

Professors accomplish this by being leaders themselves. The "faculty is very helpful and caring," providing a "world-class education" and creating an atmosphere that "just felt like home." One student notes, "If I ever need help on an assignment or anything I can get one-on-one assistance from my professors," while others confirm that the teachers here "really care," are "informative and reassuring," and "get the opportunity to get to know the students personally."

Another student sums up the Niagara experience: "It sounds corny, but there is a real sense of family here."

Northeastern University

360 Huntington Avenue
150 Richards Hall
Boston, MA 02115
Admissions: 617-373-2200
www.northeastern.edu
admissions@neu.edu
Fax: 617-373-8780

Northeastern University offers "the campus feel in an urban setting," "providing [an] outstanding campus life in the great city of Boston." A sophomore says, "It's a city school, but our campus has so much green space." Another student adds, "It's a closed-in campus in the middle of a city filled with opportunities." Students say, "We've got awesome facilities, and we're always building and improving them," and "The student population is

Type of school: private
Environment: metropolis
Total undergrad enrollment: 15,905
Student/faculty ratio: 13:1
Most common regular class size: 10–19
Range SAT Critical Reading: 600–680
Range SAT Math: 630–710
Range SAT Writing: 590–680
Range ACT Composite: 28–31

Annual tuition: $36,380

% students graduating in 6 years: 77%

Arnie Arluke, Sociology and Anthropology
Rachel Gans-Boriskin, Communication
Brad Lehman, Electrical and Computer Engineering
Alan Schroeder, Journalism
Ron Thomas, Global Management
Nizar Zaarour, Mathematics

very passionate about a wide variety of things, and that's manifested through student life and activities." Students say, "Getting involved in campus clubs and organizations is the best way to meet people and make lasting friendships," and "a good amount of students are involved in leadership activities and student organizations."

Renowned for its "unique cooperative programming," Northeastern University "integrates real-world experience and academics to form experiential learning." Students say Northeastern is an "institution that is dedicated to real-world experiences coupled with classroom guidance," and many students list "cooperative learning" opportunities as main reason for choosing the school. Additionally, the students boast about the school's "stellar academic reputation," and a junior says, "Northeastern is about equipping students with the academic prowess to have successful careers and dynamic, multifaceted lives."

A political science major says, "Professors come from a wide array of fields and bring their expertise from the outside world to the classroom and then challenge us to do the same." Another student says, "I have had amazing professors. Even the teaching assistants that have taught some of my courses have been very good instructors. Overall, I am highly pleased with the faculty at Northeastern University." While professors are generally "educated, engaging, [and] enthusiastic," students students say, "there's a range"—some "aren't as exciting," and a sophomore says, "I've had a good mix of mediocre and fantastic professors." Regardless, "they all expect a high level of dedication and hard work on [the] student's part to their classes," and they're "always looking to help us connect and apply our learning to our lives outside of the classroom." Another student said, "Transferring from a tiny liberal arts college where classes were fifteen people or less, I was initially scared about coming to such a big school. Would my professors be able to connect with me on the same level? I'm so happy to report that I was completely mistaken. I have made meaningful relationships with the majority of my professors here. They are passionate about what they teach and are willing to spend time with their students. I couldn't ask for anything more!"

Oberlin College

101 North Professor Street
Oberlin College
Oberlin, OH 44074
Admissions: 440-775-8411
www.oberlin.edu
college.admissions@oberlin.edu
Fax: 440-775-6905

Type of school: private
Environment: rural
Total undergrad enrollment: 2,839
Student/faculty ratio: 9:1
Most common regular class size: 10–19
Range SAT Critical Reading: 640–740
Range SAT Math: 620–710
Range SAT Writing: 640–730
Range ACT Composite: 27–32

Annual tuition: $38,012

% students graduating in 4 years: 69%
% students graduating in 6 years: 83%

Yolanda Cruz, Biology
David Walker, English and Creative Writing

Arguably best known for being the first American college to regularly admit female and black students, Oberlin College is viewed as a school "for laid-back people who enjoy learning and expanding social norms, allows each and every student to have the undergrad experience for which he or she is looking, all the while challenging the students to change themselves and the world for the better." Indeed, Oberlin puts the "liberal" in liberal arts, and there is a wide range of diversity in the student body, which comprises "musicians, jocks, science geeks, creative writing majors, straight, bi, questioning, queer, and trans" undergrads. Most students are left-leaning and politically active.

Professors here are seen as "the heart and soul of the school" and are dedicated educators. One student elaborates: "They treat you more like collaborators and realize that even with their PhDs, they can learn and grow from you, as well as you from them." Another notes that the professors are "excellent instructors and fantastic people" who are "focused on learning instead of deadlines." Particular praise has been given to "the sciences, English, politics, religion, music, environmental studies, and East-Asian studies" programs.

Pomona College

333 North College Way
Claremont, CA 91711-6312
Admissions: 909-621-8134
www.pomona.edu
admissions@pomona.edu
Fax: 909-621-8952

Type of school: private
Environment: town
Total undergrad enrollment: 1,546
Student/faculty ratio: 7:1
Most common regular class size: 10–19
Range SAT Critical Reading: 690–780
Range SAT Math: 700–780
Range SAT Writing: 690–770
Range ACT Composite: 31–34

Annual tuition: $39,883
Average cumulative indebtedness: $8,776

% students graduating in 4 years: 91%
% students graduating in 6 years: 94%

Richard Wesley Hazlett, Geology/
Environmental Studies
Nicole Y. Weekes, Neuroscience
Samuel Yamashita, History

Pomona College's trick in engaging students is to hire smart professors who love to teach. The "laid-back atmosphere" belies this "academically challenging institution," but professors here "have very high energy and it transfers over to what we are learning." These "engaging and accessible" teachers "are for the most part fantastic—engaging, creative, and sharp," work to "provide an amazing academic experience" for students, and "love to teach."

Dry, boring lectures are not often seen at Pomona. The "teacher/student ratio is low, providing for a lot of support," but more importantly, "many of my courses are primarily discussion-based, and there is an emphasis on collaborative learning." Here educators "will match your effort level and more" because they want students "to be happy and do everything in their power to create the best academic and social experience they can for us."

A personal touch helps. The faculty here are "cool, interesting people inside the classroom and out." The "professors really get to know their students" and "know the names of all the students, and have made a point of making themselves available outside of the classroom." Just how personal can it be? One student says, "Today, I had a class with seven people in it, then lunch with a physics professor, and then a personal tutorial with a philosophy professor." These "awesome professors" are not just "very accessible," they are also "interesting, engaging, and incredibly smart people."

Part of that energy comes from the discussions professors generate and the fact that they keep students at the forefront of their mind. They prove "to be accessible to students and are involved with campus issues and activities" and "are always there to help out a student when they ask for it." One student enthusiastically endorses the professors, saying, "They are, in my experience, incredibly smart and provide excellent flow to discussions. I have genuinely enjoyed my academic experience thus far, and the professors have a tremendous amount to do with this." The "engaging" and "incredible" professors are "generally amazing," but, far more important when it comes to teaching, they "know what they are talking about. It is very easy to pay attention in class because they make the material interesting."

Considering the gorgeous location, incredible weather, and laid-back atmosphere, the fact that students devote so much time to praising their professors speaks volumes.

Princeton University

P.O. Box 430
Admission Office
Princeton, NJ 08544-0430
Admissions: 609-258-3060
www.princeton.edu
Fax: 609-258-6743

Princeton University, an Ivy League institution, has earned its "sterling reputation" by "simultaneously providing undergraduates with all the resources of a world-class research university and all the individualized attention of a small liberal arts college." The school provides a "welcoming, accepting,

Type of school: private
Environment: town
Total undergrad enrollment: 5,142
Student/faculty ratio: 6:1
Most common regular class size: 10–19
Range SAT Critical Reading: 690–790
Range SAT Math: 710–790
Range SAT Writing: 700–790
Range ACT Composite: 31–35

Annual tuition: $37,000
Average cumulative indebtedness: $5,225

% students graduating in 4 years: 90%
% students graduating in 6 years: 96%

Joshua T. Katz, Classics and Linguistics

community atmosphere" and "does a fantastic job of offering its students a premier educational experience." Students proclaim that "Princeton is the most undergraduate-focused of the nation's top-tier institutions" and that "resources (financial, academic help, extracurricular funding, advising) are plentiful." The school's many advantages end up "creating a scholar who is also a citizen of the world."

The student population is also provided with numerous opportunities to form strong bonds with the faculty at the school. "Princeton provides an intimate campus setting where the professors and students interact on a level not seen on many other college campuses." Students praise the school's "intellectual environment" where "even freshmen are welcomed to critique the work of senior members of the faculty." According to one student, "because Princeton focuses so heavily on undergraduate education, professors love teaching, and there are many fantastic lecturers." The many "superb," "award-winning" and "down to earth" professors at this school are "leading scholars in their field" and undergrads have "a lot of opportunities to work with really big name professors." One student waxes enthusiastic: "My professors have been unfailingly brilliant, open, and inspirational." Students seem to agree that "most professors are really engaging and motivated by their subject matter." "They work hard to make students feel comfortable enough to speak up in class without remembering to be self-conscious." The professors are also focused on "teaching undergrads how to think and discuss logically and see myriad sides of issues and apply those skills out of the classroom…" The professors at Princeton also receive much praise for their "dynamic lectures and their clear passion for what they teach." Students across the board have observed that their professors "will do anything to help them, both with course material and with life in general."

Rider University

2083 Lawrenceville Road
Lawrenceville, NJ 08648-3099
Admissions: 609-896-5042
www.rider.edu
admissions@rider.edu
Fax: 609-895-6645

Type of school: private
Environment: village
Total undergrad enrollment: 4,609
Student/faculty ratio: 12:1
Most common regular class size: 10–19
Range SAT Critical Reading: 470–570
Range SAT Math: 480–590
Range SAT Writing: 470–570
Range ACT Composite: 20–25

Annual tuition: $29,870
Average cumulative indebtedness: $35,404

% students graduating in 4 years: 52%
% students graduating in 6 years: 64%

Dr. Jonathan Millen, Communication,
Liberal Arts

Located in quaint Lawrenceville, New Jersey, Rider University is a private co-ed college university that offers a "highly respected" business school program as well as strong liberal arts and science programs. Students also rave about the accounting program which one student cites as "the best in the state of New Jersey." Undergraduates mainly hail from the East Coast, but "The student body is very diverse politically, socially, and academically." Indeed, "there is a good mix of jocks, brainy people who are committed to studying, and artsy hipster types" so most "students can usually find at least one group to fit in with." Rider is also notable for its evening program, where "older, working, returning students" come to complete their studies; these attendees are known for taking their studies seriously.

Campus life is friendly and fun, and "basketball games are always a big draw." The university also hosts "major comedians, musicians, [and] film nights" in the evenings. Also, the "Student Rec Center is a great place to hang out because it's got basketball courts, a pool table, ping pong table, all the video game systems, a gym, a track, and a pool." For those students who want to have fun off campus, "there are coffee shops, frozen yogurt places, [and] a house of cupcakes" in the nearby town of Princeton, and "New York City and Philly are only a train ride away."

Rider is primarily seen as "student-oriented," and the administration "goes the extra mile in making sure all students are treated equally." One student asserts, "The science professors have been really helpful with helping me achieve my goals by introducing me to opportunities for grants, internships, and other experiential learning." There is a major focus on quality teaching at Rider, and there are "some phenomenal professors at Rider University who go out of their way to give their students a great education."

Rollins College

1000 Holt Avenue, Box 2720
Winter Park, FL 32789-4499
Admissions: 407-646-2161
www.rollins.edu
admission@rollins.edu
Fax: 407-646-1502

Type of school: private
Environment: town
Total undergrad enrollment: 1,730
Student/faculty ratio: 10:1
Most common regular class size: 10–19
Range SAT Critical Reading: 560–650
Range SAT Math: 560–650
Range SAT Writing: 550–650
Range ACT Composite: 24–29

Annual tuition: $38,400
Average cumulative indebtedness: $25,294

% students graduating in 4 years: 59%
% students graduating in 6 years: 69%

Rick Bommelje, Communication

Located in the heart of Central Florida, Rollins College is a private liberal arts college that boasts "an impressive physics department, a great theater program with professors who are working professionals, a strong pre-law program, [and] a good education department." In addition to its "beautiful" location and "amazing campus," the college also offers "many opportunities for studying abroad, and financial aid helps to pay for most of them." At Rollins, "if you've got a goal, they'll take you there." According to a very satisfied and enthusiastic student, "the environment is wonderful, [the] administration is extremely helpful, [and] the professors are one in a million! Everyone truly cares about you." A fellow Rollins student observes, "Rollins isn't just an education, it's an experience. The days and the nights will introduce you to new and exciting things…" Although "fun and relaxed," the school does challenge its students to push themselves academically and socially. Students are "always busy with school and extracurricular activities," and most of them agree that success here requires "a lot of work, much more than some people think."

Small classes also mean that students "are really forced into keeping up-to-date with the reading and with the assigned writings." An advantage of the small class size is that they offer the students a chance to participate in interactive discussion groups. One student explains, "Rollins is also a cool place to learn because many of our classes are taught around tables or in circles to stimulate discussion." Although considered "tough," the professors at Rollins seem to support the student population at Rollins by making themselves accessible and available when needed. Students observe that "some [professors] require a lot of reading and work, but if you have problems they are always available outside of class to help."

Rose-Hulman Institute of Technology

5500 Wabash Avenue–CM 1
Terre Haute, IN 47803-3999
Admissions: 812-877-8213
www.rose-hulman.edu
admissions@rose-hulman.edu
Fax: 812-877-8941

The "academically demanding" classes at the Rose-Hulman Institute of Technology, a tech school in Terre Haute, Indiana, may put students "through hell," but a "small student-teacher ratio" and heavy doses of "personal attention" mean students who run the gauntlet are "almost guaranteed a job in the field of your choice." This is a school that is "rigorously preparing students for a variety of careers."

Type of school: private
Environment: town
Total undergrad enrollment: 1,872
Student/faculty ratio: 12:1
Most common regular class size: 20–29
Range SAT Critical Reading: 570–670
Range SAT Math: 630–740
Range SAT Writing: 550–650
Range ACT Composite: 27–32

Annual tuition: $35,595
Average cumulative indebtedness: $40,619

% students graduating in 4 years: 69%
% students graduating in 6 years: 80%

Phillip Cornwell, Mechanical Engineering
Diane Evans, Mathematics
Elton Graves, Mathematics
Yosi Shibberu, Mathematics
Richard Stamper, Mechanical Engineering
William Weiner, Applied Biology and Biomedical Engineering

Rose-Hulman provides a "learning environment like nothing I have seen at other schools," one in which a "friendly and welcoming" vibe and "family atmosphere" makes students feel as if they are part of "one big family." And that's not just talk. Students here say their professors "are so personal that they will know your name, ask if you are okay if you miss a class or two, and even pull up a chair next to your table at the bar." That "friendly atmosphere between faculty, students, and teachers" means students here feel that the faculty "truly care that you do well and are there to help."

All this is aimed at one thing: providing great academics. At Rose-Hulman "the courses are challenging yet rewarding." Students are described as "smart, dedicated," and "geniuses," and they are educated by "professors who are here because they like to teach and are good at teaching, not for research." The small town of Terre Haute doesn't offer students much to do, but on-campus activities are many, and sports and the arts thrive. Yet the relatively low-key life at Rose-Hulman is exactly what serious students seek. One notes, "I live in Los Angeles, but to be a mechanical engineer I knew that I'd need to go somewhere with a good school and nothing else. Thus I chose Rose-Hulman, figuring that a great education only would happen if I could focus on it." Students like this one are helped along by "professors who know your name and are more than willing to provide extra help" and teachers who "are personal and focus on undergraduate education."

One student summarizes: "Teachers giving out cell phones numbers and knowing your name, not just a number in the system, is what college should be about." That's Rose-Hulman.

Santa Clara University

500 El Camino Real
Santa Clara, CA 95053
Admissions: 408-554-4700
www.scu.edu
ugadmissions@scu.edu
Fax: 408-554-5255

Type of school: private
Environment: town
Total undergrad enrollment: 5,158
Student/faculty ratio: 12:1
Most common regular class size: 20-29

Test scores
Range SAT Critical Reading: 550-650
Range SAT Math: 570-680
Range ACT Composite: 25-30

Annual tuition: $37,368
Average cumulative indebtedness: $25,438
% students graduating in 4 years: 78%

Laura Poe, Mathematics

A small Jesuit school located in the Silicon Valley, Santa Clara University may be best known for its liberal arts program—not to mention for being the oldest college in California—but it also boasts well-respected business and engineering programs. Classes at this cozy school are driven by discussion rather than lectures, thanks to the 13:1 student-to-teacher ratio and an emphasis on professors who are "very enthusiastic about the material they teach." The student body's focus on community service and volunteerism also deemphasizes partying and alcohol, making Santa Clara a school perfect for the socially conscious.

Small class sizes are an essential ingredient at Santa Clara. Professors routinely help students on an individual basis. This is "a small campus where each student receives personal attention to optimize their success." One student says, "[I] like the small sizes of the classes that allow me to receive the attention and help that I need." The school offers "a lot of one-on-one attention," with both professors and students who are "focused on education in order to help the greater good of the world, not simply to get a job and earn money." The philosophy of the teaching body "encourages growth in the whole person, not just the academic side of me."

Santa Clara maintains those intimate classes by capping class sizes at fifty students, "and unlike schools like Stanford, classes are only taught by professors." Those small class sizes provide an "opportunity for a real teacher-student relationship." The academic environment is a challenging one—students call it "rigorous," "challenging," and "competitive"—but "graduates say that professors create an environment for your success." Most students find that "the teachers were good at engaging the students." Santa Clara University would not be Santa Clara University with professors "who invest lots of time into their students and a faculty that is dedicated to the success of the student."

While students initially fall in love with the "beautiful, sunny location" in Silicon Valley and the school's close proximity to San Francisco and Santa Cruz —students comment that they feel at home thanks to the "slower paced feel of a smaller town"—the memory they walk away with is of having a "great experience in terms of faculty interaction and class discussion." The frequent "one-on-one engagement with professors" makes learning a highly personal experience. The combination of a highly regarded business program with an "eco-friendly" sense of social awareness results in students who feel connected to their education in a way that rises above mere academics. "I feel like Santa Clara University cares for me as a person and wants to make sure that I am happy with the decisions that are made," said one student.

And, as another student noted, it all begins with the faculty: "I'd say the staff and faculty truly make Santa Clara what it is. We have such a strong support system. No one is allowed to fall through the cracks. Most people hear Santa Clara and automatically think strict-Catholic institution and snobby students because we are private. Contrarily, students here are grounded and realistic while the entire community is open-minded to and supportive of all religions, races, and genders."

Sarah Lawrence College

One Mead Way
Bronxville, NY 10708-5999
Admissions: 914-395-2510
www.sarahlawrence.edu
slcadmit@slc.edu
Fax: 914-395-2515

Type of school: private
Environment: metropolis
Total undergrad enrollment: 1,295
Student/faculty ratio: 9:1
Most common regular class size: 10–19

Annual tuition: $42,600
Average cumulative indebtedness: $17,246

% students graduating in 4 years: 64%
% students graduating in 6 years: 73%

Joseph Lauinger, Literature

Sarah Lawrence College is a great fit for intellectually curious students who are seeking a less traditional approach to academics. Indeed, undergrads here truly have a direct hand in their studies. This results in a "personal education" tailored to each student's interests and goals. In keeping with the belief that higher education should focus on learning (not simply career prep), Sarah Lawrence does not mandate majors or provide grades. Instead, students simply choose a concentration and receive evaluations. Further, the college maintains small class sizes, allowing for lots of discussion and "close teacher relations." Undergrads are also able to work directly with professors through the conference system, whereby students conduct research with faculty on a topic of their choosing. This is an opportunity in which most SLC students revel, given that they view their professors as "passionate, engaging, and extremely intelligent." Importantly, "they take an interest in you personally to understand your goals, and then they cater their teaching to that." Additionally, faculty make themselves "readily available for any questions outside of class." And as one extremely satisfied undergrad concludes, "I couldn't ask for more."

Seton Hall University

Enrollment Services
400 South Orange
South Orange, NJ 07079
Admissions: 973-761-9332
www.shu.edu
thehall@shu.edu
Fax: 973-275-2040

Type of school: private
Environment: village
Total undergrad enrollment: 4,972
Student/faculty ratio: 14:1
Most common regular class size: 10–19
Range SAT Critical Reading: 470–570
Range SAT Math: 470–580
Range SAT Writing: 480–580
Range ACT Composite: 20–25

Annual tuition: $29,940
Average cumulative indebtedness: $16,160

% students graduating in 4 years: 41%
% students graduating in 6 years: 63%

Melinda D. Papaccio, Writing

Business, management, and diplomacy are the bread and butter of Seton Hall's strong reputation, a reputation this Catholic university maintains through the efforts of its expert teaching staff. In addition to its affiliation with the United Nations, the university would not have a reputation as one of the northeast's best schools for diplomacy and business without the "nurturing faculty who are truly great mentors with so much experience." According to students, "the faculty is what truly makes this school a blessing."

Students say "the faculty are very inviting and enjoyable to work with." The "friendly and helpful staff," led by "intelligent professors," helps students meet the challenges of Seton Hall's rigorous academic program. The word "friendly," in fact, comes up a lot among students asked about their professors, often paired with descriptors like "gifted," "helpful," and "really awesome." The "exceptional" staff "genuinely care about the well-being of the students and won't allow anyone to fall through the cracks." They are also respected as experts in their respective fields: "The professors know what it is that they are teaching, and teach it."

Seton Hall is "the perfect size because you will recognize faces even though you might not know who the people are." That means the university strikes a balance between being fairly small and providing a "robust academic program that can easily scale to how intense you want it to be." That program is administered by professors "with real experience" and a faculty that is "knowledgeable and passionate about teaching." They and administrators "will bend over backward in order to help you."

Social life and activities at Seton Hall revolve around the ever-popular basketball program and a thriving Greek scene. The campus wins few raves when it comes to entertainment opportunities—many students live in the region, commuting back home on weekends—but the short train ride to New York City, one of the world's best-known getaways, more than makes up for the lack of night life. "Life at Seton Hall," students agree, "is what you make of it." Yet night life is not why most students attend Seton Hall. Despite "lacking the social aspects of a larger, more exciting university," the school "has a great learning atmosphere where you can find your niche no matter what kind of person you are."

The "wonderful leaders and motivators" here ensure students have "an endless number of opportunities." Teachers "are there to help you and teach you, not to fail you or prevent you from graduating." They "want to see you succeed" and "care about your success and actually know your name." Students "do not feel as if [they are] a number." The goal is to give students "a great foundation beyond one's major so that students are well-rounded individuals with a variety of experiences upon graduation."

Skidmore College

815 North Broadway
Saratoga Springs, NY 12866-1632
Admissions: 518-580-5570
www.skidmore.edu
admissions@skidmore.edu
Fax: 518-580-5584

Type of school: private
Environment: town
Total undergrad enrollment: 2,703
Student/faculty ratio: 9:1
Most common regular class size: 10-19
Range SAT Critical Reading: 570-680
Range SAT Math: 570-660
Range SAT Writing: 580-690
Range ACT Composite: 26-30

Annual tuition: $40,350
Average cumulative indebtedness: $18,303

% students graduating in 4 years: 78%
% students graduating in 6 years: 84%

Victor L. Cahn, English
Linda Hall, English
Sheldon Solomon, Psychology

Reputation and location are prime reasons students choose Skidmore College, but current students discover there is more to the school. One tells us, "The campus is small and welcoming and the students always look happy. It was not until visiting that I seriously considered attending." Another freshman shares, "I originally applied because of the phenomenal art department, but I was pleasantly surprised to see how enthusiastic all the departments were about their chosen subjects." Saratoga Springs is a beautiful backdrop for academia, but there is more to this school than its beautiful location. "The academic atmosphere can be best described as a relaxed intensity," a current student explains. Students appreciate the active campus and the friendly atmosphere. Skidmore "allows students with a variety of interests to take classes that they are interested in. I have taken classes in about eight different departments." This student continues, "The school is open to all different walks of life." The small student/faculty ratio allows students to establish "personal connections with the professors and have a multitude of leadership options." This student goes on to explain that "it's normal to have at least two majors and do activities that are unrelated to those majors." A recent graduate tells us, "I loved the small classroom setting and the wide range of classes offered." She continues, "Creative approaches to learning and education are infused into the curriculum and daily life." Another current student explains, "I wanted to go to a smaller school to be able to work closely with the faculty. I knew that a larger university with graduate students would prevent me from doing any large-scale research with my advisors." Overall, it seems to be the feel of the campus, the great research opportunities, the diversity of student interests and activities, and great reviews of the professors from fellow students that make Skidmore the choice for students.

St. John's University

8000 Utopia Parkway
Queens, NY 11439
Admissions: 718-990-2000
www.stjohns.edu
admhelp@stjohns.edu
Fax: 718-990-2096

Type of school: private
Environment: metropolis
Total undergrad enrollment: 12,067
Student/faculty ratio: 19:1
Most common regular class size: 20–29
Range SAT Critical Reading: 480–590
Range SAT Math: 490–620

Annual tuition: $31,250
Average cumulative indebtedness: $32,886

% students graduating in 4 years: 36%
% students graduating in 6 years: 58%

Joyce Boland-DeVito, Esq., Business Law
Regis Clifford, Management, Marketing, Economics
Thomas Kitts, English
James O'Keefe, Criminal Justice
Andrew Russakoff, Computer Information Systems and Decision Sciences

St. John's University's students are as diverse as the borough it resides in, Queens, New York. Though steeped in tradition, the Roman Catholic school nonetheless keeps current with the cultural cutting edge of New York City.

Students have one hundred programs and concentrations to choose from in fields including arts, sciences, business, education, pharmacy, and allied health. Knowledgeable professors, 90 percent of whom hold a PhD or possess similar level of experience, are readily available to assist students when needed. In addition to arming all incoming students with brand-new laptops, the school offers freshmen the opportunity to take advantage of the innovative Passport Program, which allows students to study abroad during their very first year at St. John's.

Those seeking a longer stay overseas than the two week course, located at the university's Rome campus, can enroll in additional global studies programs.

One such class, Discover the World, allows students to earn fifteen credits while studying in three foreign cities all in one semester. In addition to St. John's three residential New York City campuses in Queens, Staten Island, and lower Manhattan, there are campuses located in Rome, Italy, and locations in Oakdale and Paris, France.

Since everything in the surrounding area "is just a subway ride away," students have access to everything from "clubs, sports events, parties, [and] restaurants." While the school's Catholic background is not a requirement, "St. John's makes it easy to incorporate a spiritual life with an academic one." There are "community-service initiatives galore" to take advantage of as well to keep the campus in balance.

Stanford University

Undergraduate Admission
Montag Hall
Stanford, CA 94305-6106
Admissions: 650-723-2091
www.stanford.edu
admission@stanford.edu
Fax: 650-725-2846

Type of school: private
Environment: city
Total undergrad enrollment: 6,988
Most common regular class size: 10–19
(36% are 2–9, 32% are 10–19)

Range SAT Critical Reading: 670–770
Range SAT Math: 690–780

Annual tuition: $40,050
Average cumulative indebtedness: $16,458

Joshua Landy, French and Italian
Mehran Sahami, Computer Science

Widely considered by many as a West Coast Ivy League school, Stanford University is a renowned college located on the San Francisco Bay peninsula. Stanford is recognized for its strong academics and unique cultural atmosphere, with one student describing it as "an alternate reality paradise filled with geniuses wearing costumes." Another student called Stanford "a surreal utopia of Nobel Prize faculty, stellar academics, and groundbreaking research." The school boasts a very diverse campus with students hailing from 143 countries, 18 territories and all 50 states. However the diversity isn't strictly related to geography; one student notes that "the intellectual curiosity and diversity of opinions" make for a rich and fulfilling experience.

Stanford has a lot to offer in terms of internships and student programs, with "nearly infinite opportunities for undergraduate research." Notable programs include the Stanford Technology Ventures Program, which grants students the chance to work with and learn from entrepreneurs in nearby Silicon Valley. Stanford is also well known for its Immersion in Medicine Series Program, which offers opportunities for premed students to shadow physicians at Stanford Hospital. The study abroad program is "fantastic" and allows students to spend a semester in Australia, Chile, China, Germany, Great Britain, Japan, Russia, France, Italy, Spain, or South Africa.

Although Stanford is a research-driven university, professors are very interested in getting to know their students. One student raves, "I have never hated a class at Stanford; I have formed deep relationships with most of my professors." In addition, many of the professors have a high level of expertise; one happy student reports taking classes by "a Nobel laureate, a former secretary of defense, and famous authors." The classroom experience is discussion-oriented, and dialogues frequently extend beyond the lecture halls.

Don't feel too daunted by the academic atmosphere; the student body knows how to have fun. Many students subscribe to the "work hard, play hard" model, and there are numerous extracurriculars available. The dorms are often compared to palaces. And the weather is quite simply beautiful with many describing the sunny California locale as "gorgeous."

State University of New York at Geneseo

One College Circle
Geneseo, NY 14454-1401
Admissions: 585-245-5571
www.geneseo.edu
admissions@geneseo.edu
Fax: 585-245-5550

Type of school: public
Environment: village
Total undergrad enrollment: 5,488
Student/faculty ratio: 19:1
Most common regular class size: 20–29
Range SAT Critical Reading: 610–700
Range SAT Math: 630–690
Range ACT Composite: 28–30

Annual in-state tuition: $4,970
Annual out-of-state tuition: $13,380
Average cumulative indebtedness: $21,000

% students graduating in 4 years: 64%
% students graduating in 6 years: 78%

Gary Towsley, Mathematics

Viewed by many as the crown jewel of the New York university system, SUNY Geneseo offers the feel of a small, private college at a fraction of the cost. Academic and social opportunities abound here. Indeed, a large percentage of students participate in study abroad, and a number conduct undergraduate research as well. As if that wasn't enough, Geneseo is located in the historic Finger Lakes region which virtually guarantees beautiful, natural surroundings. After all, *National Geographic* magazine has ranked the sunsets at SUNY Geneseo among the top ten in the world. Of course, what really seals the deal for most students is their access to a phenomenal faculty. And what's not to love about them? Professors here are "experts in their fields and their enthusiasm for [their chosen] subject shows in the way they teach class material." Moreover, the "small class sizes allow them to really get to know you as an individual." Additionally, the faculty at SUNY Geneseo bend over backward to make themselves accessible. One pleased student concurs, stating, "Professors are always open to talk to [undergrads], even during non-office hours. They are truly dedicated to helping students succeed." Impressively, professors aim to take an egalitarian approach in their classrooms. As another thankful undergrad shares, "Teachers here don't place themselves above students. Rather they regard themselves as equals [and view discussions] as a learning experience for them as well as us." Finally, a supremely content undergrad boldly concludes, "I have had some professors at Geneseo who have changed my life."

State University of New York—Binghamton University

State University of New York—
Binghamton University
P.O. Box 6001
Binghamton, NY 13902-6001
Admissions: 607-777-2171
www.binghamton.edu
admit@binghamton.edu
Fax: 607-777-4445

Widely known as "one of the top public universities of the region," Binghamton University is built on achievement, exploration, and leadership. The institution is a part of the State University of New York and works to turn out "well-rounded individuals" who are "globally aware and environmentally conscious," without too much strain on their finances.

Students have many fields of study to choose from and a wealth of faculty to support them. "All of my professors have been highly qualified for their positions, and any courses taught by graduate students have been comparable to those taught by professors. My academics have been challenging but have also allowed me time to pursue other interests such as clubs, leadership positions, and community outreach activities," says one student.

Type of school: public
Environment: city
Total undergrad enrollment: 11,745
Student/faculty ratio: 21:1
Most common regular class size: 10–19
Range SAT Critical Reading: 580–670
Range SAT Math: 620–700
Range SAT Writing: 570–660
Range ACT Composite: 26–30

Annual in-state tuition: $4,970
Annual out-of-state tuition: $13,380
Average cumulative indebtedness: $21,110

% students graduating in 4 years: 66%
% students graduating in 6 years: 78%

Jennifer Wegmann, Health & Wellness Studies
Mary Haupt, Journalism

State University of New York— Stony Brook University

Office of Admissions
Stony Brook, NY 11794-1901
Admissions: 631-632-6868
www.stonybrook.edu
enroll@stonybrook.edu
Fax: 631-632-9898

Type of school: public
Environment: town
Total undergrad enrollment: 16,045
Student/faculty ratio: 19:1
Most common regular class size: 20–29
Range SAT Critical Reading: 530–630
Range SAT Math: 580–680
Range SAT Writing: 520–630
Range ACT Composite: 25–29

Annual in-state tuition: $6,994
Annual out-of-state tuition: $16,444
Average cumulative indebtedness: $19,770

% students graduating in 4 years: 43%
% students graduating in 6 years: 65%

Catherine Marrone, Sociology

Students fortunate enough to attend SUNY Stony Brook are privy to a "large campus" that offers "a lot of diversity," "many opportunities," and perhaps most importantly, "good food." The incredible "variety of classes" means undergrads have access to nearly any academic subject they can conceive of. Moreover, students rave about their "great" professors who strive to make themselves "easily accessible," and are quick to point out that their school manages to attract "Nobel Prize winners [and] Ivy League grads/profs" while maintaining an affordable, state school price tag. These noted professors work diligently to ensure that their relationships with students extend beyond the confines of the classroom. Indeed, they provide a "huge amount of research opportunities" and help undergrads obtain internships. What more could a college student hope for?

State University of New York— University at Albany

Office of Undergraduate Admissions
University at Albany—SUNY
1400 Washington Avenue
Albany, NY 12222
Admissions: 518-442-5435
www.albany.edu
ugadmissions@albany.edu
Fax: 518-442-5383

Type of school: public
Environment: city
Total undergrad enrollment: 12,797
Student/faculty ratio: 19:1
Most common regular class size: 20–29
Range SAT Critical Reading: 500–590
Range SAT Math: 530–620

Annual in-state tuition: $4,970
Annual out-of-state tuition: $13,380
Average cumulative indebtedness: $22,092

% students graduating in 4 years: 53%
% students graduating in 6 years: 63%

Jeffrey Berman, English

Firmly rooted in New York's capital city, SUNY Albany is a moderately sized university that manages to maintain an intimate feel. With a broad range of academic programs, opportunities for intellectual exploration abound. The university loves to take advantage of its prime location to augment programs in criminal justice, business, and political science. Additional departments of merit include Japanese studies, psychology, mathematics, and a number of the hard sciences. Naturally, praise for these disciplines is due in large part to the professors who teach the material and impart knowledge. Overall, undergrads at SUNY Albany find the faculty to be "receptive, active, and engaging." A pleasantly surprised student reveals, "[The professors] are a lot more accessible than I would have thought for a school this big." A fellow undergrad wholeheartedly agrees, stating teachers truly "go out of their way to help students who are interested in learning, come to class regularly, and care about their academic work." With such attentive and assertive professors, it's no wonder why Albany students are so content with their education.

Stonehill College

320 Washington Street
Easton, MA 02357-5610
Admissions: 508-565-1373
www.stonehill.edu
admissions@stonehill.edu
Fax: 508-565-1545

Type of school: private
Environment: village
Total undergrad enrollment: 2,573
Student/faculty ratio: 13:1
Most common regular class size: 20–29
Range SAT Critical Reading: 550–630
Range SAT Math: 560–640
Range ACT Composite: 24–28

Annual tuition: $33,920
Average cumulative indebtedness: $30,435

% students graduating in 4 years: 80%
% students graduating in 6 years: 85%

Richard Capobianco, Philosophy
Jared Green, English

The "small classroom setting" at Stonehill College, a Catholic liberal arts college located outside Boston, Massachusetts, makes for a campus that "just felt like home" for students. The "personable and engaging" professors here provide a "supportive community environment" right from the start. "Everyone I met through my decision process was ridiculously nice," one student notes, "and they all seemed to be concerned about what was right for me." The sense of community here "goes unmatched," and the "incredible" support staff make the campus "seem more homey and friendly."

Yet this isn't all hand-holding, feel-good education. "Academics are taken seriously" at Stonehill. In fact, it is "probably the strongest feature of the school." Prospective students like the "high quality of [Stonehill's] liberal arts education," which lets them be "free to grow as a person and be ready for the world outside of it." The staff "emphasizes students' personal and academic interests," rewarding students who "are achievers and have worked hard to get here." Professors work hard to ensure they are available to help students. Some "give students not only their school e-mail addresses, but their cell phone or home phone numbers as well as their AIM screen names if they have them!"

"Practically everyone participates in a sport, club, or volunteer work," reports a student. However, both Boston and Providence are a mere twenty-two miles away, so "a lot of people go there to find their entertainment."

Academics, though, is the focus "hands down," which is due in no small part to professors who are "entirely dedicated to the well-being of their students.

If I don't show up to class, my professors will e-mail me to see if everything is okay [and] why I didn't show up." The warm community atmosphere does not mean students won't have professors who "challenge you to question: question your readings, your professors, yourself." Educators at Stonehill aim to teach every student "how to be a critical thinker, and to look more in depth on ideas and topics."

Swarthmore College

500 College Avenue
Swarthmore, PA 19081
Admissions: 610-328-8358
www.swarthmore.edu
admissions@swarthmore.edu
Fax: 610-328-8580

The "lovely" school of Swarthmore, located in Pennsylvania, "provides all the advantages of a great small liberal arts school" and offers a community "where everyone pushes each other towards success."

Students here succeed because "they truly love to do what they do." But an even bigger reason is the faculty. Professors "really care about your success" and don't pass their duties on to others; they "teach all the classes here." At Swarthmore, "teachers truly care about you and are there to support you." Though the education is "almost unbearably difficult sometimes," the efforts of Swarthmore's professors results in graduates who feel that "it's totally worth it."

Maybe that's because "the administration views the students as responsible adults and thus leaves them to their own devices when they are out of class." Trust is important. So is a strong level of expertise in what faculty are teaching.

Type of school: private
Environment: town
Total undergrad enrollment: 1,505
Student/faculty ratio: 8:1
Most common regular class size: 10-19

Range SAT Critical Reading: 670-760
Range SAT Math: 670-770
Range SAT Writing: 670-760
Range ACT Composite: 29-33

Annual tuition: $39,260
% students graduating in 4 years: 88%
% students graduating in 6 years: 92%

Steve C. Wang, Statistics

"Some of my professors have knocked me to the floor with their brilliance," boasts one student. Despite the "really challenging" academics, "Swarthmore is amazingly flexible." Students seeking a great education can find it here: "If they don't offer a major you want, you can design your own with ease."

The school is not large. The size means "opportunities to participate in many different programs" are available to all; the school features a student body that is "either working on extracurriculars, studying, or fighting sleep to do more work." Indeed, there is no lack of things to do at Swarthmore—students "could spend four years in non-stop activity on committees, in clubs, at shows, concerts"—yet the "awesome professors" are what makes the school special. A huge number of resources are available for students, including faculty who are "really helpful to talk to when you have major papers." Students say "whenever you need help with something, there's someone you can talk to."

While this "challenging academically" school is not widely known across the nation, those who do know of Swarthmore "also know of its wonderful reputation." Here students pursue "learning for the sake of truly learning rather than just for grades." This "academically rigorous" college is a draw for enthusiastic learners, resulting in a student body who "are 100 percent invested in their studies without coming off as total nerds because they choose to study what they are passionate about." Those who go to Swarthmore "care about the world and want to make it better."

Sweet Briar College

P.O. Box B
Sweet Briar, VA 24595
Admissions: 434-381-6142
www.sbc.edu
admissions@sbc.edu
Fax: 434-381-6152

Total undergrad enrollment: 605
Student/faculty ratio: 7:1

Range SAT Critical Reading: 500-620
Range SAT Math: 470-580
Range ACT Composite: 21-26

Annual tuition: $30,620
Average cumulative indebtedness: $27,712
% students graduating in 4 years: 57%
% students graduating in 6 years: 59%

Steve Wassell, Mathematical Sciences

Set in breathtaking rural Virginia, Sweet Briar is an all-female, liberal arts college brimming with history and tradition. The school makes it a mission to empower its students to be leaders both on campus and beyond. Academic integrity is paramount at Sweet Briar, and most undergrads take their course work rather seriously. Indeed, diligence is the norm and hard work is necessary for success in the classroom. Fortunately, the small student-to-faculty ratio allows for unparalleled access to professors. Undergrads need not be shy when asking for help. As one glowing student shares, the professors are "always incredibly involved and supportive." A fellow student chimes in, "My professors even remembered me from my pre-acceptance visits." Yes, warmth and openness is pervasive amongst Sweet Briar faculty. As yet another student reveals, "Our president, Jo Ellen Parker, keeps an online blog….Our administration takes turns having cooking nights for students to learn how to cook different meals. [And] I have personally had dinner with the dean of co-curricular life at her house along with other students." It's experiences like these that leave undergrads gushing, "Sweet Briar is smarts, opportunity, and beauty all wrapped up in one."

Texas Christian University

Office of Admissions TCU Box 297013
Fort Worth, TX 76129
Admissions: 817-257-7490
www.tcu.edu
frogmail@tcu.edu
Fax: 817-257-7268

Type of school: private
Environment: metropolis
Total undergrad enrollment: 7,804
Student/faculty ratio: 13:1
Most common regular class size: 20-29
Range SAT Critical Reading: 520-630
Range SAT Math: 530-650
Range SAT Writing: 520-630
Range ACT Composite: 23-29

Annual tuition: $32,400
Average cumulative indebtedness: $36,546

% students graduating in 4 years: 54%
% students graduating in 6 years: 74%

Ralph Carter, Political Science
Ronald L. Pitcock, Honors
Steven E. Woodworth, History

The "small, friendly campus" of Texas Christian University, a Fort Worth college that bucks the bigger-is-better trend of massive Texas schools, is as inviting as the "emphasis on the individual" the school showcases. Students say professors here "seem genuinely interested in me and give me advice right then and there about what I can do with my degree and how they can help me out." This school's "great reputation" comes in part through the work of teachers who "really care, and unlike public schools, the classes are smaller and the professors want to know you, and your name." Students frequently cite those class sizes as a major factor in their success. "The fact that all of my professors know me makes me more accountable," one reports, with another saying, "I know that I'm not just a number." Students here can "get more on-one-on time with my professors" than in larger schools. "I can talk to my professors," students note. While the "excellent academics" at Texas Christian are strong, educators don't merely care about grades. Professors here seek to "try to create an individual that is culturally aware and globalized," working to "educate individuals to think and act as ethical leaders and responsible citizens" and to "think about the world beyond their own bubble." This is facilitated by "friendly and community-oriented" professors who "really care about you" and are "very understanding and realistic." When it comes to their students, teachers here "want them to succeed, and they do everything they can to help the students make that happen." The school boasts Division 1 sports, a well-respected premed program, a "wonderfully well-rounded dance program," a renowned business curriculum, a "top-ranked football program," plenty of Greek life, a "reputation as a great journalism school," and much more. Texas Christian University is first and foremost about the students. Professors "want to see you succeed" and "are dedicated to what they teach." The "personal attention they are able to provide in the classroom can't be denied," and students are pleased that "I can find assistance wherever I might need it." Students will get a "personal learning experience from professors." The school is "very challenging academically"—no surprise there, since "most students are career-minded and success-focused"—but students can expect to "have close relationships with your professors," a recipe for success that results in many families returning to TCU generation after generation.

The Ohio State University

Undergraduate Admissions
110 Enarson Hall
154 West Twelfth Avenue
Columbus, OH 43210
Admissions: 614-292-3980
www.osu.edu
askabuckeye@osu.edu
Fax: 614-292-4818

The Ohio State University is one of the country's largest and best known colleges, a huge school with something to offer every student, a staff of professors with "prestige" who give students "every resource you could possibly need," and of course, Buckeye pride.

There are "excellent professors in the classroom" who provide an academic

Type of school: public
Environment: metropolis
Total undergrad enrollment: 40,851
Student/faculty ratio: 19:1
Most common regular class size: 20-29
Range SAT Critical Reading: 540-650
Range SAT Math: 590-700
Range SAT Writing: 540-640
Range ACT Composite: 26-30

Annual in-state tuition: $8,994
Annual out-of-state tuition: $23,178
Average cumulative indebtedness: $22,830

% students graduating in 4 years: 49%
% students graduating in 6 years: 78%

Lisa Cravens-Brown, Psychology
Joseph Irvine, Business Law
Paul Clingan, Engineering
Elizabeth Renker, English
Douglass Schumacher, Physics

atmosphere that is "top notch, but not overwhelming." The "die hard professors" here ensure students "have every opportunity to succeed in the classroom," providing an education that "helps you become the person you want to be." Students report that "the professors are interactive," affording students "opportunities to do anything you can dream up." The school may be best-known for its nationally recognized football program—Buckeye pride is a big deal at Ohio State—but academics are no walk in the park. Though teachers are helpful, the school "[does not] hold your hand though planning and logistical matters." They expect students to develop the skills necessary to succeed. Yet that does not mean they don't take an interest in students. Professors at Ohio State are "incredibly eager to work with students," provided the students, too, are eager to learn. Many are "as interesting and entertaining as they can be when lecturing" and work with students on "everything from music to biochemical engineering and anything and everything in between."

Doing "everything" is a big part of the eclectic, diverse life of an Ohio State student. This "big and friendly" school sprawls out over Columbus, Ohio, with a campus that feels "like its own city" while "still having enough green space for sports and just hanging out." There are literally hundreds of student clubs, thousands of classes, and opportunities to do just about anything. This school is "all about being yourself and having a good time doing it." For those interested in learning, "the opportunities are endless." Overall, there are "ample opportunities to get involved, and you develop your own niche."

Tufts University

Bendetson Hall
Medford, MA 02155
Admissions: 617-627-3170
www.tufts.edu
admissions.inquiry@ase.tufts.edu
Fax: 617-627-3860

Type of school: private
Environment: town
Total undergrad enrollment: 5,187
Student/faculty ratio: 9:1
Most common regular class size: 10-19
Range SAT Critical Reading: 680-740
Range SAT Math: 680-760
Range SAT Writing: 680-760
Range ACT Composite: 30-33

Annual tuition: $42,962
Average cumulative indebtedness: $16,839

% students graduating in 4 years: 86%
% students graduating in 6 years: 91%

David Denby, Philosophy
Robert Devigne, Political Science
Mary Glaser, Mathematics,

Included faculty are part of the School of
Arts and Sciences

A beautiful view of nearby Boston isn't all that the prestigious Tufts University offers. Tufts also has a lively campus bustling with opportunities for students to get involved in as well as easy access to all the culture that Boston has to offer. The campus also has options that allow for hardworking students to be studious during the week and unwind on weekends. Best known for its science and international relations programs, academic life at Tufts is also enriching and rewarding. This is because Tufts has cultivated a brilliant faculty eager to educate its students. Students can expect "top-quality professors" that are "engaging." "It's not surprising to see a text book with your professor's name on it," a satisfied student intimates. Faculty are also very accessible to students. Professors are found to have "flexible office hours that allow students to go in for extra help" for students that may need it. This is due to Tufts' "small classes" that allow a more personal relationship between students and faculty. The professors also "provide great mentorship" for the student body, helping them beyond the classroom and into life.

Tulane University

6823 St. Charles Avenue
New Orleans, LA 70118
Admissions: 504-865-5260
www.tulane.edu
undergrad.admission@tulane.edu
Fax: 504-862-8715

Type of school: private
Environment: city
Total undergrad enrollment: 7,754
Student/faculty ratio: 11:1
Most common regular class size: 10–19
Range SAT Critical Reading: 610–700
Range SAT Math: 620–700
Range SAT Writing: 620–710
Range ACT Composite: 29–32

Annual tuition: $43,434
Average cumulative indebtedness: $27,510

% students graduating in 4 years: 59%
% students graduating in 6 years: 73%

Chris W. Surprenant, Philosophy

"The spirit in this place is truly unique," says one satisfied undergraduate of Tulane, a university located, fittingly, in the distinctive city of New Orleans. It is "an academic environment that challenges each student to work to his or her full potential." Another student says, "Whether through research in the classroom or discovering the vast historical roots that are alive in the city of New Orleans, Tulane is a place where the ability to learn never stops." The school combines education with a long-standing commitment to community service. Students are "required to have completed at least forty hours of community service in order to graduate," and they are proud of their contributions. Students tell us that Tulane is "quirky, classy (with underlying chaos), optimistic, and not without a sense of humor." The student body praises Tulane effusively, as a community "bound together by a common love for the Green Wave and the Crescent City," with students being "a huge part of why New Orleans is returning to its former prominence." One undergraduate adds, "the food, the music, the history, and the culture are unlike anything anywhere else in the entire world." Tulane offers a wide selection of majors, and students report that course work is "stimulating thanks to the professors and their manner of presentation." Undergrads are constantly supported by "impressive and knowledgeable professors," "who actually want to talk to you." "Teachers are invested and enthusiastic." "Most professors know your name and who you are." Students are impressed by the fact that "professors treat each person as an individual and as an adult." One student raves that the teachers "believe what they teach" and loves "that they can spark ideas."

The University of Akron

This career-oriented school provides students with a homey feel (especially since a large majority hail from within a 200–300 mile radius of the campus). A current student explains, "The University of Akron is a largely commuter campus, but there are a lot of opportunities for socialization and personal development." Providing a 'big school' feel on a mid-sized campus, The University of Akron is a popular choice because of its location and price. One student tells us, "One of the strengths of UA is the campus size, which is not very big—so it's nice walking from class to class (especially in winter!)."

Students are greatly impressed with the growth and improvements that have been made in recent years. "For the most part, everything is very up to date and modern. There are always new projects being worked on to better our school." The location is very popular with many, as this sophomore tells us: "I think UA has everything a campus could need all within walking distance. In addition it has a wide variety of majors to choose from, and the faculty is almost always interesting and an expert on their subject matter."

UA is best known for its engineering and business programs but attracts a diverse population and has many different opportunities available for students from all walks of life. The small class sizes make it easy to be involved in discussion. Students feel that "administrators and faculty are very willing to help in any way they can," and that "the faculty and staff are experienced and involved in the success and education of their students." A recent graduate summarizes by stating, "The greatest strengths are the school's ability to meet most students' needs academically with professors who are well versed in their field and are willing to share their knowledge to help those who want to excel."

Type of school: public
Environment: city
Total undergrad enrollment: 21,378
Student/faculty ratio: 20:1
Most common regular class size: 20-29

Range SAT Critical Reading: 430-560
Range SAT Math: 430-590
Range ACT Composite: 18-24

Annual in-state tuition: $7,733
Annual out-of-state tuition: $15,389
% students graduating in 4 years: 14%
% students graduating in 6 years: 35%

Susan Young, Mathematics

The University of Alabama

Box 870132
Tuscaloosa, AL 35487-0132
Admissions: 205-348-5666
www.ua.edu
admissions@ua.edu
Fax: 205-348-9046

Type of school: public
Environment: city
Total Undergrad Enrollment: 26,234
Student/faculty ratio: 19:1
Most common regular class size: 10–19
Range SAT Critical Reading: 490–620
Range SAT Math: 500–620
Range SAT Writing: 480–600
Range ACT Composite: 22–29

Annual in-state tuition: $8,600
Annual Out-of-State Tuition: $21,900
Average Cumulative Indebtedness: $26,701

% students graduating in 4 years: 38%
% students graduating in 6 years: 67%

John Beeler, History

The University of Alabama is a ridiculously afford-able, "technologically advanced," "student-centered" institution that enjoys an outrageous degree of alumni support. "Course offerings are pretty diverse," and there are "tons of majors." Highlights include a "great" engineering college and three honors programs. Other standout programs include business, communication studies, and nursing. Some students say that the "bold and visionary" top brass runs the school "fairly well." Professors here are "top researchers or writers in their fields," and some are "very enthusiastic about having undergraduate students helping them with research." The faculty as a whole is also "approachable" and "generally very easy to get in touch with for outside assistance." Students here are "extremely friendly" and "usually well-dressed and well-mannered." "People tend to be a bit conservative," and "a lot are religious." "The typical student is active in a few organizations, makes decent grades, and finds time to relax, too." "An atmosphere of almost antebellum charm" permeates this "pretty" campus. "On sunny days in the fall and spring, students enjoy studying and playing on the quad." Recreational facilities are "excellent." "Life during football season revolves around football." So does morale. Win or lose, though, UA boasts "one of the best college football atmospheres in the country. On Saturdays when the Crimson Tide plays at home, the campus is "a sea of tents for tailgating," "and Alabama fans are singing the fight song."

University of California—Berkeley

110 Sproul Hall #5800
Berkeley, CA 94720-5800
www.berkeley.edu

Type of school: public
Environment: city
Total undergrad enrollment: 25,885
Student/faculty ratio: 15:1
Most common regular class size: fewer than 10 students
Range SAT Critical Reading: 600–730
Range SAT Math: 630–760
Range SAT Writing: 610–740

Annual in-state tuition: $9,402
Annual out-of-state tuition: $32,281
Average cumulative indebtedness: $7,000

% students graduating in 4 years: 69%
% students graduating in 6 years: 90%

Denis Auroux, Mathematics
P. Robert Beatty, Molecular and Cell Biology
Ron Gronsky, Engineering
Alan Karras, International and Area Studies
Steven Pedersen, Chemistry
Zvezdelina Stankova, Mathematics
David Wetzel, History

The University of California—Berkeley is world famous for so many things—its offbeat student body, its role in 1960s counterculture, its strong political views, its influence on popular culture—that many forget it also has the "best academic reputation of any public university in the country," a school where you will be "challenged and compete with the best." For all the talk of its role in prompting changes in American society, Berkeley also "carries a good reputation for its superior instructions and educational opportunities," something students take pride in. Thanks to its "amazing reputation and brilliant instructors," it is difficult to find a school where professors are more highly regarded by those taking their classes. Students call educators here "amazing," "brilliant," "notable," "engaging," "stimulating," "outstanding," "stellar," and overall, the "world's best professors." "You simply cannot find a school with better professors," one student enthuses. They are "some of the greatest thinkers in the world," educators who "teach students how to be independent." Their goal is "not to completely overload the students with work, but rather to teach students ways of understanding information thoroughly, whether it be conceptually or being able to apply what they have learned to real-life situations."

Students enjoy learning from "some of the most brilliant minds in [their] field," a "diverse range of professionals" who are "engaged in the classroom." "I get to pick the brains of people I only used to read about in magazines or journals," notes one student. These teachers "are superstars in their field." Because Berkeley is "is a leader in many fields," students feel confident that "whatever I end up studying I know I will be well taught." The experienced educators here "take you outside of your comfort zone, and fundamentally change the way you look at the world." There are few programs that don't win praise from students—science, business, engineering, premed, and the arts all receive high accolades—probably a reason why some call it "best public university in the nation" taught by "the most knowledgeable and inspirational professors." Students say that "the degree at Berkeley will immediately set me apart in future job applications" because "the professors here are the best in their respective fields." Educators at this "world-class" university "work on some of the most innovative and complex research," experience that translates to "limitless opportunities" for their students. "Berkeley forces students to mature into responsible citizens of the world," notes one student, "no matter what major they chose to pursue." All in all, "Berkeley pushes you to become your best."

University of California—Davis

178 Mrak Hall
One Shields Avenue
Davis, CA 95616
Admissions: 530-752-2971
www.ucdavis.edu
undergraduateadmissions@ucdavis.edu
Fax: 530-752-1280

Located in Davis, California, a short trip away from Northern California highlights like San Francisco, Sacramento, and Lake Tahoe, University of California—Davis has a relaxed and cozy setting ideal for students. Its student body is diverse, and it is home

Type of school: public
Environment: town
Total undergrad enrollment: 24,497
Student/faculty ratio: 16:1
Most common regular class size: 20-29
Range SAT Critical Reading: 530-650
Range SAT Math: 570-690
Range SAT Writing: 540-660
Range ACT Composite: 24-30

Annual in-state tuition $13,860
Annual out-of-state tuition $32,281
Average cumulative indebtedness $16,222

% students graduating in 4 years: 51%
% students graduating in 6 years: 82%

Thomas Famula, Animal Science

to many student archetypes, from sorority girl to band geek. Don't let Davis's relaxed nature fool you, though. The school has a fast-paced quarter system that doesn't leave much room for slacking. However, you'll be glad to know that you'll have professors that support you along the way. Despite the fact that some students feel that faculty are only "here to collect their paycheck," there are many who disagree. Some even go as far as to say that UC Davis offers a "world-class education" experience. "Helpful" professors seem to be the norm on campus, as well. "I feel like there isn't anyone here, whether students or professors, that [isn't] willing to lend a hand to students," an appreciative student remarks. Students also find that the classes are "interesting" and challenging. UC Davis provides an atmosphere that excites and stimulates it students. As an enthusiastic student succinctly puts it, "the professors are amazing and the campus is beautiful!"

University of California— Santa Cruz

Office of Admissions, Cook House
1156 High Street
Santa Cruz, CA 95064
Admissions: 831-459-4008
www.ucsc.edu
admissions@ucsc.edu
Fax: 831-459-4452

The University of California—Santa Cruz offers one of the nation's best combinations of "focus on scholastic endeavors in a beautiful forest setting" and is, by all accounts, "a great place to live and study!" Students attribute their enthusiasm to "intelligent, eloquent, and easily accessible

Type of school: public
Environment: city
Total undergrad enrollment: 15,666
Student/faculty ratio: 19:1
Most common regular class size: 10–19
Range SAT Critical Reading: 500–630
Range SAT Math: 520–640
Range SAT Writing: 510–620
Range ACT Composite: 22–27

Annual in-state tuition: $13,416
Annual out-of-state tuition: $22,878
Average cumulative indebtedness: $16,024

% students graduating in 4 years: 49%
% students graduating in 6 years: 74%

Walter Campbell, German

professors," academics that are "impressive and challenging," and fellow students who are "happy, open-minded, and a little bit crazy." This school is best suited to those who can motivate themselves in a "chill" environment and the sort of student whose motto might be, "There's no point in learning if you're too stressed to enjoy it." The sciences are "world-class" at UCSC, and the school also boasts "one of the finest engineering programs in the UCs" as well as "a great marine biology program." While the "professors all do research," what sets them apart from those at the typical research-driven university is that "they are very passionate about their subject even when teaching undergrads," and they "also tend to be quite approachable despite having large class sizes, and allow students to attend their office hours for extra help." The school also offers undergrads "a lot of opportunities in terms of internships, research opportunities, job opportunities, and networking." "There's a focus on undergraduate study" here, one student contentedly reports.

University of Central Florida

P.O. Box 160111
Orlando, FL 32816-0111
Admissions: 407-823-3000
www.ucf.edu
admission@mail.ucf.edu
Fax: 407-823-5625

The University of Central Florida is "an innovative, diverse, and growing university," says one undergraduate. Much like the surrounding area of Orlando, UCF is expanding constantly. And although the university is getting larger, the ease of getting around campus remains; most everything is conveniently located and accessible. The school has its own medical school opening next year, and is always eager to provide students

Type of school: public
Environment: city
Total undergrad enrollment: 47,306
Student/faculty ratio: 31:1
Most common regular class size: 20–29
Range SAT Critical Reading: 530–630
Range SAT Math: 550–650
Range SAT Writing: 510–600
Range ACT Composite: 24–28

Annual in-state tuition: $5,020
Annual out-of-state tuition: $20,500
Average cumulative indebtedness: $18,966

% students graduating in 4 years: 34%
% students graduating in 6 years: 63%

Steve Lytle, Health Professions

and faculty with the latest developments in technology to use. UCF also boasts "academic advisers and professors who actually care about the students and their futures," according to one student, and another tell us the "professors are amazing…willing to go out of their way." The school has a wide variety of internships available and provides wonderful opportunities for networking with an extensive alumni base in the area. UCF is a fine value, as well. "I am a Florida native and the tuition for public schools is very affordable, especially with the Bright Futures scholarship program," says an undergrad. Facilities, from the gym to on-campus housing, are spoken of highly by the student body. There are innumerable entertainment options to be found—students tell us that "since our new on-campus stadium was built, football has become very big," although there are "many areas to explore outside the typical college scene." "My school life is greatly enhanced by my involvement in Greek life. Through it I have become involved in philanthropies and other organizations that I wouldn't have otherwise." Also, students also enjoy taking "advantage of all of the tourist attractions that Orlando has to offer"—Walt Disney World is less than an hour from campus.

University of Cincinnati

P.O. Box 210091
Cincinnati, OH 45221-0091
Admissions: 513-556-1100
www.uc.edu
admissions@uc.edu
Fax: 513-556-1105

The University of Cincinnati is one of America's top public research institutions and the region's largest employer, with a student population of more than 42,000 and "offers students a balance of educational excellence and real-world experience"

Type of school: public
Environment: metropolis
Total undergrad enrollment: 22,893
Student/faculty ratio: 17:1
Most common regular class size: 20-29
Range SAT Critical Reading: 500-620
Range SAT Math: 520-640
Range SAT Writing: 480-590
Range ACT Composite: 22-27

Annual in-state tuition: $8,805
Annual out-of-state tuition: $23,328
Average cumulative indebtedness: $26,462

% students graduating in 4 years: 22%
% students graduating in 6 years: 59%

LisaMarie Luccioni, Communication

on an expansive campus comprised of twelve separate colleges. Students agree it's "a large school with many great programs and infinite opportunities that still retains the feeling of a small university." Many praise the "cooperative education program that gives students a real edge in the job market" by allowing them the opportunity to pursue competitive internships while enrolled. Students also feel confident that "UC provides excellent opportunities outside of the classroom to make me successful post-graduation." As one student puts it, "The University of Cincinnati is not only known for its great academics, but for all of the incredible opportunities students have including cooperative education, on-campus activities and clubs, along with athletics and one of the most beautiful campuses in the world." The university's size assures that there are "a wide variety of majors to choose from," and students name the College-Conservatory of Music, the College of Design, Architecture, Art, and Planning, and the engineering programs as stand-outs. Overall, students feel that "the professors here have so much life experience in what they are teaching. It makes me trust and respect them more." Also, "advisors have been helpful." However, they note, "the professors are as diverse as the classes offered here."

University of Delaware

210 South College Avenue
Newark, DE 19716-6210
Admissions: 302-831-8123
www.udel.edu
admissions@udel.edu
Fax: 302-831-6905

The University of Delaware sits at the halfway point between New York City and Washington, D.C. ; its alumni include three signers of the Declaration of

Type of school: public
Environment: town
Total undergrad enrollment: 16,340
Student/faculty ratio: 15:1
Most common regular class size: 20-29
Range SAT Critical Reading: 540-640
Range SAT Math: 550-560
Range SAT Writing: 540-650
Range ACT Composite: 24-29

Annual in-state tuition: $9,670
Annual out-of-state tuition: $25,940
Average cumulative indebtedness: $21,856

% students graduating in 4 years: 62%
% students graduating in 6 years: 77%

Patrick J. White, English
Christopher B. Wolfe, Business Law

Independence, a vice president, governors, Nobel Prize winner and a Rhodes Scholars. Students at the school enjoy the freedom of obtaining core education requirements in large lecture settings, with the full support of the faculty when needed. As young scholars narrow their focus and choose their majors, they find that class sizes shrink and the level of individual attention grows.

According to students there's something for everyone who calls this campus home. Those who are looking for an extra challenge have the opportunity to apply for University of Delaware's rigorous honors program. For individuals seeking to explore the world, UD has one of the top study abroad programs in the country.

The average University of Delaware student focuses diligently on academics while maintaining a healthy social life and involvement in campus activities. There is a wide range of clubs and cultural events to satisfy virtually any interest, "from the adventure club to organic cooking to ultimate Frisbee." Greek life is present on campus, and members are "very spirited, have a ton of fun, and are widely supported by our campus community."

University of Florida

201 Criser Hall, Box 114000
Gainesville, FL 32611-4000
Admissions: 352-392-1365
www.ufl.edu
Fax: 904-392-3987

A top-tier research institute that "is full of bright students who still know how to have fun," the University of Florida offers "an environment unparalleled by an other university in the world with its first-class amenities, athletics, academics, campus, and students," enthusiastic students insist.

Type of school: public
Environment: city
Total undergrad enrollment: 32,043
Student/faculty ratio: 20:1
Most common regular class size: 10-19
Range SAT Critical Reading: 570-670
Range SAT Math: 600-690
Range ACT Composite: 26-30

Annual in-state tuition: $5,657
Annual out-of-state tuition: $27,321
Average cumulative indebtedness: $16,013

% students graduating in 4 years: 58%
% students graduating in 6 years: 82%

Mike Foley, Journalism
Steven Noll, History
Sergei Shabanov, Mathematics

The school "has excellent academic programs all across the board: You're not limited to just a great engineering program or journalism program" here; the sciences (including premedical studies, which piggyback on "a strong teaching hospital on campus"), business, education, communications, and engineering are among the many standout offerings. In short, "UF is a great school" that's "not expensive, even for out-of-state students. Plus, there is a great sense of family here: You really are a part of the Gator Nation" even if it is a very large university. In fact, "there are people all over the spectrum," although the place is so big that "half of them you may never meet." "We are one of the most diverse campuses in the nation," one student explains, "and we are all Gators at heart, first and foremost." Students love the professors here. "The professors are almost always wonderful: They are helpful and definitely know their stuff."

The University of Georgia

Terrell Hall
Athens, GA 30602
Admissions: 706-542-8776
www.uga.edu
undergrad@admissions.uga.edu
Fax: 706-542-1466

Students say that the professors at The University of Georgia "are outstanding and easy to reach." "The professors really do want to see you at office hours if you have questions," and they "want to share their love of learning with you." "My major-related classes are very small, and each student receives individual attention." The honors program also receives raves: "Many of my best classes and favorite teachers have come from the honors program." "The typical student at UGA is one who knows how and when to study but allows himself

Type of school: public
Environment: city
Total undergrad enrollment: 25,709
Student/faculty ratio: 19:1
Most common regular class size: 20-29
Range SAT Critical Reading: 560-660
Range SAT Math: 560-670
Range SAT Writing: 560-660
Range ACT Composite: 25-29

Annual in-state tuition: $9,472
Annual out-of-state tuition: $27,682
Average cumulative indebtedness: $15,938

% students graduating in 4 years: 54%
% students graduating in 6 years: 82%

Audrey A. Haynes, Political Science
John Knox, Geography
Charles Kutal, Chemistry

or herself to have a very active social life." The majority are Southerners, and many students are from Georgia. Life at UGA seems to be a good mix of the two different worlds of sports and arts: football, frats, and tailgating on campus come together nicely with the coffee shops and music scene in downtown Athens. "On Saturday afternoons in the fall, nearly everyone on campus is at the football game. It's a way of life here." "Everybody really gets behind the team, and Saturdays in Athens feel like mini vacations."

University of Mary Washington

1301 College Avenue
Fredericksburg, VA 22401
Admissions: 540-654-2000
www.umw.edu
admit@umw.edu
Fax: 540-654-1857

Although located in quaint Fredericksburg, Virginia, the University of Mary Washington boasts a replace with vibrant campus life. Students are active in everything from on-campus politics to community service projects. With its small class sizes, University of Mary Washington makes academics more approachable for its students.

Many students say the school's faculty "offer the highest quality learning experience possible for [their] tuition." They report that the faculty is "well educated" and "have a superb grasp on the topics they are teaching." Remarks one

Type of school: public
Environment: city
Total undergrad enrollment: 4,271
Student/faculty ratio: 15:1
Most common regular class size: 20–29
Range SAT Critical Reading: 530–640
Range SAT Math: 520–610
Range SAT Writing: 520–620
Range ACT Composite: 23–27

Annual in-state tuition: $3,984
Annual out-of-state tuition: $15,712
Average cumulative indebtedness: $15,630

% students graduating in 4 years: 65%
% students graduating in 6 years: 72%

Beverly McCullough Almond, English
Dan Hubbard, Accounting and Management Information Systems
Miriam Liss, Psychology
Jeffrey McClurken, History and American Studies
Warren Rochelle, English
Gregg Stull, Theatre
Steve Watkins, English

student, "The professors are some of the brightest and best you could ask for." Also, "students have the opportunity for one-on-one time with professors for help in the classroom." More important, "the professors genuinely seem to want to help you succeed" and "go out of their way to make the material come to life and connect to real life." Overall, the student/professor dynamic is a special one at University of Mary Washington. As one student puts it, "Every professor is different, however, I have found [that] each professor has striven to make my education the best [it] possibly could be."

University of Massachusetts— Amherst

University Admissions Center 37
Mather Drive
Amherst, MA 01003-9291
Admissions: 413-545-0222
www.umass.edu
mail@admissions.umass.edu
Fax: 413-545-4312

Type of school: public
Environment: town
Total undergrad enrollment: 20,287
Student/faculty ratio: 18:1
Most common regular class size: 20-29
Range SAT Critical Reading: 520-630
Range SAT Math: 540-650
Range ACT Composite: 23-28

Annual in-state tuition: $11,917
Annual out-of-state tuition: $23,813
Average cumulative indebtedness: $23,614

% students graduating in 4 years: 49%
% students graduating in 6 years: 66%

Panayotis Kevrekidis, Mathematics & Sciences

With over eighty-five majors offered, the University of Massachusetts—Amherst has courses and degree programs to fit almost any student's needs. It also includes an active student life full of programs and activities that you won't have to leave the campus to attend. While UMass—Amherst might be the largest public university in New England, the passionate faculty is supportive of students despite large class sizes.

Students considering attending larger universities often worry that they'll get lost in the crowd, but UMass Amherst students are quick to allay that concern: "It isn't about the size of the student body, but the faculty to student ratio." In fact, several students feel that they get the attention they need. "Despite the large student body," one says, "I have connected personally with several of my professors and TA's who know me by name (after just one semester)." Another student agrees, chiming in to say that professors "are engaging, responsive, and dedicated to my learning." UMass Amherst also offers "an excellent online learning environment for adults returning to school" which makes getting an education more convenient. Students say that the faculty and course work offer "many opportunities to expand your horizons." "Professors are understanding and demanding," a student remarks, "which makes you want to work harder."

University of Massachusetts— Lowell

Office of Undergrad Admissions
883 Broadway Street, Suite 110
Lowell, MA 01854-5104
Admissions: 978-934-3931
www.uml.edu
admissions@uml.edu
Fax: 978-934-3086

UMass Lowell is a public research university that offers high-quality academic programs for students who are ready to pursue careers in almost any field. The university is part of the five-campus University of Massachusetts system. UMass Lowell's eight thousand undergraduate students are ethnically, culturally, and economically diverse. Students are active in a wide variety of community service activities and volunteer work. They find that one of UMass Lowell's great assets is the people themselves—people who share their aspirations and commitment and who offer them support and encouragement. Among classmates, professors, and administrators, students encounter a wide range of ideas, traditions, and

Type of school: public
Environment: city
Total undergrad enrollment: 9,615
Student/faculty ratio: 15:1
Most common regular class size: 20-29

Range SAT Critical Reading: 480-570
Range SAT Math: 500-610

Annual in-state tuition: $1,454
Annual out-of-state tuition: $8,567
Average cumulative indebtedness: $21,542
% students graduating in 4 years: 28%
% students graduating in 6 years: 44%

Stephen Pennell, Mathematical Science

languages, and UMass Lowell is surrounded by a region rich with heritage and culture. The campus is located twenty-five miles from Boston and within an hour of ocean beaches and New Hampshire mountains.

University of Michigan—Ann Arbor

1220 Student Activities Building
Ann Arbor, MI 48109-1316
Admissions: 734-764-7433
www.umich.edu
Fax: 734-936-0740

Among the many allures of the University of Michigan—Ann Arbor is that the school offers "a great environment both academically and socially." One student explains, "It has the social, fun atmosphere of any Big Ten university, but most people are still incredibly focused on their studies. It's great to be at a place where there is always something to do, but your friends completely understand when you have to stay in and get work done." With "an amazing honors program," a "wide range of travel-abroad opportunities," and "research strength" all available "at a low cost," it's no wonder students tell us that UM "provides every kind of opportunity at all times to all people." Academically, Michigan "is very competitive, and the professors have high academic standards for all the students." In fact, some here insist that "Michigan is as good as Ivy League schools in many disciplines." Standout offerings include business ("we have access to some of the brightest leaders" in the business world, students report), a "great engineering program," and "a good undergraduate program for medical school preparation." Those seeking add-on academic experiences here will find "a vast amount of resources. Internships,

Type of school: public
Environment: city
Total undergrad enrollment: 26,830
Student/faculty ratio: 16:1
Most common regular class size: 10–19
Range SAT Critical Reading: 590–690
Range SAT Math: 640–750
Range SAT Writing: 610–710
Range ACT Composite: 27–31

Annual in-state tuition: $12,634
Annual out-of-state tuition: $35,812
Average cumulative indebtedness: $27,828

% students graduating in 4 years: 73%
% students graduating in 6 years: 89%

Bruce Conforth, American Culture
Pauline Khan, Technical Communications
Thad Polk, Psychology, Electrical Engineering & Computer Science
Shelly Schreier, PhD, Psychology

career opportunities, tutoring, community service projects, a plethora of student organizations, and a wealth of other resources" are all available. The Michigan student body "is hugely diverse," which "is one of the things Michigan prides itself on." "If you participate in extracurricular activities and make an effort to get to know other students in class and elsewhere, you'll definitely end up with a pretty diverse group of friends," undergrads assure us. Although varied, students tend to be similar in that they "are social but very academically driven."

University of New Orleans

University of New Orleans Admissions
103 Admin Building
New Orleans, LA 70148
Admissions: 504-280-6595
www.uno.edu
admissions@uno.edu
Fax: 504-280-5522

Tucked into the heart of one of the country's most vibrant cities, University of New Orleans provides a fantastic education with a very palatable price tag. Historically viewed as a commuter school, UNO has grown steadily in the last few years, opening opening up new dorms and renovating the Earl K. Long library.

Of course, what attracts most undergrads is the "diverse community of students" and "some of the best academics in the country." Indeed, students warn that though it might be relatively easy to gain admission, graduating requires a lot of diligence (along with blood, sweat, and tears). Top academic departments include business, engineering, naval architecture, hotel, restaurant and tourism administration, and a phenomenal jazz program (it *is* New Orleans, after all).

Type of school: public
Environment: metropolis
Total undergrad enrollment: 8,164
Student/faculty ratio: 18:1
Most common regular class size: 20–29
Range SAT Critical Reading: 470–583
Range SAT Math: 450–580
Range SAT Writing: 450–580
Range ACT Composite: 20–24

Annual in-state tuition: $4,152
Annual out-of-state tuition: $13,740
Average cumulative indebtedness: $16,427

% students graduating in 4 years: 5%
% students graduating in 6 years: 38%

Gilda Werner Reed, Psychology

Many undergrads attribute their great education to a superior faculty that's "accessible," "dedicated," and "extremely knowledgeable." Additionally, they "have had extensive careers" and retain "good connections to the real world." Certainly, from caring and talented professors and friendly campus to the cultural opportunities of the Big Easy, it's no surprise that University of New Orleans is a great package.

University of Pennsylvania

1 College Hall
Philadelphia, PA 19104
Admissions: 215-898-7507
www.upenn.edu
info@admissions.ugao.upenn.edu
Fax: 215-898-9670

Type of school: private
Environment: metropolis
Total undergrad enrollment: 9,756
Student/faculty ratio: 6:1
Most common regular class size: 10–19
Range SAT Critical Reading: 650–740
Range SAT Math: 680–780
Range SAT Writing: 670–760
Range ACT Composite: 30–33
Annual tuition: $34,868
Average cumulative indebtedness: $19,085
% students graduating in 4 years: 88%
% students graduating in 6 years: 96%

At the University of Pennsylvania, everyone shares an intellectual curiosity and top-notch resources but doesn't "buy into the stigma of being an Ivy League school." Students here are "very passionate about what they do outside the classroom" and the "flexible core requirements." The university is composed of four undergraduate schools (and "a library for pretty much any topic"). "You can take courses in any of the schools, including graduate-level courses." Luckily, there's a vast variety of disciplines available to students: "I can take a course in old Icelandic and even another one about the politics of food," says a student. Wharton, Penn's highly regarded, "highly competitive under-graduate business school" attracts "career-oriented" students who don't mind a "strenuous course load." There are "more than enough" resources, funding, and opportunity here for any student to take advantage of, and "Penn encourages students to truly take advantage of it all!" Professors "are incredibly well-versed in their subject (as well as their audience)." If you're willing to put in the time and effort, your professors "will be happy to reciprocate." In general, the instructors here are "very challenging academically" and are "always willing to offer their more than relevant life experience in class discussion."

University of Richmond

Brunet Memorial Hall
28 Westhampton Way
University of Richmond, VA 23173
Admissions: 804-289-8640
www.richmond.edu
admissions@richmond.edu
Fax: 804-287-6003

Type of school: private
Environment: city
Total undergrad enrollment: 2,945
Student/faculty ratio: 9:1
Most common regular class size: 10-19
Range SAT Critical Reading: 580-680
Range SAT Math: 600-700
Range SAT Writing: 600-690
Range ACT Composite: 27-31

Annual tuition: $43,170
Average cumulative indebtedness: $23,070

% students graduating in 4 years: 81%
% students graduating in 6 years: 87%

Stephen Long, Political Science and International Studies
Joe Troncale, Russian

Located in the state's capital, this central-Virginia location is a favorite because of its beauty and proximity to a variety of activity. The University of Richmond is just over an hour from the Washington, D.C. area, with Annapolis, Maryland nearby on the Chesapeake Bay. To the south are the coastal cities of Virginia Beach, Newport News, and Norfolk. The temperate climate and diverse location make the university a popular choice. It provides the resources of a large university with the personalized feel of a small campus. One student tells us, "UR was unlike any other school I thought about attending, small and still distinctly elite with its academics and up-and-coming athletics programs. It's the school I wanted to root for because I felt like there was so much potential here. I still feel that way." Traditions are really important at Richmond. A current student explains, "The biggest is Ring Dance, a formal held for junior women every February at the Jefferson Hotel. Richmond's greatest strength is that it is a small, closeknit school that can compete with larger schools in all areas (academics, sports….).” Another student tells us, “The smaller size meant I would have fewer people in my classes and more accessibility to my professors. Richmond is about connecting with people on a deeper level, meeting lifetime friends, and giving back to your community.” Students are active in community service and pursue academic challenges, but also have many outlets for relaxing and having fun. As a recent graduate explains, “Richmond is about discovering yourself through your education, the activities you choose to take part in, and the life you live on campus and off.” Students are the number-one priority at Richmond—all of the professors genuinely care about seeing students grow and succeed. One student says, “The greatest strengths are its size and resources (in terms of career counseling, academic advising, etc.). You can have in-depth conversations with people you just met, and everyone (including staff and administration) continually want to do better and achieve more.” This liberal arts college has excellent international and research opportunities; a current student explains that “Richmond is about having a complete college experience with good academics and ample opportunities for expanding cultural knowledge and appreciation. The campus and its facilities are gorgeous. There is also a great classroom experience and the faculty is amazing. They try to provide as many opportunities to each student as they possibly can.”

Richmond is interested in giving students the whole package: great academics, amazing research opportunities, countless study abroad programs, and athletics, all supported by highly respected and knowledgeable faculty. As one student says, “It is a place where students feel they have the opportunity to do whatever they feel passionate about, can develop meaningful relationships with faculty and students, and are supported 100 percent.”

University of San Diego

5998 Alcala Park
San Diego, CA 92110-2492
Admissions: 619-260-4506
www.sandiego.edu
admissions@sandiego.edu
Fax: 619-260-6836

Type of school: private
Environment: metropolis
Total undergrad enrollment: 5,299
Student/faculty ratio: 15:1
Most common regular class size: 30–39
Range SAT Critical Reading: 550–640
Range SAT Math: 570–660
Range SAT Writing: 550–650
Range ACT Composite: 25–29

Annual tuition: $38,582
Average cumulative indebtedness: $29,928

% students graduating in 4 years: 66%
% students graduating in 6 years: 73%

Shreesh Deshpande, Finance
Del Dickson, Political Science
Erik Fritsvold, Criminology & Legal Studies
Barton Thurber, English

The University of San Diego couples "amazing academics" with "great weather and a beautiful campus." Indeed, this "academically challenging, Roman Catholic" institution "strives and puts into action ways to create a well-rounded student who is able to succeed out in the real world." Set in a beautiful coastal town, USD has been described as a "country club escape from the city with outstanding professors, a friendly student body, and a five-minute drive to the beach." The city of San Diego is "amazing," and there are plenty of local hot spots including "parties at the beach, downtown's Gaslamp District, and Sea World on the weekends."

Life at USD is very enjoyable, and many say that USD is a "laid-back school overlooking the ocean, so people are happy to be at school and in class every day." One liberal arts student says "I just felt an overwhelming sense of belonging the very first time I stepped on campus. I fell in love right away." The student body is "very active and fit," and while some note that they "would love to see more diversity on campus," USD boasts "tremendous opportunities to get involved at USD, local community, and abroad!" Students here are especially motivated; one student advises, "Don't let the students' good looks, high fashion, or athletic prowess and wealth fool you, these students had 4.0s in high school, have intense internships, compete for graduate and professional school spots, and are constantly serving the community."

Many students appreciate "small class sizes, potential relationships with professors, and the caring nature of the faculty." One student notes, "I love that the classes are taught by instructors with PhDs rather than TAs. It is great having your professor know you personally." USD has a prestigious undergraduate business program, and the "undergraduate research opportunities are great!"

University of South Carolina—Columbia

Office of Undergraduate Admissions
University of South Carolina
Columbia, SC 29208
Admissions: 803-777-7700
www.sc.edu
admissions@sc.edu
Fax: 803-777-0101

Type of school: public
Environment: city
Total undergrad enrollment: 21,031
Student/faculty ratio: 19:1
Most common regular class size: 20–29
Range SAT Critical Reading: 530–630
Range SAT Math: 560–650
Range ACT Composite: 24–29

Annual in-state tuition: $9,386
Annual out-of-state tuition: $24,962
Average cumulative indebtedness: $21,811

% students graduating in 4 years: 46%
% students graduating in 6 years: 68%

Bradford R. Collins, Art History
Tom Hughes, Business Law
Mariah Lynch, Accounting
Mark Sibley-Jones, Literature

The University of South Carolina combines outstanding academics with diverse student life in the heart of the South. A medium-sized state university that attracts people from all over the world while still maintaining a high percentage of in-state students, it has "an atmosphere befitting its Southern heritage," says one student. The administration is committed to improving nationwide recognition while retaining its mutually supportive relationship with downtown Columbia. "The epitome of Southern hospitality," it has "an elegant mix of history and innovation," say students, who also inform us that although big on sports, USC "doesn't let important things like academic achievement, overall student health, and research fall to the wayside." "I chose

USC because of the fact that they said that I could have great relationships with my professors," says one student; small, discussion-based classes assist in that regard. Students are lavish in their praise: "Faculty and staff make the effort to get to know you and help you flourish as a student and community member." "I receive individualized attention and encouragement in all of my classes." "We are lucky to have intelligent, dedicated, and talented professors and staff." The Honors College gives students "an entirely separate college within the larger, sports-oriented main campus," and is "very rigorous and academically challenging." One student reports satisfaction with the level of support offered: "[I have] a peer mentor, professor mentor, and am invited to special dinners and events with the President and faculty." There are plenty of tutoring and supplemental instruction options; career services and study abroad programs are highly regarded, as is USC's phenomenal International Business Program. The administration strongly promotes "student involvement in all school events and give significant funding to student groups"; student organizations "have a loud voice on campus," and the school is environmentally aware. Charlotte, Atlanta, Charleston, and Myrtle Beach are all easily accessible, and downtown Columbia is close to the beach and mountains. "The historic parts of campus are amazing, and on top of it all we get SEC football," with the "unparalleled fan support of the Gamecock Nation."

University of Texas at Austin

P.O. Box 8058
Austin, TX 78713
Admissions: 512-475-7440
www.utexas.edu
Fax: 512-475-7475

Type of school: public
Environment: metropolis
Total undergrad enrollment: 36,711
Student/faculty ratio: 17:1
Most common regular class size: 10–19
Range SAT Critical Reading: 540–660
Range SAT Math: 570–690
Range ACT Composite: 24–30

Annual in-state tuition: $9,794
Annual out-of-state tuition: $32,506
Average cumulative indebtedness: $17,000
% students graduating in 4 years: 46%
% students graduating in 6 years: 68%

Jeremi Suri, Global Leadership, History, and Public Policy

Students insist that the University of Texas at Austin has "everything you want in a college: academics, athletics, social life, location," and it's hard to argue with them. UT is "a huge school and has a lot to offer," meaning students have "an infinite number of possibilities open to them and can use them in their own way to figure out what they want for their lives." As one student tells us about arriving on campus, "I did not realize how much was available to me just as an enrolled student. There is free tutoring, gym membership, professional counseling, doctors visits, legal help, career advising, and many distinguished outside speakers. The campus is crawling with experts in every field you can imagine." Standout academic departments are numerous: from the sciences to the humanities to creative arts, UT makes a strong bid for the much-sought-after mantle of "Harvard of the south." Also, the school does a surprisingly good job of avoiding the factory-like feel of many large schools. One student observes: "Coming to a large university, there was a prejudgment that the huge classes will make it impossible to know your professor and vice versa. The university has dispelled that myth with professors who want to know you and [who] provide opportunities to get to know them."

University of Wisconsin—Madison

702 West Johnson Street, Suite 101
Madison, WI 53706
Admissions: 608-262-3961
www.wisc.edu
onwisconsin@admissions.wisc.edu
Fax: 608-262-7706

Type of school: public
Environment: city
Total undergrad enrollment: 28,897
Student/faculty ratio: 17:1
Most common regular class size: 10–19
Range SAT Critical Reading: 530–670
Range SAT Math: 620–750
Range SAT Writing: 580–680
Range ACT Composite: 26–30

Annual in-state tuition: $9,665
Annual out-of-state tuition: $25,415
Average cumulative indebtedness: $22,837

% students graduating in 4 years: 51%
% students graduating in 6 years: 84%

Bryan Hendricks, Psychology
John E. Martin, Atmospheric and Oceanic Sciences
Aric Rindfleisch, Marketing
Kevin Strang, Neuroscience/Physiology

The resources are phenomenal at University of Wisconsin—Madison. "If you are proactive, you basically have the means and resources to pursue any academic or creative feat," promises a journalism major. "The liberal arts majors are fantastic." However, Madison is mostly known as "an amazing research institution," and the hard sciences and engineering programs get most of the pub. They iodized salt here, after all, and cultivated the first lab-based embryonic stem cells. The school of business is "excellent" as well and boasts "some of the best facilities on campus." The academic atmosphere is "challenging." Madison "definitely makes you earn your grades." "Some professors are amazing." "All types of people make up the student body here, ranging from the peace-preaching grass-root activist, to the protein-shake-a-day jock, to the overly privileged coastie, to the studious bookworm, to the computer geek," explains a first-year student. "There is a niche for everyone." "There are a lot of atypical students, but that is what makes UW—Madison so special," adds a senior. "Normal doesn't exist on this campus." "Many people are passionate about many things, and it provides a great opportunity to see things from others' points of view." UW is "energetic" and mammoth. "No one's going to hold your hand and point you to what it is you want." At the same time, whoever you are, "there is a group for you and a ton of activities for you."

Vanderbilt University

2305 West End Avenue
Nashville, TN 37203
Admissions: 615-322-2561
www.vanderbilt.edu
admissions@vanderbilt.edu
Fax: 615-343-7765

Type of school: private
Environment: metropolis
Total undergrad enrollment: 6,836
Student/faculty ratio: 8:1
Most common regular class size: 10–19
Range SAT Critical Reading: 670–760
Range SAT Math: 690–770
Range SAT Writing: 660–750
Range ACT Composite: 30–34

Annual tuition: $38,952
Average cumulative indebtedness: $18,605

% students graduating in 4 years: 85%
% students graduating in 6 years: 91%

Leonard Folgarait, History of Art
John Lachs, Philosophy

Located in Nashville, Tennessee, Vanderbilt University combines the advantages of an urban environment, strong academics, traditions, and research. The school offers seventy degree programs housed in four undergraduate schools, taught by professors leading the way in fields such as neuroscience, child psychology, music education, and nanotechnology.

Vanderbilt encourages students to approach their education with vigor and integrity and offers the tools to follow through. Notable programs include the Commons, a first-year living and learning residential community, 120 research centers, global education through study abroad options, and over 300 student-led organizations. Vanderbilt Visions is another program which pairs one upperclassman with one professor or dean who mentors a group of seventeen incoming first-year students.

Three-quarters of undergraduate students on campus participate in internships, research positions, and service projects to create experiences that will ultimately shape their future and contribute to their success. Students say that they "really connected with the professors" who offer them "a great intellectual challenge."

This school is ideal for individuals "who are outgoing, social, engaged, and who like to lead balanced lives. Vanderbilt is all about the undergraduate experience. Undergrads here have the opportunity to lead in a multitude of ways, to impact decisions the administration makes, and to work with professors outside of the classroom on a colleague-to-colleague level."

Vassar College

124 Raymond Avenue
Poughkeepsie, NY 12604
Admissions: 845-437-7300
www.vassar.edu
admissions@vassar.edu
Fax: 845-437-7063

Type of school: private
Environment: town
Total undergrad enrollment: 2,408
Student/faculty ratio: 8:1
Most common regular class size: 10–19
Range SAT Critical Reading: 670–740
Range SAT Math: 640–720
Range SAT Writing: 660–750
Range ACT Composite: 29–32

Annual tuition: $42,560
Average cumulative indebtedness: $18,153

% students graduating in 4 years: 93%
% students graduating in 6 years: 99%

Bryan William Van Norden, Philosophy

One of the Seven Sister colleges, Vassar College is a private, liberal arts school in Poughkeepsie, New York. Students enjoy the privilege of carving out their own curriculum due to the unique flexibility in terms of universal core requirements. Undergraduate research is king, with small classroom settings, giving way to fifty possible majors to choose from. The mixing of disciplines and fields of study allows the option to tailor individuals' education to their needs.

Students find professors to be engaging and often available for extra help. "Every class is unique and interesting, and students regularly get together just to discuss their favorite classes."

In addition to offering the opportunity to major in a range of languages from Spanish to Japanese, Vassar has a Self-Instructional Language Program (SLIP) that offers courses in offers courses in Hindi, Irish/Gaelic, Korean, Portuguese, Swahili, Swedish, Turkish, and Yiddish. Many students take advantage of the chance to study abroad during their junior year. Programs in China, England, France, Germany, Greece, Ireland, Italy, Mexico, Morocco, Spain, and Russia are supported directly by the school, however, students may also choose approved courses at other institutions in the United States as well as overseas.

Entertainment options are limited in Poughkeepsie, but the campus does their share to provide a multitude of activities to help students unwind. From engaging lectures and theater productions to organizations and clubs, the campus, which is affectionately referred to as the "Vassar Bubble," has the feel of a community in and of itself.

Washington College

300 Washington Avenue
Chestertown, MD 21620
Admissions: 410-778-7700
www.washcoll.edu
wc_admissions@washcoll.edu
Fax: 410-778-7287

Washington College is located on Maryland's Eastern Shore, and in-state residents comprise approximately half of its student body. While the school provides a very intimate and personalized educational experience, its alumni base and proximity to three major markets (Washington, D.C., Philadelphia, and Baltimore) provide steady employment, networking, and internship opportunities. All students are required to meet with an advisor to plan out each semester beforehand; impressively, there is also a "strong English and literary focus that emphasizes good writing and reading skills as the basis of any study," according to one student. Another believes the college does "an excellent job of creating an enthusiastic and successful learning environment." The foundation here is the faculty. "Superb," "extraordinary," and "knowledgable" instructors "[teach] you to think critically and form your own opinions," say students, and present their material clearly. Professors "bring thoughtful insight into discussions," and make classes "interesting and meaningful," say a few satisfied undergrads. Others tell us that "the attention given to the students by faculty is "undeniable…it's something that many students underestimate, but once you experience it, you never want it any other way." "It is easy to grow close to professors here." Instructors are very

Type of school: private
Environment: rural
Total undergrad enrollment: 1,385
Student/faculty ratio: 13:1
Most common regular class size: 10–19
Range SAT Critical Reading: 540–630
Range SAT Math: 530–620
Range SAT Writing: 520–620
Range ACT Composite: 23–27

Annual tuition: $36,078
Average cumulative indebtedness: $35,831

% students graduating in 4 years: 68%
% students graduating in 6 years: 71%

Richard Gillin, English

approachable and "provide copious amounts of advice." They are said to greatly respect the opinions of their students who, in turn, admire them for wanting "to get to know you and help shape your education around what matters to you most," and being "inclined to assist, and very patient—I have never been made to feel incompetent by asking a question." Many students are thrilled to form actual relationships with faculty members, and often find role models as a result. "I have most of my professors' cell phone numbers and frequently visit their homes for dinners, extracurricular activities, and social outings." "I could not have asked for a group of more influential, caring, and dedicated professors." The administration promotes participation in sports as well, and many students strive to be scholar-athletes.

Wellesley College

Board of Admission
106 Central Street
Wellesley, MA 02481-8203
Admissions: 781-283-2270
www.wellesley.edu
admission@wellesley.edu
Fax: 781-283-3678

Wellesley College is "an intellectual haven for fiercely driven and deeply passionate women," says one student, and this description surely rings true for many others. The school has high expectations and "really respects its students and their ideas," reports an undergrad. Wellesley has a very open, "safe space" community on top of excellent academics and a respected faculty. Student life on campus is wonderfully diverse and engaging; students admire the "talented," "approachable," and "patient" professors, and

Type of school: private
Environment: town
Total undergrad enrollment: 2,362
Student/faculty ratio: 8:1
Most common regular class size: 10–19
Range SAT Critical Reading: 640–740
Range SAT Math: 630–740
Range SAT Writing: 650–750
Range ACT Composite: 28–31

Annual tuition: $40,410
Average cumulative indebtedness: $12,495

% students graduating in 4 years: 84%
% students graduating in 6 years: 87%

Akila Weerapana, Economics

appreciate having "amazing academic opportunities and an intense intellectual environment, and a really strong sense of community." Wellesley "empowers its students and opens up an environment that encourages discourse and exploration." The teachers interact with students on a very personal level too. Wellesley has "amazing professors that are there to teach and connect with students. They know your name and care about you. You will never be in a lecture hall with a hundred other students and a professor that has no clue who you are," one student tells us. You can cross-register at MIT (and to a limited extent at Brandeis, Babson, and Olin). Wellesley also has a very strong alumni network; internship and community service opportunities abound. Though it is an all-female school, one student reports, "the environment definitely doesn't feel stifling or super feministic." "We also like to get off campus to hit up the 'typical' college parties at MIT, Harvard, and BC." Another mentions that "Wellesley is close enough to Boston to take advantage of all the city has to offer, but you can always come home to the quiet campus." One student offers her assessment: "Wellesley will turn you into an intense, intelligent, competitive woman who's ready to take on any career challenge."

William Jewell College

500 College Hill
Liberty, MO 64068
Admissions: 816-781-7700
www.jewell.edu
admission@william.jewell.edu
Fax: 816-415-5040

Armed with a strong liberal arts program and a growing reputation, William Jewell College is a great find for students seeking a rich academic community. Indeed, brimming with Midwestern warmth, undergrads quickly feel at home here. By and large, students at

Type of school: private
Environment: town
Total undergrad enrollment: 1,060
Student/faculty ratio: 12:1
Most common regular class size: fewer than 10 students
Range SAT Critical Reading: 510–700
Range SAT Math: 500–620
Range ACT Composite: 23–29

Annual tuition: $29,600
Average cumulative indebtedness: $23,210

% students graduating in 4 years: 56%
% students graduating in 6 years: 65%

Mark Walters, English

William Jewell are active, curious, and constantly juggling multiple activities. Of course, classes take priority, and incoming freshmen should expect a heavy workload. Fortunately, we're assured that the college offers "an incredible learning opportunity, available to all who are willing to put in the work." Perhaps even more impressive, students are really able to influence their educations. One content undergrad shares, "If you want something changed in the café they'll do it; if you want to design your own major they'll do it." Moreover, "Jewell is big on getting [its] students into real-world situations as soon as possible" through internships and service projects. Most important, undergrads attribute their rewarding experience to "incredibly brilliant" professors who are truly accessible and supportive. As another grateful students reveals, mMost teachers will work with you personally should you have a problem with the class, or even on a personal level." With passionate professors, an active student body, and a friendly campus, William Jewell virtually ensures a fantastic collegiate experience.

Wofford College

429 North Church Street
Spartanburg, SC 29303-3663
Admissions: 864-597-4130
www.wofford.edu
admission@wofford.edu
Fax: 864-597-4147

Wofford College's motto is "a Quintessential education." By offering "demanding and challenging academics that expand students' intellectual independence," and a "phenomenal" faculty, with "highly intelligent and extremely effective communicators," according to undergrads, Wofford appears to accomplish just that.

Type of school: private
Environment: city
Total undergrad enrollment: 1,479
Student/faculty ratio: 11:1
Most common regular class size: 10–19
Range SAT Critical Reading: 560–675
Range SAT Math: 590–680
Range SAT Writing: 545–650
Range ACT Composite: 22–28

Annual tuition: $31,710
Average cumulative indebtedness: $23,103

% students graduating in 4 years: 78%
% students graduating in 6 years: 82%

Charlie Bass, Chemistry

Strategically situated and close to Charlotte, Greenville, Charleston, and Atlanta, with Asheville, North Carolina a bit further north, "it's very Southern. Everyone has good manners and strong values," notes one impressed student. Others mention that Wofford has a "stunning faculty-to-student ratio," and much mutual respect; "professors in each department genuinely strive to be on a first-name basis with all of their students, even after the student is no longer in their class." "It is easy to access and get to know the professors and other faculty members and receive the academic support that you need." Teachers want to help students gain research opportunities; one undergrad finds that "the fact that professors are the ones that teach the labs speaks volumes." Other superlatives from students are equally as impressive. "They are very good teachers who push their students to the limit. They will challenge you, and you WILL learn." "Serious effort has to be put into every class." "I really liked how the classes usually have no more than twenty to thirty students." Instructors are dedicated and truly care about your life and your success after school. In addition to having a well-connected alumni network, Wofford has great success in placing students in graduate and professional programs. "I am quite proud I made the decision to attend Wofford College."

Worcester Polytechnic Institute

Admissions Office, Bartlett Center
100 Institute Road
Worcester, MA 01609
Admissions: 508-831-5286
www.wpi.edu
admissions@wpi.edu
Fax: 508-831-5875

Type of school: private
Environment: city
Total undergrad enrollment: 3,537
Student/faculty ratio: 14:1
Most common regular class size: 20–29
Range SAT Critical Reading: 560–660
Range SAT Math: 630–730
Range SAT Writing: 560–660
Range ACT Composite: 26–31

Annual tuition: $40,030
Average cumulative indebtedness: $30,573

% students graduating in 4 years: 72%
% students graduating in 6 years: 79%

John Goulet, Mathematics

Worcester Polytechnic Institute prides itself on its "project-based and very hands-on" learning experience. One of the nation's earliest engineering and technology universities, WPI is renowned for its strong mathematics, science, and engineering programs. Many students are delighted to have "the opportunity to work on projects with minimal guidance from their advisors." The undergraduate class comprises a very nice mix of students here who do not fit the typical engineering student [profile]." "We're all nerdy in our own way, whether it be a love of calculus or getting excited over video games," quips another student. Virtually everyone is "very driven and self-motivated."

WPI is praised for its great computer and lab facilities, and the "social life is unbeatable." Indeed, the campus supports "a very large amount of active clubs and organizations." Most notable is the student-run committee, which is always holding really outrageous and fun events," including "concerts with really good and popular bands." There is an active sports scene, and "football and basketball are pretty popular." Students also rave about the parties here, which draws "people from all the neighboring schools" and "are always fun-themed and not sketchy."

WPI has a noteworthy grade system: If a student fails a class, it will not show up on his or her transcript. This beneficial structure allows for "freedom to take riskier classes." The healthy academic atmosphere "promotes a culture of cooperation over competition." While the quarterly academic calendar "allows students to take a more diverse array of classes," the classes themselves are rigorous, and one student notes that "if you're sick for two weeks, you have lots of make-up work to do."

One of New England's top engineering and science schools, WPI encourages undergrads to question and experiment. Promoting a "project-based curriculum," WPI allows students to put their focus towards "hands-on work" in nearly every class. Undergrads appreciate this approach, stating that it "emphasizes the understanding of technical concepts, the practical implementation of these concepts, and also an appreciation for how technological advances can benefit mankind." Further, WPI's academic calendar is based around a quarter system. This results in students' ability to enroll in a wide variety of classes. Unfortunately, it also means a heavy workload and courses that must move along rapidly. Luckily, the winning combination of supportive professors and a grading policy that doesn't account for F's on transcripts (there's simply A/B/C/NR) makes for a student that's not afraid to take risks. The faculty and administration also manage to help foster "a culture of cooperation over competition." Ultimately, between "incredible technological resources," highly supportive advisors, and a hopping social calendar, it's understandable why WPI is teeming with happy undergrads.

Yale University

P.O. Box 208234
New Haven, CT 06520-8234
Admissions: 203-432-9300
www.yale.edu
student.questions@yale.edu
Fax: 203-432-9392

Type of school: private
Environment: city
Total undergrad enrollment: 5,258
Student/faculty ratio: 6:1
Most common regular class size: 10–19
Range SAT Critical Reading: 700–800
Range SAT Math: 700–780
Range SAT Writing: 700–790
Range ACT Composite: 30–34

Annual tuition: $38,300
Average cumulative indebtedness: $12,297

% students graduating in 4 years: 98%
% students graduating in 6 years: 99%

Paul Bracken, Management & Political Science
Karen von Kunes, Slavic Languages & Literatures

One of the country's oldest and most prestigious universities, Yale is a school bursting with resources and opportunity. Not surprisingly, the university nets an intellectually curious, driven student body that's highly "committed to learning and to each other." Moreover, while Yale is at the forefront of many groundbreaking research projects, research rarely comes at the expense of teaching. Rest assured, the college "places unparalleled focus on undergraduate education," requiring all professors to teach at least one undergraduate course every academic year. Students truly appreciate this rule, noting, "[You know] the professors actually love teaching, because if they had just wanted to do their research, they could have easily gone elsewhere." One proud undergrad gushes, "The experiences you have here and the people that you meet will change your life and strengthen your dreams." Now that's a pretty spectacular promise for any university!

Index

Pressprich, Karen A.	70	Stupar, Daniel	41
Pucci, Joseph	78	Suggs, David N.	36
Rachootin, Stan	53	Sullivan, Karen	197
Rajewski, Jonathan	94	Suri, Jeremi	179
Ravillon, Stephanie	144	Surprenant, Chris W.	241
Reed, Gilda Werner	269	Tanglen, Randi Lynn	131
Renker, Elizabeth	128	Thamattoor, Dasan M.	71
Richeimer, Joel	237	Thomas, Ron	58
Rindfleisch, Aric	200	Thurber, Barton	131
Rivers, Christopher	145	Tilney, Barrett	40
Rochelle, Warren	129	Townsley, Eleanor	283
Rockwell, Paul	146	Towsley, Gary	222
Rogate, John	88	Troncale, Joe	149
Ronis, Eric	84	Tucker, Jr., Kenneth H.	284
Rosenwasser, David	130	van Es, Cindy	105
Russakoff, Andrew	89	Van Norden, Bryan William	241
Sahami, Mehran	90	Vander Griend, Doug	72
Sanderson, Catherine	270	Vishton, Peter M.	275
Saracino, Dan	217	Voguit, Steve	179
Schoepflin, Todd	281	von Kunes, Karen	150
Schreier, Ph.D., Shelly	271	Walker, Steven C.	132
Schroeder, Alan	194	Walker, David	137
Schumacher, Douglass	246	Walters, Mark	133
Schvaneveldt, Stephen	71	Wang, Steve C.	223
Scott, Jacqueline	239	Warne, Paul	224
Serrano, Roberto	103	Wassell, Steve	225
Shabanov, Sergei	217	Watkins, Steve	134
Sher, Beverly	54	Webster, Janice Gohm	135
Shibberu, Yosi	218	Weekes, Nicole Y.	230
Shiner, Rebecca	272	Weerapana, Akila	106
Shoemaker, Dr. Melinda Anne	273	Wegmann, Jennifer	163
Shoer, Shalom	147	Weiner, William	56
Shutt, Timothy	186	Wetzel, David	180
Sibley-Jones, Mark	196	White, Patrick J.	136
Simmons, Kevin M.	104	Whittenburg, James P.	181
Smith, Tony	85	Wichlinski, Lawrence	275
Solomon, Sheldon	273	Winsor, Robert D.	202
Somerville, Mark	114	Wolfe, Christopher B.	63
Sorensen, Erl	219	Wood, William	106
Spears, Trisha	55	Woodard, Craig	56
Spence Adams, Sarah	203	Woods, Ephraim	73
Stamper, Richard	115	Woodworth, Steven E.	182
Stankova, Zvezdelina	220	Wright, Colby	141
Starr Ph.D., Howard A.	274	Wurtzler, Steve J.	74
Sternstein, Martin	220	Yamashita, Samuel	183
Stone, Brad Elliott	240	Young, Susan	226
Stracke, Alan	282	Yukich, Joseph	227
Strand, Allen R.	221	Zaarour, Nizar	228
Strang, Kevin	229	Zima, Monica	115
Stull, Gregg	286	Zimmer, Marc	73